Handbook of
Municipal
Administration
and Engineering

Handbook of Municipal Administration and Engineering

WILLIAM S. FOSTER *Editor*

**Consulting Editor and Former Editorial
Director and Associate Publisher,
*The American City & County***

McGRAW-HILL BOOK COMPANY

New York *St. Louis* *San Francisco* *Auckland* *Bogotá*
Düsseldorf Johannesburg London Madrid
Mexico Montreal New Delhi Panama
Paris São Paulo Singapore
Sydney Tokyo Toronto

Library of Congress Cataloging in Publication Data
Main entry under title:

Handbook of municipal administration and engineering.

  Includes index.
  1. Municipal engineering—Handbooks, manuals, etc.
2. Municipal government—Handbooks, manuals, etc.
I. Foster, William S.
TD159.H36   628   77-14128

1234567890 HDHD 7654321098

*The editors for this book were Harold B. Crawford and
Beatrice E. Eckes, the designer was Naomi Auerbach,
and the production supervisor was Frank P. Bellantoni.
It was set in Baskerville by Monotype Composition
Company.*

Printed and bound by Halliday Lithograph Corporation.

Contents

Contributors

CRISTOFANO, S. M. *Director of Public Works and City Engineer, Santa Clara, California* (CHAPTERS 7 AND 8)

ELLIOTT, ARTHUR L. *Consultant in the design, construction, and maintenance of bridges; former head of the Bridge Department, California Divison of Highways* (CHAPTER 5)

FOSTER, RUTH S. *Landscape consultant, Boston, Massachusetts* (SECTION OF CHAPTER 12)

FOSTER, WILLIAM S. *Consulting Editor and former Editorial Director and Associate Publisher,* The American City & County (CHAPTERS 1, 2, 3, 4, 6, 9, 11, 12, 13, 14, 15, AND 16)

HENDON, WILLIAM S. *Professor of Urban Studies, University of Akron* (SECTION OF CHAPTER 12)

KURANZ, JOSEPH H. *General Manager and Chief Engineer, Waukesha, Wisconsin, Water Utility; Past President, American Water Works Association* (CHAPTER 10)

Preface

Unfortunately, the city as a subject has received a bad press ever since the days of Babylon, Sodom, and Gomorrah. The headline "Can Cities Survive?" has been popular in Sunday supplements for years. The poet Shelley wrote "Hell is a city much like London." Thomas Jefferson hated cities, and this was in a period when the largest city in the United States, Philadelphia, had a population of only 30,000.

During those times the critics had much evidence to support their arguments. Most of the townspeople had to live in unbelievably squalid and crowded conditions. Water was poisonously polluted. There was no organized collection of either solid or liquid wastes, and householders would customarily dump the night's collection of body wastes into the streets, where it would mix with the manure of the horses to make an offensively foul, odorous, and repulsive commingling. Streets were not cleaned. Street lighting was casual, consisting generally of a few smoky flares if any light was provided at all.

Badly polluted air was customary in cities. The Romans protested it with little result. In 1306 some unfortunate Briton was beheaded for illegally burning "sea-coal," but even this did little to stop the practice or to alleviate the foul London air. Until very recently, many considered smoky, dirt-filled air in a city a sort of civic virtue, symbolizing prosperity and employment for all.

In such cities epidemics were common, the death rate was high, and the life-span was short. These conditions persisted until very recently. Franklin D. Roosevelt, when he was a young man, very nearly died of typhoid fever, which is generally caused by drinking polluted water. Those who cried out against the urban environment of their times had good reason.

Nevertheless, cities or, more properly, urbanism has continued to grow and to thrive in the United States and elsewhere, primarily because talented men and women can support themselves and become prosperous by exercising their talents more effectively in an urban environment than in a rural one. Craftsmen, skilled workers, physicians, lawyers, tradesmen, artists, writers, and many others found that an urban community permitted them to develop and sharpen their skills and talents for the general benefit of all. In contrast, a rural environment required a man to become the well-known jack-of-all-trades and, unfortunately, master of none.

To permit an urban society to function and produce these benefits in the United States, the urban organization, elected by the prople being served, whether it is the government of a city, town, village, parish, borough, or county, now must provide new services that will help overcome the problems of urban societies of the past. Water must be collected, purified, and distributed in quantities large enough to serve the people's domestic needs, as well as their businesses and their industries, and to provide fire protection. Roads and streets must be built to permit circulation within the urban social structure. Bridges must be built and maintained. Streets must be cleaned of dirt and litter. Snow must be removed. Liquid wastes must be collected, treated, and allowed to be released without damage to receiving waterways. Solid wastes must be collected and disposed of in a suitable manner. Traffic and street lighting must be maintained. Parks and recreational facilities must be developed. All these services, considered rather pedestrian in the minds of many, must be performed if this sensitive urban structure is to operate to provide the benefits so valuable to the maintenance of the quality of life in the urban environment.

Neglect or mismanagement of these services can prove disastrous. Few can forget the traumatic effect on the nation of the assassination of Dr. Martin Luther King, Jr. Yet the event had its start in a dispute between the city of Memphis and its sanitation workers. Prestigious Columbia University collapsed under the impact of militant students, spurred by a parkland dispute. New York City proved helpless when its sanitation workers went on strike, and the result was a condition that posed a great risk not only to health within the city but to public safety in the form of fire hazards.

In Pittsburgh's troubled Hill district, slum dwellers told the city's redevelopment agency, during one riot-studded period, that what they really wanted was better refuse collection, improved and repaired streets, more numerous street lights, the demolition of vacant, boarded-up buildings that had become neighborhood nuisances, additional and safer playgrounds for their children, and a voice in determining what was to be done to their neighborhoods.

These, obviously, are very human and understandable wants. Those responding to them are not the sociologist, the psychologist, or the behavioral scientist but the municipal maintenance crews who provide the basic services that allow an urban society to function.

One small incident, occurring during World War II, colorfully shows how our society depends on undramatic but essential services. This involved the man who cleaned the privies in a French village during the time when it was occupied by the Germans. When the allies advanced and subsequently recaptured the village, this man disappeared into the hills with his cart and donkey, apparently fearing that he would be accused of collaborating with the Germans, probably because he had cleaned the night soil from their privies also. Very shortly, the little village was in crisis. So grave was the situation, because of the overflowing privies, that the Allied military government sent teams into the hills to find and persuade the man to return. He finally consented, and as he made his way back, the villagers cheered him and strewed flowers before his donkey and cart.[1]

Many have claimed that a free urban society, by its very nature, cannot be efficient. Alexis de Tocqueville, the French observer who wrote very thoughtfully about the United States in 1835, forecast that democracy as outlined in the Constitution would never function in an urbanized society.

Those men and women who perform the tasks that the public frequently takes for granted and who serve heroically when their cities are in great danger, during floods, tornadoes, or hurricanes, are living proof that democracy *can* be efficient and *can* function in an urban environment. This handbook is dedicated to them and undertakes to assist them in this valuable work.

William S. Foster

[1] *Jack McKee, "Messr. Le Vidangeur," Sewage and Industrial Wastes Journal,* vol. 18, p. 534, 1946.

Chapter One

Street Types and Soil Problems

WILLIAM S. FOSTER

INFLUENCE OF STREET PATTERNS ON CITY PLANNING

Street styles have changed for the better since World War II. And this change should lessen urban roadway-maintenance problems, principally because fewer miles of roadway must be used to serve a given residential or other urban area with the newer street layouts.

Origin of the Traditional Gridiron Street Layout

For centuries and perhaps even for millennia, those who built cities used the gridiron system. Their reasons for doing so were logical. The sys-

Figure 1-1   The gridiron system of street layout, while simple, is monotonous and rigid. Past practices in the use of the gridiron have produced crowded residential patterns with little concern for open space. [*Urban Land Institute photo*]

tem was orderly.   It gave the people of the community quick, easy access to other parts of town, and it promoted a sense of security.

Historically, cities developed as fortified places, generally at the crossroads of trade.   Cities were largely independent and had to defend themselves from attack.   Those charged with defense found merit in a gridiron system that permitted easy mustering of the defenders and quick mobility from one part of the city to another.   The system reflected order. People comprehended it readily and could identify their property easily with it.   It was popular because it was understandable, and it made people feel secure.

Unexpected Advantages of the Gridiron System

Insistence on use of the gridiron plan occasionally has produced enjoyable benefits.   Consider San Francisco, which is generally accepted as the most interesting and beautiful city in the United States.   Originally a Swiss surveyor laid out a gridiron street pattern in the flat area near the harbor.   Then, as the little community grew, the settlers extended these lines rigidly into the surrounding hills to make the steep, spectacular street pattern that gives San Francisco much of its charm.

In Texas, the original San Antonio Mission had trails leading to it from surrounding areas.   As the mission grew into a city, the planners superimposed a gridiron system over the trails, producing what looks like a bewildering network of streets.   Yet this irregularity enhances San Antonio's appeal.

Disadvantages of the Gridiron Pattern

However, these two cities are exceptions.   In the great majority of cases the gridiron system adds to the cost of street maintenance and destroys some of the charm and interest that an urban environment can have.

Figure 1-2   Modern city planning incorporates in the street system gentle curves that fit the natural topography and provide interest through constantly changing viewpoints.   [*Urban Land Institute photo*]

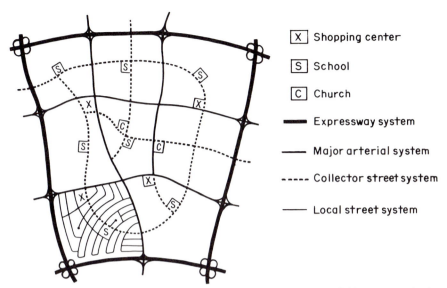

Figure 1-3   Today's urban street systems frequently fit general plans of this type. [*Portland Cement Association*]

The system is forced onto a land area without regard for the topography of the region or the convenience of the people.   It is wasteful in its use of land, requiring an inordinate number of streets, thereby increasing the original cost of roadways and streets and adding to the cost of their maintenance.   The need for a greater mileage of streets to serve a given area also increases the cost of supplying utility services such as water, electric power, sewers, gas, telephones, street lighting, and, more recently, television cables.

Curved Street Patterns

In recent years and especially since World War II, most urban planning has embraced the concept of curved street patterns.   Curves are nature's lines: they can fit the topography.   A curved street introduces change by presenting new points of view to the pedestrian and the motorist.

Innovative city planners even have introduced curved traffic lanes into existing straight downtown shopping streets.   This practice gives them the opportunity of enhancing the appearance of the downtown area by landscaping around the curves and of placing other amenities that make the area more attractive.

Alleys

With the use of curved street patterns and today's way of life, alleys now are rarely included in city patterns.   Gridiron-planned streets almost always have had them.   Alleys served the utilitarian purpose of facilitating the delivery of goods and services in an era when tradespeople were not encouraged to enter a house through the front door. Streets, in contrast, were supposed to reflect a community's charm and grace.

Alleys were especially useful when each house had a barn and each family kept a horse (and often chickens and even a pig). Kitchens were work areas in the rear of the houses that guests seldom entered.

Today, living styles have changed. The barn has become the garage and has been moved to the front of the lot or been made a prominent part of the house itself. The kitchen is as attractive as any portion of the house, and guests are welcome there. The front door, moreover, has become an easy and convenient entranceway for deliveries. The need for utilitarian alleys has largely disappeared, and in the designs for new urban areas one rarely finds them.

However, most municipalities have old homes and new ones, old street layouts with alleys, and new ones without them. Rarely do those in charge of maintaining old street systems have the opportunity of rebuilding them completely to new lines and grades. Their task is to keep the present street systems, and the alleys if they exist, in continuing good serviceable condition, making adjustments if changing conditions dictate more intensive duty.

TYPES OF URBAN STREETS

The types of streets that must carry urban traffic demand close attention because of the intensive use made of them. Urban roadways carry 54 percent of the total vehicle-miles (vehicle-kilometers) on the nation's 3,800,000 miles (6,100,000 kilometers) of roads and streets. However, they are only 16 percent of the total mileage. These urban roadways can be grouped into three major categories and a fourth that is taking on significance: local, arterial, limited-access, and rural, nonfarm streets.

Local Streets

These streets serve a specific area in which the traffic lacks a consistent destination pattern. They may be subdivided into local residential, local business or commercial, and local industrial streets.

The first of these subcategories, that of local residential streets, carries only light, convenience-type traffic. These streets probably perform best when their design discourages the entry of all traffic except that having a reason to enter or leave a specific area.

Streets of the second subcategory, local business streets, often known as downtown streets, serve the business and commercial needs of a specific area. Today such areas have been challenged by shopping centers, and many downtown streets are making drastic changes to improve their appearances and attract shoppers.

Streets of the third subcategory, local industrial streets, must be structurally strong and able to permit the movement of heavy trucks. Like the business streets, they face competition from out-of-city industrial parks that tend to cluster around freeways where truck movement is easy.

Arterial Streets

Arterial streets provide a means of carrying traffic with a common destination pattern within an urban area. They connect residential areas with business, industrial, or other areas where traffic seems impelled to go. Some of these streets may be considered semiarterial (collector) streets, feeding into more heavily traveled arteries. Unfortunately, strip-type business development occurs along arterial streets, forming unattractive "gasoline alley" business districts and damaging the attractiveness of abutting residential neighborhoods.

Limited-Access Streets

Streets in this category are the mainstay of a transportation network. They are designed to permit the movement of large volumes of traffic quickly and expeditiously among cities and points within or around cities, especially within the same metropolitan area.

The designs for this type of facility generally provide access only from an arterial street or another limited-access street. In any case, access is controlled; indiscriminate on or off movements are normally prohibited by physical barriers such as fences, landscaping, and grade differentials.

Figure 1-4 Limited-access roadways permit the easy movement of large volumes of traffic. This is a view of Franklin D. Roosevelt Drive, which borders the east side of Manhattan Island in New York. A pedestrian promenade covers the drive. [*Urban Land Institute photo*]

Rural, Nonfarm Roadways

These represent a relatively new thrust of urbanism that may cause new problems unless it is understood and analyzed. The U.S. Bureau of the Census has recognized this development in its census classification of rural, nonfarm areas. This classification embraces areas not settled thickly enough to merit a classification of urban under the Census Bureau's standards. Nevertheless, the people are oriented, at least in part, toward an urban environment. They want electric power, good water (although if they are fortunate, they can provide their own), a well-maintained road system usable the year round and free of snow and ice in winter, good refuse collection and disposal, and even some publicly supported parks and playgrounds.

However, the residents of these areas want to retain a rural appearance. They violently oppose sidewalks, curbs and gutters, street lights, and even the simpler forms of roadway asphalt surfacing. Police protection is generally casual, and fire protection almost always consists of volunteer forces, which often must bring water in tank trucks. If the thrust of urbanization continues, such an area will require a roadway system of higher quality as well as a better water-supply system, probably sewers and a treatment plant, and additional park facilities.

TECHNIQUES OF STRENGTHENING ROADWAY SUBGRADES

Most of the maintenance problems for urban roadways can be traced to failures of the supporting soils. And since the allowable legal loads for trucks seem to increase constantly, these soil failures can be expected to increase, and greater attention will have to be directed toward their correction. The characteristics of soils that create these problems can be grouped under several general headings:

Pressure   Soil will change its shape under the weight of vehicular traffic. Like most other solids, it tends to flow under pressure.

Volume Changes   Depending on the moisture content of the soil, shrinkage or swelling can be expected.

Elasticity   Many soils are resilient. They deflect and rebound with each passing vehicle, and this effect can increase with each traffic repetition.

Frost Heaving   Many soils with access to free water, especially fine-grained types that do not drain easily, will expand markedly when frozen, sufficiently to make the roadway rough and often dangerous. In spring, the soil will thaw and lose its load-carrying power.

Settlement   Coarse, granular soils can settle and become more dense under traffic if they have not been carefully compacted during construction.

Soil Variations   Varying soil types in the same roadbed produce variations in support and, consequently, changes on the roadway surface.

Soil Pumping   When the soil supports concrete pavements, it may "pump" at expansion and contraction joints or at the cracks in the pavement as the slab ends deflect under vehicle-load applications. The pumping effect is caused by the entry of water through the joints and cracks. This continuing movement and oscillation weakens the subgrade soil and can cause the concrete to break. Consequently good maintenance in sealing the cracks and joints is mandatory.

Soil Plasticity Index

One of the principal guides that determines the supporting qualities of soils is the plasticity index. If the supporting soils have a favorable plasticity index, maintenance of the roadways becomes far less troublesome.

The plasticity index is the arithmetical difference between the *liquid limit* and the *plastic limit*. The liquid limit is the maximum moisture content that permits the soil to behave as a plastic material. Above this moisture content, the soil starts to become a viscous fluid. The plastic limit, in contrast, is the minimum moisture content that permits the soil to have plastic characteristics. Below this moisture content, the soil tends to become nonplastic and no longer holds together. Both limits are determined by well-known tests.

Measuring Soil Compaction

Since compacting a soil by rolling or other means is the least costly method of improving its load-carrying capabilities, some method of measuring this compaction is necessary. For more than 40 years, the classic Proctor test in one form or another has served this purpose.

The Proctor test determines the maximum density of a soil in pounds per cubic foot (kilograms per cubic meter) at its optimum moisture content when compacted into a cylinder of $\frac{1}{30}$ cubic foot (9.4 cubic centimeters) under controlled conditions. Many specifications for the compaction of supporting soils require some percentage of this maximum density, generally between 90 and 95 percent. When stabilized bases are involved, specifications may require 100 percent.

The test does not mean that this is the maximum density which the soil can attain by compaction. It is the density that this particular test determines as the maximum when using a cylinder of $\frac{1}{30}$ cubic foot and compacting the material in three layers with a tamper of 5.5 pounds (2.5 kilograms), applying twenty-five blows per layer with the tamper exerting a free fall of 1 foot (0.3048 meter).

A modified Proctor test produces greater maximum densities, which are required when greater strengths are needed, as at airports used by heavy aircraft. This test uses a 10-pound (4.5-kilogram) hammer, dropping 18 inches (457.2 millimeters). The sample still is inserted into a cylinder of the same size, but it is placed in five layers with twenty-five blows per layer.

Compacting on the Dry Side of Optimum Moisture

When a supporting soil or a stabilized base is being compacted, the best results will be obtained when the soil or base material is slightly drier than the optimum moisture. The compacted soil structure will be stronger and less subject to shrinkage, although it may be somewhat subject to swelling.

In contrast, if the clay core wall of a dam is being compacted, the moisture content should be on the wet side of the optimum moisture figure. Under these conditions, the core wall will be able to accommodate itself to deformations without developing cracks. Moreover, compaction at this moisture content will reduce the core wall's permeability.

Determining Compaction of Roadway Soil

The test that determines whether a compacted roadway soil or a stabilized base has reached its specified density is simple. The technician carefully digs a hole in the roadway surface, collecting all the soil being removed. He or she then weighs the soil, both in its natural condition and with the moisture driven off, thus determining the moisture content.

The technician then measures the volume of the hole created by extracting the sample. One useful method of determining this volume is called "balloon density." A graduated cylinder with a rubber membrane incorporated in it and equipped with a hand pump is placed over the hole. The operator uses the pump to force water into the hole, the membrane moving into the hole first and forming an impervious lining. The cylinder is calibrated to show the volume of the hole directly by measuring how much water is pumped out of it and into the hole. Knowing the weight of the sample and the volume of the hole, the technician makes a simple arithmetical calculation to determine the density of the sample in terms of weight per unit of volume or, more simply, pounds per cubic foot (kilograms per cubic meter).

A second, more popular method of measuring the volume of the hole left by extracting the sample is to fill it with dry sand that has been graded to a uniform size. After carefully pouring the sand from a previously weighed container when the hole has been filled to the precise level of the compacted surface, the technician again must solve a simple problem of arithmetic to determine the volume of the hole. The technician, of course, must know the specific gravity of the sand in order to translate the weight of the sand poured into the hole into the volume it occupies. The test sand is normally graded to pass a No. 10 sieve (200 millimeters) and to be retained on a No. 200 sieve (0.075 millimeter).

One-Point Proctor Test

One of the major problems in any density-control program is the determination of the correct target density and optimum moisture for the soil encountered at a specific test location. When soil types vary considerably, inspectors often visually compare soils undergoing the density test with samples of soils used to determine the proper target values. This subjective visual procedure can result in errors and invalid test results.

To eliminate this human factor, many state highway departments as well as the Federal Highway Administration (FHA) use the one-point Proctor test in conjunction with a family of moisture-density curves. The inspector makes a single determination of the wet density and moisture content at the roadway where the density figure is needed. This moisture content should be on the dry side of the optimum moisture determined when the target density factor is obtained. The inspector then refers this determination to the family of curves and can select the maximum dry weight and the optimum moisture content that can produce it.

Many state highway departments have developed families of curves to fit soil conditions and operating techniques in their areas. The one-point Proctor determination normally is applied to large projects and has only casual use in most urban maintenance work.

Nuclear Moisture-Density Determinations

In contrast to these density-determination methods, the use of a nuclear meter to determine soil densities and moisture contents has a growing application. The instrument can determine soil characteristics and the densities of asphalt layers, and it can monitor backfilling in utility trenches and reduce the danger of settlement. Its use is much faster than digging a sample, measuring the hole, and drying and weighing the material. Some disparagingly call the older method "rat holing." The nuclear moisture-density test is fully as accurate and far more convenient when a number of tests must be made in a relatively short period. Several states use this method almost exclusively, particularly on large highway projects. The FHA allows the use of nuclear gauges for compaction control on federal projects and has conducted frequent demonstrations to provide assurance that the gauges are reliable.

When using the nuclear test method, the operator can employ either of two density-measurement methods: direct transmission and backscatter. To test the density of a compacted soil with the direct-transmission method, the operator first inserts the nuclear source into the soil through a punched access hole to depths ranging from 2 to 8

Figure 1-5 The nuclear determination of soil density and moisture with convenient instruments of this type is fast and accurate and requires only a minimum of training. [*Seaman Nuclear Corp.*]

inches (50.8 to 203.2 millimeters).   A 12-inch (304.8-millimeter) penetration is available with special equipment if needed.

The source transmits gamma photons to the detector, which translates them into the density of the soil being tested, since the radiation level at the detector is an inverse log function of density.   The method has many advantages, the chief of which is the fact that the inspector controls the depth measurement.

The backscatter method places both the nuclear source and the detector on the surface of the soil.   Gamma photons are directed from the source into the soil and scattered back to the detector.   The large scattering angle and other characteristics of the method lower the precision of measurement and also limit measurements to a shallow depth.   However, the ease of the method often compensates for the errors.   The backscatter method is especially useful when the compaction of a uniform material, such as asphaltic concrete paving, is being determined.

The instrument also can determine the moisture content of the compacted soil by either direct transmission or backscatter, recording the moisture content as a function of the equivalent weight of water per unit volume.   It relies on the extent of thermalization of fast neutrons by the chemically bound hydrogen in the water.

Some errors can creep in through the presence of hydrogen and other light elements in the soil.   And there may be larger errors caused by capture of the thermal neutrons by elements such as cadmium, boron, and iron.   However, these elements do not often occur in the soil.   If they are present, it may be necessary to calibrate the equipment by the comparison of soil samples with oven-dried material.

SOIL STABILIZATION

Compaction of roadway soil actually is a method of stabilization.   However, the supporting soil can be further strengthened, making it better able to carry the traffic-wearing surface without troublesome maintenance problems, through the use of certain stabilizing agents.   Such an agent can be asphalt, portland cement, or lime.   For a rough guide, the stabilizing agent can be selected on the basis of the plasticity index of the soil to be blended with it as follows:

Plasticity Index	Stabilizing Agent
0–10	Asphalt
3–15	Portland cement
10–50	Lime

Asphalt-Soil Stabilization

As a stabilizing agent, asphalt should be used with a soil that not only has a plasticity index of 10 or less but also has a liquid limit of 30 or less.   These requirements should apply to that portion of the soil passing a No. 40 sieve.   For good stabilization, the American Road Builders' Association (ARBA) suggests the following sieve analysis for the soil:

Screen Size Number	Percentage Passing
4	50 or more
40	50–100
200	35 or less

ARBA also recommends that no granular particle of the soil be larger than one-third of the depth of the compacted base.

The selection of the asphalt to be used for stabilization should depend on the type of soil to be stabilized.   For extremely sandy soils with very little clay or silt, a rapid-cure cutback asphalt works well.   As the clay or silt content increases, a medium-cure cutback should be selected.   With soils having higher contents of clay and silt (as much as 30 to 40 percent), a slow-curing asphalt should be used.

The amount of asphalt stabilizer should be no more than a ½ gallon of liquid asphalt per square yard (2.26 liters per square meter) per inch (25.4 millimeters) of compacted depth.   This is a good figure to use when making a trial mix.

The grade of asphalt should be the heaviest that can readily be worked into the soil.   If a patrol grader is to mix the soil and asphalt, a light grade of asphalt will allow more time for mixing.   If a traveling plant will do the mixing, a heavier grade can be used.   If the stabilization work takes place during hot weather, a heavy grade serves well.   In general, asphalt-soil stabilization should be a hot-weather task if this is at all possible.

The thickness of the stabilized base should be no less than 6 inches (152.4 millimeters) and no greater than 9 inches (228.6 millimeters). If greater thicknesses are required, an appropriate type of plant mix should provide them. The temperature of the asphalt when applied to be mixed with the soil as the stabilizing agent should be within the ranges shown in the accompanying table.

Type of Asphalt	Degrees F	Degrees C
RC-1, RC-2, MC-1	80–150	27–66
MC-2	100–200	38–88
RC-3	125–175	52–79
MC-3	150–200	66–88
MC-4	175–225	79–107
SC-1	80–200	27–88
SC-2	130–200	54–88
SC-3	175–250	79–121

For relatively small maintenance assignments, as found in most urban areas, mixed-in-place construction, using a patrol grader, works very satisfactorily. In the hands of a skilled operator, a grader with scarifier teeth can pulverize the soil in a workmanlike manner. It also can blend the asphalt into the pulverized soil, and by windrowing the mixture from side to side it can reduce the moisture in the mix to a figure somewhat below the optimum content that produces the maximum Proctor density. This makes the base somewhat easier to compact. On larger jobs, a rotary tiller can assist in the mixing, and a disc harrow will help aerate the mixture and lower the moisture content if that appears necessary.

For best results the asphalt application rate should be between 0.25 and 0.50 gallon per square yard (between 1.13 and 2.26 liters per square meter). The application should continue until the design content of asphalt for stabilization purposes has been reached. For large projects, traveling plants can mix and apply the stabilized base. However, improvements of this size are normally beyond standard maintenance practices and fall into the category of contract construction.

Compaction of the stabilized base is best achieved by placing the base in 2-inch (50.8-millimeter) layers and compacting it with pneumatic rollers. However, compaction of the stabilized base in a single lift, even at thicknesses of 10 inches (254 millimeters), is proving practical. Careful attention is required to make sure that the degree of compaction reaches the specified density. Nevertheless, the speedier completion of the work makes this method valuable for built-up urban areas. The single lift, often called "full-depth construction," also will enhance compaction if the mix is machine-laid and retains some of the heat in the asphalt.

When a pneumatic-tired roller is used, the tires should be inflated to from 40 to 80 pounds per square inch (276 to 552 kilopascals), and the roller should carry no more than 5 tons (4536 kilograms) per wheel. The roller can be either self-propelled or trailed. Steel-wheeled rollers can be used for a final compaction, which is undertaken principally to provide a smooth top surface. These rollers are classified as three-wheel, two-axle tandem, and three-axle tandem. The three-axle tandem type, which mounts all three rollers on a rigid frame with their axles in the same plane, can help eliminate high spots in the compacted base.

A wearing surface of some type, generally asphalt, must be placed on all stabilized bases. The base supports the traffic load, and the wearing surface provides the toughness to resist the erosion of the roadway that traffic inflicts on unimproved roads.

Reprocessing is possible with all three types of stabilized bases. All can be rescarified, remixed, and relaid if the need arises. Truck loadings on all roads seem to increase each year, and this persistent and recurring load application is bound to uncover weaknesses in the supporting subsoil that were not apparent originally.

Classification of Soil Types

To classify and understand more thoroughly the types of soil underlying a roadway, the American Association of State Highway and Transportation Officials (AASHTO) has compiled a practical and useful table (see Table 1-1). The soil groupings in the table enable maintenance personnel and others to have a common understanding of how the soil performs. AASHTO also suggests using the group index as a value measurement of the soils within the various group classifications. This index is a function of the soil's liquid limit, its plasticity index, and the percentage of the soil passing a No. 200 sieve. The lower the group index, the better the soil for supporting urban roadway traffic.

AASHTO has developed the following formula for the group index:

$$GI = 0.2a + 0.005ac + 0.01bd$$

where a = percentage greater than 35 but not more than 75 percent passing the No. 200 sieve

b = percentage greater than 15 but not more than 55 percent passing the No. 200 sieve

c = portion of liquid limit greater than 40 but not more than 60

d = portion of plasticity index greater than 10 but not more than 30

All the letters in the formula are expressed in positive whole numbers.

As an example, let us consider a soil with 25 percent passing the No. 200 sieve, a liquid limit of 40, a plastic limit of 25, and thus a plasticity index of $40 - 25$, or 15. If we refer to Table 1-1, we see that from the percentage of the soil passing the No. 200 sieve the sample must be one of the A-2 types. On the basis of its liquid limit, it could be either A-2-4 or A-2-6. On the basis of its plasticity index, it would have to be A-2-6. We then substitute in the formula $a = 0$ (since only 25 percent of the

Table 1-1 Soil Classifications

General classification	Granular materials (35 percent or less of total sample passing No. 200)							Silt-clay materials (more than 35 percent of total sample passing No. 200)			
	A-1		A-3	A-2				A-4	A-5	A-6	A-7
Group classification	A-1-a	A-1-b		A-2-4	A-2-5	A-2-6	A-2-7				A-7-5 A-7-6
Sieve analysis percent passing:											
No. 10	50 maximum										
No. 40	30 maximum	50 maximum	51 minimum								
No. 200	15 maximum	25 maximum	10 maximum	35 maximum	35 maximum	35 maximum	35 maximum	36 minimum	36 minimum	36 minimum	36 minimum
Characteristics of fraction passing No. 40:											
Liquid limit				40 maximum	41 minimum	40 maximum	41 minimum	40 maximum	41 minimum	40 maximum	41 minimum
Plasticity index	6 maximum		NP*	10 maximum	10 maximum	11 minimum	11 minimum	10 maximum	10 maximum	11 minimum	11 minimum
Group index†	0		0	0		4 maximum		8 maximum	12 maximum	16 maximum	20 maximum

*Nonplastic.
†Group index (GI) = $0.2a + 0.005ac + 0.01bd$.

sample passes the No. 200 sieve and this is less than 35 percent), $b = 10$ (since 25 percent is 10 points larger than 15 percent specified), $c = 0$ (since the liquid limit is equal to the lower figure specified), and $d = 5$ (since the liquid limit is 15). This makes the group index $0 + 0 + (.01)(10)(5) = 0.5$, or the whole number 1. Thus the complete AASHTO description of the soil is A-2-6(1), indicating that it is a very satisfactory soil for compaction and stabilizing.

Soil-Cement Bases

Bases combining soil and cement have had a long and dependable career on both rural and urban roadways, although recent heavy loads have tended to give some of them trouble. Producing a soil-cement stabilized base consists essentially of pulverizing the soil so that at least 80 percent passes a No. 4 sieve and 100 percent passes a 1-inch (25.4-millimeter) screen.

A grader with scarifier teeth can pulverize the soil satisfactorily, but mechanical soil pulverizers can do the job faster if the work is extensive enough to warrant their use. If clay balls form during pulverizing, they should be moist. Dry clay balls will expand when they absorb moisture and spall the base.

The next step is to blend portland cement with the pulverized soil in measured amounts and to add water to produce a calculated moisture content in the mix. Then the moistened mix is spread and immediately compacted to a specified density, shaped and rolled to a smooth surface, and immediately sealed, preferably with a cutback asphalt that prevents the moisture from evaporating and permits full hydration of the cement. The seal also can serve as the prime coat for an asphalt wearing surface, which should be placed on every stabilized base regardless of the type.

Figure 1-6 Mechanical mixing of soil and cement is useful in providing a firm, supporting stabilized base. [*Portland Cement Association*]

Preliminary design tests are required to determine the quantity of cement required for stabilization and the optimum moisture content. One of them is the Proctor test to determine the maximum density at optimum moisture content. Others are the freeze-thaw and wet-dry tests, which show the lowest content of cement that will harden and strengthen the soil adequately. In addition, tests can be made for grain size and for unconfined compressive strength if desired. Most state highway department testing laboratories, as well as private testing laboratories, can conduct these tests if a local government does not maintain the necessary facilities. These tests should enable the laboratory to recommend a precise figure for cement requirements, as well as the recommended density and optimum moisture content. For smaller maintenance requirements, however, the normal range of recommended cement content for the various soil groups identified in Table 1-1 can be estimated from Table 1-2.

TABLE 1-2   Cement Content in Soil-Cement Bases

	Cement required (percent)	
Soil group	By volume	By weight
A-1-a	5–7	3–5
A-1-b	7–9	5–8
A-2-4, 5, 6, 7	7–10	5–9
A-3	8–12	7–11
A-4	8–12	7–12
A-5	8–12	8–13
A-6	10–14	9–15
A-7	10–14	10–16

Lime Stabilization

This type of stabilization follows the general plan used for soil-cement bases with one or two differences. First, a smaller quantity of lime is generally needed than that of cement. The amount varies from 2 to 4 percent by weight, based on the dry weight of the soil for granular soil (more than 50 percent passing the 40-mesh screen), to 3 to 6 percent by weight for stabilizing fine-grained clays. Generally a soil with a high plasticity index requires more lime than one with a low index.

The second difference lies in the lime-stabilization procedure. As with soil-cement bases, the steps are (1) scarifying the soil in place; (2) spreading measured amounts of lime; (3) thoroughly mixing the two and adding controlled amounts of water, bringing the moisture content of the mix to a point somewhat less than the optimum; and (4) compacting the mix and curing.

In the case of heavy clays, however, mixing proceeds best in two stages, with an intervening curing period of 1 or 2 days. During this time the lime mellows the clay so that it can be pulverized readily in the second mixing operation. Compaction should then proceed promptly and be complete within 6 hours after the final mixing.

If the lime-stabilization maintenance work is extensive, pneumatic bulk tank trucks can apply the lime through a spreader bar. For the commoner small maintenance tasks, bagged lime is more practical. If dusting is a problem, the lime can be applied as a slurry, prepared in a batch tank or on a continuous basis with the use of a slurry maker. Conventional water trucks with spray bars would do the spreading. The slurry method requires care to avoid imparting to the mix an excessively high moisture content beyond the optimum obtained in the Proctor test. If the mix exceeds this content, it must be worked with a patrol grader or a harrow until enough moisture has evaporated to bring the figure close to the optimum content.

Figure 1-7 will help to determine the rate of application of hydrated lime for a stabilized base with a specified compaction density. The type of lime to be used should be either quicklime or hydrated lime; it should not be pulverized lime or "ag-stone," which is used in agriculture as a soil conditioner. Quicklime is produced from limestone in kilns operating at 2000 to 2500°F (1090 to 1360°C). Hydrated lime, made by adding water to quicklime to form a powder, is preferred for soil stabilization because it is convenient and trouble-free.

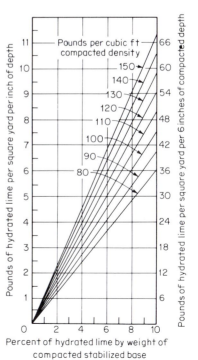

Figure 1-7 Hydrated lime-stabilization chart for determining the rate of application. [Lime Stabilization Construction Manual, *National Lime Association, Washington, 1965*]

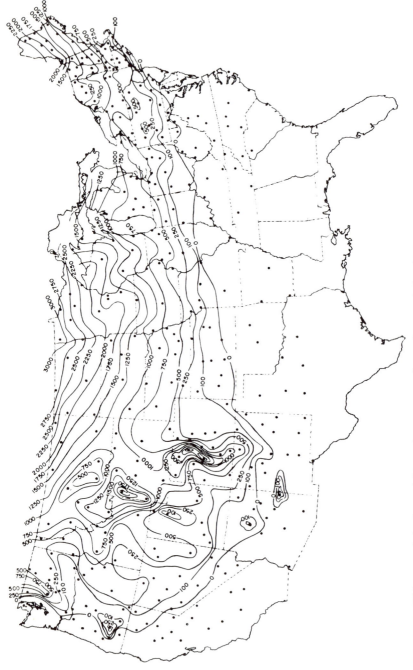

Figure 1-8 This map of the forty-eight contiguous states shows the cumulative degree-days below 32°F (0°C) on the basis of data from 361 National Weather Service stations. Areas with high freezing indices can expect problems with soil frost heaving. [*U.S. Army Technical Manual TM5-818-2*]

Depth of a Stabilized Base

Whether the stabilizing agent is asphalt, cement, or lime, the depth of the base should depend on the amount of traffic, the supporting soil, and the use of the stabilized roadway. There are formulas to help establish the depth, but the following thicknesses will serve in almost all cases:

Traffic Condition	*Base Thickness*
High volumes	8 inches (203.2 millimeters) or more
Moderate volumes	6 inches (152.4 millimeters)
Low volumes on a strong subgrade	5 inches (127 millimeters)
Very low volumes; parking areas	4 inches (101.6 millimeters)

EXCESS-MOISTURE PROBLEMS

Excess moisture in the subsoil is the enemy of any roadway.   It weakens the carrying power, subjects the roadway to frost heaving in northern climates, and complicates maintenance problems.

The U.S. Army Corps of Engineers, in its design recommendations for airfields, advises that subgrade drainage be provided when seasonal fluctuations of groundwater rise in the subsoil beneath a surfaced area to less than 1 foot (0.305 meter) below the bottom of the base course.   The troublesome water may originate from underground springs, from

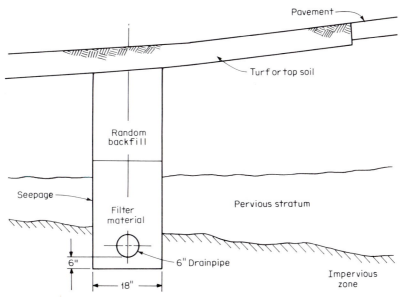

Figure 1-9   Typical installation of intercepting drains.   [*U.S. Army Corps of Engineers*]

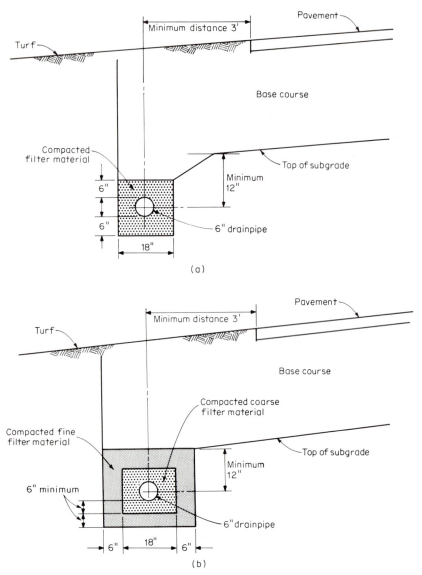

Figure 1-10 Typical details of base drain installations: (*a*) one gradation of filter material; (*b*) two gradations of filter material. [*U.S. Army Corps of Engineers*]

exposed rock that carries water in its layered formations, and from pervious soil layers. The problem is aggravated in spring, when melting snow increases the amount of water that is received in such trouble-prone areas.

To intercept this water and remove it, the Corps recommends the use of drainage pipe. Suitable types of pipe include almost all except farm tile with butt joints.   Farm tile works satisfactorily in agricultural fields but cannot be relied upon where traffic may cause some movement in the soil.

A standard or an extra-strength perforated pipe works well.   This type of pipe can be made of vitrified clay, nonreinforced concrete, corrugated metal, asbestos cement, or cast iron.   If the perforations do not go completely around the pipe, the pipe should be placed with the perforations downwater.

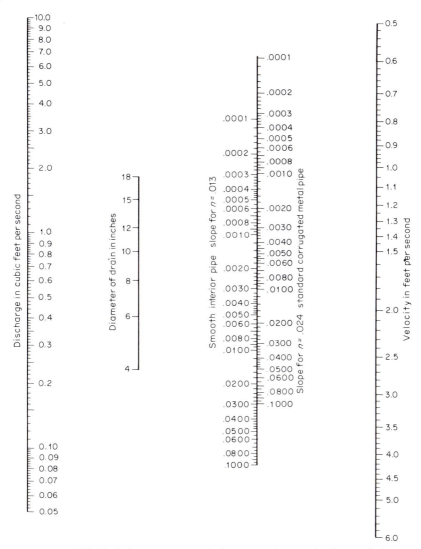

Figure 1-11   Airfield drainage nomograph for computing required size of circular drain, flowing full ($n = .013$ and $n = .024$).   [*U.S. Army Corps of Engineers*]

Nonperforated bell-and-spigot pipe also will serve if the pipe is laid with open joints, partially mortared, and with the joints surrounded with coarse rock to ensure the continuous entry of water.   This pipe can be of vitrified clay, nonreinforced concrete, or cast iron.

A porous concrete pipe with sealed joints also can be used.   However, with any concrete pipe, a check should be made to ensure that the water to be removed is not aggressive and has a low pH.   Aggressive water has a tendency to erode the pipe by reacting with the cement.

For the design of the drainage system, a 6-inch (152.4-millimeter) pipe, laid at a slope of at least 0.15 percent, generally will do.   Manholes should be supplied at least once every 1000 feet (304.8 meters) to expedite cleaning.   To calculate the capacity of the line in cubic feet of flow per second and also the velocity of the water flowing in the pipe, the Corps of Engineers has developed the nomograph in Figure 1-11.   A roughness coefficient n of .013 applies to smooth-barreled pipe and a coefficient of .024 to corrugated metal pipe.

To illustrate how to use the nomograph, a smooth-barreled pipe 6 inches (152.4 millimeters) in diameter, laid at a slope of 0.030, will carry water at the rate of 0.3 cubic foot (0.0085 cubic meter) per second at a velocity of 1.54 feet (0.469 meter) per second.   This velocity should make the line relatively self-scouring.

The line should be embedded in coarse sand, such as concrete sand, as indicated in Figure 1-10.   Where a coarse filter material is indicated, a pit-run gravel will be satisfactory.

BIBLIOGRAPHY

Soil Analysis

Bowles, Joseph E.: *Engineering Properties of Soils and Their Measurements,* McGraw-Hill Book Company, New York, 1970.
Nuclear Testing, Construction Variability, Materials Control and Acceptance, National Academy of Science, Transportation Research Board, Washington, 1969.
PCA Soil Primer, Portland Cement Association, Skokie, Ill., 1962.
Soils Manual for the Design of Asphalt Pavement Structures, Manual Series No. 10, 2d ed., Asphalt Institute, College Park, Md., 1971.

Soil Stabilization

Essentials of Soil-Cement, Portland Cement Association, Skokie, Ill., 1969.
Soil-Cement Stabilization: A Committee Report, American Road Builders' Association, Washington, 1966.

Chapter Two

Asphalt Street Maintenance

WILLIAM S. FOSTER

Basically, the surfacing on improved streets can be grouped into two general types: *flexible*, although most flexible surfacings have some structural strength; and *rigid*, even though rigid surfacings also experience a certain amount of flexibility, deflection, and movement when loads are applied. More specifically, surfacings can be classified as some form either of *asphalt* or of *portland-cement concrete* paving.

Many use the term "concrete" to mean portland-cement concrete. The popular press frequently and incorrectly describes portland-cement concrete as "cement." Concrete is a controlled blend of coarse and fine aggregate bonded together by a cementing agent. The agent may be portland cement, asphalt, occasionally natural cement, or some other cementing agent.

MAINTENANCE OF FLEXIBLE PAVEMENTS

The types of asphalt paving failures requiring the attention of maintenance crews can generally be classified into those caused by weaknesses of the supporting soil and those caused by some deficiency in the asphalt mix itself. Problems caused by weaknesses in the supporting soil can be grouped into these four categories:

1. Alligator cracking, consisting of random interconnected cracks caused by settlement or movement of the soil. The cracks form irregular blocks in the surfacing that somewhat resemble the skin of an alligator.

2. Edge cracking, which occurs longitudinally along the edge of the

Figure 2-1 These random interconnected cracks are known as alligator cracking. [*Asphalt Institute*]

flexible pavement, especially when the edge is not supported by curb and gutter.

3. Ruts or channels, which are generally caused by the consolidation and settlement of the base or the supporting soil without producing fractures in the surface, as is the case with alligator cracks. They may also be caused by the movement of the asphalt surfacing itself if the mix lacks sufficient stability.

4. Heaving, which is caused by the freezing of a water-saturated soil. (It occurs in both flexible and rigid paving types.)

Other flexible-base maintenance problems, which may be traced to deficiencies in the asphalt mix, to improper placement, or to other construction weaknesses, can be grouped into these twelve categories:

1. Longitudinal-joint cracks, which are caused by poor jointing of adjacent spreads of hot-mix, machine-laid asphalt.

2. Reflection cracks, which are most liable to occur when an asphalt surfacing is placed over an old concrete pavement containing cracks and joints.

3. Shrinkage cracks, which are associated with low-penetration asphalt used to surface streets that carry low volumes of traffic.

4. Slippage cracks, which occur when the wearing-surface layer does not bond well with the base course below it. Slippage generally occurs when the base is poorly primed or is not primed at all. Poor compaction of the base may cause added settling and a break in the bond between the surface and the base.

5. Traffic channeling, which generally occurs when concentrated traffic loads cause the supporting soil to settle or displace the asphalt surfacing itself.

6. Washboarding, which results from unstable mixes that contain either too much asphalt or too many fines.

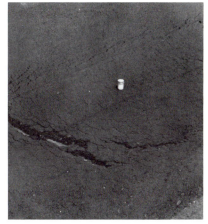

Figure 2-2 Reflection cracks form as the pavement base moves below the surface overlay. [*Asphalt Institute*]

Figure 2-3 Slippage cracks are caused by a failure of the surface course to bond with the base of supporting layer. [*Asphalt Institute*]

7. Potholes, which generally result from a weakness or an imperfection in the mix. Poor drainage also may be a cause.

8. Raveling, which is caused by a lack of asphalt in the mix, by placing the surfacing during wet or cold weather, by using dirty aggregate, or by overheating the mix.

9. Bleeding, which is caused by excess asphalt in the mix or by too heavy a prime coat in the surface treatment.

10. Slippery aggregate, which results from using a soft aggregate, such as certain limestones that polish in traffic and produce a slippery pavement surface.

11. Loss of cover aggregate applied on surface treatments. The cover aggregate may not have been applied promptly, it may not have been rolled quickly enough, or it may have been rolled with steel-tired rather than rubber-tired equipment, which kneads the aggregate more thoroughly into the asphalt.

12. Streaking, which is evidence of an imperfect asphalt distributor that does not spread the asphalt evenly. Streaking can occur along the length of the road or across it. In the latter case, a worn pump or clogged orifices have probably caused the imperfections.

Types of Asphalt

The asphalt to be used for urban-roadway maintenance should be selected carefully. The types used most commonly are cutback asphalts and emulsions.

Cutback Asphalts Cutback asphalts are produced by blending an asphalt cement with a solvent. Depending on the solvent used, the blends can be subdivided into rapid-cure (RC), medium-cure (MC), and slow-cure (SC) cutbacks.

The RC cutback asphalt uses a volatile solvent, such as naphtha or gasoline, which evaporates relatively quickly, thus permitting early use of the surfacing. The surfacing work must be done quickly, before evaporation takes place. The quick-curing feature makes the RC cutback attractive for work in urban areas where traffic must be allowed to use the roadway as soon as possible. As described below, light grades of RC cutback asphalt also work well as prime and tack coats.

The MC cutback asphalt uses kerosine as the solvent. Its slower action makes it useful in street-maintenance operations for which a little more working time is helpful.

The SC cutbacks, or road oils, are a blend of asphaltic residual oils with virtually no volatile portions or of asphalt cement and a residual oil. They are often used for dust laying on unimproved roadways.

Emulsions Asphalt emulsions are a combination of asphalt cement, water, and an emulsifier. The manufacturers prepare them by heating asphalt sufficiently to liquefy it and mixing it with water and the emulsifier. The emulsions generally are about 60 percent asphalt cement and 40 percent water. Asphalt prepared in this way is very convenient to use.

Although standards for emulsions change, the most recent grouping consists of rapid-setting (RS-1 and RS-2), medium-setting (MS-1, MS-2, and MS-2b), and slow-setting (SS-1 and SS-1h) emulsions. The numbers indicate the degree of viscosity, or readiness to flow.

The RS emulsions "break" rapidly; that is, the asphalt cement sets up, and the water drains or evaporates. RS-1 flows more readily than RS-2, which generally requires heating to 130 to 150°F (54.4 to 65.5°C) before it can be pumped through a distributor. RS-2 has about 5 percent more asphalt than RS-1 has.

The most useful of the three MS emulsions is MS-2. It must be held at temperatures between 100 and 160°F (between 37.7 and 71.1°C) to be applied effectively in a bituminous distributor. Because it breaks more slowly than RS emulsions, it is well suited to road mixes, to surface treatments, and to the filling of large voids in penetration macadam.

The slow-setting emulsions do not break immediately when in contact with soils or aggregate and thus are well suited to road-mixing operations. The SS-1h emulsion is made from hard-based asphalt with a penetration of 40 to 90 and works well in slurry seals. The SS-1 uses an asphalt with a penetration of 100 to 200.

Emulsions may be cationic or anionic. Cationic emulsions are made in an acid solution and carry the designation C, as in CRS-1, a rapid-setting cationic emulsion. Anionic emulsions are made in an alkaline solution. Since one type is acid and the other alkaline, they cannot be mixed or stored together. The anionic type stores well, but the choice for a particular application depends on the aggregate that will be used with the emulsion.

The American Association of State Highway and Transportation Officials (AASHTO) cautions against trying to blend any asphalt material with an emulsified asphalt. It also warns against mixing water with an asphalt emulsion. Exceptions are the SS types, which can be diluted if desired.

Air-blown Asphalts These asphalts are a special type that deserves some attention. The manufacturing process changes the thermoplastic character of the asphalt so that its consistency changes very little with variations in temperatures. Air-blown asphalts are thus valuable in joint sealing, subsealing of concrete slabs, and waterproofing concrete structures. To produce air-blown asphalt, the manufacturers use an asphalt obtained from the distillation of crude oil.

Aggregates The aggregates used with asphalts should be clean, free of dust, and dry, with no more than 1 percent moisture, unless they are being used with asphalt emulsions. They should retain the asphalt well. If the asphalt tends to strip off the aggregate surface, between 0.5 and 1 percent of lime may be required in the mixture.

Faulty Mixes Bad asphalt mixes that should be rejected and not be used in a resurfacing program can be identified by some simple rules. The city of Los Angeles instructs its inspectors to reject asphalt paving materials according to these guidelines:

1. Excessively hot mixes can be identified by blue smoke rising from the mix in the truck or in the hopper of the paving machine. If a yellow smoke rises, the material has been burned. Suspected loads should be checked with a thermometer.

2. Excessively cold mixes can be detected if the mix appears stiff or the larger aggregate is poorly coated. Here again, loads should be checked with a thermometer.

3. Too much asphalt can be detected if the mix slumps and levels out in the truck. A good mix remains stiff enough to resist slumping. Excess asphalt in the mix leaves a slick surface after passing through the paver.

4. Too little asphalt is indicated by a brownish, dull appearance. After such a mix goes through the paver, it will not compact properly, and the surface will ravel badly under traffic.

5. Nonuniform mixing will show patchy areas of lean, brown, dull material intermixed with areas that have a shiny, black appearance. Mixtures of this type should be rejected.

6. Excess coarse aggregate will appear to have too much asphalt and will tend to slump in the truck. After the mix goes through the paver, it will produce a surface with a coarse texture.

7. Excess fine aggregate will appear to have insufficient asphalt. The mix will not be adequately coated.

8. Excess moisture is accompanied by steam rising from the mix when it is dumped into the paving hopper. The mix may appear to have too much asphalt and be dark and rich.

9. Segregation of material and contamination by dirt, trash, or debris also are causes for rejection.

Repair Procedures

Asphalt repair procedures must respond to the reason for the failure of the asphalt surfacing. When an asphalt paving surface breaks down, the causes can be grouped under one of three headings:

1. A failure of the base due to insufficient compaction

2. A failure to provide drainage of both surface and subsurface water, with the result that the supporting soil becomes saturated and weak

3. A defect in the mix itself

Insufficient compaction often can be a problem in maintaining new roadways when attention to subsoil compaction was negligent. Drainage problems cause continuing difficulties. Breaks in the paved surface aggravate the danger, and a surprising amount of surface water can enter the subsoil through them. A test at the University of Maryland using portland-cement concrete and a simulated rain of 2 inches (50.8 millimeters) per hour showed that the amount of the water falling on the pavement and entering the cracks ranged from 70 to 95 percent. It is therefore urgent to seal surface breaks promptly.

Cracks   Cracks become a source of damage when they are more than $\frac{1}{8}$ inch (3.2 millimeters) wide. To seal them effectively, they should be cleaned with a hard-bristled broom and compressed air. They should then be filled with a liquid asphalt, generally one of the lighter grades of RC or MC cutbacks. If necessary, the asphalt should be heated so that it will pour easily. A flame torch should not be used to heat a cutback asphalt because it might ignite the naphtha or kerosine.

In the usual practice, one worker pours the liquid asphalt, and another follows with a small U-shaped squeegee, pushing the open end of the squeegee forward to confine the asphalt and work it into the crack. Another worker later scatters sand or small chips onto the sealed cracks.

A maintenance crew in the San Jose, California, Public Works Department was able to simplify the work so that it requires only two workers instead of three, who can fill the cracks faster and more thoroughly. The customary funnel that applies the crack-filling asphalt is hard to operate accurately if the funnel is held waist-high. Moreover, the work is arduous for persons of normal height if they must lean over all day to make sure that the funnel hits the crack accurately. So the San

(a)   (b)

Figure 2-4 (*a*) After a crack has been cleaned, a lead worker fills it with asphalt, while another works the asphalt into the crack with a squeegee. (*b*) A third then scatters sand or small chips onto the sealed crack. [*Asphalt Institute*]

Jose maintenance crew mounted the crack-filling funnel on a pair of wheels. They also mounted a U-shaped squeegee on the wheel axle, with the open end of the U pointed forward so that the operator could cover the crack easily and work the filler into the crack, all without having to bend over. A second operator using a similar wheel-mounted funnel applies the chips or sand over the freshly placed crack filler. This funnel has a small steel roller to embed the chips.

If the cracks are very wide, sand or chips can be mixed with the asphalt to give it more body. The sand content should not be so large that it will interfere with the flow of the asphalt. Hot paving-grade asphalts should not be used for crack filling. They simply bridge over the cracks and do not fill them.

For cracks wider than ½ inch (12.7 millimeters), stronger crack-filling action is desirable. The winter's ice and snow can enter in large enough quantities to do considerable damage to the pavement. The simplest corrective action is to open the crack with a pneumatic hammer and then fill it with a suitable patching mix.

A faster and more effective method is in use in Minneapolis. There the maintenance crews open the crack with a Tennant joint-cleaning router, which removes the distressed asphalt for a width of 5 to 8 inches (137 to 203.2 millimeters) and to a depth of ¾ inch (19.1 millimeters). The routed opening is given a light prime coat or tack coat and then is filled with patching material and rolled. This procedure produces a smooth, bump-free surface. The relatively shallow depth (¾ inch) has proved able to hold the patching material more firmly than a greater depth, and when the roadway is resurfaced, the crack has less tendency to reflect through to the surface and cause fresh damage.

Potholes Potholes, or chuckholes, probably do greater damage to a community's reputation than bad politics does. They are an aggravation, and they are dangerous. If a pothole occurs in winter, during bad weather and in a cold climate, probably the best that a maintenance crew can do is to fill it temporarily with a cold patching material, roll the patch, and hope that the surface holds until spring, when the patch can be replaced with something more permanent. By that time the patch probably will have been pushed out by traffic.

In permanently repairing a pothole, one should realize that something probably was wrong with the mix at this point in the first place. The unsound material should therefore be removed, and the hole trimmed back to the good surfacing. The edges should be cut vertically, and the hole trimmed to a square or a rectangular shape so that it will have a workmanlike appearance.

The exposed subgrade soil should then be examined. It may be wet and soft because of intruding water that entered it through the pothole. The wet material should either be removed or be dried with an infrared heater or a flame torch. As an alternative, a thin layer of portland cement placed on the exposed wet soil will help remove the moisture. If the soil tends to be clayey, hydrated lime may work better.

When the base is firm and dry, the sides and base should be given a light tack coat of MC cutback or an emulsion. This can be applied with a brush or a hand spray. Sufficient time should be allowed to permit the emulsion to break or the volatiles in the cutback asphalt to evaporate;

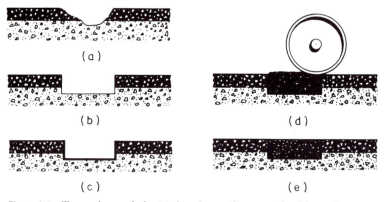

(a)

(b)

(c)

(d)

(e)

Figure 2-5 To repair a pothole, (a) clean it out, (b) square the sides and excavate to sound base material, (c) apply a tack coat to the sides and base, and (d) fill with asphalt patch material and compact with either a roller or a vibrating plate to produce (e) a finished patch level with the adjacent pavement. [*Asphalt Institute*]

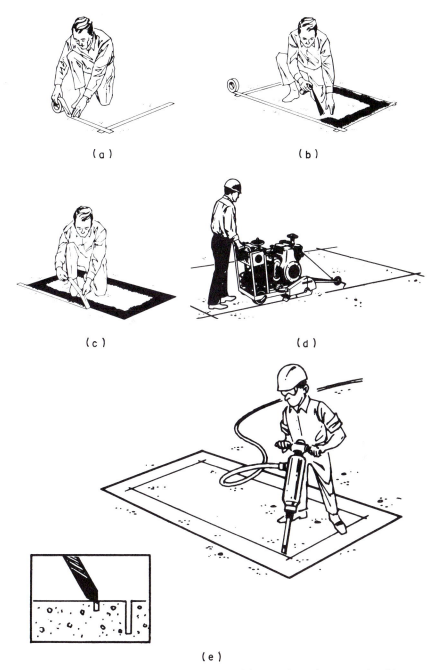

Figure 2-6 For a clean patch, (*a*) mark the area with tape, (*b*) apply spray paint, (*c*) remove the tape, and (*d*) make the cut. (*e*) Use a shallow cut as a guide and get a professional job. [The American City, *September 1972*]

then the patching mix is placed in the hole.   The mix should be compacted thoroughly and placed in 1½-inch (38.1-millimeter) layers. If available, a hot mix should be used.   The temperature should be held around 200°F (93.2°C) at the time of placing.   The hole should not be overfilled.   If it is overfilled, the repair will create a permanent bump in the pavement.

To give a patch a really professional appearance pleasing to the public, the maintenance crew should go to a little extra trouble in marking the area to be removed.   The area should be outlined with masking tape in a square or a rectangular shape.   Paint is then applied with an aerosol can to the interior area outlined by the tape, and the tape is removed to leave the area sharply outlined.   A concrete pavement saw is employed to cut around the outlined area, and a pneumatic hammer is used to cut the area away.   A series of shallow cuts in the area will help the operator of the jackhammer remove the damaged material.   This method also is useful when the pavement is being cut to repair broken water or sewer lines.

Slippage Cracks and Corrugations   As noted above, slippage cracks represent a failure of the surfacing to bond with the base.   To correct this condition, the damaged material should be cut away to the point where the asphalt is bonded to the base.   A trim square or rectangular opening should be made and then primed and filled, as in the method used for potholes.

Corrugations in the roadway surface also damage its usefulness.   If they are extensive, they should be leveled with a heater-planer.   The asphalt surfacing left after the heater-planer has done its work should be very good.   It will have been thoroughly compacted by traffic to a more dense condition than that of new asphalt.   If a seal coat is placed on the planed surface, the result should be a very serviceable pavement.

Depressions   Depressions, or settlements, in paved surfaces are sources of trouble because they allow standing water to collect.   This water is an annoyance to the motorist as well as a hazard.   Moreover, it creates locations of water entry and, thus, of pavement deterioration.

In good maintenance work, the roadway surface should be brought to a grade and crown that approximate the original design.   If the roadway has no formal design, the corrective action should provide quick, positive drainage.

If a depression deepens in the roadway surface so that alligator cracking forms, water can enter and damage the base.   A depression merits corrective action if it is ½ inch (12.7 millimeters) or more in depth. The Asphalt Institute suggests outlining the depressed area with chalk and then grinding the pavement inside the marks, near the edges.   This procedure produces sharp, vertical sides at least ½ inch thick and helps to hold the corrective patching in place.   However, a conscientious worker should be able to fill the depression without this extra effort.

Figure 2-7 Depressions, or "birdbaths," often are indicated by water trapped on the surface. [*Asphalt Institute*]

The first step should be to sweep the area thoroughly. A light tack coat of an emulsion or a cutback asphalt, amounting to not more than 0.05 gallon per square yard (0.23 liter per square meter), should then be applied. When the tack coat becomes sticky, the asphalt mix should be placed in the depression and molded to the correct crown and grade of the roadway.

The mix should contain aggregate no larger than ½ inch (12.7 millimeters), and for stability it should be fairly lean. A template is useful in bringing the pavement to the proper elevation. If the depression is large in area, a skillful operator on a patrol grader can bring the patch to the proper elevation. Rolling should finish the operation.

To correct excessive depressions in chip-sealed or inverted-penetration surfacing on a roadway that has not been built to a precise grade and crown, the maintenance crew can apply added inverted-penetration coats. The first step is to sweep the depressed area carefully. Then a very light tack coat of MC asphalt or emulsion should be applied. Cover aggregate should be placed in the coat and given a light rolling. (Excessive compaction may crush the aggregate.)

These applications should be continued until the correct grade and crown have been obtained. The asphalt should be used sparingly. Too much asphalt will cause instability and surface bleeding. A string line or a template may be used to see that the elevation of the surface is satisfactory.

Fabric Reinforcing Fabric reinforcing for many of the asphalt patches described above is being used increasingly. Asphalt surfacing has a very low tensile strength, which allows cracks in the supporting base to reflect through to the surface. This defect is particularly troublesome when an asphalt surfacing is placed on an old concrete pavement.

Figure 2-8   Polypropylene fabric provides a protective covering for this bridge deck, preventing water from infiltrating through the asphalt into the concrete to corrode the steel.

   The reinforcing is generally made of nonwoven polypropylene, which is nondirectional in character and has a relatively high tensile strength. It also forms a moisture barrier, and is reportedly able to resist a certain amount of movement of the asphalt without rupture.   Typical of these fabrics is Petromat, produced by the Phillips Petroleum Company.

   The fabric has found use on bridge decks, as a reinforcing of surfacing prior to an asphalt overlay, and as a reinforcement for patched pavement.   It is placed directly on the prime or tack coat.   Enough of the tack coat will pass through the fabric to permit the surface coat to adhere to the base.   The employment of fabric reinforcing as a moisture barrier on a bridge deck carrying a hot-mix overlay helps reduce damage from deicing salts.

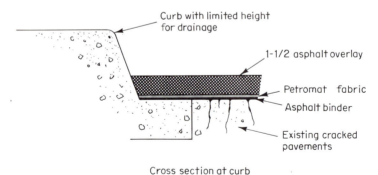

Cross section at curb

Figure 2-9   This sketch shows how polypropylene fabric can be used on a curb section abutting a cracked concrete base to prevent moisture from entering the subbase.

Repair Crews

An effective repair crew is important not only to the efficiency of the work but also to the public, which watches the performance of the repairs.   The public has a tendency to be critical, but if the work crew comes onto the job well equipped and the maintenance personnel do the work promptly and skillfully, the public gains confidence in its local government.

The street-maintenance operation in Kansas City, Missouri, built around a specially designed truck, is an example of this confidence-winning practice. The truck has a long wheelbase but carries a flatbed body of standard size. The flatbed is mounted on the rear of the truck chassis, thus providing room immediately behind the cab for an air compressor and an asphalt-emulsion priming tank mounted on the frame beneath the compressor. A 50-foot (15.24-meter) length of hose with dual connections joins the prime and air tanks to separate nozzles on an extension rod. In preparing a pothole for repair, the operator can use the air blast to clean the hole and employ the other nozzle on the same extension rod to apply the tack coat.

The flatbed portion of the truck contains a "hotbox," a 110-cubic-foot (3.11-cubic-meter) insulated rectangular container with an integral propane heating unit. It has two top opening doors for loading and two rear elevator doors, mounted side by side, for dumping. Below the rear doors is a full-width V-shaped shoveling apron. The apron may be rotated to allow direct dumping from the hotbox to the pothole being filled. By raising the bed, the maintenance personnel can dump large quantities of patching mix for the repair of substantial street areas.

A sideboard on the flatbed provides a convenient carrying place between it and the hotbox for shovels, rakes, and other equipment necessary for the repair operation. A towable roller attached behind the truck is used for the rolling operations once the appropriate quantity of mix has been placed.

The propane heating unit with the hotbox allows hot plant-mixed material to remain heated to the proper temperature over a much longer period of time than is the case with conventional insulated boxes. More of the material is actually used for patching, since this method eliminates the inevitable cooling off of the material otherwise experienced.

This specially designed truck has enabled one crew to be scheduled to do the work formerly required by two crews. Three workers are assigned to the truck for areas of light traffic, and five for heavy-traffic areas. The two extra workers serve as construction traffic directors.

Another street repair combination, which was developed in a somewhat smaller city, Bartlesville, Oklahoma, is built around the use of a trailer rather than a truck. The trailer is a 10-ton (9071.8-kilogram) farm-type vehicle equipped with pneumatic tires. In the rear is a large storage compartment for aggregate, with adjustable slots in the tailgate so that maintenance personnel can shovel out chips for patching purposes. The trailer carries an 850-gallon (3.218-cubic-meter) cationic-emulsion tank in its forward portion; a pipe and hose connection and spray nozzle lead to the rear for convenient application of the emulsion.   In this area, the cationic emulsion adheres best to the aggregate.   An air compressor at the maintenance yard pressurizes the emulsion tank each morning.

The forward portion of the trailer also carries three smaller tanks with capacities of 50 gallons (0.189 cubic meter) each.   These contain water, anionic emulsion, and diesel oil for cleanup work.   Tools are stored in a compartment at one side under the trailer platform.

On the opposite side of the trailer, mounted beneath the trailer floor, is a 100-yard (91.44-meter) roll of polypropylene fabric reinforcing to strengthen the patched areas.   The trailer also carries a small butane-powered hand torch to soften (if necessary) the edges of an area to be patched and a portable vibrator to compact the patches and (if necessary) the subsoil.

SEAL COATS

Seal coats are the final applications placed on an asphalt surfacing after its flaws have been corrected.   If the work is neat and well done, they give the appearance of new roadways.   A veteran director of public works who eventually became manager of his city once said that if he saw a neighborhood beginning to decline, he would provide a good, workmanlike seal coat to the street surface.   Invariably the people in the neighborhood would clean up their yards, often do some painting on their homes, and generally upgrade their surroundings.

Seal coats can be classified into inverted-penetration types, thin, hot mixes, and slurry sealing.   All three kinds should provide a continuous

Figure 2-10   A well-placed seal coat often is all that is needed to improve the appearance of a street and a neighborhood.

surface that is impervious to the entrance of surface water and tough enough to support the traffic that the roadway must carry.

Inverted-Penetration Seal Coats

Inverted-penetration types are the commonest and the least expensive kind of seal coats. The surface must first be carefully broom-cleaned. If the surface is open and porous, it should be primed with a low-viscosity asphalt, which should be given the opportunity of penetrating the surface. The application rate should be between 0.2 and 0.5 gallon per square yard (between 0.91 and 2.26 liters per square meter), and the asphalt should be allowed 24 hours to penetrate the surface. If this time is not allowed, the porous surface being seal-coated will absorb the subsequent application of asphalt, and the seal coat will not adhere well.

The asphalt used for priming should be a light grade if the surface is relatively dense and fine-graded. A heavier grade will perform better on open-textured, porous surfaces. If all the asphalt has not been absorbed during the 24 hours, a light application of sand should be used to absorb the remainder.

On the primed surface, the maintenance crew should apply a liquid asphalt, either an emulsion or a cutback, at a rate of 0.25 gallon per square yard (1.14 liters per square meter) and immediately cover it with rock chips with a maximum size of ⅜ inch (9.53 millimeters). Not more than 1 minute should elapse between the time that the asphalt is placed and the cover material applied so that the aggregate can become firmly embedded. Rolling, preferably with pneumatic rollers, should follow promptly.

Figure 2-11 A pressure distributor applies a prime coat to a roadway surface prior to sealing.

For a good application, the liquid-asphalt binder should embed the rock chips to a little more than half of their thickness. A greater depth will immerse the aggregate and cause "bleeding." A lesser amount will not hold the aggregate and will permit raveling. For a rule-of-thumb guide, 10 pounds (4.536 kilograms) of cover aggregate should be applied for each 0.1 gallon (0.38 liter) of asphalt binder.

The avoidance of any overlapping of asphalt binder is important to obtaining an even surface without bumps. If the distributor does not have a precise set of shutoff and turn-on valves, a good way to get a smooth connection is to stretch wrapping paper across the roadway at the place where the run should end and thus give the distributor operator a little leeway in shutting off the flow of asphalt. When the chips have been placed to cover the binder, the paper should be placed on the freshly laid seal coat at the end of the run. The distributor operator can start on the paper and be sure that the asphalt binder precisely meets the previous run.

To apply the chips, a tailgate spreader works somewhat better than the spinner type. It applies the chips to a precise width with little risk of excess aggregate being lost on the edges. The aggregate must be placed and rolled promptly to avoid its being whipped off by traffic.

A conventional street sweeper has often been used to remove excess aggregate, thus permitting its salvage and reuse. However, this work is heavy duty for a sweeper, and the sweeper hopper should not be loaded more than about half full.

Hot Mixes

A thin, hot-mix layer is frequently preferred in many maintenance programs. A prime coat is required before the hot mix is placed. The

Figure 2-12   Some municipalities prefer a thin, hot mix for a seal coat.

surface will be from ½ to ¾ inch (12.7 to 19.1 millimeters) thick and will have a clean, professional look. The drawback of this method (and that of inverted penetration as well) is that it gradually will raise the elevation of the roadway and wipe out the curb. This can be prevented by featheredging the layer at the gutter and running the risk of future raveling of this thin application.

Slurry Sealing

In the opinion of many, slurry sealing is a superior alternative to either of the two surface treatments. As the name implies, this method of sealing pavements by means of an asphalt slurry makes use of a stable suspension of crushed stone in liquid emulsified asphalt. It requires no heat and releases only water vapor during its cure.

Asphalt emulsions used in slurry seals are either anionic, cationic, or nonionic, depending on whether the electrical charge on each droplet of asphalt is negative, positive, or neutral. The emulsion selected should be in harmony with the aggregate used, particularly when it is required to break on the aggregate and to bond to it in a matter of minutes. Since opposites attract, the emulsion works best with an aggregate having an opposite charge. Most limestone aggregates, for example, work best with an anionic (negatively charged) emulsion; most crushed-gravel types work best with a cationic (positively charged) emulsion. Some prefer gravel to limestone because it is harder and resists crushing or wear. On rare occasions, in places where there is a strong interest in recycling, crushed glass has been used successfully as an aggregate.

Slurry surfacing can be placed in thicknesses varying from ⅛ to ⅜ inch (3.2 to 19.1 millimeters), depending on the size of the aggregate used. The thinner surface reduces the effect of "wiping out" the curb.

For optimum service, the slurry mix will coat each aggregate particle with a film of asphalt 8 micrometers (0.000039 inch) thick. This precise proportioning requires a laboratory test before the slurry is used. In general, the proportions of asphaltic material used in making acceptable slurries are as shown in the accompanying table (the percentages are based on the weight of the dry aggregate plus mineral filler).

	Fine Seal	General Seal
Percent asphalt emulsion	17–27	12.5–28.5
Percent pure asphalt	10–16	7.5–13.5

Several kinds of continuous-mix machines for properly proportioning, mixing, and laying slurry seals are available commercially. Many municipalities find it advantageous to own and operate their own slurry machines. Others award contracts for the work to firms specializing in this type of surfacing.

A pavement to be sealed with slurry must first be cleaned to remove all loose material and vegetable matter. Large cracks should be filled and

Figure 2-13 Slurry sealing places a thin, tough, and frequently skid-resistant surfacing on the roadway without excessively raising the level of the pavement and destroying the usefulness of the curb.

potholes patched.   Spalled-concrete, old-brick, and oxidized-asphalt surfaces should have a tack coat of dilute asphalt emulsion applied prior to slurry sealing.

Optimum atmospheric conditions for the application of slurries are temperatures between 60 and 70°F (between 15.6 and 20.1°C), a relatively low humidity, and a complete absence of rain.   With very quick-setting combinations, however, rain will do little harm to slurries that have been in place for at least 15 minutes before the rain begins.

The machine itself normally applies a light fog coat of water just prior to laying the slurry.   The operator must see that the slurry is neither too wet nor too dry and that the break of the emulsion has not progressed too far before the slurry is finally in place.   In quick-setting combinations, the time available between the start of mixing and the stiffening of the slurry decreases as the temperature of the air and the materials rises.

Cured-slurry surfaces, made with properly proportioned and strong aggregates, provide effective seals against penetration by moisture; they have a relatively long life and are skid-resistant.   The work leaves no loose particles of aggregate that must be picked up and can be thrown by traffic.   This is particularly important at airport runways, where loose stones can cause extensive damage to jet engines.

CORRECTION OF ASPHALT SURFACE PROBLEMS

As indicated above, raveling of the asphalt surface usually is the result of insufficient asphalt in the mix.   If the asphalt raveling has not progressed to the point of approaching disintegration, it can be corrected by a light application of relatively soft cutback asphalt or emulsion with a penetration of 200 to 300. This should be applied at a rate of 0.1 to 0.25 gallon per square yard (0.45 to 1.14 liters per square meter) and covered with clean sand at a rate of 15 to 25 pounds per square yard (8.1 to 13.5 kilograms per square meter).

Oxidized asphalt, or the rapid aging and weathering of the asphalt surface, can produce a general breakdown of the surfacing. Its symptoms are dryness, brittleness, pitting, and shrinkage cracking.

To renew the life of the oxidized surface, a rejuvenating agent can be applied. One that has been studied by the Federal Highway Administration with favorable conclusions is a stable cold-water emulsion of petroleum oils and resins known as Reclamite.[1] The report suggests that the agent can prolong pavement life and serviceability by from 2 to 5 years.

However, the report warns that the rejuvenating agent should not be used on an asphalt surface having air voids of more than 4 percent; nor should it be used on a dense surface or on one having an excess of asphalt, which causes instability. The agent should be used when the weathering problem can be controlled by increasing the penetration and ductility of the asphalt in place.

The product also can be beneficial in improving new construction if the mix is underasphalted or the resulting surface has voids in excess of 4 percent. The treatment will seal the surface and restore fractions of the asphalt driven off at the hot plant and will reduce raveling and the loss of fines. However, the report warns that using the product in new construction can reduce skid resistance.

The product is usually diluted at a ratio of 2 parts Reclamite to 1 part

[1] Reclamite is a product of the Golden Bear Division, Witco Chemical Corporation. The Federal Highway Administration's report is HO-31, dated Sept. 15, 1971.

Figure 2-14 A stable cold-water emulsion of petroleum oils and resins can be applied by a pressure distributor to renew oxidized asphalt.

water and applied by an asphalt distributor in a nonheated condition, although it can be heated if desired. Application rates range from 0.026 to 0.185 gallon per square yard (0.12 to 0.84 liter per square meter) of the diluted combination with an average of about 0.09 gallon (0.34 liter). The manufacturer provides a grease-ring permeability test to determine the application rate. The product is pink when applied, but the color disappears when the material is absorbed. The manufacturer recommends spreading clean sand on the surface after treatment at a rate of 2 pounds per square yard (1.1 kilograms per square meter).

OPEN-GRADED SURFACES

Open-graded asphalt surfaces command a growing interest among many persons in roadway-maintenance work. This type of surface builds skid resistance into the roadway, it minimizes the dangerous effect of hydroplaning of cars on wet pavements, and it reduces the water spray from tires that hampers visibility. In addition, lane-striping paint is considerably more visible during a rain and remains more durable than it does on a dense-graded surface. The Federal Highway Administration considers that this type of surfacing, when properly designed, using good-quality, skid-resistant aggregate, and carefully placed on good, tight, structurally sound, and well-sectioned pavement surfaces, represents the best bituminous skid-resistant surface available at the present time.

An open-graded plant mix contains a large percentage of coarse aggregate, a minimum amount of fine material, and a relatively high asphalt content. The Federal Highway Administration has surveyed current practice in a number of states using this type of surfacing and has discovered that the aggregate gradation shown in the accompanying table would normally produce a mix capable of resisting consolidation from high traffic volumes and high pavement temperatures as well as severe cold-weather conditions.

Sieve Size	Percentage Passing
⅜ inch (9.5 millimeters)	100
No. 4	30–50
No. 8	5–15
No. 200	2–5

An asphalt content of 6 percent appears to be popular for very heavy traffic, and one of 7 percent for medium to light traffic. The asphalt can have a penetration of 85. In very hot weather, the percentage passing the No. 8 sieve can be reduced to 0–10 percent, and that passing the No. 200 sieve to 0–2 percent. The asphalt content would remain unchanged.

A minimum amount of aggregate passing the No. 200 sieve permits a somewhat higher mixing temperature and may produce a tougher mix that is better able to resist snowplow damage. Some use a tack coat before laying the open-graded mix, especially if the existing surface is old and weathered. The tack coat generally is a light application of dilute emulsion.

The aggregate should be crushed gravel, produced either from a quarry or from crushing gravel larger than ¾ inch (19.1 millimeters). The aggregate must resist polishing by traffic, degradation, or stripping the asphalt from the surface.

The mix should be placed to a depth equal to double the size of the maximum aggregate, or ¾ to 1 inch (19.1 to 25.4 millimeters). This will prevent the mix from dragging under the screed. Any "fat" spots (accumulations of excess asphalt) should be raked to spread the asphalt or removed before rolling. Excess asphalt on the surface being covered also should be removed to prevent it from filling the voids in the mix.

Since the layer is thin, it loses heat rapidly and consequently should be placed during warm, dry weather when the pavement surface is at least 70°F (21.1°C). One or two passes of the roller should suffice.

A more permeable form of open-graded asphalt, called "gap-graded," has attracted the attention of environmentalists, who argue that when it is laid on a permeable base structure it will immediately collect the surface water in the subsoil without the need for catch basins or sewers. This, they believe, will eliminate the need for catch basins and storm sewers as well as recharge the groundwater supply.

Some subsoil structures probably can carry the traffic load even when saturated with water. These might be fast-draining subsoils predominantly of coarse sand or gravel or limestone areas, such as exist in Florida. Elsewhere, with a loam or clay subsoil, the advocates propose a 10- to 12-inch (254- to 304.8-millimeter) layer of crushed stone, which they believe will provide the strength.

Experienced highway engineers and maintenance people regard gap-graded asphalts with some doubt. They recognize that water is well known for its ability to reduce the bearing capacity of a subgrade soil and to weaken all the pavement components. Water causes some subgrade soils to swell and others to consolidate. Freezing of the water-soaked soil not only can cause roadway damage but can result in an over-accumulation of water that will further damage the soil structure at the time of thaw. Virtually all agree that moisture is the greatest deterrent to maintenance-free pavement, and virtually all support the current practice of trying to seal water out of the pavement subsoil structure instead of inducing it to enter.

ASPHALT CURBS

Asphalt curbs offer a convenient and attractive means of strengthening asphalt-surfaced streets. They can be built quickly at relatively low cost,

Figure 2-15 Asphalt curbs can outline traffic islands, median barriers, and parking lots, as well as perform the conventional duty of strengthening street edges.

and while they are not as sturdy as portland-cement concrete curbs, they are more resistent to the salt and calcium chloride commonly used in snow and ice control. Machines are available that can place the curbs quickly, at rates of 4 to 7 feet (1.2 to 2.1 meters) per minute. However, the mix can be hand-tamped into the curb forms if a machine is not available. The curbs can be used to outline off-street parking lots and provide traffic islands and median barriers.

For the construction of curbs, the asphalt mix must be stronger than that used for roadway surfacing. The asphalt cement should be harder, usually a grade with a penetration of 60 to 70. If that grade is not available, the penetration can be lowered by the addition of powdered asphalt, which consists of hard or solid asphalt crushed to a fine powder. A penetration grade of 85 to 100, for example, will be reduced to a penetration grade of 60 to 70 by the addition of 15 pounds (6.8 kilograms) of powdered asphalt per 100 pounds (45.4 kilograms) of the 85–100 penetration grade.

The mix also can be strengthened by adding 1 to 3 percent of asbestos fibers.   The Asphalt Institute suggests the classification 7M, Quebec standard testing-machine method.   The asbestos requires an increase in the asphalt content of 1 percent for each 1 percent of asbestos fibers added when using hard asphalt.   If asbestos fibers are used, the grade of the 85–100 penetration asphalt cement need not be lowered with a powdered-asphalt addition.   The asbestos should be added to the heated, dried aggregate in the pug mill no more than 10 seconds before adding the asphalt content.

The aggregate gradation and asphalt content of typical mixes used for asphalt curbs, as suggested by the Asphalt Institute and also by the Federal Housing Administration (FHA), are as shown in the accompanying table.

	Percentages passing by weight	
Sieve size	Asphalt Institute	FHA
¾ inch (19.1 millimeters)	100	100
½ inch (12.7 millimeters)	85–100	95–100
⅜ inch (9.5 millimeters)	. . .	85–95
No. 4	60–80	60–80
No. 8	50–65	44–60
No. 50	18–30	22–32
No. 200	5–15	8–15

The Asphalt Institute suggests an asphalt content of 6 to 9 percent by weight of the total mix, and the FHA suggests one of 6 to 8.5 percent. Both suggest using a 60–70 penetration asphalt cement, and both recommend using the upper penetration limits when the aggregate is slag or another absorptive material.

When the mix is being placed, it should be held to a close range of temperatures, between 275 and 325°F (between 135 and 162.8°C).   Too low a temperature will not permit compaction, while too much heat will present the risk of a slumped curb or material sloughing off.   When placed, the mix should have a low air-void content, between 5 to 10 percent.   The curb should be protected by barricades until it has cooled sufficiently and the asphalt cement has hardened.   The curb-laying machine should not continue to run when empty.   Such a practice produces vibrations in the forms that deform the curb, causing it to slump.

Before the curb is placed, the asphalt surface should be cleaned and primed with a very light application of cutback asphalt or emulsified asphalt in the lighter grades.   The FHA recommends a tack coat applied at 0.08 to 0.2 gallon (0.30 to 0.76 liter) per 15 linear feet (4.57 meters) of curb, depending on the width of the curb and the age of the pavement receiving the curb.   An older, more absorptive surface should, of course, receive a heavier tack coat.

On any extensive work, it becomes necessary to form a joint in the curb at the end of a day's run.   The following day, the exposed end should be primed with a cutback asphalt or an emulsion so that the new curb will bond firmly.

Occasionally curbs must be painted for traffic-control purposes or other reasons.   If the need to paint arises, an oil-based paint should not be applied directly on the curb, since it will soften the asphalt and bleed through the paint.   The curb should first be primed with an asphalt-based aluminum paint; then any type of paint desired may be used.

BIBLIOGRAPHY

AASHTO Maintenance Manual 1976, American Association of State Highway and Transportation Officials, Washington, 1976.

Asphalt in Pavement Maintenance, Manual Series MS-16, Asphalt Institute, College Park, Md., 1967.

Asphalt Overlays and Pavement Rehabilitation, Manual Series MS-17, Asphalt Institute, College Park, Md., 1969.

Asphalt Surface Treatments and Asphalt Penetration Macadam, Manual Series MS-13, Asphalt Institute, College Park, Md., 1964.

Construction Specifications for Asphalt-Concrete and Other Plant-Mix Types, Series 1 (SS-1), 4th ed., Asphalt Institute, College Park, Md., 1969.

Lime Stabilization Construction Manual, National Lime Association, Washington, 1965.

Open-graded Plant Mix, Report HNG-23, U.S. Department of Transportation, Federal Highway Administration, Washington, May 28, 1973.

Specifications and Construction Methods for Asphalt Curbs and Gutters, Series 3 (SS-3), 2d ed., Asphalt Institute, College Park, Md., 1960.

Specifications for Asphalt Cememts and Liquid Asphalts, Series 2 (SS-2), 5th ed., Asphalt Institute, College Park, Md., 1963.

Stabilization of Soil with Asphalt, American Road Builders' Association, Washington, 1965.

Thickness Design, Manual Series MS-1, 8th ed., Asphalt Institute, College Park, Md., 1969.

Chapter Three

Concrete Street Maintenance

WILLIAM S. FOSTER

RIGID PAVEMENT USE IN URBAN AREAS

The term "rigid pavement" refers to portland-cement concrete pavement. It is a type of roadway surfacing with a structure strong enough to overcome many weaknesses in the subbase that would cause distress to flexible pavement. Nevertheless, it has a certain amount of flexibility, just as flexible pavement can be built with some structural strength.

Rigid pavements respond rather actively to temperature, expanding and contracting by measurable amounts each day. This characteristic creates many of the maintenance problems associated with this type of roadway.

These pavements have a higher first cost than most flexible types do, but their maintenance cost is generally much lower. Since maintenance costs rise each year through the forces of inflation, this strong economic advantage should make rigid pavements popular, especially in urban areas.

Offsetting this advantage is the general practice of making special assessments against property owners for the construction of the street improvement. Moreover, these assessments cannot be listed as tax deductions in federal income tax statements. Maintenance costs, in contrast, come from the general tax fund and are deductible. So, by virtue of existing tax laws, a street improvement with a high first cost and a low maintenance cost has substantial artificial disadvantages.

Of course, flexible pavements are not always associated with high maintenance costs. Under favorable conditions, if the supporting soil is stable and is not subject to freezing and thawing in winter or to excessively high temperatures in summer, flexible pavements can be as nearly maintenance-free as rigid types can.

MATERIALS FOR RIGID PAVEMENTS

Portland cement is the distinctive ingredient of rigid pavements. Manufacturers produce portland cement by first grinding a carefully measured mixture of calcareous, aluminous, and siliceous materials, then burning the mixture in a rotary kiln until it just begins to vitrify, and finally regrinding the vitrified clinker while adding a small amount of gypsum.

The resulting gray powder combines chemically with water to form a strong, dense mass, which continues to harden as long as it has access to moisture, but at a steadily diminishing rate. Theoretically, portland-cement concrete continues to harden indefinitely. However, the forces of deterioration and decomposition eventually overcome this trend.

The addition of sand and coarse aggregate to the cement paste forms what is known as concrete. The strength of the concrete is controlled principally by the developed strength of the cement paste. The smaller the amount of water used in the cement paste, the greater the developed strength of the cement mortar. To a lesser degree, the strength is a function of the maximum size and structural characteristics of the coarse aggregate and of the cement-aggregate ratio.

Water-Cement Ratio

Since the amount of water is of such importance, designers use a water-cement ratio when specifying concrete strength. Concrete shows its greatest strength when it bears compressive loads. However, since critical stresses in concrete pavement are flexural rather than compressive, the structural design of a concrete pavement is based on its flexural strength as determined by the familiar beam test. The modulus of rupture in flexure for concrete that is 28 days old, a common test period, may be 500 pounds or as high as 1000 pounds per square inch (3447 or 6895 kilopascals).

Generally, the water-cement ratio is expressed in terms of United States gallons of water per sack of cement, and this is a convenient method for most urban maintenance work, which frequently involves small mixers and bagged cement. As Figure 3-1 shows, the lower the water-cement ratio, the stronger the concrete, if it is assumed that the mix is designed to be workable.

Many prefer to express the water-cement ratio in terms of pounds of water per pound of cement, especially on larger projects that make use of cement in bulk. However, the figures are easily interchanged, since a gallon of water (0.0038 cubic meter) weighs 8.345 pounds (3.785 kilograms) and a sack of cement 94 pounds (42.64 kilograms).

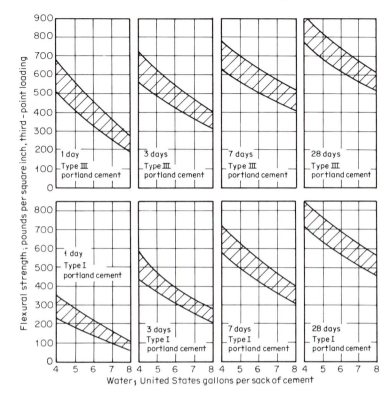

Figure 3-1 The water-cement ratio governs the strength of the concrete. The upper curves show the variations at differing ages for Type III high-early-strength cement. The lower curves show the same variations for Type I standard cement. [*Portland Cement Association*]

For most pavement work in areas subject to harsh winter weather, concrete mixes are designed on the basis of a water-cement ratio of 5.5 to 6 gallons (21 to 23 liters) per sack of cement. In more moderate climates, the ratio can be between 6 and 6.5 gallons (between 23 and 25 liters) per sack.

Mixing

The time required for the cement paste to set is important in the orderly processing of the work. It depends basically on the fineness of the cement grind, which is reflected in the heat of hydration. The heat of hydration is most critical in mass concrete as in dams and least critical in relatively thin slabs as in pavements. The time needed for setting also can be controlled by the amount of tricalcium silicate in the chemical composition.

The setting time must permit the concrete to be placed and finished while it is plastic and workable. The time for mixing generally is set for

Figure 3-2 Truck mixers, which provide concrete for much municipal maintenance work, must be subject to detailed control if the quality of the concrete is to remain reliable.

at least 1 minute, or long enough for the cement and aggregate to be mixed thoroughly.

Occasionally, in maintenance work concrete is left standing in the mixer, and the concrete tends to stiffen before the cement has hydrated to its initial set. The Portland Cement Association advises that such concrete need not be wasted but may be used if, upon remixing, it becomes sufficiently plastic so that it can be placed in the forms and compacted. A small amount of water can be added if this does not result in exceeding the water-cement ratio or the maximum specified allowable slump. The concrete should be remixed for at least half the minimum time required for a normal batch, or half the specified number of revolutions of the mixer drum. Concrete that is remixed in this manner can be expected to harden quickly.

Frequently concrete for this maintenance work will be delivered by a truck mixer. When the concrete is completely mixed by such a unit, the drum should rotate from 70 to 100 revolutions at the speed recommended by the manufacturer. Specifications by the American Society for Testing and Materials (C94) require that the concrete from truck mixers be discharged within 1½ hours, or before the drum has revolved 300 times, after the introduction of water to the cement and aggregates or of the cement to the aggregates.

Types of Cement

The difference in brands of cement may be a slight problem in street maintenance, especially if the work is large enough to require more than one plant to supply the concrete on a given day. Cements manufactured by a particular company generally produce a concrete of a distinctive color. To avoid a patchwork effect on the pavement, the producers of the concrete should be required to use cements with the same coloring, preferably from the same manufacturer.

At least five types of portland cement, as well as a variety of special cements, should be familiar to urban maintenance personnel. A knowledge of them will assist materially when effective maintenance practices are planned and unusual conditions must be faced. Three types are commonly used in most pavement work and normal concrete maintenance and repair:

Type I cement is the standard cement used for the great bulk of construction and maintenance work.

Type II cement has been designed to provide good resistance against sulfate and alkali attack. It should be specified for concrete subject to attack by seawater, alkaline water, or alkaline soil.

Type III cement attains high early strength through its extremely fine grind and the addition of tricalcium silicate.

Other cements, less frequently used, will respond to the needs of special conditions. The principal types are as follows:

Type IV cement will generate a low amount of heat of hydration while setting. This makes it useful in massive concrete structures where the heat of setting generated by the more commonly used cements might be troublesome.

Type V cement is highly resistant to sulfate damage. In some areas of the United States, soil and water are highly alkaline and will damage concrete even though it has been made with Type II cement. Type V sets slowly and attains a higher ultimate strength.

Waterproof cement used in concrete walls and similar structures will prevent the flow or seepage of water through the concrete.

White portland cement is used principally in architectural concrete and for other decorative purposes.

Oil-well cement will set and form a strong concrete even when subject to high temperatures.

Plastic cement is used in cement mortar mixes. However, a little hydrated lime or fireclay can improve the workability of Type I cement if plastic cement is not readily available.

Aggregates

Aggregates used with cement paste are much less costly than the cement itself. Consequently the more aggregate that can be placed in the concrete mix, the more economical the concrete will be. This circumstance frequently tempts designers to produce dry, harsh mixes, and often these can be placed with the use of vibrators. However, the workability of the mix for the purpose cannot be overlooked. Both workability and strength are mandatory.

The strength of the concrete depends not only on the water-cement ratio but also on the strength and characteristics of the aggregate.   A crushed-gravel coarse aggregate with fractured surfaces permits the mortar to bond more firmly and to develop greater strength.   Similarly, a sand that is "sharp" and not rounded produces a stronger concrete.

Aggregates can be divided into two categories, fine and coarse.   Fine aggregate is sand, coarse aggregate is gravel or crushed stone, often limestone.

The fine and the coarse aggregate in the mix should provide an evenly graded combination so that they will blend well with the cement paste when placed in the mixer.   Too large a coarse aggregate will interfere with mixing operations.   As an absolute maximum, the largest size should never exceed one-third of the thickness of the pavement slab. Too much fine material in the sand will require excessive amounts of cement paste because of the additional surface area that must be coated. Both fine and coarse aggregates should be free from dirt and silt, organic matter, and soft material such as clay, shale, and mica.

For gunite or shotcrete work, which are described in Chapter 4, the moisture content of the sand must be held to a close range.   It should not be more than 5 to 6 percent or less than 3 percent.   Too wet a sand will clog in the pneumatic gun, and too dry a sand will develop uncomfortable amounts of static electricity that will trouble the nozzle operator.

Occasionally lightweight aggregate is needed for specialized construction and maintenance work on structures other than pavement.   Normal concrete weights about 150 pounds per cubic foot (2403 kilograms per cubic meter).   Lightweight aggregate can reduce this weight to as little as 40 pounds (641 kilograms per cubic meter), which is helpful in minimizing dead loads.

Lightweight aggregate can consist of (1) expanded blast-furnace slag; (2) natural deposits of volcanic cinders, pumice, diatomite, and similar materials; (3) industrial cinders; and (4) heat-expanded clays, shales, and vermiculite.   Since all these materials are porous, they must be moistened thoroughly before use.   Because of their rough, irregular shapes, they require large amounts of fine aggregate to make them workable. Expandable, lightweight aggregate, of course, will not produce a concrete with the compressive strength of that made with normal aggregates.

Extra-weight aggregates are useful in making concrete for purposes such as counteracting buoyancy in underwater construction.   The most convenient type is steel scrap such as punchings.   These should be placed directly in the concrete and not be run through the mixer because of possible damage to the mixer blades.   The concrete should have a low slump, and it should not be vibrated internally because this will cause the steel to settle.   External vibration also should be held to a minimum.

An iron oxide aggregate such as magnetite or ferrous sulfide also can be used. These aggregates can produce a concrete as heavy as 240 pounds per cubic foot (3844 kilograms per cubic meter), or 90 pounds per cubic foot (1441 kilograms per cubic meter) heavier than normal concrete. The aggregate can be used in a standard mixer, but it may overload conventional ready-mix trucks.

CONCRETE-MIX DESIGN

The precise design of a concrete mix is important on large construction projects involving substantial quantities of material. For most urban maintenance work, for which the quantity of concrete is much smaller, standard mixes such as those suggested below should serve well. In general, unless the governmental unit is large and maintains a well-equipped materials and testing laboratory, the design of a mix should be left to a commercial testing laboratory or to the facilities of the state highway department if they are available.

Actually, the procedure is simple and straightforward, being based on the consideration of absolute volumes, or theoretical voidless volumes of the material used in the concrete. The first step is to select the strength of concrete wanted. For most work on street maintenance, a water-cement ratio of 5.5 to 6 gallons (20.8 to 22.7 liters) per sack provides ample strength. The second step is to make a trial batch based on the ratio selected. The calculations below can serve as a good start in selecting the quantities of cement, sand, and coarse aggregate needed. The quantities of each material should be carefully weighed, and the quantities of fine and coarse aggregate varied until they produce a mix that is easily workable.

After the quantities in the trial mix have been determined, the next step is to translate the quantities into absolute volumes, or the volumes of water that the materials will displace, thus providing the volume of each ingredient. This is done by dividing the weight of each ingredient by its specific gravity and then dividing this figure by 62.4 pounds, the weight of a cubic foot of water. The specific gravity of cement generally is 3.14; of most sands and coarse aggregates, between 2.65 and 2.70. The specific gravity of water is, of course, 1.

To illustrate how this calculation is made, let us assume that a satisfactory mix would require these quantities per sack of cement:

Cement	94 pounds (1 sack; 42.64 kilograms)
Sand	205 pounds (92.99 kilograms)
Gravel	365 pounds (165.56 kilograms)
Water	6 gallons* (0.0227 cubic meter)

*50.0 pounds at 8.34 pounds per gallon.

The water represented by moisture in the sand and gravel must of course be determined and included as part of the 6 gallons used in the mix.

The yield of the mix then can be calculated as follows:

Cement $\dfrac{94}{3.14 \times 62.4}$ = 0.480 cubic feet (specific gravity, 3.14)

Sand $\dfrac{205}{2.65 \times 62.4}$ = 1.240 cubic feet (specific gravity, 2.65)

Gravel $\dfrac{365}{2.65 \times 62.4}$ = 2.207 cubic feet (specific gravity, 2.65)

Water $\dfrac{6.0 \times 8.34}{62.4}$ = 0.802 cubic feet (specific gravity, 1)
Total $\qquad\qquad\qquad$ $\overline{4.729}$ cubic feet

Thus, on a void-free basis, the mix selected will yield 4.725 cubic feet (0.1338 cubic meter) of concrete per sack of cement. Some minute voids (no more than 1 percent) probably will be present but not in sufficient quantity to harm the accuracy of the calculation. If the cement selected is the air-entraining type, an additional 5 percent of volume must be added to represent the air voids introduced to make the concrete more resistant to scaling.

COLD-WEATHER CONCRETE PLACEMENT

A few precautions should be followed when it becomes necessary to place concrete in weather that approaches freezing:

1. Concrete should not be placed by ordinary fair-weather methods when the air temperature in the shade at the site is 35°F (1.7°C) and descending.

2. If concreting must be performed during freezing weather, the mixing water and the aggregates should be heated but not to more than 90°F (32.2°C). High-early-strength cement should be used if available.

3. Concrete placed in freezing weather, when the temperature is expected to drop below 32°F (0°C), requires protection by some sort of insulation such as hay or straw to a depth depending on the degree of temperature drop expected but not less than 3 or 4 inches (76.2 or 101.6 millimeters). The hay or straw should be held in place by burlap or a similar secure method. It should be kept in place for 3 or 4 days.

4. Concrete work by ordinary warm-weather methods can start when the air temperature in the shade is 35°F (1.7°C) and rising.

5. When ready-mix concrete is used and the air temperature at the site is 45°F (7.2°C) or less, the delivered concrete must have a temperature of at least 65°F (18.3°C).

CONCRETE EXPANSION, CONTRACTION, AND JOINTING

Often the maintenance of concrete pavement involves the repair of an area around a crack or an expansion or contraction joint. Consequently an understanding of how concrete performs in expansion and contraction is helpful.   It is recognized that portland-cement concrete expands and contracts in this general manner:

1. It contracts during setting.

2. It will not expand to a length as great as it occupied when it was poured and before its initial set.

3. It expands and contracts each day with the change in air temperature.   It also has a tendency to curl slightly, because the surface of the slab will be warm and dry and the base relatively cool and moist.

Maintenance work will also be better performed if those in charge know clearly what a joint or a crack in the pavement is and how they perform.

A *joint* in a pavement is a separation of the slab made artificially during construction.   It may be a contraction joint placed to relieve the stresses of tension in the pavement caused by shrinkage.   The contraction joint may be transverse, dividing the slab into segments of 15 to 20 feet (4.57 to 6.09 meters), or longitudinal to prevent random cracking down the center of the pavement.   A joint can be an expansion joint, installed to permit greater movement of the slab if conditions of construction require it; or it can be a construction joint, created at the end of a day's work.

A *crack*, in contrast, is a pavement separation that occurs naturally despite a designer's efforts to anticipate and prevent its occurrence.   A concrete expert once observed that he did not believe that God ever made any stonelike material more than 20 feet (6.09 meters) long without providing cleavage in it.   A crack may form despite the careful placing of contraction joints.   One should not assume that concrete is faulty if cracks occur within 6 feet (1.83 meters) of any artificially placed joint.

Expansion and Contraction Joints

Since concrete is as long as it ever will be when it is poured and before setting, there is really no need for expansion joints to accommodate a greater length. As a result, most concrete pavement designs omit or markedly reduce the use of these joints, confining their employment to locations where the concrete abuts some fixed object, such as a building, a manhole or valve box, or a bridge abutment.   Most designs surround the concrete in the center of an intersection with expansion material to accommodate pavement movement at right angles.

Frederick G. Lehman states that concrete can be expected to change in length by 0.66 inch (16.76 millimeters) per 100 feet (30.48 meters) for an air-temperature change of 100°F (55.6°C).[1]   So if the concrete did not crack or had no joints, the ends would move between 6 and 7 inches

---

[1] "Materials for Reinforced Concrete," in W. S. La Londe, Jr., and Milo F. Janes, *Concrete Engineering Handbook*, McGraw-Hill Book Company, New York, 1961, p. 1–51.

Figure 3-3   A contraction joint placed in concrete pavement by a saw ensures that the joint will be straight and the pavement remain relatively smooth, with little tendency to spall at the joint.   This joint is in an airport runway.

Figure 3-4   The saw that makes the contraction joint uses a blade of this type, which is provided with industrial diamonds for cutting.

Figure 3-5 When the pavement must be cut to repair or service buried utilities, the opening should be made with a concrete saw. [The American City]

(between 152.4 and 177.8 millimeters) in 1000 feet (304.8 meters) of pavement subject to a 100° change in temperature.

Pavement designs anticipate this shrinkage and cracking by supplying contraction joints across the pavement for every 15 to 20 feet (4.57 to 6.09 meters) of its length. The designs also supply longitudinal joints that generally divide the pavement into traffic lanes and reduce the incidence of random cracks down the center. These joints may be in the form of a weakened plane, provided by a metal or a polyethylene strip, or they may be made by a concrete saw that cuts about 1 inch (25.4 millimeters) into the pavement shortly after the concrete has taken its initial set.

For pavements subject to heavy traffic, the designs provide extra reinforcing at the ends, especially at the corners of the slabs, and smooth dowel bars that keep the ends of the slabs in alignment, preventing faults or offsets in elevation at the joints. On the dowel bars provided for transverse joints, grease or paint is applied to the portion extending into one of the slab ends so that it will not bond to the concrete but will slip and permit the concrete slab to expand and contract with the air temperature. For pavements carrying relatively light traffic loads, as in residential areas, the load transfer across the joints can be provided by the interlock of the aggregate at the joint fracture instead of by dowel bars.

Joints also must be provided for separate concrete curb and gutter sections, which are used frequently to support and supply drainage for a bituminous pavement surface. Weakened-plane joints every 10 feet (3.048 meters) and expansion joints every 30 feet (9.144 meters) should be sufficient to meet the most difficult conditions.

Sealing of Cracks and Joints

Pavement blowups occasionally occur, suggesting that expansion joints are needed. However, not lack of expansion space but inadequate maintenance is the reason for this problem. The blowups are caused by the entrance of sand, dirt, and other incompressible material into the open crack when the slab has contracted, especially during cold winter weather. This incompressible material takes up the space that the slab normally would occupy during warm weather. As this process occurs and reoccurs, the intruding sand and dirt generate compressive stresses in the concrete too great for it to withstand. The result can be a spectacular blowup.

Prompt and thorough sealing of the cracks and joints by the maintenance crews can prevent this difficulty. Consequently this work is an important part of the maintenance of concrete pavement. Sealing the cracks and joints also prevents the entry of water from the surface that would soften the supporting soil and weaken its ability to carry the traffic load. It also prevents "pumping" at the joints, a problem that is discussed in Chapter 4.

Joints and cracks require sealing whenever the old sealing material becomes hard and brittle and cannot move with the movement of the slabs. Although this condition can occur at any time, resealing in the spring and fall is critical and is often badly neglected, resulting in unnecessary damage to the pavement.

Sealing material for both joints and cracks falls into two general classifications: rubberized sealers, applied both hot and cold; and polysulfide-base sealers.

The hot-applied rubberized sealers should meet either of two federal specifications, SS-S-164 or 167b. Both must be applied at a temperature of 350°F (176.7°C), heated in a double-shell kettle, fired indirectly. The kettle should have mixing equipment to agitate the sealer so that it will be heated uniformly. It should also have a pump and a pressure hose with an applicator to place the material in the cleaned joint. Small double-boiler types of portable applicators that apply the sealer by gravity also are available.

The polysulfide sealer is a two-part self-vulcanizing material meeting federal specifications SS-S-00200e. It requires a bond-breaking tape, either of pressure-sensitive aluminum foil or of polyethylene placed at the bottom of the joint. A special proportioning, mixing, and placing machine applies the sealer at a temperature of not less than 60°F (15.6°C).

To prepare joints for sealing, the maintenance crew must first remove the old inelastic sealing compound. Self-propelled power cutters and routing machines can be used to cut away the material without damaging the edges of the pavement joint. A power brush then should be run through the joint to clear away any remaining sand and dirt.

To seal the joint, the first step is to blow the opening clean with oil-free compressed air. Next, the joint should be filled from the bottom to within ⅛ inch (3.17 millimeters) of the top. The sealed joint is then covered with paper, sawdust, or sand to prevent tracking. If hot-applied rubberized sealers are used, no attempt should be made to reheat and reuse the material once it has been heated and then allowed to cool.

To prepare cracks for sealing, the maintenance supervisor must recognize which cracks should be sealed. Hair cracks, which are surface cracks that extend for only a limited depth, should not be sealed. Although they represent a weakness in the concrete slab, placing a sealer on such cracks will not correct the weakness and will only make the pavement rough and unattractive.

Cracks that require sealing must pass through the entire slab depth, and they must be opened wide enough for the cutters, routing tools, and sealer to enter. If the sealing material merely lies on the surface, traffic will soon displace it.

A routing tool to be used on cracks should have a vertical rotating bit that will mill the sides of the crack to a width of about ⅜ inch (9.52 millimeters) and a depth of 1 inch (25.4 millimeters). This opening will permit the crack to receive the sealing material and allow the material to penetrate the remainder of the crack. The debris should be removed from the opened crack with a power brush, compressed air, or both. The crack may then be sealed by the procedure outlined for joints.

Spalled Joints

Spalled joints, joints with a portion of the concrete near the surface, may disfigure the pavement. If they are small, they can be filled with a joint-sealing material. If they are large, a cement mortar patch is preferred because it matches the appearance of the pavement.

In the past, maintenance crews have found it difficult to place cement mortar patches in relatively thin layers in locations such as this and feel sure that they would remain in place. However, new epoxy adhesives permit these layers to bond securely and to withstand the impact of heavy traffic. Where traffic is less heavy, careful workmanship can generally produce a sufficiently strong bond without epoxy.

Spall repair starts with the removal of all unsound material, exposing the firm, strong concrete. This material must be chipped away, and any dust or remaining fine material must be blown or brushed out thoroughly.

Commercial hydrochloric or muriatic acid should then be applied carefully because of possible danger to the person making the application. The acid should be placed on the bottom and sides of the spalled area while it is still moist. It should be allowed to react with the alkalinity of the exposed concrete and then flushed away until a check with litmus paper shows that a neutral condition exists on the exposed surface.

The next step is to brush a coating of epoxy grout or sand-cement grout mixed at a ratio of 1 part epoxy or cement to 1 part of sand. Then the spalled area should be overfilled with a cement-sand mortar of a 1:2 mix. The mortar should be stiff and barely workable. It should then be tamped firmly into the patched area to ensure that it makes solid contact with the concrete. The finish of the patch should be as close to the texture of the adjoining concrete as possible.

None of the mortar should be permitted to bridge across the joint. If mortar does cross the joint, it can cause disruptive stresses in the patch when the slabs move. If the spalls occur on both sides of a joint, the patch can be extended across the joint but must be cut open with a concrete saw to separate the slab. The repaired joint should then be cleaned and resealed in accordance with previously outlined procedures.

Extensively spalled areas can be repaired by the same general method. However, the area to be repaired should be outlined by a concrete saw making a 1-inch (25.4-millimeter) vertical cut, shaping it to a neat, rectangular shape. By making several cuts to the same depth within the spalled area, workers can remove the defective material more easily. The cuts should parallel one side of the outlined area and be about 6 to 9 inches (152.4 to 228.6 millimeters) apart.

After treating the area with acid and placing the bonding grout, the maintenance crew can resurface with a low-slump concrete, preferably one using an air-entraining cement. The mix can be 1 part cement to 3 parts sand. Small, coarse aggregate can be used to advantage, the largest size being no greater than half the depth of the area being patched. If cement, sand, and coarse aggregate are to be used, they should be mixed at a ratio of 1:1½:1½. The water-cement ratio should be no more than 4 or 5 gallons (15.1 or 18.9 liters) of water per bag of cement. This mix, of course, must be tamped firmly into place with a vibrating screen, if one is available. The finish should resemble that of the adjoining concrete.

BIBLIOGRAPHY

Air-entrained Concrete, Portland Cement Association, Skokie, Ill.
Design and Control of Concrete Mixtures, 11th ed., Portland Cement Association, Skokie, Ill., 1968.
Fast Concrete Pavement Patching, Portland Cement Association, Skokie, Ill., 1964.
Maintenance Practice for Concrete Pavement, Portland Cement Association, Skokie, Ill., 1956.
Portland Cements, Portland Cement Association, Skokie, Ill., 1971.

Chapter Four

Miscellaneous Street-Maintenance Practices

WILLIAM S. FOSTER

UTILITY CUTS

Utility cuts, especially in concrete pavement, are the most common and, to the public, the most aggravating maintenance work, especially if a cut must be made in new pavement. In a well-run municipality, the director of public works frequently conducts regular meetings with appropriate representatives of the other utilities so that all can coordinate their work and minimize these disagreeable pavement openings.

Nevertheless, in an emergency, such as a break in a water pipeline, the pavement frequently must be opened, the repair made, and the concrete replaced. If the work is not done well, a substantial investment in street surfacing can be badly damaged, and the results are clearly visible to an annoyed public.

Since the pavement must be opened, the work should be done as neatly as possible. A concrete saw should make a cut about 2 inches (50.8 millimeters) deep at right angles to the pavement center line. The cut should provide an opening in the pavement about 1.5 to 2 feet (0.4572 to 0.6096 meter) wider than the trench that will be excavated. The concrete then can be broken with a pneumatic hammer or similar pavement-breaking equipment. This will provide a trim upper edge and an irregular fractured face below the cut that will interlock with the patch when it is placed and help to hold it firmly. Any reinforcing steel should be cut and bent back to permit excavation of the trench. (See Figure 3-5 for procedure.)

After excavation and repair of the utility, the most important task is to replace the excavated material. The best results are obtained when the density of the soil being used for backfill approaches that of the soil adjacent to the trench. When the density of the soil is consistent throughout the pavement area, settlement problems will be minimal.

First, the utility pipe must be carefully bedded. Clean sand makes a good bedding material when it has been compacted into place. Next, the trench backfill, using the excavated earth, should be replaced in lifts no greater than 1 foot (0.3048 meter) and compacted to a density approaching and slightly greater than that of the surrounding soil. The most convenient tool to determine this is a nuclear soil-density meter (see Chapter 1). The tamping preferably should be done by a mechanical tamper or vibrating plate. Rocks larger than 6 inches (152.4 millimeters) should not be placed in the fill, nor should frozen soil be used. However, in cold winter weather modern power equipment can make excavations even though the ground is badly frozen, thus permitting year-round work in areas that in the past have had to remain closed for the winter.

When a trench is being backfilled in subfreezing weather, the fill should consist of granular material placed at the bottom of the trench for bedding; it should cover the pipe or conduit to within 5 feet (1.524 meters) of the ground surface. The rest of the trench can then be filled temporarily with frozen material and topped with a temporary bituminous cover so that the street can remain in service. In the spring, the bituminous material can be removed, and the frozen material allowed to thaw and be recompacted as described above.

FULL-DEPTH PAVING PATCHES

According to the Portland Cement Association, the depth of a patch reaching the full depth of the pavement slab should be from 10 to 30 percent greater than the concrete it replaces. The deepest portions should be in areas with unprotected corners. If the portion of the concrete to be replaced involves an expansion or a contraction joint, the patch should be at least 6 feet (1.8288 meters) wide. In general, reinforcing steel will not be needed for these thicker patches. However, existing reinforcing bars that remain when the concrete has been broken away can be reused and will help to tie the patch to the existing slab.

The cement used in concrete for patching, for the convenience of the public, should be high-early-strength Type III cement. The water-cement ratio should be low, with no more than 4 gallons (15.1 liters) of water for each sack to provide a strong concrete. If high-early-strength cement is not available easily, calcium chloride, amounting to 2 percent of the weight of the cement, can be added. For best results, the calcium chloride should be dissolved in the mixing water. It can be added dry by placing it with the aggregate in the hopper, but not in contact with the cement. No more than 2 percent calcium chloride should be used. Greater amounts will injure the strength of the concrete and unduly hasten settling, making the concrete difficult to finish.

If the work must be performed in an area with a cold climate, in which snow and ice are controlled by the use of chlorides, the concrete for the patch should be made of air-entraining cement. If this cement is not easily available, an air-entraining agent should be added, or, lacking this, the finished concrete should be given an application of linseed oil.

To minimize inconvenience to the public, a large patch should be placed over the width of one traffic lane at a time.

SLAB JACKING

Slab jacking, or mud jacking, is a very useful method of correcting many of the problems of concrete pavement without having to relay a portion of the pavement. It restores the elevation of concrete slabs that have settled because of subsoil problems and fills voids that have developed beneath them.

This practical method has resolved many of the difficulties that have arisen as the loads that pavements are forced to carry have steadily increased, both in number of vehicles and in their gross weights. Voids frequently develop beneath the pavement slabs, particularly near bridge abutments and fixed structures. Soils of different types in the subgrade may compact differently and leave voids. And, as mentioned earlier, pumping can occur at joints, especially when fine-grained soil supports the pavement. When this pumping action persists, it can dislodge enough soil so that the concrete breaks.

Material and Equipment

Originally, slab jacking actually used mud, which was pumped under pressure through holes bored in the concrete. Later, those doing the work discovered that they obtained better results by adding cement to the mud. Today mud has been replaced with a fine-grained sand or limestone mixed with cement, occasionally with fly ash added, and often with a wetting agent to increase the flowability of the slurry.

The American Association of State Highway and Transportation Officials (AASHTO) suggests a fine mortar sand with at least 30 percent passing through the No. 200 sieve. When limestone is used, AASHTO suggests that 100 percent pass through the No. 50 sieve and not less than 60 percent through the No. 200 sieve. For a mix, the association suggests a ratio of cement to sand or limestone of 1:4 or 1:5. If fly ash is

available the ratio of fly ash, cement, and sand or fine limestone may be
1:1:6. Frequently, specifications require the slurry to have a minimum
strength of 300 pounds per square inch (2068.4 kilopascals), as determined by compression tests on a 6- by 12-inch (152.4- by 304.8-
millimeter) cylinder 7 days old.

The Federal Highway Administration suggests a soil-cement slurry.
The soil should be A-4 classification, silty, or preferably A-2-4
(AASHTO standards, discussed in Chapter 1). It should be free of clay
balls or aggregations of any kind, with 35 percent passing through the
No. 200 screen. One or two bags of cement should be used per cubic
yard (0.7645 cubic meter) of material. The cement prevents some of
the shrinkage and aids the mixture in setting up. Water should be
added to produce the consistency desired. A wetting agent can be
added at the rate of 1 part per 1000 parts of water to improve pumping.[1]

The jacking equipment should consist of the following:

1. Pneumatic hammers with drills to open holes varying from 1¼ to
2¼ inches (31.75 to 57.15 millimeters) in diameter
2. A jacking unit of the positive-displacement type
3. A slurry-mixing machine
4. A supply of tapered wood plugs to close holes temporarily
5. An air compressor
6. A water tank or other source of water supply

Procedures and Precautions

The spacing of the holes in the pavement for the slab-jacking operation
is important. Raising the slab requires holes about 6 feet (1.8 meters)
apart but not closer than 3 feet (0.9 meter) to any joint. Small-
diameter holes do less damage to the slab bottom.

If the slab has settled firmly against the subgrade soil, the holes must
be drilled into the soil to provide a cavity for the slurry to start its work.
If the soil is very firm, it may be necessary to blow a cavity open before
starting the pumping operation. If the slab rests on one of the stronger
stabilized bases and is bonded to it, the hole should penetrate through
the base so that the grout can lift the base as well as the paving slab.

To adjust an incorrect vertical alignment, such as a dip or a sag,
pumping should start where the settlement begins and move to the low
point on a rotating basis, working longitudinally and staggering the
application of material in the holes transversely. Lifts should be limited
to ¼ inch (6.35 millimeters) per location at any one pumping operation.
Normally a string line or a straightedge can detect an elevation change
that indicates that the jacking has begun to raise the slab. However, if

[1] *Maintenance Aid Digest:* MAD 2, "Mudjacking," U.S. Department of Transportation,
Federal Highway Administration, April 1971.

Figure 4-1 The success of slab jacking depends largely on the careful location of the holes for the entry of the grout. The slab jacking is adjacent to a bridge abutment. [*Portland Cement Association*]

the sag covers a distance of 50 feet (15.24 meters) or more, a survey crew should be summoned to establish the elevation precisely.

The work of realigning faulted joints by slab jacking should be scheduled during cool weather, when the joints are open and adjustment will not be hindered by contact between the faulted slab ends. If the faulting is not corrected and one end of the slab continues to be lower than the other end, there will probably be a break in the slab as well as a general disintegration of the slab itself.

A few precautions should be adopted to ensure that the slab-jacking work will be effective. The principal precautions are as follows:

1. Pyramiding of the grout immediately around the hole at the underside of the slab can be a problem; if not corrected it can break the slab. To prevent pyramiding, the slab-jacking crew should make sure that the grout appears in adjacent holes and does not simply solidify beneath the pavement around the hole being pumped.

2. Thin, watery grout appearing in adjacent holes indicates that the mix is harsh and is not flowing readily along the underside of the slab. When the grout does appear in the adjacent holes, it should have a firmer consistency than it did before being inserted by pumping.

3. Leakage of grout at the edge of the pavement may be troublesome. It can be reduced, if not corrected, by pumping a little grout into the holes along the edge and allowing the grout to set.

4. A blowup in slab jacking means that the pumped grout has burst out of the side of the pavement. This indicates a weakness in the subgrade at that point, but it will tend to be corrected by the grout if the

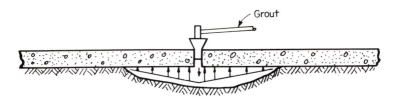

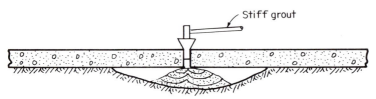

Figure 4-2   A slab-jack grout of good consistency (above) will distribute itself through the subgrade weakness area and exert a supporting pressure on the concrete slab.   A stiff grout (below) tends to pyramid and leave portions of the slab unsupported.   [Slabjacking Concrete Pavements, *Portland Cement Association, Skokie, Ill., 1968*]

blowup can be contained.   Generally the blowup can be stopped by driving a truck on the earth adjacent to the pavement, thus compacting the soil sufficiently to prevent the escape of the slurry.

JOINT PUMPING

Joint pumping in rigid pavements is another maintenance problem requiring attention.   It results from deflections in the slab as traffic passes over a joint.   Water first must enter the joint, penetrate the subgrade, and soften it.   A fine-grained subsoil is particularly susceptible.   Evidence of the problem appears on the surface as muddy soil works its way through the joint.   The pumping can produce a void under the pavement, ultimately causing it to break.

Careful sealing of the joint, preventing the entry of water, is an obvious way to prevent pumping.   However, sealing the underside with asphalt is a more thorough way to contain the water and prevent its softening the soil.   This can be a messy job if it is not done carefully.   Crews must take special care to avoid disfiguring the pavement and also to protect themselves from the hot asphalt.

Asphalt subsealing of the pavement somewhat resembles slab jacking, with asphalt being used instead of slurry.   The work requires no more than two holes near the center of the slab and from 1 to 1.5 feet (0.3048 to 0.4572 meter) from the joint in the direction of traffic.

Hot asphalt, either air-blown asphalt or asphalt with a penetration of 20 to 30, should be used for subsealing.   It should be applied by a truck

Figure 4-3 Pumping joints are evidence of failure to seal the joints to exclude surface water. Note the weakening of the shoulder and the appearance of a crack in the pavement caused by the pumping action. [*Portland Cement Association*]

equipped with asphalt-heating equipment, pressure pumps, metal hoses with return lines, and special nozzles. The pumps should develop at least 80 pounds of pressure per square inch (551.6 kilopascals).

To protect the appearance of the pavement, it should either be wet thoroughly or be covered with sand. Any spilled asphalt can thus be removed with a minimum of marring of the pavement.

There must be a connecting device that will permit the asphalt to be pumped through the holes without spilling onto the pavement. Pumping should continue until the slab shows some evidence of movement or the asphalt appears to be ready to blow out the side of the pavement. Then pumping should stop immediately. The connecting device should remain in place until the asphalt has cooled, when it should be removed and the drilled hole filled with grout.

SHOTCRETE REPAIRS

Shotcrete, or gunite, is a versatile and effective means of renewing deteriorated concrete. A pneumatic "gun" applies a strong cement-sand mortar to the prepared concrete surface, renewing the concrete so that it is as strong as, and often stronger than, it was originally.

The mix of the pneumatically applied concrete is generally 1 part by volume of portland cement to 3½ or 4 parts of sand. The sand should have a moisture content of no less than 3 percent and no more than 5 or 6 percent. The water content of the mix should be no greater than 3 to 3.5 gallons (11.4 to 13.2 liters) per sack of cement, including moisture in the sand.

The cement and sand must be mixed separately and screened to remove lumps that might interfere with the operation of the gun, or nozzle. Water is applied separately at the nozzle. When the pneumatic

Figure 4-4   Shotcrete material must be prepared carefully in equipment such as this.

equipment is operating correctly, the mix leaves the nozzle at a pressure of 30 to 60 pounds per square inch (206.8 to 413.7 kilopascals), depending on the size of the gun. Water must be introduced at a pressure of about 15 pounds per square inch (103.4 kilopascals) more than the air pressure.

Shotcreting has been employed to rebuild curbs, retaining walls, culverts, and deteriorated bridge members as well as to build swimming pools and water reservoirs. It was used to renew the structures on the spectacular highway to Key West, Florida, including the Seven-Mile Bridge. Because of the unusual aspects of shotcreting, a contractor who specializes in the technique generally does the work.

The operators apply the shotcrete in layers. On overhead areas, the layers are no more than 1 inch (25.4 millimeters) thick. For vertical walls, the layers may be 1½ inches (38.1 millimeters) thick, and for horizontal, nonoverhead surfaces the thickness of the layer can be increased until the application appears wet.

The surface receiving the shotcrete must be clean and free of oil and all loose, weakened material. Shotcrete should never be applied to a frozen surface or to a surface with water running over it.

Before the shotcrete is applied, the surface must be cleaned with water under pressure, or with a strong blast of air. This procedure also

Figure 4-5   The shotcreting technique often is used to repair deteriorated concrete bridges such as this one.

should be followed for each succeeding layer of the pneumatically applied concrete.   Rebounding sand should be cleaned away so that it will not leave sand pockets when subsequent layers are being placed.

Shotcrete must be moist-cured and not allowed to dehydrate quickly. If reinforcing is involved, the operator must make sure that it is well embedded.   A common specification for reinforcing should require that at least 0.4 percent of the wall cross section in each direction consist of reinforcing steel.   Reinforcing ends should be lapped at least 4 inches (101.6 millimeters) and preferably 6 inches (152.4 millimeters).

Figure 4-6   The shotcreting process can restore concrete curbs, retaining walls, culverts, and similar concrete structures.

SIDEWALKS

The provision of sidewalks, particularly in residential areas, unfortunately can generate emotional problems. Many people, in their efforts to produce a rural atmosphere in their neighborhoods, bitterly oppose sidewalks and even curbs and gutters, hoping to create a nonurban "charm" in their areas. Some, of course, oppose sidewalks simply to avoid the cost of their installation.

Sidewalks ought to be supplied along routes that will permit schoolchildren to have a safe walkway to school or to the school bus stop. Sidewalks also should be provided on streets with a moderate amount of traffic to avoid forcing children to use the roadways for play areas. Streets with traffic of this type do not make good pedestrian ways. People out for an evening stroll should not be forced to use the roadways.

Many heart-rending accidents have involved children playing in the streets. Drivers of delivery trucks constantly fear that small children may dart in front of their trucks where the children cannot be seen and then be hit and badly injured. The danger is real, and sidewalks help to reduce it.

However, this danger will not be enough to convince determined homeowners who passionately argue for a "country lane." If those in charge of street maintenance cannot get the needed sidewalks, they should go plainly on record, in writing, as wanting them. Then if an accident occurs, they will have a legal defense against a charge of negligence.

Figure 4-7 Although sidewalks and curbs impart safety and neatness to an urban area, many persons oppose them, arguing that they prefer a rural, unimproved appearance.

Placement

Sidewalks preferably should be required on both sides of the street in new developments that will generate an urban-type population density. The U.S. Bureau of the Census identifies an area as urban if it has 2500 or more people in it per square mile (965 or more per square kilometer).

In other areas with existing housing, sidewalks should be scheduled on a priority basis, taking into account such factors as (1) traffic volume, (2) average vehicle speed, and (3) the amount of pedestrian traffic. Vehicle speed is critical and lethal. At 25 miles (41.2 kilometers) per hour, the average driver needs 66 feet (20.1 meters) to stop his or her car. At 35 miles (57.3 kilometers) miles per hour, the driver requires 112 feet (34.1 meters). These speeds are relatively slow and are common in residential areas.

Concrete sidewalks should be 5 inches (127 millimeters) thick and, in a residential neighborhood, preferably 5 feet (1.52 meters) wide. In snow-belt areas, they should be set back from 3 to 4 feet (0.9 to 1.2 meters) from the curb so that plows will have a place to put the snow and still not interfere with pedestrian traffic. The sidewalks should normally pitch ¼ inch per foot (20.8 millimeters per meter) toward the street, and the area between the sidewalk and the curb also should be sloped toward the street by at least the same amount.

In snow-free areas, residential sidewalks frequently adjoin the curb. This practice works well for both the property owners and local government. Tree-lined streets, with trees growing between the sidewalk and the curb, are very appealing. However, trees so located aggravate street cleaning in the fall when they drop their leaves; and unless they have small-caliper trunks, as they grow, their roots lift the sidewalk and break it, causing a hazard for pedestrians. If property owners can be persuaded to put the trees farther from the street, on their own property, they can still enjoy the beauty of the trees while reducing leaf problems and damage to the sidewalks and curbs from root growth.

A sidewalk built to adjoin the curb should be constructed so that it is about ½ inch (12.7 millimeters) above the top of the curb. In some cases the sidewalk can be built monolithically with the curb, generally without a gutter section. In such cases, the curb should extend well below the base of the roadway, or not less than 15 inches (381 millimeters) below the top of the curb.

Construction

Sidewalks should be built in a single course, never with a rough base course and a plaster topping. Adoption of the latter method, which is still urged in some areas, will result in the top layer's quickly scaling off, leaving a bad sidewalk surface.

For appearance, sidewalks should be divided into squares equal to the sidewalk width. The joints should be finished to form weakened planes, preferably about 1 inch (25.4 millimeters) deep and ¼ inch (6.35 millimeters) wide. Those building the sidewalks can work interesting patterns into the surface, as is the practice in certain European cities. The added cost should be nominal.

Sidewalks need expansion joints since it is impractical to seal the contraction joints, as can be done on roadways. Constant expansion and contraction, with the intrusion of dirt and sand, can eventually cause a sidewalk to push the curb out of place at the intersection where the sidewalk butts against it. A good rule is to place ½-inch (12.7-millimeter) expansion joint material in the sidewalk at intervals of not more than 150 feet (45.7 meters) and to reduce this distance to 100 feet (30.5 meters) during the cooler weather in the late fall. Joint material also should be supplied between the sidewalk and any curb or building that it adjoins. Joint material should be used around hydrants or poles in the sidewalk.

Figure 4-8 Carefully selected, sturdy small trees can thrive and help make even a busy neighborhood attractive.

Provision for Trees

Trees should be retained if at all possible. Because the public sets great store by trees in front of their houses, sidewalk designers should go to great lengths to preserve them. Sidewalks may be aligned to miss trees, or ample openings can be left in the walks for trees. In the latter case, a steel grating should be fitted into the opening around the base of the tree to prevent excessive compaction of the soil by pedestrian traffic and to help allow rain to enter and irrigate the tree.

As an attractive alternative, bricks can be placed loosely without mortar in the area surrounding the tree, the tops of the bricks being set at the same elevation as the sidewalk itself. The bricks will support pedestrian traffic and also permit the entry of rainwater.

In either case, a pipe or other passageway should be supplied to permit water to enter the lower portions of the tree roots. A 4-inch (101.6-millimeter) porous pipe can be inserted at each corner of the excavation for the tree. As an alternative, a 4- by 4-inch length of wood can be placed at each corner of the excavation and then be carefully removed after backfilling; the resulting opening can be refilled with coarse rock.

SELECTION OF STREET TREES

Street trees, those planted between the curb and the sidewalk, preferably should be types that develop relatively small trunks so that the growing trunk will not dislodge either the curb or the sidewalk. Large, towering trees are admittedly attractive, but they suffer during heavy windstorms, and when they fall, they can cause great property damage. Moreover, the past practice of planting a single type of tree throughout a community has had disastrous effects. Both the American elm and the American chestnut have been decimated by blights that have spoiled the appearance of many communities. At present, certain palm trees in Florida appear to be similarly in trouble.

A sounder practice is to choose a variety of trees, with a generous use of flowering types. This introduces change in the community, always a good quality, and offers protection from the wholesale loss of trees affected by some new disease.

Good practice also suggests the use of hardy trees, able to survive in an urban environment and tolerant of the salt used to help remove snow and ice from the streets. If street trees and shrubberies can be selected for their tolerance to salt and if the snow-removal crews reduce the amount of salt and apply it more skillfully, the difficulty will be minimized.

Many varieties of trees resist salt damage. A University of New Hampshire study of salt tolerance of common roadside trees in that state disclosed twelve species that tolerate salt and ten that do not. The agronomist Edward F. Button of the Connecticut Bureau of Highways found that trees and shrubs that are tolerant and moderately tolerant to salt include those in the accompanying list. He warns that it is difficult to rate the trees because of other factors such as type of soil, soil permeability, soil reaction, rainfall frequency, winter winds, and the general health of the plants themselves.

Salt-tolerant	*Moderately Salt-tolerant*
Pfitzer's juniper	Privet
Creeping juniper	Tartarian honeysuckle
Adam's needle	Black locust
	Thornless honey locust
	Most oaks
	Weigela

The selection of trees that will survive on streets in an urban environment must include those that are expected to grow under difficult conditions. The most common of the special considerations are a narrow aboveground growing area and restricted root space. Trees that appear able to thrive in most urban conditions would generally include those in the accompanying table. Not all will thrive everywhere, in all climates, but those that are adaptable to a local climate also should be able to thrive in most urban environments.

Urban Trees

General planting	Narrow spaces	Restricted root space
Norway maple	Norway maple	Norway maple
Indian laurel fig	Weir maple	Indian laurel fig
Maidenhair tree	Maidenhair tree	Red horse chestnut
Ornamental pear	Ornamental pear	Weeping bottlebrush
Goldenrain tree	American sweet gum	Goldenrain tree
Silk tree	Red maple	Red maple
Washington thorn	European hornbeam	European hornbeam
Green ash	Cajeput tree	Cajeput tree
Thornless honey locust	Tulip tree	Carriere hawthorn
Southern magnolia	European mountain ash	English hawthorn
Amur cork tree	Littleleaf linden	European ash
London plane tree		Modesto ash
Yew pine		Sweet shade
Japanese pagoda tree		Crape myrtle
Saw-leaf zelkova		Japanese privet
		Oleander
		Carolina laurel cherry
		Purple-leaf plum
		Brisbane box

DRIVEWAYS AND WHEELCHAIR RAMPS

When concrete sidewalks cross concrete driveways, the walks must be thickened by at least 2 inches (50.8 millimeters). No concrete sidewalk

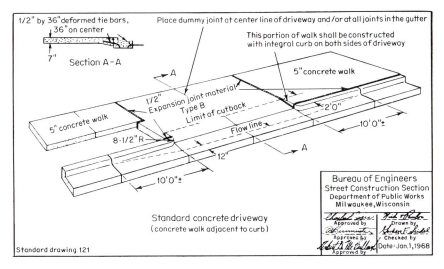

1/2" by 36"deformed tie bars, 36"on center

Section A-A

7"

Place dummy joint at center line of driveway and/or at all joints in the gutter

This portion of walk shall be constructed with integral curb on both sides of driveway

5" concrete walk

A

5" concrete walk

1/2" Expansion joint material Type B
Limit of cutback

8-1/2"R

Flow line

2'0"

10'0"±

12"

A

10'0"±

Standard concrete driveway
(concrete walk adjacent to curb)

Bureau of Engineers
Street Construction Section
Department of Public Works
Milwaukee,Wisconsin

Approved by   Drawn by
Approved by   Checked by
Approved by   Date: Jan.1,1968

Standard drawing 121

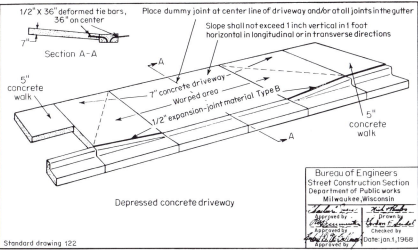

1/2" X 36" deformed tie bars, 36" on center

Section A-A

7"

5" concrete walk

Place dummy joint at center line of driveway and/or at all joints in the gutter

Slope shall not exceed 1 inch vertical in 1 foot horizontal in longitudinal or in transverse directions

A

7" concrete driveway
Warped area
1/2" expansion-joint material Type B

5" concrete walk

A

Depressed concrete driveway

Bureau of Engineers
Street Construction Section
Department of Public works
Milwaukee,Wisconsin

Approved by   Drawn by
Approved by   Checked by
Approved by   Date:jan.1,1968

Standard drawing 122

Figure 4-9   Concrete driveways can take a variety of forms.   In general, they should lead smoothly from the sidewalk to the pavement without creating problems either for the pedestrian or for the motorist.   These are two of six designs adopted by Milwaukee. [Street Construction Specifications, *Milwaukee Department of Public Works, Milwaukee, Wis., 1968*]

that forms part of a driveway should ever be less than 7 inches (177.8 millimeters) thick.

The two drawings in Figure 4-9 showing plans for driveways are representative of good practice in this field.   They were prepared by the Milwaukee, Wisconsin, Department of Public Works.   Milwaukee also specifies that if two or more driveways are constructed on the same property, they must be separated by a safety zone of at least 10 feet

(3.048 meters).   The city requires that asphalt driveways be at least 10½ inches (266.7 millimeters) thick and consist of 5 inches (127 millimeters) of crushed stone, 3 inches (76.2 millimeters) of asphalt base, and 2½ inches (63.5 millimeters) of surfacing.

One should avoid depressed driveways that are built with curbs and force pedestrians to step down as they cross.   These are unexpected obstacles that create danger points for pedestrians as well as barriers for the physically handicapped.

Wheelchair ramps represent a response to those persons in an urban society who are physically handicapped and yet are able to contribute constructively and productively.   The number of such people is growing, and the ramps have value for many other people as well.   Persons pushing baby carriages or grocery carts, for example, find ramps useful.   Persons using crutches prefer them.   Many elderly persons would rather use ramps than step up and down curbs.   The Federal Highway Act of 1973 states that no state highway safety program will be approved

Figure 4-10 Sidewalk ramps for the handicapped, such as persons confined to wheelchairs, are becoming mandatory. Here is a suggested layout prepared by the American Public Works Association.

for funding unless it provides access that is safe and convenient for the physically handicapped, including those in wheelchairs.

The American Public Works Association has developed guidelines that assist in placing these ramps for the greatest convenience to all who would use them. These guidelines can be summarized as follows:

1. The ramp should always be placed within the marked crosswalk.

2. The preferred location is the center of the curb arc that forms the corner of the intersection. If possible, the ramp should be at the same location at all corners for the assistance of the blind.

3. The ramp should have an access width of 4 feet (1.22 meters) at the curb and can narrow to 3 feet (0.91 meter) at the point where it rises to the sidewalk elevation. Its slope should preferably be 12:1 (8:1, if necessary). An absolute maximum slope should be 6:1, which may be troublesome in icy weather.

4. The ramp should have a ½-inch (12.7-millimeter) rise above the pavement at the curb face so that the blind will not inadvertently walk off the ramp and into the street without realizing their misapprehension.

5. The ramp should have a transition area on each side. This should have a slope of 12:1 at the curb face, or a width of 6 feet (1.83 meters) for a 6-inch (152.4-millimeter) curb. The width can be reduced to 4 feet (1.22 meters) if landscaping or poles interfere.

6. The texture of the ramp surface should be noticeably rougher than that of the adjoining sidewalk so that it will be easily identified and have a more nonskid character.

7. If street-drainage conditions permit, the flow line of the gutter should be raised to reduce the curb height and thereby shorten the length of the ramp or flatten its slope. This procedure is useful when the sidewalk is relatively narrow.

8. If the flow line of the gutter cannot be raised and the sidewalk is narrow, the elevation of the back of the sidewalk may be dropped to accommodate the ramp.

Ramps can also be provided at crosswalks at midblock by adopting these general guidelines to conditions there. Occasionally conditions may dictate the provision of two ramps at each corner, one in the direction of each crosswalk. Here again, the guidelines can be adjusted to these requirements.

LOCATION OF UNDERGROUND UTILITIES

Today's streets and roadways, as any urban administrator knows, do not simply carry vehicular and pedestrian traffic. Beneath the surface is an ever-increasing network of utilities of various types that are necessary for the orderly functioning of urban life. In the downtown areas of large cities this tangled maze of utilities is hard to comprehend without

Figure 4-11 For easier maintenance of many utilities, some municipalities use precast concrete utility corridors; the cover forms a sidewalk. This section can be lifted relatively easily for access by the use of removable eyebolts.

seeing it. To avoid aboveground visual pollution, cities often create underground congestion.

Utilities that should be located beneath the street right-of-way customarily include the following:

Water mains	Street-lighting cables
Sewer lines	Traffic-control circuits
Gas mains	Steam lines
Power lines, both primary and secondary (preferably)	Fire and police signal cables CATV cables
Telephone cables (preferably)	Rapid-transit subway lines

In addition, street-maintenance work often is complicated by induction loops placed in the pavement surface to record and control traffic, especially on the busier streets. If street maintenance is to be effective, the municipal maintenance department must know where all these utilities are and have their precise locations in accessible and permanent records. Unfortunately, in many cases the records are in the offices of the various utility companies and frequently are difficult to obtain.

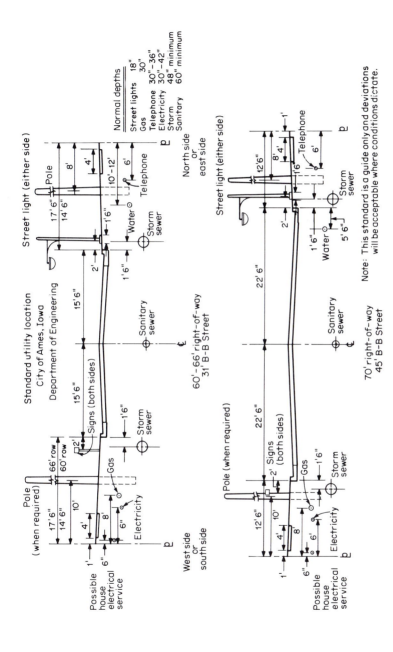

Figure 4-12 A general guide of this type, developed by Ames, Iowa, will simplify many of the problems associated with the maintenance of underground utilities.

An interutility coordinating committee is a useful means of avoiding problems from conflicting utility lines. Its work can be stimulated most effectively by the municipality, whose appropriate officer should invite each involved utility to designate one or more members of its staff to serve on the coordinating committee. Committee members should meet on a regular schedule to discuss immediate and long-range plans that involve underground utility conduits. Thus, if one utility plans work that will involve street cuts in a specific area, the others can attempt to schedule their work at this place at the same time, thus minimizing street disruption. The local governing body, as owner of the street right-of-way, should initiate these meetings, retain control of the utility conduit or cable placement, and keep records of utility locations.

Utility location in residential areas is not as complex as that of downtown districts. In general, the street right-of-way provides ample space. A plan such as the one in use in Ames, Iowa (population 40,000), illustrated in Figure 4-12, should serve. The information should be kept current and up to date, because at the request of the public additional utilities are placed underground each year.

An alternative to this method is to place all utilities in a single trench. The proposal is to excavate a trench 3 feet (0.91 meter) wide and at least 5½ feet (1.68 meters) deep. In it would be placed all utilities at varying and specified levels (the sewer mains, which flow by gravity, are an exception). The trench should be backfilled with sand to facilitate reexcavation.

In business and commercial districts, a "utility corridor" that can also serve as a sidewalk offers many advantages of convenience. The corridor units are generally precast concrete, in 10-foot (3.048-meter) lengths containing twin 2- by 2-foot (0.61- by 0.61-meter) channels. The units rest on a bed of sand or gravel about 3 inches (76.2 millimeters) deep. They are capped by precast sections that bolt onto the ducts and form the sidewalk. Ordinarily the corridors do not carry water mains. However, they carry other utility conduits such as electrical cable, telephone, and traffic, fire, and police communication cables. They could carry gas mains.

The great advantage of corridors is their easy access. The top sidewalk sections have four bolt holes arranged so that lifting bolts can be inserted to remove the sections for quick repair of the utility if needed. One maintenance worker likened them to "a long manhole."

"Utilidors," or large utility tunnels, may be the future way to unravel the complexities of underground utilities in downtown areas. And the opportunity appears more nearly realizable as more downtowns undergo renewal in some form or another.

Utility tunnels should be considered whenever a city undertakes a major improvement, such as a large-scale street reconstruction or the construction of a rapid-transit subway system.   The utility tunnel can carry all normal utilities with the exception of sewers, which flow by gravity.   The designs must anticipate the problems that may arise within the utility conduits.   Primary difficulties would be heat, humidity, and leakage, and the problems may be serious.   Nevertheless, they can be resolved, especially with the easy access afforded by the tunnels.   The water utility especially must provide frequent connections not only for services but for fire hydrants and valves.

Utility tunnels are scarcely an ordinary urban maintenance item. Nevertheless, they can make the maintenance of urban areas much more efficient and less costly.

BIBLIOGRAPHY

Shotcrete, Portland Cement Association, Skokie, Ill., n.d.
Slabjacking Concrete Pavements, Portland Cement Association, Skokie, Ill., 1967.

Chapter Five

Urban-Bridge Maintenance

ARTHUR L. ELLIOTT

All bridges pass through three life phases regardless of whether they serve in an urban or a rural area or whether they carry vehicular, rail, or other traffic. These phases are planning and design, construction, and service life and maintenance. Oddly enough, even though the last phase takes by far the most time, it almost always receives the least attention. And when a bridge must carry urban traffic, this lack of attention becomes increasingly critical.

Designers will strive to perfect their theory and calculations, and materials men will carefully check each item that goes into the structure,

Figure 5-1 A pair of strikingly designed welded steel bridges serving a limited-access highway provides a frame for an old wooden bridge used by local traffic. Each has its own maintenance needs.

Figure 5-2 Often bridges in outlying areas tend to be neglected. The abutment wing wall of this bridge has deteriorated.

but once construction is complete, the bridge is often left to fend for itself against the ravages of man, nature, traffic, and the weather. In fact, paradoxical as it is, the designer frequently never finds out how well the design performs. Often awkward details are perpetuated year after year simply because the designer has no line of active communication with maintenance personnel.

Such lines should be kept open and be well used. The people on each end of the line should be equally anxious to see that information is exchanged on both the good and the bad points of a structure's design. Too often, maintenance personnel seem to accept the problems of the bridges assigned to them as their personal challenge to be solved by their own ingenuity, with the result that the policy makers and administrators, let alone the designer, may never know that a difficulty exists.

A bridge should be regarded as a manufactured product. If it does not perform properly, the designer and the manufacturer should be responsibly concerned. Better structures will result.

IMPORTANCE OF RECORDS

Good bridge maintenance must include an accurate record of the inspection and the corrective action, if any is needed. This record must document the fact that the maintenance has been well planned and that it is long-range. It must embrace the following:

    1. The essentials of what is in the bridge—its plans and any unusual features of its design and construction

    2. The dates and circumstances of regular and unscheduled inspections that have occurred throughout its life

    3. Complete information on the results of inspections, repairs, and damage if this has occurred

Each of these points is vital to the performance of the bridge. Unless the bridge inspector makes a record of what is found, the inspection has little value. When a crisis arises, it is important for those responding to it to have complete documentation of what inspections have been made, what was found, and what was done to correct any discovered defects. The records should contain all available basic information such as data on design and construction, sufficient structural details to make it possible to determine the structure's load capacity, several photographs of the bridge, important dimensions, and data on alignment and age.

An agency responsible for the maintenance of any number of bridges should set up and maintain a detailed set of these bridge records. It is astounding and deplorable to discover the number of cities and counties that keep totally inadequate records of their valuable and expensive investment in bridges. As the years go by, good records will provide the type of information that extends the useful service life of a bridge, improves the design of new bridges and makes them more nearly trouble-free, and ensures the effectiveness of bridge-maintenance work.

Record Format

Records can be kept in several ways. One good arrangement is a combination of a card file and a set of 8½- by 11-inch (216- by 279-millimeter) screw-post binders.

The card file should contain a card for each bridge (see Figure 5-3). On the card should be information that identifies the bridge's physical dimensions, its location, and its load capacity. In many cases, a quick reference to the file will give all needed information.

If more detailed information is needed, the 8½- by 11-inch binder file

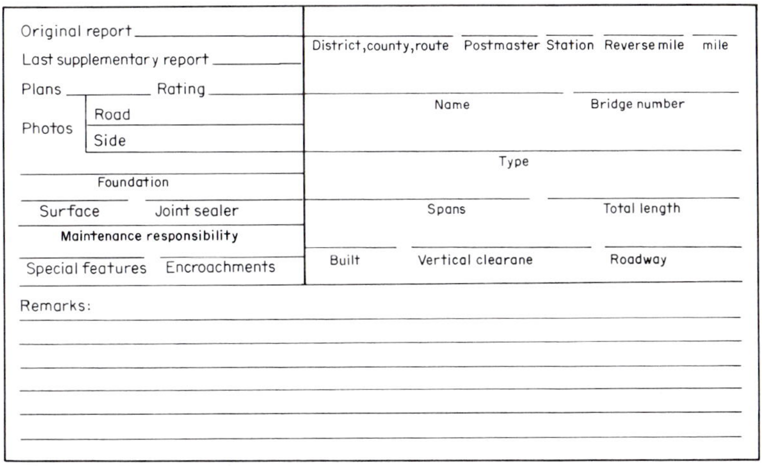

Figure 5-3 This simple bridge-inspection file card can carry enough pertinent information to identify a bridge.

may be consulted (see Figure 5-4). There one should find a few reduced sheets of the plans of the bridge if they are available. If plans are not available, the bridge should be measured and all dimensions of members, roadway width, span lengths, and clearances recorded. The file should also contain complete data on the following:

1. Bridge identification—the location and enough photographs to show any unusual features. The photographs should include, at a

```
┌─────────────────────────────────────────────────────────────────────┐
│                                                                       │
│   Bridge report                  Bridge No. _____   │
│                                  Other No. _____   │
│                                  Public utility commission No. _____   │
│                                  Location _____   │
│                                            District,community,route,postmaster,city │
│                                  Date of investigation _____   │
│                                                                       │
│   Name _____  │
│   Latitude _____ Longitude _____                             │
│   Structural data and history                                         │
│   Year built _____ By _____ Contract No. _____   │
│   Date of revisions _____ │
│   Designed by B.D. □ _____ Plans available at: ___  │
│   Description:                                                        │
│                                                                       │
│                                                                       │
│   Spans _____   │
│   Length _____ Skew _____ Design LL _____   │
│   Ratings: Inventory _____ Operating _____ Permit _____  │
│   Description: on structure                                           │
│   Bridge width _____   │
│   Total width _____ Lanes _____ Tracks __  │
│   Median _____ Rail type _____    │
│   Vertical clearance over deck _____ Approximate roadway width _   │
│   Wearing surface _____ Deck seal _____     │
│   Alignment _____   │
│   Description: under structure                                        │
│   Roadway sections _____   │
│   Clearance: Vertical _____ Horizontal _____ Left _____ Right │
│   Lanes _____ Tracks _____ Pump plant: None □ See bridge No. _  │
│   Facilities crossed _____   │
│                                                                       │
└─────────────────────────────────────────────────────────────────────┘
```

Figure 5-4 To include more detailed information than can be given on a file card, this 8½- by 11-inch (216- by 279-millimeter) sheet may be used in an appropriate binder.

minimum, one looking down the road across the bridge and one showing the side of the bridge.

2. A record of all inspections with a quick system for determining the date of the latest inspection and a description of any needed repairs.

3. A cost sheet containing the original cost of the bridge and the costs of subsequent repairs.

4. Copies of any posting or load-reduction orders if these are less than the legal limits as well as overloads that may be permitted.

Even though an inspection shows nothing to be amiss, the record still must indicate that an inspection has been made. Use may be made of a rubber stamp saying:

An inspection was made on _____(date). No repairs were required.

Signed _____ (Engineer)

In general, an annual inspection should be adequate for bridges in good condition. For older bridges and those with some structural inadequacy, more frequent inspections may be necessary.

Thus, the first step in a well-organized bridge-maintenance program is

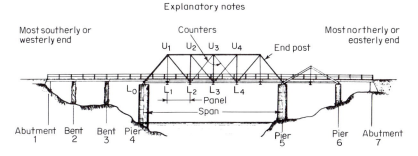

Typical support numbering system

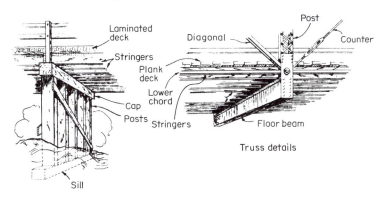

Typical timber bent

Figure 5-5 This sheet identifies the elements of most bridges so that they can be labeled properly on inspection reports.

threefold: (1) a good set of records; (2) information on the physical characteristics and dimensions of each structure; and (3) the provision of fully qualified engineers who make regular inspections.

Inspectors

Persons making inspections should be well qualified to detect and evaluate evidence of bridge deterioration.   It is wasteful and dangerous to assign personnel to make inspections if they do not know what they are looking for.   Inspectors should be registered engineers who have undergone a thorough training covering the basic points in bridge inspection discussed in this chapter.

Each type of structure has its own points of typical weakness and kinds of failure.   Alert inspectors check all these spots to be sure that no trouble is developing.   If a number of bridges must be maintained, inspectors should be assigned to this work alone.   It is not wise to use maintenance inspection as a fill-in job to be done when people are available from other tasks.   Maintenance inspection is an important function and merits performance as a full-time assignment by people trained to know what they are looking for.

TIMBER-BRIDGE MAINTENANCE

Each type of bridge has its own Achilles' heel.   A knowledgeable engineer recognizes at once just where to look for trouble.   This is especially true of timber bridges carrying urban traffic.

Although comparatively few timber bridges are being built today, many old bridges of this type carrying both rural and urban traffic remain in service.   Moreover, in some areas developers use timber bridges for vehicular and pedestrian traffic to create rustic charm in new areas.

Tools for Timber-Bridge Inspection

The inspector should be equipped with a *miner's pick* as an essential tool for digging out suspect areas.   Merely sinking the point of the pick into the wood will immediately show whether the wood is sound or decayed. A carpenter's *brace and bit* also is very handy.   If internal rot is suspected, the inspector can detect it by boring a hole in the timber.   If rot is present on the inside, the bit will appear to hit a void and drop through.

If the timber is sound and free from rot, the inspector should carry some short sections of *hardwood dowel* to drive into inspection holes. These will seal off attractive access points for the entry of insects into the heart of the timber.

Another very useful tool, not only for inspection but also for mainte-

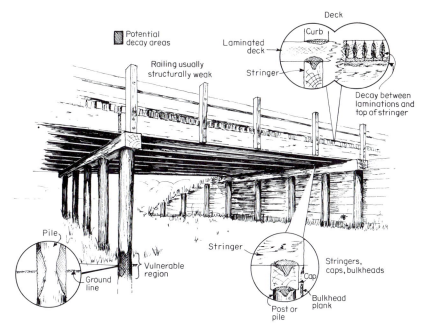

Figure 5-6 This drawing points out the potential decay areas in most timber bridges.

nance, is a *small hoe* that can be used to rake dirt from between the stringers and keep these areas clean and dry.

Location of Timber-Bridge Vulnerable Areas

Timber is subject to two main types of failure: breakage and attack by rot and insects. Broken members are easily identified by visible deflections. However, attack by rot and insects is more subtle and harder to detect. In general, it occurs where dirt and moisture can accumulate.

When examining a timber structure, the inspector should look first for trouble between the stringers on top of the caps (see Figure 5-6). Here dirt accumulates, and termites and other insects find a home. If the bearing area of a stringer has been attacked by rot or insects, some settlement should be evident unless the damage is in the early stages. If the damage is advanced, the stringer will appear to be sinking into the cap, and both members will be badly decayed.

Rot also may be found in the contact surface between the cap and the post or pile upon which it rests. If the bridge is a pile structure, decay and insect infestation are usually severest at the ground line or adjacent to the water in a tidal zone. The inspection should be carried at least 1 foot (0.3048 meter) below ground, and the soundness of the wood thoroughly tested with a pick throughout the area.

If the bridge has timber bulkheads, there will certainly be rot on the back of the bulkhead timbers unless they have been well treated with preservative. The inspector must decide how far the rot can progress before it will destroy the planks' ability to hold back the earth. The planks probably can be rotted at least halfway through before they must be replaced.

If the bridge has a timber deck, made either of planks or of laminated wood, the inspector should look for rot under the deck planks, between the layers of planks or laminations, and under the curbs or scuppers, which are usually bolted to the deck.

Well-treated timber will withstand attacks by rot and insects over a long period of time. Treatment in place has some delaying action but is not highly successful as a long-time protection. Unfortunately, scattered across the United States are still thousands of bridges which lack treatment and protection and of which rot and termites have been in possession for a long time.

Often, one hears the petulant comment, "The bridge stood all these years and seemed to be in good shape. Why did it fall down now?" The only answer is that no one insisted that inspectors examine the bridge earlier and find the trouble before it happened.

Repairs for Timber Bridges

Although timber bridges are susceptible to many types of creeping failures, they can be repaired successfully and rather inexpensively. When the stringers become decayed in their bearing areas, new stringers can be slipped in beside them and wedged up to carry the load.

It used to be a common practice to turn the stringers over, and it is still possible to find bridges on which this has been done. When the tops of the stringers became decayed and would not hold the deck nails, the stringers were turned over, bringing sound wood onto the top so that the deck could be renailed to it.

Although this procedure solved the nailing problem, it was a poor solution because the stringers had been severely weakened. Since the bottom, or tension edge, of the stringers had been rotted and weakened, the bridge's load-carrying capacity was markedly curtailed.

Repair of Posts and Piles

If decay has occurred under the caps and on top of the posts or piles but has not penetrated too far into the posts, half caps and scab supports may be bolted onto the sides of the posts to pick up the loads of the stringers in a new and solid wood area. Many bridges have been given an additional 10 years of life by measures of this sort. Piles decayed at the ground line or water line may be shaved to remove the bad wood, then given a coat of preservative and a jacket of concrete to protect the wood and help carry the load.

The fact that an old timber bridge is being used at all usually indicates that funds are not plentiful and that temporary measures which will postpone the inevitable day when complete replacement is necessary are welcome. Once difficulties have been detected, alert maintenance crews can devise many ingenious ways to patch and prop up a wooden structure to keep it serviceable for a few more years.

CONCRETE-BRIDGE MAINTENANCE

Unfortunately many persons have the impression that a concrete bridge is a permanent structure that needs no maintenance. Although concrete does have long life, it is subject to deterioration, which prompt and thorough maintenance can correct.

Traffic is one source of maintenance problems. Traffic may run on the concrete deck of the structure or on an asphalt wearing surface. In either case the term "wearing surface" is very appropriate. Traffic does cause wear, and the surface does erode. Traffic results in accidents, and accidents can fracture portions of the bridge.

Weather also creates bridge maintenance problems, chiefly through temperature changes that induce expansion and contraction in the bridge members. Salt used for snow and ice control is a special source

Figure 5-7   A vehicle colliding with a bridge railing created this troublesome maintenance problem. Railings of this type are structurally inadequate by today's standards.

Figure 5-8   This outside beam of a concrete bridge, hit by a truck with an overheight load, presents a serious maintenance problem.

of deterioration. It damages the concrete and corrodes the steel, causing spall "pop-outs" in the bridge deck.

Correction of Salt Deterioration

If salt is used to melt snow and ice, the deck surface can deteriorate rapidly. If the asphalt wearing surface is porous, salt water may penetrate and attack the concrete beneath without giving any surface indication of trouble until the damage becomes severe.

When salt is to be employed for ice control, the deck should be sealed effectively and a wearing surface placed over the seal to protect it. Many sealing systems have been tried, and the best has probably not yet been developed. At present the most thorough seal seems to be a solid-sheet membrane of an inert material, cemented to the deck with an adhesive and covered with at least 2 inches (50.8 millimeters) of asphalt wearing surface.

This also is the best available solution for the repair of a deck that has deteriorated. The deteriorated salt-damaged concrete should be removed, the reinforcing steel cleaned, and the void filled with epoxy concrete or with regular concrete in the thicker sections. The repaired deck must then be covered with a membrane seal and a wearing surface. (Additional information on the mechanics of these repairs is found in Chapter 3.)

If the deck delamination can be discovered before it pops out on the surface, valuable time may be bought by pressure-grouting the horizontal cracks in the concrete deck with epoxy. This procedure restores a measure of soundness to the deck and postpones the day when complete repairs will be necessary. However, the basic solution is to keep the salt from penetrating the concrete in the first place.

Expansion-Joint Maintenance

The expansion joints of concrete bridges should be carefully inspected. If the expansion detail "locks up" or becomes inoperative, stresses induced by temperature may be transmitted to the members, spalling out concrete under the sole plates and cracking abutment walls or stubby columns. If damage has occurred, the only solution is to provide a temporary support, jack up the structure, and replace the defective detail as well as the damaged concrete.

Simple, easy-to-clean expansion details are best. For anticipated movements of a maximum of 2 inches (50.8 millimeters), elastomeric pads are popular because they have no moving parts. A single large steel roller usually works well if it is kept clean. A roller nest, providing a number of small steel rollers between two steel plates, formerly was used extensively. Unfortunately, such a nest deteriorates into an immovable mass of rust unless it has extremely good maintenance. The

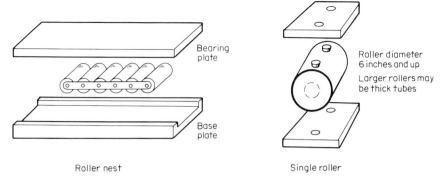

Roller nest   Single roller

Figure 5-9   Bridge expansion joints can use a single roller or a nest of rollers.   The former is less liable to cause maintenance problems.

only practical solution is to replace a rusted roller nest with a simpler, more satisfactory expansion unit.

Correction of Other Defects

Expansion is the root cause of other problems that make the maintenance of concrete bridges difficult.   For example, the expansion of adjacent pavements or the movement of earth fill may slowly push the abutments and jam all the joints in the bridges and also crack abutment walls and columns.

Usually this threat can be eliminated by cutting off a section of the pavement adjacent to the abutment, excavating a slot of earth behind the abutment, and then backfilling the gap with compressible material. Nevertheless, the damage may require extensive repair.   This is an instance of a rather expensive maintenance and repair job that could have been avoided by early and thorough inspection.

Concrete structures also are subject to damage from vehicles in collision, from foundation settlement, and occasionally from earthquakes. The proper corrective measure becomes an individual matter for each structure.   Nevertheless, the importance of prompt and thorough inspection and the early detection of problems should not be minimized.

Maintenance of Prestressed-Concrete Bridges

Increasingly, prestressed-concrete bridges are being used in both urban and rural highway systems.   When properly made and placed, they present few maintenance problems.

Bridges of this type range from huge, complicated structures to small, simple bridges with precast girders.   The plant-manufactured precast girder is a very attractive structural element for small bridges.   In some parts of the United States, suppliers carry prestressed girders as shelf items and deliver them on short notice.   Either as stock items or as structural members fabricated to order, these convenient and serviceable beams offer an economical and relatively maintenance-free solution to the small-bridge problem.

Bridge Widening with Prestressed-Concrete Members

Prestressed members offer one very good solution to a common difficulty encountered when widening a bridge, that of making a smooth connection between the old and the new concrete. The older portion, of course, has taken its full shrinkage and plastic flow, but the newer part has not. The work crews may construct a smooth joint, but as soon as the new conventional concrete takes its permanent shrinkage and plastic flow, it will sag a bit and longitudinal discrepancies will appear in the deck surface.

However, if the widened portion is designed as a prestressed member with at least some posttensioning, the newer portion may be cured and then posttensioned so that it is pulled back up to match the older surface perfectly. The prestressing will hold the two slabs in good agreement, and the connection will remain smooth.

Fracture of a Prestressed-Concrete Member

Probably one of the worst problems that a maintenance crew faces occurs when a vehicle hits and breaks a prestressed member. The concrete may be battered, and some of the tendons may be cut or damaged. If a concrete deck has been placed on the prestressed beams, removing the damaged beam becomes a major chore.

If the removal expense or inconvenience to traffic is too great, it is possible to clean away sufficient concrete to clamp onto the ends of the tendons, take a strain on them, and then weld in a short connecting piece of tendon. This procedure is not easy, but it can be carried out if alternatives cause too much difficulty. The best solution is to replace the damaged beam.

Prestressed-Concrete Riding Surfaces

At times, the riding surface of a bridge consists of precast sections such as T's or channels that have been set side by side and then covered with an asphalt wearing surface. Unless the keys between the beams are very strong and serviceable or there is lateral prestressing, the beams often break loose and begin to work up and down, especially at the edge of the lane used by heavy trucks. Two corrective solutions (other than endlessly patching the deck) can rectify this fault:

1. A slot may be cut in the surfacing, and the joint between adjacent beams opened far enough so that a stronger key may be placed between them.

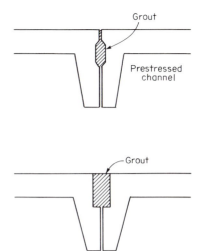

Figure 5-10 When prestressed concrete sections are used for bridge decks, strong keys between the sections are important. The lower key is the better type, better able to withstand heavy differential loads. The upper type will probably break out under heavy loading on either section.

2. The asphalt surfacing may be completely cleaned away, and a 4-inch (101.6-millimeter) concrete slab placed over the entire deck and topped with an asphaltic surface to ensure smooth riding. This procedure will usually spread the load and keep the cracks from reflecting through the surfacing.

Prestressed beams occasionally develop longitudinal cracks that are not structurally dangerous. If an examination discloses that the cracks can be tolerated structurally, they may be sealed by injecting them with an epoxy mixture to prevent the entry of water that would corrode the tendons. Preventing anything corrosive from attacking the tendons is probably the most important consideration in the maintenance of any prestressed-concrete structure.

MAINTENANCE OF STEEL BRIDGES

The maintenance of steel bridges usually centers on (1) corrosion, (2) wear of moving parts, (3) fatigue of the metal, and (4) damage from vehicular collision. Possible corrosion damage varies widely with the atmospheric exposure of the steel. Near the ocean the corrosion may be rapid and severe. In high mountains or on dry deserts, steel may go for years with little paint maintenance needed and little loss from corrosion. Modern paint systems using zinc-based paints give excellent protection for 10 years or more in the most severe exposures. The secret of paint longevity, other than paint quality, is extreme care and thoroughness in the preparation of the steel and the application of the paint. Economy in the quality of paint or in the thoroughness of preparation and application is a false saving.

Figure 5-11 An overloaded truck ran into trouble when trying to cross this light pin-connected truss bridge. An adequate inspection report could have warned the trucker not to use the bridge (unless he was attempting to cross it illegally).

Maintenance of Pin-connected Truss Bridges

Modern steel bridges have few moving parts, and they are seldom subject to mechanical wear. However, many older pin-connected truss bridges that are still in service will have experienced considerable wear both of the connecting pins and of the I bars. Counter rods, often used with turnbuckles for adjustment, are usually badly worn and may rattle and bang as vehicles cross the bridge.

Badly worn pins should be replaced. I bars may have to be welded and rebored if they cannot be adjusted. Counter rods should be made snug by adjusting their turnbuckles but should not be made tight if they are to perform their functions properly. Some enthusiastic maintenance personnel, seeing a turnbuckle, will tighten a rod until it sings like a fiddle string. If the rod is left in this condition, it may break under a heavy load. It should be loosened to a snug condition.

Portals for Through-Truss Bridges

An old through-truss bridge will certainly have suffered damage to its portal bracing from overheight loads. This damage may or may not be important to the load-carrying capabilities of the bridge. In some cases, the best solution is to remove the largely decorative portal braces and, if necessary, to strengthen the interior panel cross bracing, which is usually high enough to avoid being hit.

If the portal brace is bent and must remain, it often can be heat-straightened. Heat straightening is an art that can save costly repairs of damaged steel members. It is no job for an experimenter, but personnel who know their business can skillfully bring members back into line with a minimum of cost and effort. Badly bent main members may often be straightened without removing them from the bridge.

Detecting Fatigue Cracks

Steel is subject to fatigue, and inspectors must be alert for cracks starting in steel members.   With the advent of welding and the use of higher-strength steel, the fatigue threat has become more important.

Engineers inspecting steel bridges should be well versed in fatigue and its effects.   Certain details, such as cover-plated beams and acute corners, are prone to induce cracking if the steel is susceptible.   A crack caught in its early stages may be repaired, whereas a neglected crack may cause the fracture of a member and a possible catastrophe.   Engineers must know what to look for and where to look.

Detecting Vandalism Damage

Vandalism is always a threat.   Inspecting engineers should be alert for evidence of anything that is out of place or missing.   Pins have been stolen from steel expansion joints.   Any part of a bridge that is removable seems to be fair game, and its removal may leave the bridge in a highly dangerous condition.   Inspectors should watch for missing retaining nuts or cover plates on pins or for any other part that can be carried away.

General Defects   Inspectors should check the possible existence of the following defects:

1. Missing parts
2. Improperly placed expansion details
3. Tilted shoes
4. Sags in the bridge rail or deck
5. Abutments or piers out of plumb
6. Fill slip-outs or washouts around abutments or footings

INSPECTION TOOLS AND AIDS

Bridge inspectors may have either simple or exotic tools at their disposal, but simple tools usually permit a very thorough inspection.   In the last analysis, the most effective tools are a pair of eyes backed by an alert and inquisitive mind.   Often inspectors will uncover a major difficulty by recognizing that "Something just doesn't look right."

For the inspection of timber bridges, as mentioned above, a prospector's pick and a brace and bit can detect most trouble.   For the inspection of concrete bridges, inspectors depend primarily on visual observations.   However, a *small gauge* is useful for measuring crack widths to detect progressive movement.   To sound out laminated deterioration in a bridge deck, an inspector can drag a *heavy chain* over the deck.   The flawed areas generally are the result of rust on reinforcing steel, causing horizontal cracks and starting potential spalls or pop-outs.   The chain creates a hollow noise over a lamination.   The hammer end of a prospector's pick also can aid in assessing the

Figure 5-12 To find laminated weaknesses in bridge floors, inspectors frequently drag chains across the surface and listen for hollow sounds. [Civil Engineering]

soundness of old concrete. For the insection of steel bridges, a *jackknife* is useful to probe paint blisters and find rust. Electronic *thickness gauges* to determine paint thicknesses are convenient but not essential.

A pair of *field glasses* is necessary to check places difficult to reach without scaffolding. *Dye penetrants* or *Magnaflux* outfits also are useful in detecting suspected cracks. These more refined instruments and tools are usually required when an inspector has detected something amiss that is not easily apparent.

Ultrasonic equipment may be used on steel members to seek unseen cracks when trouble is suspected. Highly sophisticated instruments, which manufacturers claim are able to "listen" to cracks in the steel as they develop and thereby to assess the danger, are being developed. No doubt these will be improved and be of great use on major structures.

These fine instruments all have their uses and are invaluable in tracing defects under difficult circumstances. For the usual difficulties faced by someone charged with maintaining a number of moderately sized bridges, however, no better inspection instrument exists than an alert, trained inspector who has both eyes open and is equipped with a few simple tools with which to probe, scrape, and examine the structure.

Maintenance of Records as an Inspection Tool

The responsibility of keeping a bridge file up to date is a heavy one, but most of the effectiveness of an inspection program is lost if records are not carefully maintained. With commendable zeal, a maintenance department may have established a fine set of files, but if the complete inspection program has not been adopted, the records probably will never be touched thereafter. If the records are not current, the entire system falters.

A trucker may ask for an overload permit. With good records, an engineer requires only a moment to run through the cards that give data for the bridges along the trucker's proposed route to see if they will carry the overload safely.

Cost sheets are equally valuable. Large sums of money spent each year on maintenance quickly reveal themselves, and their record provides facts essential in judging the need for a replacement bridge. Damage records carefully kept often prove invaluable in explaining an otherwise-mysterious failure. Up-to-date records are also of great assistance in answering design, operational, and administrative questions about bridges.

To anyone having the responsibility of maintaining a number of bridges and keeping them in good operating condition, a complete set of well-kept records can be of the greatest aid. The maintenance head knows exactly what bridges the department has, their capabilities, and the current condition of each structure.

BIBLIOGRAPHY

Manual for Maintenance Inspection of Bridges, American Association of State Highway and Transportation Officials, Washington, 1974.

Standard Specifications for Highway Bridges, 10th ed., American Association of State Highway Officials, Washington, 1969.

Chapter Six

Street-cleaning Practices

WILLIAM S. FOSTER

HISTORICAL DEVELOPMENT

Urban street sanitation, for that is what street cleaning is, has had a long and neglected history in the United States. In the early days, in the period when New York City had just ceased to be New Amsterdam, householders were expected to clean the street in front of their homes. Moreover, ordinances prohibiting the emptying of "tubbs of odour and nastiness" into the streets were passed. The city's first American-born mayor, Stephanus Van Cortlandt, tried to initiate a systematic program of street cleaning. Somewhat later the city awarded a contract for street cleaning at £30 per year, but this plan apparently did not work satisfactorily and was dropped. Consequently, until early in the nineteenth century residents were again given the responsibility of cleaning the street in front of their homes.[1]

The Horse and Sanitation

People today forget the impact of the horse on urban sanitation. From the standpoint of the long history of human civilization, the horse has been the principal means of transportation, and the motor vehicle and the train are merely newcomers. Only recently have people been relieved of the discomfort and dangerous risk of disease caused by the odorous, fly-and-insect–attracting filth that the horse placed on the streets.

[1] *Outline History of the Department of Sanitation, New York City*, City of New York, Department of Sanitation, New York, 1954.

At the turn of the twentieth century, sanitary engineers attempted to measure this source of pollution. The results sound humorous today, but they were serious at the time. Engineer George Soper, for example, estimated that in each working day one horse would deposit a half gallon (1.9 liters) of urine and 20 pounds (9 kilograms) of manure on the city streets.[2] This is an aspect of street sanitation that fortunately does not concern today's urban environment.

Introduction of Whitewings

The first major step to eliminate this mixture of manure and debris on the streets of American cities was taken in 1895 in New York, where the problem was especially acute. Mayor William L. Strong appointed a vigorous and dedicated Civil War engineering officer, Col. George E. Waring, Jr., and gave him a free hand in cleaning away the odorous, unsightly contribution to urban discomfort and disease.

Colonel Waring organized his crews along paramilitary lines, paid them well, instructed them that they were saving lives as well as improving the quality of life in their city, and provided them with smart white uniforms, thus introducing the term "whitewing." His results were spectacularly successful, even though he had virtually no mechanical equipment as we know it today.[3] Unfortunately his successors

[2] George A. Soper, *Modern Methods of Street Cleaning,* Engineering News Publishing Co., New York, 1907, p. 163.

[3] Martin V. Melrose, "Out of Sight, Out of Mind," *Historian,* August 1973, pp. 621–640.

Figure 6-1   In the nineteenth century, innovative men attempted to develop horse-drawn and horse-powered mechanical sweepers. None was successful enough to be practical. [*Drawing courtesy of Dr. John Horton*]

and his contemporaries in other cities did not maintain his high standards, and for many years street sanitation suffered from neglect.

Horse-drawn Mechanical Sweepers

During this period, innovative men did attempt to develop horse-drawn mechanical sweepers, a rotating broom being powered by a gear drive connected with the rear wheel of the sweeper wagon. One sweeper was developed by C. H. Bishop in 1847, and another by a sanitation company in 1860. Neither performed well on the rough streets of the time, and both were abandoned around the turn of the twentieth century.[4]

Push Brooms

The push broom and the shovel were about the only tools that worked on the roadways typical of the urban streets of the nineteenth century. Roads and streets were rough and uneven in the days of the horse and wagon. Steel-rimmed wagon wheels and iron horseshoes did great harm to roadway surfaces. Pneumatic tires reduced this damage, permitting the use of concrete and asphalt pavements. Mechanical sweeping was possible only when smooth pavements became common.

Modern Methods

Despite mechanization, the worker with a cart, a push broom, and a shovel remains an important part of many contemporary street-sanitation organizations. This is particularly true in areas that still have streets paved with blocks and in districts of intensely high traffic with much truck loading and unloading. Some debris is difficult to pick up in any other way.

However, the United States is almost alone among nations in its use of the stiff-bristled push broom. Almost everywhere else, street-sanitation crews use the attractive birch broom with its fibers cut at an angle. The man or woman (in the Soviet Union women do most of the street cleaning) who operates it uses a semicircular motion, pushing the heavy material with the short stub fibers and collecting the lighter material with the long, whiplike flexible ends. Cleaning crews in other nations use these brooms because they do a better job, but in the United States there is so much street litter that crews consider themselves fortunate if they can clean up the heavy material. The reputation that Americans have of being the most litter-prone people in the world is scarcely a proud achievement.

Motorized Whitewings

To provide push-broom street cleaners with a little greater scope, they have been mechanized to some extent. In some municipalities with large land areas, whitewings have been provided with a small scooter-

---

[4] Correspondence with Dr. John J. Horton, president of Ecolotec Inc., Oct. 25, 1974.

Figure 6-2   Frequently the effectiveness of a push-broom sweeper is enhanced by providing motor-scooter equipment like this to increase the range of the sweeper's operation.

Figure 6-3   In some business areas, a sidewalk sweeper such as this can do the work of a sweeper with a push broom.

Figure 6-4   After World War II the modern mechanical sweeper became increasingly popular as a means of using labor more effectively.

Figure 6-5 In many commercial and high-traffic areas, keeping streets clean is challenging. Note the two sweepers operating in tandem in this heavily littered area.

type vehicle carrying a box with a capacity of about half a cubic yard (0.382 cubic meter) and with space provided on the vehicle for a broom and a shovel. This permits them to patrol larger areas than they can when they are equipped with conventional pushcarts.

Mechanical Sweepers

Mechanical sweepers have grown in popularity, particularly since World War II. The cost of labor has risen so substantially that even small municipalities find themselves served more economically by one worker on a sweeper than by three or four with push brooms, even though the sweeper may be used for only a portion of the day. On a per capita basis, small cities own greater numbers of mechanical sweepers than large ones do.

Mechanical sweepers clean most downtown areas at least once a day for a minimum of 6 days a week. Often those areas are cleaned twice a day. It is good practice to sweep industrial areas daily and to sweep residential areas with high population densities (predominantly of apartment buildings) two or three times weekly. Areas consisting of single-family dwellings preferably should be swept once a week (once a month is an absolute minimum). In a good program, sweepers should average between 20 and 25 curb miles (between 32 and 40 curb kilometers) per shift.

Problem of Parked Cars

The chronic problem complicating good performance in street sanitation is the parked car. Curiously, the parked vehicle has always been a problem. In the days of horse-drawn vehicles, laws had to be enacted to prohibit the overnight parking of unharnessed wagons and carriages on city streets because of the difficulties they caused to those trying to keep the streets clean.[5] Parking-ban legislation, incidentally, draws on an old English law stating, "The King's highway shall not be used as a stableyard."

Today's parking restrictions can take the form of complete bans at night, when traffic is at a minimum and sweepers can operate freely on both sides of the street. In areas not requiring daily sweeping, there may be bans on alternate sides of the street, as, for example, a parking ban on Mondays and Wednesdays on one side and on Tuesdays and Thursdays on the other side. In heavily built-up areas, the ban may be in effect for a limited time that is long enough to let the sweeper pass by. For example, there may be a ban from 8 A.M. to 10 A.M. in one section, from 9 A.M. to 11A.M. in an adjoining area, and from 10 A.M. to noon in a third, with the work progressing in a continuous manner until the streets have been cleaned with a minimum of annoyance to residents.

Although on-street parking prohibitions aid those in charge of street-cleaning operations, they may meet with strong opposition. Residents of cities with high residential population densities rely heavily on public streets for overnight storage of their cars. Frequently people with single-family homes having one-car garages own two or three cars and use the streets for storage. University towns, with or without dormitories, rely heavily on streets for the storage of students' cars, and efforts by local governments to enforce parking bans are frustrating.

Any parking-restriction program must win community acceptance, or at least tolerance, before being put into effect. Some years ago, the mayor of Philadelphia attempted to put into effect a parking restriction, but the opposition was so violent that for a time his aides feared that he would suffer physical harm.

Water Pollution from Street Debris

While community appearance is the most obvious reason for good street-cleaning practices, it is not the only one and never has been since the days when householders cleaned their own streets. At one time, most authorities considered storm water from city streets sufficiently free from pollution so that it would not affect the quality of the receiving water. Today careful studies have shown that storm water carrying street debris, especially fine dust, is a matter for growing concern. The

---

[5] "Outline History of the Department of Sanitation, New York City."

Detroit Metropolitan Water Department, in its May 1968 report on dirt and debris problems in streets and alleys, estimated that its waste-water purification costs could be reduced by $3 million annually if its treatment plants need not receive such a heavy load of storm water polluted by street debris.

A study by Prof. Raymond C. Loehr[6] identifies pollution sources from urban runoff as:

- Street litter
- Motor-vehicle combustion products
- Ice-control salts
- Rubber and metals lost from vehicles
- Decaying vegetation
- Domestic pet wastes
- Fallout from industrial and residential combustion products
- Chemical fertilizers and insecticides applied to home lawns and to parklands
- Lead, presumably from automobile and truck exhausts

Concentration of Pollutants near the Gutter

A study of selected areas in seven large cities has shown that 97 percent of the solids left on the street are within 40 inches (1016 millimeters) of the curb, or, unfortunately, where the conflict between the street sweeper and the parked car is greatest. The runoff from these street surfaces is surprisingly polluted. The runoff contributed during the first hour of a storm with rainfall amounting to ½ inch (12.7 millimeters) per hour would bear a considerably greater pollution load than the city's sanitary sewage would bear during the same period.

The significant finding is that the polluting portion of the street-surface contaminants is in the fine solids, smaller than 43 microns (43 micrometers; 0.00017 inch). This fraction accounts for only 5.9 percent of the total solids, but it is responsible for about 25 percent of the oxygen demand and between one-third and one-half of the algal nutrients. It also accounts for more than half of the heavy metals and nearly three-fourths of the total pesticides (see Table 6-1). Yet conventional street-sweeping practices, which are geared basically to appearance, have great difficulty in collecting this fraction, leaving behind 85 percent of the material smaller than 43 microns and about half of the material smaller than 246 microns (0.0096 inch).[7]

The problem that this presents to pollution-control authorities is that

---

[6] Raymond C. Loehr, "Characteristics and Comparative Magnitude of Non-point Pollution Sources," *Journal of the Water Pollution Control Federation,* vol. 46, no. 8, pp. 1862–1864, 1974.

[7] James D. Sartor and Gail B. Boyd, *Water Pollution Aspects of Street Surface Contaminants,* EPA-R2-72-081, U.S. Environmental Protection Agency, November 1972.

TABLE 6-1   Fraction of Total Constituent Associated With Each Particle Size (Percentage by Weight)

	Less than 43 microns	43–246 microns	More than 246 microns
Total solids	5.9	37.5	56.6
Biochemical oxygen demand (5 days)	24.3	32.5	43.2
Chemical oxygen demand	22.7	57.4	19.9
Volatile solids	25.6	34.0	40.4
Phosphates	56.2	36.0	7.8
Nitrates	31.9	45.1	23.0
Kjeldahl nitrogen	18.7	39.8	41.5
Heavy metals (all)	51.2		48.7
Pesticides (all)	73		27
Polychlorinates biphenyls	34		66

SOURCE: James D. Sartor and Gail B. Boyd, *Water Pollution Aspects of Street Surface Contaminants,* U.S. Environmental Protection Agency, November, 1972.

concentrations of pollutants in urban runoff can vary widely. Results from three representative cities, shown in Table 6-2, typify these inconsistent results.[8]

The contribution of pollutants from street debris generated in various sections of an urban land area also is not clear, although some trends appear evident. Studies of ten large cities show that commercial and shopping districts contribute the smallest amount, presumably because sweeping is more frequent there. Residential areas contribute more, with the older and presumably less affluent areas contributing the largest amount in this land-use category. This fact probably indicates that a more frequent sweeping schedule would lower the contribution. Industrial areas contribute the greatest amount, with areas having light industry making by far the largest contribution. Only the most limited and inconsistent evidence is currently available to show how quickly these pollutants tend to concentrate after the streets have been cleaned or after a heavy rain.

Nevertheless, the evidence of damage to receiving waters is often convincing. Apparently street runoff contributed by Bucyrus, Ohio, to the Sandusky River has been responsible for much of the river's polluted condition and the loss of fish life.[9]

Street-cleaning Effectiveness

Street cleaning practices in use in well-run cities today can remove from 95 to 100 percent of all large street litter, such as paper, wood, and leaves. They can remove almost 80 percent of the material smaller than 2000 microns (0.078 inch) and about 15 percent of the fraction smaller than 43 microns (0.00017 inch). Overall, they can remove about 50

[8] Loehr, op. cit.
[9] Sartor and Boyd, op. cit.

TABLE 6-2   Street Pollutants

City	Suspended solids (milligrams per liter)	Five-day biochemical oxygen demand (milligrams per liter)
Cincinnati, Ohio	5–1200	1–173
Tulsa, Oklahoma	84–2050	8–13
Washington, D.C.	26–36,200	6–625

percent of the dirt and dust.   However, James D. Sartor is of the opinion that they can remove 70 percent either with a second pass or with a slower operation of the sweeper.   He feels that no sweeper in use today can remove 90 percent of the fine material.   Whether this degree of cleanliness will be necessary has not been confirmed.

SWEEPERS

Most present mechanical street sweepers can be grouped into three-wheel and four-wheel types.   The categories can be subdivided into sweepers using mechanical brooms and those using air suction; some sweepers use both.

Three-Wheel and Four-Wheel Types

The three-wheel, broom-type sweeper is the familiar tricycle model with the hopper in front and the steering wheel or wheels at the rear.   This model can be provided with a hoist-type hopper that enables the operator to discharge a load of dirt and debris directly into a waiting truck rather than dumping it on the street for reloading.   It will travel at speeds of 20 to 30 miles (32 to 48 kilometers) per hour when moving

Figure 6-6.   The flexibility of the tricycle type of sweeper has been enhanced by lifting arms that permit it to discharge its load of debris directly into the truck.

Figure 6-7 In the postwar period a sweeper body mounted on a conventional truck chassis won adherents through its ability to move at relatively high speeds when not sweeping.

from location to location. The four-wheel sweeper mounted on a truck chassis can move at higher speeds when traveling to its assignment. It is especially useful in serving areas that are not densely populated and where sweeping duties are widely scattered. Both types carry hoppers with capacities varying from 3 to 4.5 cubic yards (2.29 to 3.44 cubic meters).

All types can be equipped with either automatic transmission or a hydrostatic drive. These make the work of the operator easier and also permit varying the speed of the broom. The hydrostatic drive allows sweeping both forward and backward and also "sitting down" on a heavy load of debris until the broom has picked it up.

Separate Engine for the Main Broom

The four-wheel, truck-mounted sweeper frequently is equipped with a separate engine as a power source for the brooms. This engine provides the operator with an opportunity to adjust the cleaning work to the debris on the street. The disadvantage of the separate engine is that it offers one more opportunity for mechanical breakdowns. It also adds to fuel requirements and contributes a certain amount of air pollution.

Truck-mounted, Trailer-Type Sweeper

One truck-mounted sweeper makes use of a trailing type of main broom, which can remain in contact with the street surface independently of the truck chassis. At present this is the only truck-mounted unit that can dump debris directly into an awaiting truck. The hopper, ranging in capacity from 3 to 6 cubic yards (2.29 to 4.58 cubic meters), can be hoisted to tilt to one side and discharge into the receiving truck.

Figure 6-8   The vacuum sweeper is gaining popularity because of its ability to pick up fine material that contains a high proportion of pollutants. [*Elgin photo*]

Vacuum Sweeping

Responding to a demand for a higher degree of cleanliness free of the dust fraction, sweepers that clean by an air-suction system are being produced.   They may have rotating side brooms as optional equipment. The purpose of the brooms is to bring street dirt in the center of the pavement to the suction nozzle.

These sweepers are truck-mounted and can travel from site to site at truck speeds.   They are designed to operate at 2 to 5 miles (3.2 to 8 kilometers) per hour, or more slowly than conventional mechanical sweepers.   When equipped with gutter brooms, they have cleaning paths of 6 to 7 feet (1.83 to 2.13 meters).   Downtime is reported to be less with these sweepers than with conventional units.

Main-Broom Performance

Over the years the main brooms of conventional mechanical sweepers have been made of a variety of fibers.   The kinds may be grouped into natural fibers (bass, hickory, or imported palmyra), synthetics (nylon, polypropylene, or polystyrene), crimped wire, or a combination of these. The selection of fibers has varied with economic conditions and availability.   Currently very little natural fiber is being employed, and what is in use is chiefly bass.   In the synthetic group, only polypropylene is in use.   This choice, of course, can change and undoubtedly will.

Many experienced operators have observed that an old main broom picks up more street debris than a new one does.   This superiority is due not so much to the age of the fiber as to the flicking action that moves the dirt to the sweeper conveyor and to the storage hopper. The fibers of a new broom are longer and have weaker flicking action. As they wear, they become shorter and the flicking action stronger. However, as the fiber continues to wear, to lengths of 3 to 4 inches (76.2 to 101.6 millimeters), the stiffness becomes so great that the flicking action ceases to be effective and the fibers must be replaced.[10]

Broom Patterns

The broom pattern defines the width of the area in which the main broom actually makes contact with the pavement. It is a major factor in appraising the cost-benefit relationship of the sweeping activity. Too wide a pattern results in excessive wear on the broom fibers, and too narrow a pattern lowers the ability of the broom to pick up dirt and other debris.

Broom patterns vary from 4 to about 9 inches (101.6 to about 229 millimeters) and depend on the condition of the street surface and the type of dirt and debris that must be collected. With predominantly sandy street debris, such as would be encountered in a shore area, a wide pattern would be required. An uneven pavement surface reduces the effectiveness of the broom by decreasing the width of the pattern. For example, a 2-inch (50.8-millimeter) pavement dip can result in the

[10] Correspondence with Richard Fenton, assistant administrator, Environmental Protection Administration, New York City, Dec. 12, 1974.

Figure 6-9   A broom pattern, the width of the contact that the broom makes with the pavement, can vary from 4 to 9 inches (101.6 to 228.6 millimeters), depending on sweeping conditions.

sweeper's leaving almost 3 times as much dirt and debris as it would on a smooth pavement.

Broom mileage is extremely variable. Some records suggest as much as 1000 curb miles (1609 curb kilometers) per broom, and others as little as 200 curb miles (322 curb kilometers). The difficulty is that no way of relating the quality of cleaning to broom mileage has yet been developed, although a means of measuring the quality of sweeping will be discussed later in the chapter.

Broom-filling Methods

Maintenance forces formerly made their own brooms. This was a laborious and costly task. An operator had to thread the broom fibers onto the rope by hand as the broom core was turned in a specially designed frame. Today suppliers can provide prefabricated broom coils with the fibers already in place, and these can be quickly and easily wound onto the broom core. Or they can provide broom-fiber "wafers," individual sections of brooms that can be slipped onto specially prepared cores.

Figure 6-10   Prefabricated brooms of various types simplify the provision of sweeper main brooms.

Gutter Brooms

Many persons overlook the performance of gutter brooms when they analyze the performance of mechanical sweepers. These brooms have the important duty of transporting debris from the gutter, where most

Figure 6-11 The action of the gutter broom on a mechanical sweeper is highly important because it must transport the debris from the gutter to an area in front of the main broom.

of it accumulates, into the path of the main broom, which in turn picks it up for removal.

Gutter brooms also formerly were made in maintenance shops. Today these brooms can be provided in segments that can be clamped quickly onto a polyethylene holder that appears resistant to moisture, warping, separation, and impact. Virtually all gutter brooms use crimped wire for fibers. They vary from 20 to 47 inches (508 to 1193.8 millimeters) in diameter, and the broom fibers have an operating life varying from 300 to 600 gutter miles (from 483 to 966 gutter kilometers).

One of the problems in using gutter brooms is that their sweeping action can be so strong that they sweep the debris beyond reach of the main broom, thus leaving the center of the roadway dirty. To prevent this, sweepers generally are equipped with a flexible baffle that can stop the debris.

The strategic role of the gutter broom can be illustrated by a simple calculation. If both the main broom and the gutter broom are 80 percent effective, the machine itself has an effectiveness of 80 times 80, or 64 percent, which is not as great as most administrators would like it to be.

Operator Comfort

A pressurized, air-conditioned cab on the sweeper can add greatly to the comfort and efficiency of the operator. The job is normally hot and dusty, and an air-conditioned cab should permit the operator to improve the quality of the work. Hydrostatic drives and automatic transmissions in sweepers also can ease the work of the operators and reduce sweeper maintenance costs as well.

Diesel Engines

Although diesel engines have a higher first cost than that of gasoline-fueled engines, for most conditions their long-term improved performance should make them a more economical power source. Diesel fuel is less expensive than gasoline and gives substantially more curb miles of performance per gallon (curb kilometers per liter). Diesel engines do not need spark plugs, points, or carburetor adjustments. Overall, they last longer and perform more economically than gasoline-fueled engines do.

From an environmental standpoint, diesel exhaust gases do not contain as many of the more harmful air pollutants such as carbon monoxide. If the engine is powered to meet its service requirements and is not underpowered and if it is properly maintained, it will not discharge the odorous black exhaust that characterizes the operation of many commercial trucks and buses with diesel engines.

Data on commonly used street sweepers are shown in Table 6-3.

GENERAL PROCEDURES

The effective programming of sweeper routes is as important as the sweeper operation itself. Careful routing of sweepers often can reduce the number of sweeping units needed while improving cleaning performance.

Sweeper routes must be based on the number of curb miles (curb kilometers) selected for each machine. The total should not exceed 20 to 25 miles (32 to 40 kilometers) per shift, and should be based on a sweeper operation of 4 to 6 miles (6.4 to 9.6 kilometers) per hour. (Higher speeds mean only that the sweeping is not thorough.) Sweeper routes then can be assembled into districts. Downtown commercial districts should be considered separately because sweeping there is more frequent and preferably should be scheduled at night.

Dumping Sites and the Disposal of Collected Debris

In the less densely populated residential areas, the assembly of routes into districts permits several sweepers to use a common disposal site from which the debris can be picked up for transfer to the place of ultimate disposal. These sites can be carefully selected on-street or off-street points. On-street sites must be provided with traffic warning

TABLE 6-3   Some Commonly Used Street Sweepers

Type	Manufacturer	Model	Number of wheels	Number of engines	Main-broom width (inches)	Side-broom diameter (inches)	Sweeping path*	Sweeping speed (miles per hour)	Maximum travel speed (miles per hour)	Water spray	Hopper capacity (cubic yards)	Comments
Pickup broom	BLH Austin-Western	70	3	1	60	36	9 feet	1–10	25	Yes	4½	Model 40-B has 2-cubic-yard hopper.
	Elgin	475 (White Wing)	3	1	68	36	8 feet	1–15	22	Yes	4½	Model 375 has 3½-cubic-yard hopper.
	Elgin	Pelican	3	1	68	36	8 feet	1–15	22	Yes	2½	Self-dumping (8-foot 6-inch lift).
	MB	Cruiser	4	1	60	47	n.a.	¾ and up	50	Yes	4⅓	Dumps from rear.
	Mobil	TE4	4	2	60	42	7 feet 6 inches	1–12	55	Yes	4	Model TE-3 has 3-cubic-yard hopper.
	Wayne	984	3	1	58	45	9 feet	2–8	25	Yes	4	Model 973 has 3-cubic-yard hopper.
	Wayne	945	4	2	58	45	8 feet	1–15	55	Yes	4	Self-dumping (94-inch lift).
	Wayne	933	3	1	58	45	8 feet	1–15	55	Yes	3	Self-dumping (side dump).
	Murphy	4032	4	2	58	45	10 feet	1–12	55	Yes	3	Self-dumping (side dump).
	Murphy	4042	4	2	58	45	10 feet	1–12	55	Yes	4	Self-dumping (side dump).
	Murphy	4062	4	2	58	45	10 feet	1–12	55	Yes	6	Self-dumping (side dump).
Air	Tymco	300	4	2	80	Optional	6 feet 8 inches	1–8	55	Optional	3	Uses "regenerative" air system.
	Tymco	600	4	2	96	Optional	8 feet	1–10	55	Yes	6	Uses "regenerative" air system.
Vacuum	Tennant	100	3	1	42	32	6 feet	0–12	15	No	1¾	Uses vacuum system for dust control.
	Elgin	Whirlwind	4	2	60	28	87 inches	n.a.	55	Yes	5.5	Has auxiliary pickup nozzle.
	Ecolotec	Vacu-Sweep	6	2	60	20	72 inches	n.a.	55	Yes	6.3	Has auxiliary pickup nozzle.
	Coleman	Metro-Vac	6	2	...	20	94 inches	n.a.	55	Yes	11½	

*This list is not comprehensive but does include the most commonly used sweepers. Sweeping-path data are based on using one side broom. The Tymco sweepers have no broom; the broom width specified is actually the width of the pickup head.

SOURCE: James D. Sartor and Gail Boyd, *Water Pollution Aspects of Street Surface Contaminants*, EPA-R2-72-081, U.S. Environmental Protection Agency, November 1972.

equipment such as cones, barricades, or flashers. Off-street sites should be as well screened from view as possible and preferably be located adjacent to vacant lots or in otherwise remote areas. The pickup and transfer of the debris should be as prompt as possible.

If the sweepers have elevating hoppers that can discharge directly into a truck box, no central transfer points are needed. However, this procedure requires coordination between the truck and the sweeper to avoid waste time. With a four-wheel sweeper on a truck body, the operator can attain a higher traveling speed, frequently permitting the sweeper to deliver its load of debris directly to the final dumping area.

Sweeper Visibility

A sweeper should be as visible and as attractive as possible. It should carry the customary triangular warning sign indicating a slow-moving vehicle, and when operating in heavy traffic or at night, it probably should carry rotating warning lights. Yellow has generally been recognized as the most visible color, but white has a good degree of visibility and connotes sanitation, thus winning favor with the public being served.

Whenever practical, sweepers should operate when the public will see them. This scheduling should stimulate operators to do a more thorough job, and it will remind the public that the equipment and the municipality are doing what they can to keep neighborhoods clean and attractive.

Pickup and Transfer of Dumped Sweeper Debris

At a central transfer point, the commonest practice is to load the debris that has been collected and placed on the street by means of a tractor-mounted front-end loader bucket. Another useful unit is a dump truck with a front-end loader bucket equipped with lifting arms that carry the bucket over the cab, unloading it into the truck dump box. Its employment eliminates the need for one equipment unit and one operator.

A growing number of municipalities use the popular truck-mounted vacuum loader that discharges into a large closed body, generally with a capacity of 16 cubic yards (12.2 cubic meters). One of these units frequently can pick up the debris collected by four or more sweepers. The vacuum loader has a flexible collecting hose. The driver can back the truck to the pile of debris and then get out of the cab and use the hose to pick it up. Thus only one operator is involved. The strong suction from the hose does a very thorough job, and debris does not pass through the fan.

Figure 6-12   To collect sweeper debris that has been stockpiled in the street, many municipalities use vacuum loading units of this type.

Two-Way Radio

If at all possible, for the general good of the community the sweeper operator should be equipped with a two-way radio and be thoroughly instructed in how to use it.   Not only does the radio give the supervisor contact with the sweeper operator, but it also allows the operator to reach a truck if the sweeper has a hoisting, direct-dump hopper.   It permits the operator to advise the supervisor that a sweeper load is being discharged at the designated central point.   The loading equipment can then be dispatched to the central point to transfer the debris to its ultimate disposal point, generally a landfill area.   Furthermore, the two-way radio gives the community an additional opportunity to provide prompt response to accidents, emergencies, unreported danger points in the streets, and other urgent civic problems.

Sweeper-Operation Monitor

As it has become clear that street-cleaning operations must be more highly concerned with thoroughness, there has arisen a need for some type of monitor that will record when the sweeper is operating and at what speed.   Ideally, the monitor should record (1) when the machine is sweeping, (2) at what speed it is traveling, and (3) how fast the brooms are rotating.   It also should record when the sweeper is traveling to its assigned route, when it returns, and when it is traveling to the disposal area.

Recording this type of information would help and protect conscientious operators, who today lack a real method of showing the quality of their work. Operators could and should be encouraged to evaluate the records with notes so that good performance could be recognized.

Instrumentation like this is within the capabilities of manufacturers and would not be difficult to assemble. However, the only monitoring equipment now available is a mechanical, clockwork-powered recorder mounted on the sweeper that documents when the sweeper is operating. It can provide at least some of the information to record good performance.

OTHER EQUIPMENT

For certain applications, a "regenerative" air sweeper is becoming popular. This unit replaces the rotating broom with a strong current of air that moves the dirt and debris into the hopper. The sweeper can be supplied with a water spray for dust control. A dust-separation system vents a portion of the air used in the cleaning.

Small industrial sweepers also are occasionally used for specialized street-cleaning work. However, their commonest use is found in cleaning parking lots, parking garages, and sidewalks.

Street Flushers

Street flushers have had a long history in urban street care. Originally, their use was confined to moistening the dirt surface so that water would "lay the dust." Later, suppliers used pumps to provide pressure so that the water would transport the dust to catch basins.

The most effective use of the flusher is to provide a polishing action by transporting the dust and dirt that the mechanical sweeper has missed and washing it to a catch basin. This practice poses a problem with

Figure 6-13 The most effective modern use of a flusher is that of providing a polishing action behind a mechanical sweeper.

water-pollution control agencies, which do not want dust to enter the waste-water flow. How this difference will be resolved is still undetermined. The thrust of water-pollution control is toward removing pollution from all sewage, whether it is sanitary sewage or storm water.

It can be argued that a rainstorm places all the dust and dirt into the sewer as a shock load that strains the treatment facilities, both hydraulically and from the standpoint of removal mechanisms. However, flushing introduces this dust and dirt in small increments that should not cause problems for the treatment plant. The principal criticism of flushers is the assertion that they cannot provide enough water to move the debris to a catch basin. However, if the curb is open and free of parked cars and if the water pressure is adequate, the flusher should be able to transport the debris to a catch basin without difficulty. Flushers carry from 800 to 3000 gallons (3028 to 11,356 liters) of water.

Commonly used street flushers and eductors are shown in Table 6-4.

LEAF COLLECTION

Concern about air pollution has added to the problems of municipal street cleaning. Statewide bans on open burning now are common, and they have forced street-cleaning crews to collect the entire accumulation of leaves each fall. Leaf collection can be difficult and exasperating.

TABLE 6-4   Commonly Used Street Flushers and Eductors

Company	Model	Tank capacity (gallons)	Flushing width (feet)	Pump size (gallons per minute)	Comments
Etnyre	Leader	800–3000	Variable	750	Flusher only
Etnyre	Clipper	800–3000	Variable	750	Flusher only
Etnyre	Superliner	800–3000	Variable	750	Flusher only
Rosco	MTA	1200; 1600; 2100	Variable	750	Flusher only
MS	Vactor	2500	42	650	Used as a vacuum truck
Wayne	Sanivac 1600	3300	45	600	Used as a vacuum truck; capacity, 6 cubic yards
Wayne	Sanivac 1300	2600	45	600	Used as a vacuum truck; capacity, 13 cubic yards
Central Eng. Co.	VAC-ALL	1700–2200	42	650	Used as a vacuum truck; capacity, 10–16 cubic yards

SOURCE: James D. Sartor and Gail Boyd, *Water Pollution Aspects of Street Surface Contaminants,* EPA-R2-72-081, U.S. Environmental Protection Agency, November 1972.

Leaves are light and bulky and are hard to load with ordinary materials-handling equipment.

In the past, the fall burning of leaves was a community activity that encouraged neighborliness. However, investigations have disclosed that for every 100 pounds (45.36 kilograms) of leaves burned, 20 pounds (9.1 kilograms) of troublesome air pollutants are produced. These pollutants have been identified as hydrocarbons, oxides of nitrogen, oxides of sulfur, and solid particulate matter. All adversely affect the cardiorespiratory systems of many people and cause problems to others who are allergic to leaf smoke. Dirt in the air resulting from the burning also is a factor.[11]

Since residents no longer are permitted to burn the leaves, some municipalities permit and even encourage householders to rake their leaves into the gutter for collection by municipal forces. Others offer to pick up the leaves by the regular refuse-collection service if the leaves are in plastic bags or other suitable containers.

Collection Methods

A leaf rake mounted on the front of the street sweeper frequently is used to gather leaves into piles after they have been deposited in the gutter. If the leaves are wet, they often are easier to handle.

To pick up leaves, cleaning crews have used almost any type of loading equipment even though most of it is designed for handling heavier material and therefore is not particularly efficient when handling light, bulky leaves. Vacuum-type equipment, both truck- and trailer-mounted, has proved more effective. It has the added advantage of

[11] "Leaf Burning: An Economic Case Study," *Air Pollution Notes,* College of Agriculture and Environmental Sciences, Rutgers University, New Brunswick, N.J.

Figure 6-14   A leaf rake mounted on the front of a sweeper is a common means of stockpiling leaves for pickup.

Figure 6-15 In the past street crews have used a wide variety of equipment for leaf pickup that is not particularly well suited to the task. This loader designed to handle sand and gravel is a typical example.

shredding the leaves, transforming them into a dense mass, and thus permitting the truck or trailer to carry a larger quantity of leaves.

To dispose of the leaves, some municipalities compost them for use in parks and also for the convenience of residents. Occasionally a municipality makes a small charge for this compost, if this does not complicate municipal bookkeeping. Directions on an effective method of composting leaves appear in Chapter 12, "Urban-Park Maintenance."

Figure 6-16 A variety of vacuum leaf loaders, such as this trailer-mounted equipment, has been developed.

Figure 6-17   This large-capacity vacuum leaf loader is self-contained and, if necessary, can be assigned to other tasks such as cleaning catch basins.

Palm-Frond Collection

While Northern cities can expect leaves to become a problem each fall, municipalities in the South have a continuing task of picking up palm fronds and other trimmed shrubbery, since ornamental landscaping grows fast in these areas.   The most successful unit has been a truck-mounted hydraulic crane with a grapple on the boom.   One effective crane has a reversible driver's seat in the cab, allowing the driver to operate the crane while the seat is turned to face the back of the truck.   The seat is then reversed while the truck is driven to the next loading point.   The crane delivers its load to large-capacity open trucks with dump bodies.

CATCH-BASIN CLEANING

Catch basins are a feature of the past and probably should be phased out.   They first were installed when streets were unpaved, good sewer-cleaning equipment was unavailable, and the installation of sewers was primitive.

Catch basins are small, roughly designed settling basins that can remove heavy material as their storage capacity permits.   Their limited retention time prevents the capture of the fine material that contains pollutants.

Cleaning Frequency

Catch basins require cleaning whenever the storage space in them is exhausted.   They should be cleaned in spring to remove the collected sand and abrasives used to prevent skidding and in fall to make sure that they have enough capacity to receive the winter's contribution of sand and other debris.   Of course, many other types of debris find their way into catch basins.   They may contain newspapers bundled with baling wire, rocks, sticks, discarded toys, and even money and watches.

Cleaning Equipment

The principal equipment used to empty catch basins successfully include the following:

- A hydraulic eductor
- A truck-mounted crane with a small bucket that can fit well into the catch basin
- A truck- or trailer-mounted vacuum unit

The eductor is a truck-mounted unit with a large water tank. It also has a reel carrying about 20 feet (6.1 meters) of 3-inch (76.2-millimeter) hose for suction and a small jet hose to loosen the debris in the basin. The truck carries pumps that provide water to create the jet action and to produce the suction that removes the debris. This material settles to the bottom of the water tank, permitting the water to be recirculated until it has collected all the catch-basin contents that it can hold without interfering with its work. When the load is complete, the truck transports it to a dumping area and discharges the material and water together.

The advantage of the eductor is that it works quickly and neatly, with a minimum of dripping on the street surface. The one drawback is that it cannot pick out debris larger than the diameter of the suction hose. Larger material, and there always is some, must be picked out manually.

The truck-mounted crane is a simple, direct combination. The crane is supplied with a small bucket that can fit handily into the catch-basin well and remove practically all the debris regardless of size. Moreover, it can lift off and replace the catch-basin cover, thus relieving the workers of a laborious task. The bucket places the debris in the truck dump box, permitting the truck-crane combination to clean the basins and also to transport the debris to the disposal point.

In some large municipalities the crane is a separate unit so that it can

Figure 6-18 A vacuum unit performs catch-basin cleaning work.

Figure 6-19 Catch basins frequently are cleaned by hydraulically actuated units like this one. The large hose removes the debris with the small hose loosens any caked material. [*Elgin photo*]

load several trucks.   However, in most municipalities the simplicity of a truck that carries its own crane and does its own loading and transporting has great appeal.

The truck- or trailer-mounted vacuum unit is the same piece of equipment that picks up piles of debris from street-cleaning operations. The flexible hose extending from the back of the truck body can quickly vacuum out the debris, often at a rate of about 35 basins per crew of three workers per day.

STREET-CLEANING MEASUREMENT YARDSTICKS

The question of how thoroughly a street should be cleaned has never been answered with great precision.   A pragmatic administrator once said that a street should be as clean as the public wants it to be.   If he received no more than three or four complaints per month about street cleaning, he felt that the task was being performed adequately.   This is a negative approach to street cleanliness.   Often the public is dissatisfied with the appearance of the streets but will not complain unless conditions become acute.   Another method should be available.

In the eyes of the general public, the measure of street cleanliness is primarily cosmetic.   If the streets appear clean, if the gutters are free from debris, and if the street area generally is not troubled with visible litter, then to most people the streets are commendably clean.

Over a century ago, the English biologist Thomas Henry Huxley said that science is nothing but trained and organized common sense. Trained and organized common sense should provide a means of measuring cleanliness that can be made a part of performance records.

The city government of Washington, D.C., together with the Urban Institute, has developed a rating system based on the cosmetic approach that can be made a part of a reporting program.[12]   The investigators first took hundreds of photographs of street conditions throughout the city and then sorted the prints into four categories, assigning ratings for each as follows:

Classification	Rating
Clean	1
Moderately clean	2
Moderately littered	3
Heavily littered	4

The district government then provided inspectors with typical photographs of streets with conditions fitting each of the classifications.   The inspectors made a value judgment of each street by comparison with these photographs.   This system provides a rating of the street condition that, while not absolutely precise, is sufficiently close so that others can understand the degree of visible street cleanliness.

This method, of course, leaves unclassified the amount of fine dirt and dust that remains on the streets and that is undetected in the photographs.   Since this fraction contains the troublesome pollutants that will degrade water resources, one can reasonably expect water-protection agencies to become sufficiently concerned to require its measurement as part of the rating of street cleanliness.   However, until these agencies do enforce this requirement and provide a simple and accurate means of making this measurement, the Washington method should provide street-sanitation administrators with a means of measuring and recording the quality of their work that is more enlightening than simply listing the curb miles swept or the broom mileage obtained. (For additional information on the photographic rating of cleanliness, see Chapter 16.)

MECHANICAL STREET-CLEANING COSTS

Obviously, mechanical street-cleaning costs will vary from one geographic area to another under the influence of topography, climate, frequency of sweeping, labor costs, and other factors.   More important, no commonly accepted method of measuring costs so that they can be

[12] "How Clean Is Our City?" Urban Institute, Washington, 1974.

compared among municipalities has ever found sufficiently wide acceptance to be useful.

Santa Clara, California, maintains a meticulous accounting system, and its cost and performance figures, shown in Table 6-5, provide a guide in cost measurements.

TABLE 6-5   Street-cleaning Cost and Performance Data, Santa Clara, California

Street-cleaning data:	
Curb miles cleaned	440
Number of sweeper routes	17
Average route length (miles)	26
Number of operators	3
Number of sweepers	3*
Type of sweepers	Four-wheel
Sweeping frequency	6–8 working days
Curb miles swept in 1973–1974	19,000
Street-cleaning cost distribution:	
Salaries and wages	$42,511
Materials, supplies, and equipment	35,484
Fringe benefits (33 percent)	14,156
Utility expense	300
Amortization of maintenance yard	810
Administrative overhead	6,367
Total	$99,637
Cost per curb mile swept	$5.24

*Plus a spare sweeper.

Sweeper Leasing

In a period of rising labor costs and militant municipal labor unions, many knowledgeable urban administrators are exploring the cost effectiveness of leasing equipment rather than owning and maintaining it. The results appear to be attractive.

The great advantage to the street-maintenance crews is that this plan assures that equipment will be available and operable. In virtually all municipally owned departments, at least 10 percent of the mechanical sweeping equipment is inoperative at any one time, and the figure can approach 60 percent even in well-run cities. Another advantage is that the plan places the leasing costs in the operating budget rather than making equipment a capital expense. Some will argue that, as a third point, the annual cost to the municipality will be lower under a lease arrangement than under outright purchase.

The key to an effective leasing program is that the contract must guarantee operable units on the street at agreed schedules. It also should specify the types of sweeping equipment to be used. Whether the lessor or the municipality provides the operators is a decision that will fit the needs of the individual governing body. If the latter is the choice, the lessor should be expected to train the operators.[13]

See also the accompanying lease agreement used by Kansas City, Missouri.

Contract Street Cleaning

Contract street cleaning is an arrangement that should appeal to small government units within a metropolitan area. As noted above, small municipalities own more sweepers than large ones do on a per capita basis. Moreover, they probably are less able to make effective use of sweepers because of the limited mileage of streets to be cleaned.

If a street-cleaning contractor can conclude agreements with several nearby governmental units, the contracting firm can make effective use of the equipment because it is operating over a larger land area. As a result, a small community should be able to have the advantage of a wider range of cleaning equipment, a greater number of skilled operators, and lower costs than would be possible if it owned its own equipment.

LEASE AGREEMENT USED BY KANSAS CITY, MISSOURI,
FOR SWEEPER RENTAL

This agreement made and entered into this ___(date)___ day of ___(month)___, 197__, by and between Kansas City, a municipal corporation of the State of Missouri, hereinafter referred to as the "City" acting by and through its Director of Public Works, and ___(leasing company)___, a ___(corporation, company)___, hereinafter referred to as the "Lessor".

WITNESSETH: That

WHEREAS, the City desires to lease ___(number)___ three-wheel sweepers, ___(number)___ four-wheel sweepers, and ___(number)___ 16-cubic yard vacuum type cleaners complete with street flushing attachments, which are the necessary street sweepers and support equipment to equip a street sweeping program as outlined in the attached specifications. All equipment furnished under this agreement shall be in accordance with specifications as hereinafter set out.

NOW THEREFORE, for and in consideration of the mutual covenants and conditions hereinafter contained, it is mutually agreed by and between the City and the Lessor as follows:

1. The Lessor agrees to lease street sweepers and necessary support equipment which shall meet all the specifications as advertised in the invitation for bid, which invitation for bid, the Lessor's bid and specifications are attached hereto and made a part of this Agreement the same as if incorporated and fully set out herein.

2. Lessor hereby agrees to rent to the City, and the City hereby agrees to rent from the Lessor, said street sweepers and necessary support equipment for a term of ___(months)___, said term to commence on ___(date)___, said

[13] Myron Calkins, "Leasing Sweepers Can Be Better Than Owning Them," *The American City,* March 1973, pp. 55–56.

equipment is to be delivered to and received into the possession of City. Provided, further, that the said term of said lease may be extended at the option of the City for subsequent and continuing periods of one year, each, subject to and in accordance with all the terms, as contained herein, unless the City delivers to Lessor 30 days written notice of its desire and intention to not exercise its option to renew and extend said lease for a one-year term to commence upon the last day of the first one-year term, otherwise this Agreement and all obligations thereunder shall continue. Minimum length of contract not to exceed four one-year options after the initial term.

3. City hereby agrees to pay Lessor as rent for said street sweeping and necessary support equipment for the term of _____(number)_____ months, the sum of _____ DOLLARS ____(sum in numbers)____ per month.

4. Lessor hereby agrees to lease to City the said street sweeping and necessary support equipment up to three additional terms of one year each, unless the City delivers to the Lessor 30 days written notice of its desire and intention not to renew and extend said lease. The Lessor hereby agrees to lease to the City the said street sweeping and necessary support equipment for the said additional one-year terms for a rental price of ____(write sum)____ DOLLARS ____(sum in figures)____ per month; provided, however, that in no event shall the City become obligated to pay Lessor rental payments in the stated sums for the additional term if the City delivers to the Lessor 30 days written notice of its desire and intention not to renew and extend said lease as provided in Paragraph 2 of the agreement and prior to the expiration of the first term as provided herein.

5. City's obligation to pay Lessor rents, and Lessor's right to rental payments as provided in Paragraph 3 herein, shall not be incurred or commenced until said term of the lease commences as provided in Paragraph 2 hereof, that is, upon the date of delivery to and possession of said street sweeping and necessary support equipment by City, and rental payments to be paid and due to Lessor shall correspond to the term of said lease and use of said street sweeping and necessary support equipment, and the date of this Agreement has been executed by said parties is not to be used in computing the date upon which the lease commences or the date upon which City's obligation to make rental payments for said street sweeping and necessary support equipment begins.

6. The Lessor agrees for and in consideration of the rental payments paid by the City to provide all parts, labor and other necessary services required to maintain the said equipment in a safe and fully operable condition so as to ensure the maximum availability of said street sweeping and necessary support equipment for full use during the entire period of this Agreement, and that any and all cost and expense incurred by the Lessor in this respect are contained in the total lease price paid by the City.

7. The Lessor shall furnish the City sufficient information as to the type and grade of fuel and lubricants recommended to be used in the operation and maintenance of said equipment; and the City shall furnish at its own expense the operators and fuel for said equipment. All oils and lubricants shall be furnished by the Lessor to be used in the operation and maintenance of said equipment.

8. The Lessor agrees to perform all routine maintenance work at non-

scheduled work times for all equipment. All equipment shall be made available for preventive maintenance at the regularly assigned work area of the equipment. The City shall not be required to furnish garage or work space for maintenance. The City shall return all equipment to the regular assigned work area in the event of an equipment failure.

9. The Lessor agrees to maintain and repair all equipment such that ___(number)___ sweepers and necessary support equipment shall be available for each scheduled work shift, not to exceed 40 hours per machine per week. The City has two sweepers which will be made available as standby equipment to maintain the sweepers in the field. The City shall assume all operating and maintenance of these two sweepers at no cost to the Lessor. The Lessor shall also supply and maintain a minimum of two additional standby sweepers. The Lessor agrees to repair all furnished equipment and place same in a fully operable condition within 24 hours or one working day after notification of a breakdown by the City or to furnish similar equipment in good operating condition at no cost to the City. Such equipment shall be delivered by the Lessor to the maintenance yard from where it was picked up. Should the Lessor fail to have available ___(the agreed number of sweepers)___, liquidated damages at the rate of $200.00 per machine per day shall be assessed. All liquidated damage assessments shall be deducted from current amount due the Lessor.

10. The Lessor shall include initial operating instruction for all equipment furnished under this Agreement. The Lessor further agrees to provide training for any new operators who may be required to man the equipment during the contract period and shall also provide operator review and retraining sessions at no additional cost to the City.

11. The Lessor shall furnish to the City a performance bond executed by an incorporated surety company authorized to do business in the State of Missouri in an amount of 30 percent of the total rent to be paid by the City for said equipment, such bond guaranteeing the Lessor will truly perform the covenants contained herein, and will provide the equipment to be leased to the City and all parts, labor and necessary services required to maintain the same in a fully operable condition.

12. The title of said equipment shall, at all times, be vested in the Lessor, and the Lessee shall give the Lessor immediate notice in event said equipment is levied upon or for any cause becomes liable to attachment.

13. The City shall ensure equipment against fire, theft, vandalism and public liability, storm damage, and collision.

14. The Lessor shall not be responsible for the following items:
   a. Tire repair and replacement.
   b. Daily lubrication and adjustments normally performed by the operator, including air-cleaner maintenance.
   c. Abuse and neglect—repairs caused by operation of the machine in a manner other than the purpose for which the machine was designed.
   d. Internal and external cleaning of the machine.
   e. Brooms, other than installation.

15. The payment of the sums set forth herein shall be made by the City on a monthly basis in equal installments to be paid in advance, except that the first payment thereof shall be made within the first month following delivery, which

said first payment shall include the first and second months of lease and use by the City. All succeeding payments shall be paid monthly, subject to reduction for liquidated damages as provided elsewhere herein.

IN WITNESS WHEREOF, The City by its Director of Public Works and __(leasing__ __firm)__ , by its authorized officer have caused this Agreement to be executed the day and year first above written.

KANSAS CITY, MISSOURI

A Municipal Corporation

By _____

Director of Public Works

_____

(Lessor)

By _____

Title:

Chapter Seven

Urban Maintenance Buildings

S. M. CRISTOFANO

The construction of a municipal maintenance facility, also known as a corporation yard or service center, involves a substantial community commitment. It is the type of building complex that is constructed no more often than once every 30 or 40 years, so an error in judgment incorporated into construction may cause trouble and inconvenience for decades. Good maintenance facilities do not happen accidentally. They are the result of careful and sound planning.

CHARACTERISTICS OF A MUNICIPAL MAINTENANCE FACILITY

What is a maintenance facility? It is a balance of space with time and movement. The structural complex may serve a single function only or a multiplicity of functions. It may be built in various shapes and sizes. It can be a command post in case of disaster, a warehouse, a repair center, a fuel depot, or a gathering place for personnel. Generally it is all of these.

It is unfortunate but true that many municipal maintenance yards, like the well-known Topsy, have grown without serious long-range planning. Most eventually consist of a conglomeration of makeshift buildings, lean-tos, and sheds that create chaos rather than order.

As a practical matter, some public agencies do not have the financial capability to build new, carefully planned facilities. Unfortunately they must resort to the incidental shed here and the lean-to there, until the sheer inefficiency and cost of the arrangement force a more effective

Figure 7-1 Although a municipal maintenance center should be attractive, it should emphasize efficiency. It should be a "balance of space with time and movement." This is the entrance to the Santa Clara, California, maintenance center.

solution. But even under these makeshift circumstances some planning and forethought can be exercised to make the facility as functional as possible.

One does not mass-produce an effective maintenance center. Those responsible for designing it must respond to the special needs of the community. Here are some examples.

Canton, Ohio, constructed a modern automotive-service center in 1968, replacing an old "central garage," designed in 1915 and used as a barn for horses with the second floor employed as a haymow.[1] Sheboygan, Wisconsin, fared a little better. Its new service center replaced an obsolete structure with the pragmatic name of toolhouse.[2] Both were primarily for use by public-works crews.

In contrast, Riverside, California, decided not to confine its service building to public works. In 1964 it built a 93,000-square-foot (8640-square-meter) structure on a 22-acre (8.9-hectare) site, and now the city's public works department, public utilities, parks and recreation, and central stores all operate with great advantage from this multipurpose facility.[3]

Most of these service centers are constructed to replace complexes that are old and decrepit. However, old age is not always the critical parameter. A physically sound structure or group of structures may have to be abandoned solely because of obsolescence. A city may grow so rapidly that the increased demands of personnel, material, and

[1] L. C. Dubs, Canton, Ohio, "More Than Just a Building," *The American City,* June 1970, p. 119.

[2] R. E. Fleischer, Sheboygan, Wisconsin, "Designed for Six Major Functions," *The American City,* September 1967, p. 104.

[3] R. W. Broffle, Riverside, California, "New Maintenance Center Brings Order Out of Chaos," *The American City,* October 1964, p. 93.

Figure 7-2 Many centers develop haphazardly, responding to the needs of the moment. Here a water-utility meter shop is thrown together with a welding shop in an old building. Note, however, that the area is well maintained.

Figure 7-3 The central maintenance building used by Riverside, California, provides facilities for public works, public utilities, parks and recreation maintenance, and central storehouse space.

equipment create a strain that cannot be absorbed by existing facilities regardless of their sound condition.

Several years ago, Phoenix, Arizona, analyzed its needs and produced an innovative solution to its service-center problem. To understand the Phoenix situation, it is necessary to realize that in a span of 16 years the population of this desert-located city of the Southwest had grown from 106,800 to more than 500,000 and that its area had zoomed from 17 to 246 square miles (from 44 to 637 square kilometers). As a result, some street-maintenance equipment and refuse-collection trucks had to travel as much as 15 miles (24 kilometers) just to reach job sites. Such nonproductive travel badly eroded the effectiveness of the city's services.

To overcome this costly handicap, Phoenix began constructing satellite service centers (also called area stations) designed to put workers and equipment where the work had to be performed. Today employees report directly to a center located in the middle of their work districts and are only a few minutes away from their job sites. This development has increased productive time appreciably.[4]

In contrast to a large city with its satellite service centers, a smaller city may not be faced with excessive travel time to work locations, particularly if its growth is restricted by the boundaries of adjoining cities. For

[4] Fred Glendening, Phoenix, Arizona, "Satellite Service Centers," *The American City*, May 1967, p. 102.

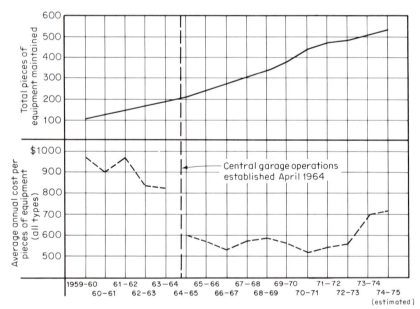

Figure 7-4 Note how the unit cost of equipment maintenance drops through the use of an efficiently designed and operated maintenance center. The graph lists costs variations at Santa Clara, California.

this situation, the best solution still appears to be a single centrally located facility. One such example is Covina, California, a vibrant community of 30,000 people. Its maintenance yard is located in a residential area and has been carefully planned to harmonize with its neighbors. Design requirements leaned heavily toward minimizing noise and unsightliness and emphasized architectural appearance and composition.[5]

The city of Santa Clara, California, which has owned and operated its electrical and water utilities since the nineteenth century, found itself with two separate corporation yards, one for the electrical department and the other for the water department. Both had become woefully inadequate through departmental expansion. Santa Clara chose to build a single facility on a newly purchased site of sufficient size to accommodate the personnel, materials, and supplies of both departments, including all telemetering and supervisory-control equipment. Staggering the work hours of each department by as little as 15 minutes was sufficient to relieve any peak demands on warehouse and automotive servicing facilities.

APPLYING SYSTEMS ANALYSIS

Systems analysis,[6] as an approach to problem solving, has catapulted to national attention mainly during the last 15 years, although most of the techniques have been developed since 1942. It is generally applied to large and complex problems and is almost always carried out by a team of specialists representing different disciplines. This does not imply that a highly sophisticated systems-analysis program is necessary to design a functional service center. It does suggest, however, that since the systems approach can be viewed as a general process within a wide variety of specific techniques, almost any public agency, large or small, can improve existing programs or develop and institute new ones by using this method. The design of a service center or a maintenance yard is one such application and a very important one.

What is the process of systems analysis? The diagram in Figure 7-5 shows its vital elements and also the relationship of the various elements to each other in the analysis. The process begins with the development of a problem that requires action, in this case action by a local government jurisdiction. The next step is to define the real need that has given rise to the problem in terms of the results to be achieved. This statement of need, or results to be achieved, must be converted into

---

[5] M. Hubiak, Covina, California, "This City Yard Is Neighborly," *The American City,* June 1967, p. 114.

[6] *Introduction to System Analysis,* Report No. 298, International City Management Association, November 1968.

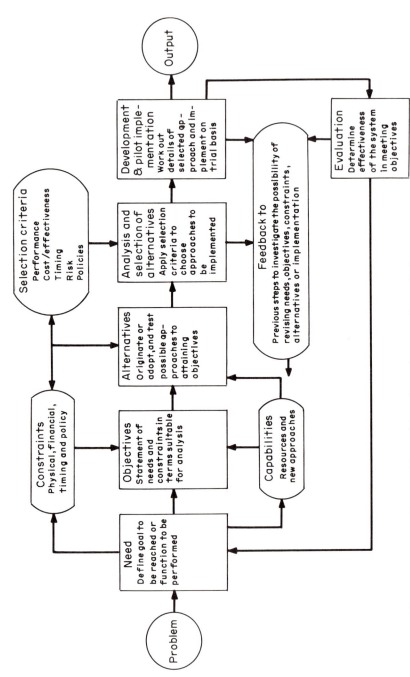

Figure 7-5   The systems approach to problem solving, shown here, can be applied advantageously to the development of an effective maintenance center.

clearly defined objectives that identify the specific conditions that are to be attained. The objectives must be measurable, and the important constraints and capabilities that limit the flexibility of the organization in achieving them must be identified.

Next, alternatives for meeting the objectives must be generated. The alternatives are differing courses of action that could be taken to meet all or some of the objectives. They must be analyzed in terms of their probable consequences, including both costs and benefits. For this purpose, criteria must be established to determine the relative merits of the alternatives and to allow selection of the preferred alternative. The alternative that best meets the selection criteria and offers the greatest possibility of achieving the objectives within the constraints is then developed into a complete action plan and implemented on a trial basis.

In the case of a municipal maintenance building complex, it is impossible to implement the action plan on a trial basis. However, it is possible to test the various elements of the plan on a simulated basis by using practical examples of actual situations that will arise when the facility becomes functional. This simulation process may point up the need to recycle certain elements of the process or the entire process itself until each element affects the others in a thoroughly satisfactory manner.

EIGHT STEPS REQUIRED FOR SYSTEMS ANALYSIS

From this general discussion of systems analysis, eight major steps can be identified: (1) determination of need, (2) definition of objective, (3) identification of constraints, (4) generation of alternatives, (5) analysis and selection of an alternative, (6) development and pilot implementation, (7) evaluation, and (8) feedback and modification.

Determination of Need

Of the eight steps, the first is probably the most easily identified criterion. An inspection of existing maintenance-yard facilities will generally establish the need for new or additional facilities. Normally, inefficient or inadequate space allocations for equipment, supplies, and personnel are ample reasons to establish the need.

Definition of Objective

The second step, definition of the objective, follows logically after the need has been established. Objectives may be broadly stated, or they may be concise and detailed. The city of Riverside identified the following broad objectives for its new maintenance center:

1. Provide closer cooperation among various city maintenance departments.
2. Minimize excessive and unproductive travel for materials and supplies.
3. Provide quicker and easier servicing of vehicles, resulting in less downtime.
4. Improve morale among employees.
5. Provide better service to the community.

Covina, with a critical need to avoid any nuisance problems with its close neighbors, outlined these more precise objectives:

1. Minimize noise and unsightliness.
2. Provide adequate facilities by using an economical type of construction.
3. Create a functional complex, with efficient traffic, materials-handling, and building-area allocations.
4. Emphasize architectural appearance and composition.

It is important to reemphasize the nature of agreed objectives. If objectives tend to be stated broadly in terms of philosophy or concept, their number is usually minimal. If the objectives are precisely identified, the list becomes much longer, and a tendency toward confusing technical design criteria with objectives can arise. Sometimes the two may be difficult to differentiate.

Identification of Constraints

The third step in the analysis causes the designer to analyze the factors that stand in the way of achieving the objective. Constraints always are there. If there were none, it would be easy to achieve any objective.

Covina's objectives properly reflect the constraints of siting its maintenance complex in a residential area. If money were not a constraint, and it always is, the designer could provide each worker with private quarters equipped with an easy chair, a deep-pile rug, and a shower and sauna. Designers and planners should not list every conceivable factor that limits reaching an objective. Rather, they should confine themselves to listing constraints that a reasonable person might consider applicable to the objectives.

The constraints most difficult to identify are those that could develop in the future but cannot be envisioned initially. Let us assume, for example, that the primary objective is to build a maintenance facility that will house services currently provided by the city. Let us assume, further, that the city does not provide refuse collection with its own forces but employs a private contractor and that it therefore does not anticipate this service in its new facility. However, let us assume also that one year after the new maintenance center goes into service, the contractor chooses not to renew the franchise, forcing the city to organize and equip its own refuse-collection crews. The question then arises: where in the new center shall the refuse trucks and personnel be placed? Planning that anticipates a constraint like this requires the judgment of a Solomon but must be faced, generally by recycling the entire complex through the systems-analysis approach in an effort to compensate for these unanticipated new activities.

Generation of Alternatives

The fourth step basically involves assembling as many different ideas as possible to accomplish the objectives. Ideas should be solicited from as many sources as are practical. The people who will occupy or direct the operations of the maintenance facility must be encouraged to submit their ideas. One good technique is brainstorming, in which positive ideas are requested from involved people of varied backgrounds and negative thoughts are not accepted. It is important not to reject any idea, no matter how impractical it may seem at first. One is bound to get a diversity of ideas. A warehouse worker, for example, may suggest that the floor of the warehouse be set at the same elevation as the ground outside the building. The driver of a truck may then offer the thought that the elevation of the floor be the same as the bed height of the truck. It is better to have both ideas, even though they conflict, than neither.

On the management level, one participant may urge that the municipality build and own the maintenance center. Another may suggest that it be built by a public nonprofit organization and leased to the city, with the lease retiring the indebtedness, and that the building then be transferred to the city. Still another may propose outright leasing from an appropriate landlord.

During this step, the following alternatives almost always will present themselves for discussion:

1. Should one large structure be built, or would a series of small structures be more efficient?

2. Should the on-site circulation plan for equipment be placed along the periphery of the facility, as opposed to a more centralized layout that might conflict with the walking movements of personnel or the outside storage of equipment?

3. Should the building or buildings be single-story or multistoried?

4. What reasonable distance should employees have to work to go from the locker room to their work assembly area and back again?

5. Should the entire facility be heated and air-conditioned, or should heating and air conditioning be restricted to certain areas? If so, to which areas?

This type of discussion should produce a wide range of ideas, and further analysis will disclose which are of sufficient merit to warrant study. Some will be rejected. Nevertheless, they should be retained as part of the record for future reference and comparative purposes.

Analysis and Selection of an Alternative

The fifth step requires that each of the alternatives be analyzed in sufficient detail to obtain a valid comparison. The views of those most knowledgeable about the operation and functioning of the alternatives should be solicited.

For example, let us consider a maintenance facility constructed to accommodate various activities not necessarily related to or under the control of one department. The maintenance activities that must be served at the center will include streets, water distribution, sanitary sewers, parks, and automotive maintenance. The automotive-maintenance section presents a problem of alternatives. What arrangement is the most effective for working on the underside of vehicles? The maintenance supervisor, the most effective person in this matter, can have hoists that will require a ceiling high enough for the largest unit or pits that will require excavation and concrete masonry. The supervisor recommends a combination of pits and hoists, but this recommendation must be analyzed on a cost-effective basis to determine whether the supervisor's plan serves the best interests.

To probe this decision on alternatives further, let us assume that the supervisor has a pet solution. Let us suppose that the supervisor doesn't like pits at all and wants all hoists to be capable of lifting the heaviest piece of equipment. Under the systems-analysis approach, such unreasonable solutions can be better controlled.

Santa Clara used the fifth step in systems analysis to great advantage. The ideas offered by personnel in the water and electric departments were reviewed, analyzed, and summarized in nine pages of data and instructions to the architect, who in turn used this material to analyze the various alternatives that arose as a result of preparing the construction plans and specifications. The basic data and instructions of the departments consisted of information that the architect was not the most knowledgeable about or in the best position to provide. The data furnished the architect included:

1. A detailed inventory of existing personnel, equipment, and supplies for each department

2. The projected size of each department commensurate with the city's ultimate population

3. The present and anticipated future activities of each department

4. A résumé of land uses adjacent to the proposed site

5. Requirements for covered and uncovered storage

6. Percentage and number of employees who might be expected to drive their own cars to work

7. Existing and future office and shop space

8. Special conditions such as the need for a constant and controlled atmosphere for supervisory-control equipment

One cannot lose sight of the fact that cost plays a significant role in the consideration of alternatives, and the cost factor should be ascertained and be readily available throughout this step. The original ideas and concepts for this service building would have produced, if built, a lovely but financially extravagant facility. The systems-analysis approach produced a proper balance with reality.

However, an excessive dependence on low cost can be damaging. Regardless of how spartan one makes a design, some decision makers will still demand even lower costs. One of the first areas that they attack is the apparently large space allocations for future requirements. This attempt must be resisted vigorously. Activities will expand, and the thriftiest investment will be for land to accommodate them. If unreasonable attempts to cut costs are not resisted, the entire systems-analysis process loses meaning.

Development and Pilot Implementation

The sixth step is extremely valuable. Some mistakenly consider systems analysis at an end when alternatives have been generated and selections made. However, no matter how good the selected alternative course of action may be, it cannot achieve the objectives unless it is tested in advance in as practical a manner as possible.

It is impractical to make a full-scale simulation, but one can devise a site-development plan and then use templates made to the proper scale for office furniture, sanitation fixtures, and stationary and mobile equipment. By applying these to what can be visualized as working conditions, the designers may be able to identify conflicts that would not otherwise become apparent.

In making this analysis step, employee movements should be traced throughout the facility, beginning at the point where the employees leave their automobiles to report to work in the morning and return to them at the end of the workday. Where will the employees normally go first? Most employees arrive from 5 to 15 minutes before their work shifts begin. They generally congregate at a central location, which may be the sanitation facilities or the locker room.

Does the design provide a direct route between the parking lot and these facilities? Or must the employees meander through open equipment or material storage areas? Worse yet, when entering the building, must employees walk through administrative offices or areas that should discourage indiscriminate or unnecessary foot traffic? What movements must employees make to report to their work assembly areas? Can they make this trip in safety, without conflict with moving equipment?

Templates should be used to simulate the effect of the anticipated

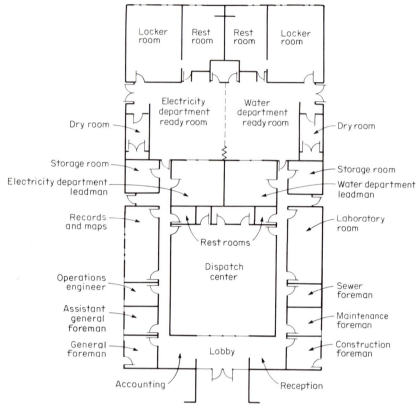

Figure 7-6 Systems analysis can produce a floor plan for a maintenance center building along these typical lines. Note that the movement of foot traffic for workers is centralized and separated from administrative functions.

number of trucks attempting to get fuel at the same time. The congestion that may develop when trucks back up to the warehouse to stock up with supplies needed for the day's work should also be anticipated. When conflicts are uncovered, the designers must decide whether to resolve them by changing the physical layout of the center or by changing operating procedures.

The purpose of pilot implementation is to prove that the new approach is possible despite organizational inertia that insists that it is not. It is to demonstrate that the new methods will produce the best possible results when implemented by the new construction.

Evaluation

The seventh step in this particular systems analysis requires the designers to make a formal analysis of the results just determined to assure themselves that the alternative selected performs as well as expected. To do this, they must review the original statement of objectives and constraints and modify them if circumstances have changed during the period of analysis and pilot implementation. On the basis of the revised objectives and constraints, if any, new simulations must be developed and applied to determine the degree to which the alternative meets all the objectives within the constraints.

As part of this evaluation, citizen participation and public response and acceptance are vitally important. Perhaps the community or at least some segments of it feel that a new park is needed in preference to a maintenance facility, arguing that a park will benefit everybody and not just a few city employees.

The city of Riverside first talked about a new service center in 1958, but 2 years had to elapse before the proposal won sufficient citizen support to merit a feasibility study by a citizens' committee. The fact that the process culminated in a maintenance center shows the astuteness of the city's administrators, who recognized the value of citizen input and support.

Today citizen participation plays a far more active role in all phases of government. Citizens demand emphasis on projects and programs that are more people-oriented. Policies of local governments, as well as financial resources, are being channeled increasingly toward social issues and decreasingly toward purely physical improvements. Consequently the designers, when making their evaluation, should direct attention to the social benefits that improved services provided by the maintenance center can provide. Although most administrators have never associated social benefits with municipal services such as these, the benefits do exist.

Feedback and Modification

The final step in systems analysis for an improvement such as this responds to the need for at least minor modifications in the overall project to gain complete achievement of the objectives. In some cases, an alternative that showed great promise may fail completely to achieve its objectives and should be abandoned.

While the major emphasis should be directed toward modifying the alternative selected to achieve the objectives, in some cases the objectives themselves or the criteria for evaluating systems performance may be found to be unrealistic. Before accepting modifications in objectives, however, the designers should insist on convincing evidence that the alternative was actually implemented as planned and that every effort was made to ensure successful performance.

COST AND FINANCING

Although maintenance centers can be built and are being built in all shapes and complexities, there seems to be a general range of costs that can be used as a rough guide in developing initial estimates. Current

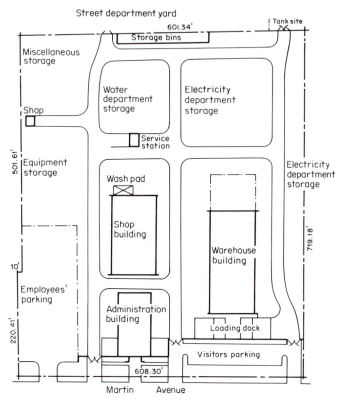

Site development plan

		Building areas (square feet)	
Engineering and administrative	$ 50,500		
Land acquistion	322,500	Administration building	9,000
Construction	603,000	Shop building	16,000
Equipment	45,000	Warehouse and dock	22,300
Total	$1,021,000	Total site area	10 Acres

Figure 7-7 Through systems analysis and input from many sources, including persons who work in the center, Santa Clara, California, developed this plan.

building costs only, excluding land, site improvements, portable equipment, and design fees, generally run in the neighborhood of $5 to $12 per square foot ($54 to $129 per square meter), with a median value of about $9. Total project costs range between $15 and $25 per square foot ($161 to $269 per square meter), applied to the building area. The average value is about $19.

Maintenance facilities are normally considered major capital projects, and their total cost therefore represents a substantial financial commitment. In the discussion of each step of systems analysis, the importance of cost has been emphasized. It has repeatedly been implied that there must be a balance between need and cost.

The financing method that administrators prefer is one that pays for

Figure 7-8 This is an aerial view of the site of the Santa Clara, California, center with the buildings in place.

the facility from available funds as the municipality constructs the maintenance center. This method is the least expensive, since it avoids interest payments and the uncertainties of a bond election. The difficulty is that it generally will require an increase in taxes, and a tax increase is difficult for the public to accept.

A second, more generally popular method is by bond issue. It has the advantage of sharing costs with present and future beneficiaries of the improved services that the municipal maintenance center will make possible. Two types of bonds are generally available: general-obligation bonds and revenue bonds. The first pledges the faith and credit of the local government and, in most states, requires a referendum vote. Such bonds are paid from ad valorem taxes levied on property. Revenue bonds are obligations to finance self-supporting facilities from fees, charges, or other earnings. Since maintenance centers do not generate revenue directly, revenue-bond financing is impractical.

A more rarely used system is that of employing a nonprofit corporation, which is organized by local people who build the center and then lease it to the city for a sum large enough to meet the cost of construction. In this way, it is possible to use revenue bonds, issued over a 25- to 30-year period, that will retire the project indebtedness. At the end of the period, the nonprofit corporation sells the center to the municipality, generally for a token sum such as $1, and then goes out of existence. The advantage of this system is that it eliminates the need for a bond referendum. Some cities have even used this method to build new city halls.

There are other methods of financing, such as special subsidies, grants, or loans, that are outside the realm of discussion here.

CONCLUSION

Any local administrator who has a responsibility for planning and implementing a new program or project must invariably approach it in a systematic fashion.   Some may unwittingly use the systems-analysis method.

Systems analysis is a valuable technical and administrative tool.   Its application is more readily apparent in some areas than in others, but there is rarely a problem area in which the process does not have some application.   Administrators who become aware of it, and use it more often, will find that it will assist them in getting the public and financial support needed to build a new municipal maintenance center.

Chapter Eight

Equipment-Maintenance Management

S. M. CRISTOFANO

ROLE OF EQUIPMENT-MAINTENANCE MANAGEMENT IN ADMINISTRATION

The maintenance of the equipment needed to provide the services required in an urban society is a vital management function. Today, when the forces of inflation have caused the prices of new equipment to rise to remarkably high levels, the urban administrator has an increas-

Figure 8-1 An urban government that promises its people that it will maintain a refuse-collection schedule and then fails to do so because of equipment breakdowns loses public confidence. Here a driver brings a truck in for preventive-maintenance inspection.

ingly strong reason to keep present equipment operating effectively for as long a period as is practicable.

The maintenance of equipment is a function that is as important as, if not more important than, any other municipally provided service. As an example, let us consider its role in the support of municipal refuse collection. The public must have confidence in its urban government. If this government establishes a refuse-collection schedule but cannot maintain that schedule because of equipment breakdowns and unproductive downtime, the public becomes cynical and the government loses effectiveness.

Central versus Departmental Equipment Maintenance

According to the American Public Works Association, equipment-maintenance management can follow two basic policies: centralized maintenance serving all municipal departments and separate departmental maintenance shops. Each of these policies must be viewed in the light of local needs and capabilities.

To avoid misunderstandings, each policy should be defined. Centralized maintenance is the performance, under the direction of a single governmental agency, of all maintenance, inspection, repairs, and rebuilding of motor equipment. As an organizational policy, it can apply either to a single garage, supporting the entire motor-equipment fleet, or to a complex of several maintenance facilities. Conversely, separate departmental maintenance means that each municipal department maintains and operates its equipment on an individual basis. There is no direction or administration by a single governmental agency.

Advantages of Centralized Maintenance

The advantages of centralized maintenance over departmental maintenance are many, and the disadvantages are few. One of the most obvious advantages is that of eliminating duplication of effort. Another is that this policy allows the purchase of spare parts at substantial savings. A third is the increased effectiveness of supervision reporting, through a chain of command, to a single director of maintenance activities. And a fourth is the development of greater mechanical skill through training and opportunity to become familiar with a wide variety of equipment. Against these and other lesser advantages, the only significant demerit is the possible increased cost of travel time by personnel and equipment between storage areas and the central shop or shops.

Response to Policies of Other Departments

To operate a successful centralized equipment-management program, the chief administrator or the administrator's delegate (garage supervisor) must be intimately familiar with the goals and objectives of

Figure 8-2 Equipment-maintenance practices must respond to the policies of the department using the equipment.   In this case, a police patrol car is being serviced.

operating line departments.   For example, typical objectives of the patrol division of a police department would include (1) the suppression of criminal activity, (2) response to routine and emergency calls, (3) investigation of traffic accidents, and (4) the apprehension of traffic violators.

The administrator of the equipment-management program therefore will realize that vehicles assigned to patrol duty, to detectives, and to undercover units represent tools needed to fulfill these objectives.   Police officers responding to an emergency situation must have full confidence in the mechanical soundness of their vehicles, thus allowing their attention to be focused upon arriving at the scene on time and in safety. They should not have to be concerned that their vehicles are poorly maintained and cannot perform as they should.

Police departments are not alone in the need for dependable equipment.   Any department that relies on automotive equipment to enable it to perform in accordance with its objectives must be able to depend on that equipment.   The philosophy of equipment-maintenance management is that all assigned equipment must perform to expectation, provided that such equipment is operated according to its intended use.

OBJECTIVES OF EQUIPMENT MANAGEMENT

The principle of management by objectives is a legitimate and effective guide to the conduct of municipal affairs.   Kapner[1] states that mainte-

[1] Sylvan L. Kapner, "Maintenance Management," in Harold B. Maynard (ed.), *Handbook of Business Administration,* McGraw-Hill Book Company, New York, 1967.

nance management has as its objective the maintenance of equipment at the optimum level. This implies that a good maintenance-management program will eliminate the vast majority of breakdowns and lengthen considerably the useful life of a particular unit of equipment. It also will save the municipality substantial sums by minimizing equipment downtime.

Kapner also observes, correctly, that to achieve these aims the administrative program must incorporate a substantial amount of *preventive maintenance*. His definition of maintenance management provides the broad-based foundation necessary to formulate the precise subobjectives consistent with the overall goals. Some of the more precise subobjectives might include the following:

1. Establish and maintain an automotive and equipment pool to supply the needs of the various departments, and keep necessary records for charging each department for the use of assigned equipment.

2. Prepare and maintain complete and accurate operating and maintenance records.

3. Prepare automotive and equipment specifications, rental charges, and replacement schedules.[2]

4. Conduct sound and effective preventive-maintenance programs for all equipment included within the maintenance management program.

5. Provide on-the-job and in-service training to assigned personnel.

6. Assist and instruct, as necessary, all equipment operators in the proper care and operation of equipment assigned to them.

Each operating level should be supplied with objectives that reflect that operational activity but will be in harmony with the overall objectives. For example, a clerk responsible for keeping gasoline records as accurately and as completely as possible may be provided with this type of objective: Compute monthly the total amount of gasoline disbursed against the gasoline on hand for the same period of time.

MASTER RULES

At one time, a major United States firm adopted eighteen rules for effective equipment-maintenance management. The same rules were subsequently adopted by the United States Navy. Because these rules have proved to be sound over the years and can be used by large as well as small urban governments, they are repeated here as a guide to policy determination:

---

[2] Rental charges used by the Santa Clara, California, Equipment Maintenance Department are listed at the end of this chapter.

1. Set up a responsible organization. Establish a separate maintenance-control group with overall control of procedures, inspections, and analysis of maintenance-cost information.

2. Use a work-order system. A written work-order procedure requires that every maintenance job be requested on a standard form that becomes the basis for equipment records, job analysis, work scheduling, and work measurement.

3. Keep equipment records. An accurate inventory and a permanent record of maintenance work performed are essential.

4. Analyze and plan jobs. The importance of an analysis of each repair order should be stressed. Moreover, a separate planning organization leaves supervisors free for direct supervision and personnel problems.

5. Make a weekly forecast. Schedule each week's work no later than the middle of the previous week. Generally, about 75 percent of the work included in the weekly forecast can be performed as specified.

6. Prepare daily schedules. Supervisors should prepare schedules for the next day prior to 3 P.M. daily to ensure that maintenance personnel need not wait for assignments each morning.

7. Set up human-power control. Human-power control includes a backlog control of worker requirements that indicates when a crew is too large or too small for the work ahead in each function, area, or shop.

8. Set up a preventive-maintenance program. Emphasize the need to do maintenance work at times when it will assure that the work force is continuously busy instead of working in surges.

9. Use budgetary control. A maintenance budget must be prepared on an annual basis and broken into monthly subdivisions. The annual budget can be fixed; the monthly budget can vary to meet changing situations.

10. Provide material control. Establish accurate maximum and minimum amounts for all stores items, material, and replacement parts as well as firm adherence to an established distribution and issue system.

11. Plan for shutdowns. Determine the expected life of various critical components in each equipment group, and then plan how to operate when any of these groups is out of service.

12. Set up major overhaul procedures. Determine the best method for overhauling any piece of equipment, including a description of the tools, parts, and worker requirements.

13. Develop standard practices for minor repetitive jobs or shopwork.

14. Use engineered work measurement. Evaluate labor performance by recording the actual amount of time taken on a series of jobs and comparing it with standard times established through engineered work measurement.

15. Improve equipment.   This is a long-range objective aimed at making maintenance easier by improving design, materials, or manufacture.   Standardization of design also is essential.

16. Train supervisors.   In the training, emphasize that maintenance controls have the strong support of management.

17. Train maintenance personnel.   Training is essential for new employees and new installations and also to increase the effectiveness of experienced personnel.

18. Analyze performance and costs.   Analyze performance and costs by continuing self-criticism of the total maintenance effort.

ORGANIZATIONAL STRUCTURE

Once the objectives of an equipment-management program have been identified and firmly established, it is possible to develop an organizational structure best suited to their attainment.   Fortunately, equipment maintenance lends itself well to a line and staff organization.   Figure 8-3 shows a typical organization chart, indicating the position of each job title in relation to other positions, both vertically and horizontally, within the department.   This chart is a guide that can be enlarged or reduced to fit the requirements of a particular community.   It typifies an

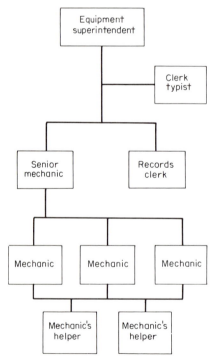

Figure 8-3 This typical line and staff organizational chart for central equipment maintenance can serve in cities with populations of 75,000 to 100,000.

equipment-maintenance organization in a community of 75,000 to 100,000 people. Maintenance and administration functions are clearly separated, and there are no connecting dashed lines. Generally the use of dashed lines suggests multiresponsibility, whereby orders or work assignments may reach an employee from more than one source. Since biblical times, experts have warned, "No man can serve two masters."

Once an organization chart has been prepared, it should reflect the actual operations of the unit. If the charts do not accurately interpret how each employee fits into the organization and how others fit in relation to him or her, the charts are useless and should be discarded.

PLANNING AND SCHEDULING WORK

Work assignments should be based on both short-range and long-range planning. Both are vital for effective operation. Long-range planning and scheduling consist of establishing preventive-maintenance routines and planned overhauls. Included also are reviewing and analyzing

Figure 8-4 Planning and scheduling maintenance work on both a short-range and a long-range basis permit maintenance to proceed smoothly with effective utilization of mechanics' time.

historical information and revising preventive-maintenance routines and planned overhauls. Short-range planning and scheduling consist in assigning jobs to maintenance workers on a day-to-day or week-to-week basis. Short-range planning decides how to perform the jobs and also how to coordinate schedules with production needs to minimize any conflict with normal operation of the equipment.

Unless long-range planning and scheduling are carried out thoroughly and thoughtfully, preventive-maintenance routines will be neglected. Lubrications will be missed, inspections will not be complete, and cleaning will not be performed adequately. In addition, the work force will be poorly utilized, and schedules will be inadequately revised to meet changed conditions. Control is gained by feeding back information. The longer the program is in operation, provided adequate planning is undertaken, the more accurate will be the preventive-maintenance routines.

Short-range planning and scheduling must be carried out on a continuous basis. Inadequate short-term planning can lead to interference with the operating needs of the equipment, poor utilization of a mechanic's time, or both.

PREVENTIVE MAINTENANCE

Preventive maintenance (PM) is the systematic inspection, cleaning, lubrication, and servicing of equipment. Its objective is to discover incipient malfunctions, correct them, and prevent breakdowns. With PM, good maintenance management should reduce the number and intensity of breakdowns to a point at which 15 percent or less of a mechanic's time is devoted to them. Without PM, breakdowns have been found to account for 85 percent or more of the time of a mechanic.

PM Personnel Requirements

Often a PM system is introduced without full consideration of personnel requirements. There will usually be a net reduction in total maintenance personnel after the program has been fully installed and is operating correctly, but because the benefits of PM are long-range, additional personnel may be required at first. Also, the realignment of duties and responsibilities may require different types of people. Generally, more clerical and fewer mechanical personnel will be required.

PM is based on the scheduling of equipment inspections, cleanings, and lubrications, the written reporting of deficiencies in the equipment, the repair of these deficiencies, and the subsequent recording of the repairs in permanent equipment-history records. These records must then be analyzed and evaluated for cause and remedial action. PM also requires estimating, planning, scheduling, and controlling maintenance repair work.   An efficient PM system must have built into it controls that indicate the need for revising routines and procedures.   All these functions generally require a change of organizational responsibilities and duties from those generally found where PM has not been used.

Classification of PM Work

All PM work can be separated into two classifications, mechanical work and paper work.   Both are important.   Mechanical work in turn can be classified into six operations: (1) inspecting, (2) adjusting, (3) tightening, (4) cleaning, (5) lubricating, and (6) routine replacing of parts.

The first item, inspecting, is probably the most vital.   PM inspecting is the art and science of discovering and diagnosing incipient failures, breakdowns that are about to happen.   These breakdowns may occur immediately, within a few weeks, or within months, but they will occur and disrupt the orderly operation of the affected department.   PM inspection is aimed at finding something wrong rather than something right.   Inspection procedures include the following:
1. Look for frayed or damaged wiring.
2. Feel the motor to detect overheating.
3. Listen for noisy bearings.
4. Test for insufficient or excessive belt tension.

Emphasis on the Negative in Reports

Psychologically, most people look for good conditions.   Consequently inspectors must discipline themselves to prepare their reports in a negative manner.   They should not write, "Test for *proper* belt tension; look to see if the pulley and shaft are *aligned*."   Instead, they should write, "Test for *insufficient* or excessive belt tension; look for a *misaligned* pulley and shaft."   When the instruction is written in the negative, the inspector will be alert for poor, potentially breakdown-prone conditions.

PM Duties of Equipment Operators

Operating personnel generally should not attempt to make repairs on the units assigned to them or to do any PM work that requires special skill or the dismantling of equipment.   Equipment operators, however, should do a certain amount of inspecting, cleaning, adjusting, and lubricating.   Any PM operation requiring tools or equipment other than a screwdriver, pliers, and a small oilcan should be performed by maintenance personnel.   Moreover, many screwdriver-and-pliers operations should also be restricted to skilled maintenance personnel because of the time needed, the intricacy of the work, or safety requirements.

Some examples of PM operations that operating personnel may be expected to perform are:

Figure 8-5 The equipment operator should be expected to perform preventive-maintenance tasks that require a pair of pliers, a screwdriver, and an oilcan.

Figure 8-6 The mechanic should be assigned preventive-maintenance duties requiring greater skill and knowledge.

1. Checking oil levels
2. Checking tires for inflation and for general condition
3. Checking the electrolyte level in a battery
4. Checking the coolant level and antifreeze
5. Checking brakes, windshield wipers, belts, and hoses
6. Checking the horn, lights, and directional and warning signals

Measuring PM Effectiveness

The most useful measures of PM effectiveness are (1) feedback from the personnel who operate the equipment and (2) the cost effectiveness of the equipment as measured by reports. Operator feedback is the most immediately revealing. If operators repeatedly complain about breakdowns, downtime, or excessive time spent at the garage, a problem that requires prompt and positive remedial action exists. No operators will be awed by an impressive array of records that show on paper excellence of performance and cost efficiency of equipment management. All that concerns operators is the fact that their equipment units are not performing as they have a right to expect.

Favorable operator feedback, in contrast, is soothing music to maintenance personnel. However, an administrator should not be lulled into relaxed contentment with this happy condition. The administrator's obligation is to reexamine the records to see if the cost or service level can be adjusted downward without jeopardizing maintenance performance.

PM cost effectiveness must be determined on a case-by-case basis for each equipment unit maintained. Information must be obtained and processed so that it will show at a glance the cost trend to maintain equipment on a total basis. Santa Clara has prepared a graphic representation of such a record (see Figure 7-4 in Chapter 7). This record shows (1) the amount of equipment maintained annually and (2) the cost experience of maintaining city equipment both before and after the inauguration of a centrally operated maintenance facility.

Paper Work

PM paper work includes PM checklists, PM route sheets, and equipment-history records. Supplementing these are necessary work on inventory, bookkeeping, and the preparation of work orders and control reports.

The first type of records, PM checklists, normally can be separated into two classes, PM inspection checklists and PM cleaning and lubrication checklists. Most of the operations on the inspection checklists require diagnosing incipient malfunctions, that is, finding the cause of trouble before the trouble itself occurs. The type of skill and experience needed for this work is greater than that required for normal troubleshooting when the problem has become apparent.

Work on the PM cleaning and lubrication checklists normally requires less skill. Given proper training, most mechanics' helpers can do it adequately. Making adjustments that require a high degree of skill and experience should be included in the PM inspection checklist, whereas most tightening and adjusting that require little skill can be included in the cleaning and lubrication checklists.

In general, a complete motor-equipment record system must answer these questions:

1. What equipment is owned?
2. How effectively is it being used?
3. What cost is involved in owning it?
4. Can this cost be reduced without a sacrifice of service?

Avoidance of Unnecessary Records

With the advent of computers during the last 20 years, it has become possible to develop and maintain generous amounts of statistics, some more meaningful than others. However, this capacity should not tempt an administrator to overburden the office with unneeded and unused records. Record systems should meet legally imposed requirements and also provide information that will assist management in decision making. Records not directly or only indirectly meeting these requirements should be subject to critical review. No records should be kept solely for the sake of keeping them.

Records must be reliable, and no record is any more accurate than the basic input. If the basic, or raw, data are misleading, fabricated, or otherwise inaccurate, any additional statistics, particularly those extrapolated from the basic data, will also be wrong and meaningless.

Style of Record Systems

The style of record systems probably varies as widely as the number of systems kept, but for illustrative purposes the following brief review discusses records in use in Santa Clara.

Records start with the introduction of a new unit, either a vehicle or another piece of equipment, into the record-keeping system by assigning it an identification number. This number remains with the unit throughout its service life until its disposition by auction, trade-in, or destruction. The number consists of six digits; the first three designate the department to which it is assigned, and the last three classify the unit within the department.

When a new unit is received, the mechanic who prepares it for service and the office clerk complete the preprinted information sheet shown on the form entitled "Repair Order." Next, the clerk initiates a 12- by

For new equipment		Make of car		Office copy	Repair order		
City of Santa Clara		Model					
Automotive services		Serial		Date			
		Motor		Material			
		Mileage		Quantity	Part No.	Description	Amount
Phone	Time wanted	Entered by	License	Make history folder; pull old folder			
				Make warranty folder; pull old folder			
Oper. No.	Instructions		Amount	Make air compressor file card if applicable			
Lubricate☐ Change oil☐ Flush tran.☐ Flush diff.☐ Wash☐ Polish☐				Make serial number file card; pull old card			
New vehicle information:				Make license number file card: pull old card			
Common identifier or body type:				Make lube card; insert 3 months from month			
GVW:				received			
Special equipment mounted on unit:				Make rental card and amortization; pull old			
Oil filter type:				card			
Air filter type:				Make entry on vehicle number system			
Tire size:				Send blue purchase order to purchasing			
Fan belt number:				Send copy of rental order to finance			
Transmission type: Auto, Manual, 3 speed,				department (Al Chung)			
4 speed, 5 speed, other				(new, transfer, and out of service)			
Special body manufacturing:				Fill out motor vehicle registration			
Air compressor installed: Yes___ No___							
if yes, fill out certificate							
Vendor:							
Purchase price:				Additional material on reverse side			
Rental rate classification:				Total material			
Conditions	Total labor			Labor			
We propose to make the above repairs to your car under the terms and conditions hereinafter specified. The prices quoted are for labor only. Additional charges will be made for all material and parts supplied. Your car will be driven by our employees to make required tests at your risk. We will not be responsible for loss or damage to your car or its contents caused by fire, theft, accident or any cause beyond our control. Your signature hereunder will constitute acceptance of this proposal.	Accessories			Accessories			
				Tires and tubes			
	Total accessories			Gas, oil, grease			
	Tires and tubes						
	Gallon gas	@					
Work authorized by	Quarts oil			Sub total			
	Pounds grease			Tax			
Posting reference	Total: gas, oil, grease			Total			

Figure 8-7 Records are started when a new unit is acquired with this initial repair-order document, the required information being provided by the mechanic and the office clerk. The same type of report is used to schedule repairs on older operating equipment.

17-inch (305- by 432-millimeter) preprinted manila history folder. This folder documents each cost item and all salient information connected with the unit during its service life.

In connection with these two records, other miscellaneous records and card files are maintained. They include the equipment warranty, registration forms, special diagrams or instructions, the license plate number (especially useful in case of theft), the vendor, cross-numerical filing by department and identification number, scheduled PM and lubrication checks, and amortization and rental rates. Many of these records are kept on standard 3- by 5-inch (76- by 127-millimeter) index cards.

REPAIR AND REPLACEMENT

Despite the most meticulous PM, at some time equipment will break down and require repair. Also, at some time equipment will require replacement for various reasons. Procedures must be developed for both contingencies.

Before any scheduled or unscheduled repairs are made on equipment, a repair order must be initiated. The repair order is identical in format to the one issued when new equipment is received, except that it does not have the preprinted new-vehicle or instructional information.

Repair orders are assigned to specific mechanics or mechanics' helpers and, in fact, represent the basis for their written workload. As the repair work progresses and is completed, the assigned maintenance employee completes the form in all respects by noting exactly the type of work performed, including total time of labor and materials used. After the mechanic signs the repair order, the supervisor reviews it. If the supervisor approves, the repair order is directed to an office clerk, who converts the mechanic's entries into dollars. This information is then posted to the history folder along with a brief description of the work done. At the same time, the clerk deducts from the inventory cards the parts taken from stock.

Contract Maintenance and Repair

Sooner or later in every maintenance operation, the administrator must decide whether certain specialized types of equipment should be maintained and repaired by the department's own forces or whether a maintenance contract with a private repair shop would be preferable. Several general rules will help guide those who must make these decisions. One should consider entering into a contract with a private repair shop for maintenance and repair when the following conditions obtain:

1. Mechanics with specialized skills that the maintenance shop cannot provide are required.

2. Specialized equipment is required but is used so infrequently that it is not economically sound to acquire it.

3. The estimated number of employee hours per year for this type of maintenance operation is low.

4. The maintenance can be combined with a leasing agreement if leasing is more economical than purchasing the equipment outright.

Replacement Analysis

The administrator's decision to replace a particular piece of equipment at a particular time is determined largely by analyzing the economic feasibility of owning and operating the equipment beyond that time. Maintenance and repair costs may have risen so high that they would amortize new equipment. Also, there may now be available more modern and efficient equipment with such great productive capacity that the savings would amortize new equipment.

To assist the maintenance administrator in making this decision, the equipment-replacement analysis form has been developed. This vital record, which is preprinted on 11- by 17-inch (279- by 432-millimeter)

Equipment No. _____

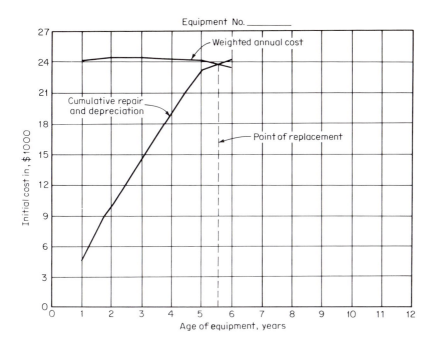

		(1)	(2)	(3)	(4)	(5)	(6)
Description International refuse truck 1968 Initial cost (basic unit) $16,863.81 Cost of special equipment ... Total cost (including tax) $16,863.81 Purchase date 9/68 Date received 9/23/68 Estimated salvage value $1,686.38 Estimated replacement cost $19,500.00 Estimated useful life 5 years Special equipment mounted on unit None	Y e a r	Annual repair cost	Cumulative repair cost	Annual deprec- iation	Cumulative deprec- iation	Cumulative repair & deprec.	Weighted annual cost
	1	$1,633.36	$ ...	$3,035.48	$ ...	$4,668.84	$24,168.84
	2	2,484.06	4,117.42	3,035.48	6,070.96	10,188.38	24,594.19
	3	1,664.51	5,781.93	3,035.48	9,106.44	14,888.37	24,462.79
	4	1,433.35	7,215.28	3,035.48	12,141.92	19,357.20	24,339.30
	5	823.18	8,038.46	3,035.48	15,177.40	23,215.86	24,143.17
	6	888.88	8,927.34	...	15,177.40	24,104.74	23,517.48
Remarks _____	7						
	8						
	9						
	10						
	11						
	12						
	13						
	14						
	15						

Note: Annual repair includes all repair costs excluding fuel cost. Weighted annual cost equals replacement cost + cumulative repair and depreciation

Equipment replacement analysis
City of Santa Clara   7/71

number of years

Figure 8-8 This form provides guidance in deciding when to replace an equipment unit. It identifies the unit and documents its replacement cost (lower left), discloses its annual cost (lower right), and graphically compares these two figures by curves (top) whose intersection indicates the time when the equipment should be replaced.

paper, maintains on a yearly basis cumulative repair and depreciation values. On the upper half of the form, the cost of cumulative repair and depreciation is plotted against the weighted annual cost. The point where the two curves cross is identified as the time of replacement. By examining past annual plottings, the garage administrator may be able to predict more closely the approximate time when the two curves will intersect.

The decision to replace a particular piece of equipment at a particular time is not bound irrevocably to the intersection of two curves; rather, the final decision must be tempered with other factors. Perhaps a special overhaul of modernization that will extend the useful life of the unit may be preferable. In any case, the utilization of a record similar to the equipment-replacement analysis form provides information vital to making the best decision possible.

Equipment Retirement

When a unit is retired from service, the garage manager initiates a prepare-for-disposition order. All records pertaining to the unit are closed by noting the date of retirement and the manner of disposition: auction, trade-in, or destruction. The license plates are returned to the state motor vehicle department, as is the completed transfer-of-owner form. The retired dossier is maintained on file for 2 years and then is destroyed.

EQUIPMENT SPECIFICATIONS

The equipment manager, despite specialized knowledge, should not attempt to write equipment specifications unilaterally but consult with the department that will operate the equipment. Operating-department personnel can provide valuable answers to such questions as how the equipment will be used, how frequently it will be used, and where it will be used. With these answers, the manager is able to prepare the specifications that best fulfill the anticipated demands. Some equipment managers may permit personnel of the operating department to prepare a draft copy of the specifications. Regardless of the particular procedure used, however, it is mandatory that the specifications bear the approval of the equipment manager before distribution is made to prospective vendors.

In some instances, equipment specifications are cluttered with minute and unimportant details. Some specifications have been filled with so many meaningless technicalities and superfluous language that bidders have had great difficulty in knowing what is expected of them. The specifications that are easiest to understand are those that limit details to salient mechanical or performance parameters. If specification writers wish to receive bids in the best interests of their organization, they will, insofar as is practical, pattern their specifications after equipment that is standard with the manufacturers whose bids they are attempting to solicit.

PERSONNEL TRAINING

No discussion of equipment management would be complete without some reference to personnel and personnel training. The administrator should develop three types of training for equipment-maintenance personnel:

    1. Preentry training in the knowledge and skills required of recruits for the various positions to which they may be assigned

    2. On-the-job training to instruct employees in their duties and related activities

    3. General training to keep experienced employees conversant with new developments and techniques and to enable them to qualify for higher positions

The inclusion of educational requirements in a recruiting program will materially aid the administrator in obtaining and promoting individuals with appropriate background and training. It also will assist in accommodating personnel to the more complex equipment that urban services now require. However, to make recruitment as valuable as possible, there should be optional alternatives that will permit applications and competition by candidates with experience and skills equivalent to the training requirement.

New-Employee Instruction

No position in a centralized equipment department can be filled satisfactorily merely by telling recruits to go to work. They must be informed of their titles, salary, hours of work, and other salient terms and conditions of employment. They must receive a clear understanding of their duties so that they will know what their supervisors expect of them.

As the employees gain experience on the job, their supervisors must advise them of the quality of their performance, particularly during the formal probationary period, if the department has one. Many public agencies have some sort of structured employee performance-evaluation program. In most instances, employees are rated once a year (more often during their probation). Supervisors should not withhold comment on good or bad performance until the next formal rating is scheduled. Employees should receive appropriate comments as quickly as possible after the particular performance.

In-Service Training

Instruction of employees in their duties is the responsibility of the immediate supervisor. The process of supervision is, to a large extent, a matter of training subordinates to enable them to assume new responsibilities.

The training of supervisory officers in the art of supervision will help them carry out this important responsibility. New employees will derive benefit from lectures and prescribed reading on the objectives and work of the department. Employees who understand the significance of the activities of the department and see how their work contributes to departmental goals will take added interest in their jobs.

Staff conferences should be held between supervisors and employees. The frequency of the conferences should be dictated largely by the amount of material to be covered. No conference should be held without careful advance preparation for the problems to be discussed. Supervisors must be given a real opportunity for discussion at these staff conferences. They must be accessible to employees and receptive to the suggestions that employees may make to improve work methods or techniques. This attitude will stimulate employees to devote more thoughtful study to their jobs and to take increased pride in their work.

Administrators should refer regulations, administrative orders, progress reports, and work and cost estimates to their supervisors, and they in turn should refer them to their employees. This procedure will help to keep subordinates informed both of their responsibilities and of the results of their joint efforts.

Seminars and Short Courses

No equipment-management department, regardless of its size or resources, can expect to satisfy all its training needs within the department. A policy of strict self-sufficiency not only would be extremely costly but would deny to employees many outside training facilities that the department could not possibly duplicate. Meetings of equipment organizations and periodic or special seminars sponsored by equipment manufacturers, professional groups, and others all offer splendid opportunities for in-service training.

Interdepartmental Training Policies

Equipment-management personnel need training, but operators of equipment in the various service departments also require training, and equipment-management employees frequently have the knowledge and experience required to assist in this training effort. The utilization of equipment-maintenance personnel as an integral part of the on-the-job training of operators in other service departments may extend over a protracted period or be offered on a demand basis. Calling on a mechanic to observe the driving techniques of an operator may quickly explain why the equipment suffers from frequent and unusual needs for clutches, brakes, and other items. Sound management techniques should dictate that equipment-maintenance personnel be readily available to assist the on-the-job training of equipment operators.

ANNUAL RENTAL AND AMORTIZATION RATES
SANTA CLARA, CALIFORNIA, FISCAL YEAR 1974–1975

Description	Number of units	Rate per unit	Total rental	Amortization rate per unit	Total amortization
Portable auxiliary:					
Burners	1	$ 66	$ 66	$ 147	$ 147
Compressors	3	66	198	71	213
Generators	18	66	1,188	38	684
Power edgers	15	66	990	38	570
Pumps	17	66	1,122	36	612
Sewer rodders	2	66	132	43	86
Sod cutters	1	66	66	55	55
Aerifiers	2	66	132	50	100
Spreaders	1	66	66	50	50
Power vacuums	5	66	330	79	395
Garden sprayers	2	66	132	19	38
Compactor-tampers	5	66	330	90	450
Augers	1	66	66	35	35
Power saws	1	66	66	25	25
Multisaws	1	66	66	35	35
Concrete mixers	4	66	246	50	200
Chain saws	2	66	132	35	70
Shears	1	66	66	20	20
Auxiliary on chassis:					
Air compressors	1	267	267	768	768
Rototillers	1	66	66	47	47
Auto wash	1	267	267	38	38
Chipper	3	267	801	359	1,077
Trailer-mounted generators	1	289	289	236	236
Flail mowers	1	144	144	79	79
Howard Rotovators	2	267	534	150	300
Renovators	1	66	66	79	79
Leaf pickers	3	267	801	437	1,311
Power buckets	2	267	534	140	280
Stump cutters	1	267	267	354	354
Tar kettles	1	66	66	62	62
Sprayers	3	267	801	68	204
Pickups	56	597	33,432	445	24,920
1½-ton trucks	14	737	10,318	698	9,772
2-ton trucks	12	1,004	12,048	749	8,988
Backhoes	5	1,664	8,320	1,011	5,055
Bookmobiles	1	1,906	1,906	1,701	1,701
Compressors	10	668	6,680	508	5,080
Crane trucks	5	1,334	6,670	2,195	10,975
Forklifts	6	935	5,610	100	600
Generators	1	1,201	1,201	2,195	2,195

ANNUAL RENTAL AND AMORTIZATION RATES
SANTA CLARA, CALIFORNIA, FISCAL YEAR 1974–1975

Description	Number of units	Rate per unit	Total rental	Amortization rate per unit	Total amortization
Bucket ladder trucks	3	$2,420	$ 7,260	$3,239	$ 9,717
Large line markers	1	330	330	698	698
Michigan loaders	1	1,906	1,906	1,370	1,370
Case loaders	2	1,906	3,812	898	1,796
Mowers	22	190	4,180	76	1,672
Triple mowers	7	341	2,387	289	2,023
Gang mowers	2	2,002	4,004	945	1,890
Police sedans	30	1,398	41,904	559	16,770
3-ton rollers	2	267	534	340	680
Vibrating rollers	5	267	1,335	567	2,835
Sedans	53	560	29,680	559	29,627
Shu Packs (refuse trucks)	12	2,669	32,028	4,000	48,000
Yard-trash trucks	1	2,669	2,669	1,397	1,397
Slurry seal pavers	1	801	801	2,835	2,835
Sweepers	4	4,002	16,008	2,120	8,480
Case tractors	1	1,004	1,004	1,247	1,247
Caterpillar tractors	1	1,004	1,004	1,802	1,802
Clark tractors	1	1,004	1,004	50	50
Patrol sedans	28	1,398	39,144	1,785	49,980
Motor grader tractors	1	1,004	1,004	2,095	2,095
Trailers	36	66	2,376	189	6,804
Trenchers	2	2,002	4,004	998	1,996
Vans	6	432	2,592	698	4,188
Washers	4	572	2,288	473	1,892
Sewer cleaners	1	1,756	1,756	2,993	2,993
"Frost" loaders	1	2,669	2,669	2,412	2,412
Cable-splicing vans	3	1,334	4,002	1,707	5,121
Rescue trucks	1	668	668	1,134	1,134
Battery forklifts	1	2,669	2,669	479	479
Rescue saws	2	66	132	42	84
Fire trucks	12	1,815	21,780	2,233	26,796
Aerial trucks	3	2,287	6,861	2,758	8,274
One-axle trailer-cable pulling reels	1	286	286	714	714
Two-axle trailer-cable pulling reels	1	350	350	1,418	1,418
High-pressure cleaners	2	367	534	677	1,354
Pickups with cab-over camper	1	668	668	388	388
1-ton trucks	12	597	7,164	399	4,788
Concrete saws with trailer	1	338	338	253	255
Cycles	11	1,271	13,981	520	5,720
Sewer rodders	1	877	877	509	509
2½-ton trucks	2	1,144	2,288	1,218	2,436
Landscape tractors	2	1,004	2,008	788	1,576
Stationary generators	7	288	2,016	500	3,500
Water trucks	2	1,004	2,008	1,748	3,496
Small line markers	1	66	66	179	179
Light utility pickups	8	444	3,552	359	2,872
Small bucket ladder trucks	1	956	956	1,380	1,380
Small sweepers	2	352	704	665	1,330
Lamplighter bucket trucks	1	1,760	1,760	4,250	4,250
Total	519		$379,887		$361,208

BIBLIOGRAPHY

Kapner, Sylvan L.: "Improving Maintenance Performance through Labor Standards," *Proceedings,* Thirteenth Annual Industrial Engineers' Conference, Seattle, Wash., Apr. 14, 1967.

———: "Maintenance Management," in Harold B. Maynard (ed.), *Handbook of Business Administration,* McGraw-Hill Book Company, New York, 1967, pp. 7-50–7-64.

Motor Vehicle Fleet Management, Special Report No. 37, American Public Works Association, Chicago, 1970.

Municipal Public Works Administration, International City Managers' Association, Chicago, 1957.

Chapter Nine

Sewer Maintenance

WILLIAM S. FOSTER

Sewers, the conduits beneath the streets that carry away the unwanted waste water to a point of treatment and disposal, undoubtedly have done more to improve the quality of life in a community than any other social or technological advance, with the possible exception of water supply. They have improved the community's quality of life more than art, literature, or drama.

Before the advent of sewers, a human settlement that now is known as a city rarely contained more than 250,000 people, and these people, both the wealthy and the poor, had to endure conditions that were pestilentially filthy. Shelley once wrote that hell is a city much like London. Thomas Jefferson railed against cities, and he had ample reason, even though at that time the United States had no cities with populations of more than 50,000.

In those presewer cities, housewives emptied the night's collection of body wastes by dumping chamber pots out of windows into the streets. These wastes, together with manure from horses and mules, made a foul and odorous mixture, polluting wells and encouraging rats, lice, and other disease-bearing nuisances. Plagues were frequent and epidemics common. Sewers that quickly removed these wastes from the living environment did much to save human life, relieve human misery, and make the urban environment more livable.

United States communities of more than 2500 people now have close to 460,000 miles (740,000 kilometers) of sewers serving them.[1] But since this investment is hidden beneath the ground, out of sight, it tends to be neglected. In many small communities and in poorly operated

---

[1] John B. Scott, "Survey of Sewer Pipe Used by Utilities Serving Populations of More Than 2500," *The American City,* August 1975.

Figure 9-1 Although sewers represent a substantial community investment in improving the quality of life, they often are forgotten and neglected because they are hidden beneath the ground. Here a deep interceptor sewer is being placed where the soil needs support during construction. [*The American City*]

large cities, maintenance policy often appears to be based solely on responding to complaints. Unfortunately, complaints represent flooded basements, which today often are family rooms where flooding does much costly damage.

SEWER-MAINTENANCE PROBLEMS

A sewer system, if it performs as the designer intended, should flow at a self-scouring rate, be free from blockages, and be able to resist breaks, leaks in the joints, and intrusion from roots. With modern improved pipe, stronger and more resilient pipe joints, and more meticulous construction, problems should disappear. However, most sewers are old, more than a century old in some cases, often made of material subject to deterioration, and jointed with hard mastic, occasionally even with cement mortar that cannot accept ground movement. In such situations a great deal of maintenance is required to retain the investment in the sewer system.   Maintenance problems can be grouped into five main categories:

1. Infiltration of groundwater into the sewer through breaks in the pipe, leaks in the joints, and poor connections at the manholes, usurping the hydraulic capacity of the sewer itself, overloading the treatment plant with water that needs no treatment, and often causing waste-water backups into homes, businesses, and industries that can cause inconvenience and costly damage.

2. Inflow into the sewer system of storm water from roof leaders connected to the sewers, drains from parking lots connected to the sanitary sewers, and similar sources.   These connections overload the sewer system unnecessarily and in most localities are illegal.

3. Clogging by sand, debris, grease, and roots that rob the sewer of capacity.

4. Breaks in the sewer pipe, caused by faulty installation, impact loads, or movement of the ground itself.

5. Damage caused by wastes that should not have been introduced into the sewer.   This generally is the result of the introduction of liquid wastes from industry that may be flammable or excessively hot or contain material that is difficult to convey in a gravity sewer.   Damage may be caused by sulfuric acid vapor generated in the waste water if the sewer is made of material susceptible to it.

Corrective Maintenance Measures

There are many measures that a sewer-maintenance organization may adopt to rectify these problems, but for general convenience they may be grouped under seven general headings:

1. Types of infiltration-resistant pipe that may be used to replace damaged pipe or to place new lines

2. Improved methods of backfill using the nuclear soil-density meter to monitor the backfilling operation

3. Methods of sewer cleaning

4. Flow-measurement techniques that help to determine the amount of infiltration and inflow that is usurping the capacity of the sewer and also to ascertain whether the sewer is being overloaded

5. Inspection and testing of the sewer by closed-circuit television, photographic means, low-pressure air, and smoke

6. Grouting the sewer to stop infiltration through leaks in the joints and in certain breaks

7. Safety measures that should be followed when working in sewers

Sewer Maps and Records

Before undertaking a meaningful sewer-maintenance program, a municipality should have or acquire accurate maps of the system. These should record accurately the sewer location, depth, slope, pipe size, pipe material, and location of services, both in use and installed for future use.   The location of other utilities in the street or alley right-of-way, both publicly owned and private, should also be recorded. This procedure should conform generally to the recommendations covering the location of underground utilities in Chapter 4.   Records also should show when the sewer was installed, when any trouble developed in various portions of the lines, and what corrective measures were taken.

Infiltration-resistant Sewer Pipe

Sewers carrying human wastes from homes, businesses, and industries are classified as *sanitary sewers*.   Those carrying both sanitary liquid wastes and storm water are called *combined sewers,* although at present municipalities rarely build this type because of the possibility of pollution to the receiving water.

Sewers carrying rainwater exclusively are *storm sewers*.   Sewer pipes carrying sanitary waste water most commonly used today are made of (1) vitrified clay; (2) concrete, either unreinforced, reinforced, or pre-stressed; (3) asbestos cement of the nonpressure type; (4) plastic, either single-wall or truss-type; and (5) cast iron or ductile iron.   Occasionally corrugated metal pipe may be used to convey sanitary waste water or combined waste water, but it is employed chiefly as a conduit for storm water.   On rare occasions fiber pipe will also be used as a sewer, but more commonly it serves as a lateral connection between the house and the sewer.

Infiltration Limits

In the past, many persons adopted a casual attitude toward the infiltration of groundwater into a sewer system, where it would usurp its capacity.   However, the concern of the U.S. Environmental Protection Agency (EPA) and others over the costly wastefulness of receiving and treating water that does not pose a pollution threat has forced a revision in this type of thinking.   One estimate of infiltration and inflow, for example, states that this source of unwanted water is usurping at least 15 percent of the total sewer capacity in the United States.[2]

Some have ambitiously proposed infiltration specifications as low as 50 gallons per inch of diameter per mile of pipe per 24 hours (46.3 liters per centimeter of diameter per kilometer of pipe per 24 hours), but requirements rarely need to be that strict.   Actually they should be based on the cost of collecting and treating the infiltrating water, matched against the cost of preventing its entry.   Most working specifications now vary between 100 and 250 gallons per inch of diameter per mile of

[2] *Hearings before the Committee on Public Works,* House of Representatives, 92d Cong. 1971, p. 2070.

pipe (between 93 and 232 liters), and some go as high as 400 gallons (370 liters).

A few will argue that some infiltration is desirable, particularly at the upper ends of the collection system, where the flow may not be great enough to carry the solids away. However, it would appear to be better to flush these upper ends periodically rather than to build a leaking sewer system deliberately.[3]

PIPE AND FITTINGS

The principal formula governing pipe size for a given flow was developed early in the twentieth century by an Irish engineer, Robert Manning. The significant part of the formula, which has remained substantially unchanged throughout the years, is the n factor, which appears in the denominator. Thus, for any pipe size, the smaller the n factor, the greater the flow that can pass through the pipe. Stated another way, for a given flow, the smaller the n factor, the smaller the pipe diameter required to carry the flow.

The n factor reflects the smoothness of the interior pipe surface. With pipe of asbestos cement or plastic, just fabricated and prior to use, the factor may be as low as $n = 0.008$. However, after the pipe has been placed in service, carrying complex waste water containing grease, oils, and other products, the factor can be expected to increase. Consequently, most regulatory bodies insist on a higher figure. A minimum of $n = 0.013$ is the lowest limit permitted in the *Recommended Standards for Sewage Works* (1973), prepared by the Great Lakes–Upper Mississippi River Board of State Sanitary Engineers, which is known more popularly as the *Ten States Standards*.

Vitrified-Clay Pipe

Vitrified-clay pipe is an overwhelming favorite among designers of sewer systems and accounts for about two-thirds of the total sewer mileage in the United States today.[4] If not fractured by unanticipated loads, this type of sewer pipe has compiled a long record of service life because of the chemically inert characteristics of its material. Clay does not corrode, rot, or deteriorate with age, and it resists attack from corrosive gases, wastes, and soils. It is strong, is not subject to deflections in diameter, and has a smooth interior surface.

In the past, when designers did not particularly concern themselves with infiltration, suppliers provided the pipe in shorter lengths, making it easier to install and at the same time creating greater numbers of joints. As previously mentioned, the jointing material frequently was

[3] "Sewer Pipe: Infiltration Is the Issue," *Civil Engineering*, July 1974, p. 79.

[4] Scott, op cit.

Figure 9-2 Clay sewer pipe is being produced in greater lengths and with improved infiltration-resistant joints. [*Logan Clay Products photo*]

cold mastic or cement mortar, neither of which can stand much ground movement.   Today clay pipe is being fabricated in greater lengths, with greatly improved jointing systems.   All sewer joints should be installed to anticipate some ground movement and permit flexibility while being watertight and resistant to root intrusion.

Bell-and-Spigot Clay Pipe   Suppliers of bell-and-spigot clay pipe customarily provide a compression joint consisting of plastic thermosetting resin applied at the factory to form concentric surfaces in both the bell and the spigot.   If the resin is rigid, an O-ring rubber gasket must be installed on the spigot end to provide the compression seal.   In other designs, an elastomeric resin, which may be urethane or plasticized polyvinyl chloride, is molded into a bead or a fin on either the bell or the spigot end to provide the seal.

Plain-End Sewer Pipe   This type of pipe is another departure from past practices.   To provide trouble-free sewers, designers attempt to eliminate any features that might create trouble.   The bell on a bell-and-spigot pipe is one such feature, and the O ring can be another.   A

Figure 9-3 Plain-end pipe is a recent innovation that eliminates the need for bell holes by the use of a polyvinyl chloride collar instead of the conventional bell.

Figure 9-4 A conscientious contractor makes sure that the O ring is carefully placed and stressed equally around the pipe. [*Oliver Tire & Rubber photo*]

conscientious contractor and an alert inspector will make sure that a bell hole is provided so that the pipe, when installed, rests on the barrel and not on the bell, since the backfill alone may fracture it. However, not all contractors are conscientious. Many omit the bell hole if they feel that the omission will not be immediately detected.

Similarly, conscientious contractors make sure that the O ring is placed carefully on the spigot in the groove where it is designed to be placed. They also make sure that the rubber ring is not unduly stressed at any one point but is equally stressed around the spigot. However, sloppy contractors may not be so careful and may even omit the O ring if they are not watched.

Plain-end pipe with a factory-applied joint avoids these problems. The joint consists of a polyvinyl chloride collar that replaces the bell. Since it is thin, it needs no special excavation. A molded band, generally of urethane rubber, is provided on the spigot end. The collar frequently has a double bead to ensure a tight seal. The joint provides sufficient flexibility to allow deflections of ½ inch (12.7 millimeters) or more per foot (0.3048 meter) of length.

Concrete Pipe

Concrete pipe, either unreinforced, reinforced, or prestressed, constitutes about 16 percent of the total sewer systems in the United States. However, in the larger sizes, with diameters of 24 inches (609.6

Figure 9-5 Concrete pipe is especially useful in sewers in the larger diameters. This example has a diameter of 9 feet (2.7432 meters). [*The American City*]

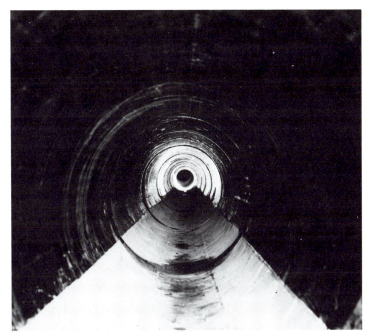

Figure 9-6 To prevent the deterioration of concrete pipe through the action of sulfurous acid gases, the interior above the low-flow line is given a protective coating. [*The American City*]

millimeters) or more, it accounts for more than 60 percent of the sewer mileage.[5]

If this pipe is required to carry a waste water that tends to become septic and generate sulfurous acid vapor, as would be the case with long lines laid on flat grades in a warm climate, the vapor will cause the upper portion of the pipe to deteriorate and eventually to fail. To prevent this damage, the pipe can be lined, either at the factory or in place. Linings are generally liquid-applied epoxy, coal-tar epoxy, or vinyl. Since the acid vapor is the cause of the difficulty, the linings need extend only from the points of low flow on each side to the top.

Unreinforced- and reinforced-concrete pipe can be used to carry waste water by gravity. Prestressed concrete pipe can carry waste water pumped under pressure through a force main. It also can be used to carry waste water by gravity when pressure-tight joints are needed, as in an area with a high water table.

Joints for concrete pipe are either bell-and-spigot or tongue-and-groove. In either case, a rubber gasket forms the watertight seal.

A continuously laid, cast-in-place concrete pipe also can be utilized in the larger sizes, from 24 to 120 inches (from 609.6 to 3048 millimeters)

[5] Ibid.

in diameter. This type of pipe has a wall thickness varying from 3 to 12 inches (from 7.6 to 304.8 millimeters). A slip-form machine with vibrators places the concrete, which is designed to develop a compressive strength of 4000 pounds per square inch (27,579 kilopascals). The producers recommend a Manning n factor of 0.014. Since the pipe is placed continuously, it will crack with any ground movement, but the supplier states that the cracks can be repaired with an expandable epoxy.

Asbestos-Cement Sewer Pipe

The first concerted effort to prevent infiltration was made by adapting the asbestos-cement pipe used for water mains to waste-water transport. This type of pipe now accounts for about 5.5 percent of the total sewer system, but its share of the market has been growing in recent years. The pipe is generally known as nonpressure pipe to differentiate it from asbestos-cement water pipe.

The interior of the pipe is smooth, encouraging good flow characteristics. The suppliers assert that the dense surface of asbestos and cement is able to resist the corrosion that would be expected if the waste water is septic. The pipe can be produced in lengths from 10 to 13 feet (from 3.048 to 3.962 meters) and is joined by ring couplings fitted with rubber gaskets. The couplings have an annular groove at each end to receive the gaskets. The pipe ends that are thrust into the coupling are machined for a closer, more infiltration-resistant fit. Since each pipe length is relatively long, it requires careful bedding and backfill to prevent unexpected loads from causing stresses in the pipe in case of ground movement.

Figure 9-7 Asbestos-cement pipe was among the first to be provided with joints to make sewers highly resistant to infiltration or inflow. [*The American City*]

Plastic Sewer Pipe

Plastic pipe is relatively new to the waste-water field, probably because the industry has been interested in other markets that have appeared more promising. At this time, most suppliers limit the size of the pipe

Figure 9-8 Because single-wall plastic pipe frequently is flexible, it can be used as a liner to rehabilitate old, deteriorating sewers. Here is a large-diameter pipe about ready for insertion. [*Du Pont photo*]

offered to diameters of 15 inches (381 millimeters) or less. Neverthe-less, plastic pipe comprised about 20 percent of the sewer pipe being in-stalled in 1974 and about 2 percent of the total sewer mileage in the United States.[6]

The pipe has a smooth interior and is made of a plastic that the suppliers state will resist chemical and biological corrosion and also

[6] Ibid.

Figure 9-9 Before the insertion of the plastic pipe, a "proofing tool" must be pulled through the sewer that is to be rehabilitated to ensure the absence of any obstacles that will prevent entry of the liner. [*Du Pont photo*]

Figure 9-10   Plastic pipe can be butt-welded in the field to form a long, continuous length.   [*Du Pont photo*]

Figure 9-11   The weld will form an internal bead at the joint that will interfere with the flow.   This reamer can remove the bead.   [*Du Pont photo*]

abrasion. It is light and easily handled, and can be produced in virtually any length specified. The pipe can be jointed by solvent cementing, heat fusion, or elastomeric seals (gaskets), all of which are tight and root-resistant.

Plastic pipe is somewhat flexible, allowing some accommodation to minor ground movement without fracture. This feature makes it able to serve as an insertion liner in deteriorated sewers, permitting them to be restored to usefulness without the inconvenience and expense of excavation and replacement. Although the liner reduces the effective diameter of the sewer, the smooth interior of the pipe probably counteracts some of this loss.

Single-wall plastic pipe, because of the flexibility of the pipe walls, requires greater care in backfilling. Good practice would dictate that backfilling comply with recommendations of the American Society for Testing and Materials (designation D 2321-74), which asks for soil densities of 85 to 90 percent of the optimum obtained by the Proctor test for various portions of the backfill. Since it is impractical to determine

Figure 9-12 A double-wall plastic truss pipe is being used in sewer systems. It is rigid and light in weight, and it utilizes joints that strongly resist infiltration. [*Armco photo*]

Figure 9-13 A plastic saddle, attached by heat fusion, can provide a leakproof and rootproof connection to a plastic sewer. [*Du Pont photo*]

Figure 9-14 A composite pipe with a polyvinyl chloride core and an epoxy-coated fiberglass outer shell is one of the newer types of sewer pipe. Note its long length and its light weight, which makes possible its transportation by a small helicopter. [*The American City*]

these densities by conventional sample excavations, a nuclear soil-density meter would be much more convenient. The use of the meter is discussed below.

Most plastic pipe is made of polyvinyl chloride; some consists of polyethylene. One supplier, Armco Steel Corp., produces a double-wall, truss-type plastic pipe with the annular space filled with lightweight concrete. The plastic for this pipe is acrylonitrile butadiene styrene. Another firm, Johns-Manville, produces a composite pipe consisting of a polyvinyl chloride core covered with a layer of epoxy-coated fiberglass.

Cast-Iron and Ductile-Iron Sewer Pipe

The advent of tighter infiltration requirements has increased the interest in these types of pipe for gravity-sewer use. In the past, their principal use was to transport waste water under pressure through force mains.

Tests by the Cast Iron Pipe Research Association indicate that non-pressurized cast-iron and ductile-iron pipe using the single-gasket push-on joint show no infiltration when exposed to external pressures as high as 430 pounds per square inch (2965 kilopascals) and no exfiltration at internal pressures of 1000 pounds per square inch (6895 kilopascals).[7]

These types of pipe represent about 4 percent of the sewer mileage in use in the United States today.[8] They are generally produced in lengths of 20 feet (6.1 meters) and can be lined with a protective coating such as

[7] Correspondence, American Public Works Association Research Foundation with Cast Iron Pipe Research Association, Apr. 28, 1975.

[8] Scott, op. cit.

Figure 9-15 Asbestos-bonded, corrugated metal pipe is occasionally used to carry sanitary sewage; more often it conveys storm water. [*National Corrugated Steel Pipe Association photo*]

heat-fused, bonded polyethylene to protect them from damage by the hydrogen sulfide generated by septic waste water.   If soil conditions are corrosive, as they are in certain portions of the nation, the pipe should be protected by encasing it in an 8-mil (0.203-millimeter) loose polyethylene envelope.   For underwater installations, use can be made of ball-and-socket joints able to resist infiltration and exfiltration while permitting deflections as great as 15 degrees between pipe sections.

Nuclear Monitoring of Trench Backfill

As mentioned in the discussion of the use of plastic pipe, careful attention must be paid to backfill operations to ensure that the pipe will work satisfactorily.   Careless backfilling is one of the danger points in any waste-water–pipe installation.   Moreover, to prevent trench settlement, many regulations require imported backfill material, which often adds to the cost of the work.

The nuclear soil-density meter can monitor backfilling and improve the results.   This meter, which has been widely accepted in the highway

Figure 9-16 Because of its flexibility, single-wall plastic pipe requires careful backfilling with mechanical compaction in 1-foot (0.3048-meter) lifts to designated Proctor soil densities.   [*Seaman Nuclear Corp.*]

Figure 9-17 A nuclear soil density-moisture meter can verify compaction quickly and accurately. [*Seaman Nuclear Corp.*]

field, facilitates making determinations quickly, requires no special training, and allows an inspector to make a number of determinations in a short period.   The meter and its use are described in Chapter 1.

To use the meter to monitor trench backfill, the inspector should take a density reading prior to excavation of the trench.   Then, after the pipe has been placed, the backfill should be replaced in 1-foot (0.3-meter) lifts and compacted to a density equal to or not more than 10 percent greater than that of the unexcavated earth.   With the backfilled earth at the same density as the surrounding soil, settlement should be at a minimum.   Moreover, the pipe itself should be firmly bedded and covered so that it is not subject to movement (see also page 9-13).

Pipe Fittings and Manhole Connectors

Accessories to sewers include the fittings that connect the sewer to the house laterals and the connectors that join the sewer to the manhole. Since the sewer pipe and the laterals may be of differing pipe material, most fittings must be adaptable to these conditions.   Fittings must be infiltration-resistant and must form no obstruction to the interior of the pipe.   Manhole connectors are being produced in a variety of types. The principal requirement is that they have flexibility, since the manhole structure itself will remain relatively fixed while the ground around it may be subject to some movement.   Infiltration through the manhole connection can be a substantial source of unwanted water.

SEWER-CLEANING METHODS

Sewer cleaning is the most important activity in a maintenance program, because the maintenance of clean sewers ensures that the system transports the waste water promptly to its point of treatment and ultimate disposal.   Maintenance crews have at least six different types of cleaning equipment and methods available to them:

1. Bucket machines
2. Rodding equipment of both rotating steel and jointed wood
3. High-velocity water jetting
4. Hydraulically propelled cleaners, including sewer balls and hinged-disc types
5. Plain flushing
6. Chemicals for root control

Another category might be included: debris removal.   Methods 2 through 5 simply transport the debris to a downstream manhole, where it must be removed, and equipment is available that will do this job quickly.   The sixth method, the use of chemicals for root control, does not actually remove the roots, but it inhibits their growth over an extended period.   The growth of roots is easily one of the most troublesome sewer-maintenance problems.

Bucket Cleaning Equipment

The use of bucket cleaning equipment, while it is somewhat more time-consuming than other methods, can open heavily blocked sewers

Figure 9-18 Some bucket-type cleaners drop debris on the ground adjacent to the cleaning equipment.   [*Rockwell International photo*]

Figure 9-19 Other bucket cleaners transport the bucket up a conveyor chute to discharge debris directly into a truck. [*The American City*]

that may be clogged by large masses of roots, sand, or clay. When the bucket machine has completed its work, the sewer, if it is not broken, will be in excellent flowing condition. The bucket can dislodge and transport mud and grease and remove the debris from the sewer, placing it in an awaiting truck.

The machine consists of two powered winches connected by about 1000 feet (304.8 meters) of steel cable, or enough to reach between two adjacent manholes. One winch is centered over the influent manhole and the other over the effluent manhole, the winch that removes the bucket generally being at the downstream end. The steel cable pulls a specially designed cleaning bucket. The cable is separate in the center, and each of the separated ends is secured to the bucket so that the winches can pull it in either direction. The bucket has been designed so that the bottom will open as the winch pulls it into the debris to be removed. When it is full, the other winch pulls it out, closing the bottom of the bucket through a mechanical linkage. The cleaner draws the bucket completely out of the downstream manhole and transfers the debris to the truck, either through a small swinging boom or through a conveyor chute.

When the bucket cleaner has removed the bulk of the debris from the sewer, the operator replaces it with a "porcupine," a cylindrical device with stiff wire cables protruding from its side. By drawing the porcupine back and forth in the sewer, the operator can remove roots, grease, and other material that have escaped the bucket cleaner. Finally, to provide a clean interior, the operator can replace the porcupine with a squeegee that fits snugly inside the pipe. After the squeegee passes through the pipe, this section of the sewer will have been restored to a condition approximating its free-flowing original design. The squeegees are frequently shop-fabricated from old ½-inch (12.7-millimeter) belting, but they can be purchased from the manufacturers of the bucket cleaners.

One detail needs attention: to permit the bucket cleaner to operate, the maintenance crew must first thread the cable through the sewer to be cleaned. The crew can do this by floating a light rope through the pipe if the flow in the sewer is great enough to support it. A more positive way is to push the cable through, using lengths of steel or wood sewer-cleaning rods.

The bucket machine may have difficulty in cleaning sewers which have been badly laid or which have service laterals that are thrust into the pipe barrel instead of being fitted neatly to the inner circumference. It also does not work well if the sewer is placed on a curve.

Rotating-Rod Sewer Cleaners

Sectional rotating-rod equipment also works well in cleaning sewers. The rods are usually high-strength, oil-tempered spring steel ⅜ inch (9.5 millimeters) in diameter, although ½-inch (12.7-millimeter) rods are sometimes used. The rods are produced in sections and clamped together so that if one rod breaks, the broken section can be removed and the equipment returned to service. Normally, the operator posi-

Figure 9-20 Rotating-rod cleaners should be placed so as to minimize sharp turns in the rods. Note also the placement of protective traffic cones. [*Rockwell International photo*]

Figure 9-21 Rotating-rod cleaners have removed some spectacularly large root growths from clogged sewers. [*The American City*]

tions the rodding machine from 8 to 10 feet (from 2.4 to 3 meters) downstream from the manhole connecting the length of sewer to be cleaned. The operator then inserts the rods upstream and withdraws them and the debris to the downstream manhole. When the machine is at this 8- to 10-foot distance, the rods feed into the guide channel without having to make any sharp bends.

On every rodding machine is a footage indicator, which must be placed at zero before the rods are inserted so that the operator will know at all times how far the equipment has entered the sewer. The indicator automatically adds and subtracts as the rods enter the pipe and are withdrawn.

The operator should increase the rotating speed of the machine to its maximum when inserting the rods and cleaning tools. With a fairly clean sewer, the rods will advance quickly and easily. If cleaning becomes difficult, the overload safety device will indicate pressure or may release and stop the rotation. If the pressure is minor, the cleaning can continue, but the forward speed should be reduced while the rotating spin remains at a maximum. With most equipment, the operator can exert additional power and penetrate difficult obstructions by tightening the overload safety device slightly. This procedure is helpful if the sewer being cleaned is badly sanded.

The operator can withdraw the rod without rotation but in most conditions should not do so. The operation should normally be started at the downstream manhole and the rod forced forward. However, if the operator has used a "spear" or "corkscrew" device on the rotating rod to open the line, spring-bladed cutters can be attached at the upstream end, and the rod and cutter pulled back carefully while the rod is rotated at high speed.

The operator has a number of cleaning tools to be used with the rotating rods. The principal units are as follows:

1. Root saws.

2. Spears and corkscrews with back-cutter edges.

3. Expandable cutters with knife-shaped blades that can be adjusted to the diameter of the sewer being cleaned. The blades are removable for sharpening.

4. Sand cups, rubber discs that block the flow of waste water but allow a small portion to pass through holes in the discs. This action creates hydraulic jets that flush debris to the downstream manhole.

5. A pickup tool to retrieve broken rods from the sewer.

The rotating-rod equipment can clean sewer sections as long as 1000 feet (304.8 meters) and to some extent can maneuver around bends. In one extremely critical incident, rodding equipment removed a latex spill that had plugged a 10-inch (254-millimeter), two-barrel sewer siphon for 250 feet (76.2 meters).

However, because the rods tend to bend, the equipment has difficulty in operating successfully in sewers with diameters larger than 15 inches (381 millimeters). The rotating-rod equipment does not transport heavy solids well, and other equipment must be used to remove the debris from the manhole where it is deposited. The equipment can be mounted on a truck or a trailer.

Spring-Cable Sewer Cleaner

The spring-cable sewer cleaner finds its greatest use in opening house laterals and clogged plumbing, but it is also used occasionally in smaller sewers. It consists of a double-spiral cable, with one spiral inside the other: the spirals turn in opposite directions so that one cable can assume the load regardless of the rotation. The unit is powered by a small gasoline or electric motor.

Jointed Wood Cleaning Rods

This type of cleaning equipment, the oldest of all sewer cleaners, probably originated with a pole thrust into the sewer to create an opening. Rods in use today vary from 3 to 4 feet (from 0.9 to 1.2 meters) in length. Each rod has a special metal coupling on each end so that operators can connect the rods and push them into the sewer for as great a distance as they are physically able to do so. Since the rods must be lifted to an angle of 45 degrees to be disconnected, the possibility of their becoming uncoupled in the sewer is remote. Operators can choose from an assortment of cleaning tools to be attached to the leading rod to perform the work.

Figure 9-22 High-velocity water-jet cleaning is proving effective in most sewer-cleaning assignments. [*The American City*]

Water-Jet Sewer Cleaners

High-velocity water-jet cleaners are one of the most recent developments in sewer cleaning. Under most conditions, these units can clean lines faster, more thoroughly, and with less work than any other equipment can. The risk of damage to the pipeline itself is low, but such a cleaner is potentially damaging to deteriorated pipe. Moreover, a water-jet cleaner is not particularly effective in removing heavy debris. Several passes of the cleaner may be required to remove some of the more resistant debris, and a substantial amount of water is necessary. The cleaner is not particularly effective in sewers with diameters greater than 36 inches (914.4 millimeters) and works best in sewers of intermediate sizes.

If the water-jet cleaner is to be used in sewers where there is a danger

Figure 9-23 This clear plastic pipe section shows how the jet cleaner operates. Note the single forward jet that opens a path and the multiple rearward jets that force the cleaner forward and transport debris to the downstream manhole for removal. [*The American City*]

Figure 9-24 If the jet cannot remove heavy growths of roots, it can be assisted by a hydraulically operated, rotating root cutter. [*Aquatech photo*]

of basement flooding, laterals should be plugged. This method also requires supplemental equipment to remove the debris from the manhole. It does not create any risk for well-prepared sewer joints.

Each cleaning unit carries an independent supply of water, generally 1000 gallons (3.8 cubic meters). The pump on the cleaner operates at about 60 gallons per minute (0.0038 cubic meter per second) at 1000 pounds per square inch (6895 kilopascals). The cleaner carries from 500 to 600 feet (from 152 to 183 meters) of 1-inch (25.4-millimeter) heavy-duty hose.

The cleaning action is developed by a special nozzle attached to the hose, which is inserted in the downstream manhole. The nozzle provides a single forward jet that opens a path for the hose. Several openings at the rear of the nozzle force the hose forward while loosening the debris and washing it downstream. When the hose reaches the end of the section of sewer being cleaned, the operator pulls it back so that the back-spray jets scour the sewer and move the debris to the downstream manhole, where other equipment removes it. As mentioned above, additional passes may be required. Normally, the jets clear away intruding roots, but if the root intrusion is strong, a hydraulically operated rotating cutter can be attached to the nozzle to remove them. The units can be either truck- or trailer-mounted.

Hydraulically Operated Sewer Balls

Air-filled sewer balls offer a practical approach to sewer cleaning that was developed by practical maintenance workers. The sewer ball floats tightly against the upper portion of the sewer being cleaned, clearing away clinging grease, roots, and other debris. The waste water flows below the ball at a high velocity generated by the head of water developed behind it, which washes the debris forward to the downstream manhole. The balls are made of heavy-duty rubber. Each is supplied with a clevis so that a controlling rope or cable may be attached. The balls vary in diameter from 6 to 60 inches (from 152.4 to 1676.4 millimeters), sizes from 8 to 36 inches (from 203.2 to 914.4 millimeters) being the most common. The balls do their best cleaning work when removing sludge, mud, and sand, but they are reasonably effective in removing heavy debris such as brick and rock and also grease and other material that adheres to the pipe sidewalls.

A sewer-cleaning crew using these balls should be supplied with the following equipment:

1. At least 600 feet (183 meters) of ½-inch (12.7-millimeter) synthetic-fiber rope mounted on a spool supported on a reel that permits free movement. For balls with diameters greater than 15 inches (381 millimeters), steel cable should be used.

2. At least 400 feet (122 meters) of 2½-inch (63.5-millimeter) hose connected to an air-break gate valve that will prevent cross-connections when the value is connected to a fire hydrant.

3. A hole jack with a small, free-running wheel for use by the rope or cable in controlling the movement of the ball.

4. Safety harnesses, rubber boots, rubber buckets, and nonsparking shovels for use when maintenance workers must enter the manhole (see page 9-48, "Safety in Sewers").

As a precaution, basement drains served by the section of sewer being cleaned should be plugged to prevent flooding of adjacent residences and businesses.

To perform cleaning work with this type of equipment, the maintenance crew first places the hole jack in the influent manhole of the sewer section being cleaned. The jack has a screw adjustment that secures it firmly in place. The wheel of the jack should be above the opening where the ball enters to permit complete removal of the ball and allow the backed-up waste water to escape. A metal elbow trap can be placed in the downstream manhole to trap much of the solid material and still allow release of the waste water.

The operators then thread the rope or cable through the jack pulley, fasten it to the ball, and push the ball about 3 feet (0.9 meter) into the pipe. They fill the manhole with water to a depth of not more than 3 feet. Next the operators start the ball moving by a few sharp tugs on the rope or cable, which must be kept tight to prevent it from overriding the ball. The ball flutters rather than spins in the pipe. If it becomes trapped in the sewer, the operators can release it by sharp, short withdrawals of the rope or cable. This will level the debris that stops the ball's forward progress and allow it to continue. Normally the ball should be inflated sufficiently to require the operators to force it gently into the sewer. However, underinflation may be required, especially with heavy deposits of debris.

In addition to cleaning sewers, some municipalities use the balls to inspect new sewers when other means of inspection, such as closed-circuit television and air testing, are not conveniently available.

Hydraulically Propelled Hinged-Disc Sewer Cleaners

This type of cleaning equipment operates very much like the sewer ball in principle. It consists of a metal disc or plate with a flexible rubber perimeter mounted on a carriage that holds it in a vertical position. The disc is hinged so that about the upper third can fold back, allowing the waste water to flow over the top. Control ropes handled by the operator can release the upper portion of the disc so that it snaps to a vertical position. The kinetic energy of the flowing waste water then forces the disc forward to perform the cleaning operation. The disc pushes the debris to the downstream manhole, where other equipment removes it.

Plain Flushing

This simple and crude technique probably finds its most justifiable use in flat sewers and at the upper ends of collection systems where solids may settle out and become septic and odorous. A fire hose connected to a nearby hydrant is the basic equipment. The hose should be equipped with a reliable vacuum breaker to prevent the possibility of back siphonage into the water mains if the water pressure drops. The flushing hose should not be used for the transmission of potable water without first being sterilized.

Removal of Debris from Manholes

As has been noted, most of these cleaning methods simply transport the debris to the appropriate manhole, where other means must be used to remove it. Some sewer departments do the work manually, using long-handled shovels with special right-angle shapes. Others may use small cranes equipped with orange-peel or other small, specially designed buckets that can pass through the manhole openings. However, most prefer pneumatic and hydraulic equipment that can remove debris without creating a nuisance at the street level.

Pneumatic Vacuum Removal Equipment Vacuum units are proving extremely versatile. They can pick up leaves, clean catch basins, and pick up street-cleaning debris deposited on the street, as well as remove debris from a manhole. A typical unit consists of a large body mounted on a truck or trailer and a high-pressure blower generally mounted on the body or adjacent to it. The blower develops the required vacuum in the body, which performs the removal work.

Figure 9-25 To remove the debris brought to a downstream manhole by jet cleaning or other means, a pneumatic vacuum unit often is employed. In this case, the vacuum unit is combined with a jet cleaning unit. [*Central Engineering photo*]

A flexible tube, generally 12 inches (304.8 millimeters) in diameter and long enough to reach into the manhole, draws out the debris. The debris need not pass through the blower itself but enters the body directly. When the body is full, the truck or trailer travels to a suitable dumping area and discharges its load by the usual dump-truck method.

Hydraulic Debris Removal The hydraulic method has a longer service record than vacuum equipment does. Developed originally to clean catch basins, it takes advantage of the Bernoulli hydraulic principle to remove the debris. Two pipes, one a small jetting pipe and the other a larger cleaning pipe, are mounted together. The small pipe delivers high-pressure water at about 100 pounds per square inch (689 kilopascals) to the larger pipe through an elbow and a venturi. This high-pressure water creates a sufficient pressure drop in the cleaning pipe to remove both the water and the debris. The larger pipe transports the debris to a watertight body of 6 to 10 cubic yards (4.6 to 7.6 cubic meters). Since the debris and the water tend to separate, the water can be reused until the body is appropriately full.

The chief drawback of this type of equipment is that it cannot pick up debris larger than 4 inches (101.6 millimeters) in diameter. Consequently some of the debris must be removed manually.

General Sewer-cleaning Precautions

While inspecting the manhole before cleaning operations begin, the maintenance crew may observe earth or fragments of pipe in the manhole trough. This debris is a sign that the upstream portion of the sewer may have sections that are broken or have collapsed. If portions

Figure 9-26 A hydraulic-actuated catch-basin cleaner can be used to remove debris, as this diagram shows. [*Elgin-Leach drawing*]

of the sewer have histories of erosion or corrosion caused by sulfide generation or, possibly, by strong industrial wastes, the sewer may collapse during cleaning operations.   In both cases, an attempt should be made to inspect the sewer by closed-circuit television, although such an inspection is difficult in an uncleaned sewer.

Chemical Root Control

The prevention of root intrusion into sewers is one of the most challenging problems in the sewer-maintenance program.   Roots are surprisingly persistent, forcing their way wherever moisture can enter, by forming a single cell, one at a time, to create the passageway.   Many sewer-maintenance personnel have tried chemicals to inhibit the growth of roots with varying degrees of success.   One of the most commonly used chemicals is copper sulfate, which is placed in the manhole invert or occasionally is flushed down a toilet bowl.   However, the copper sulfate dissolves in the flowing waste water, and since the roots enter the sewer from the top, they still can form the familiar and troublesome root curtain and ultimately block the sewer without coming in contact with the treated waste water.

Experiments in the Sacramento, California, County Department of Public Works, supported by research at the University of California at Davis, have demonstrated the value of treatment with a chemical of the soil-fumigant or weed-killer type. The fumigant consists of anhydrous metham, or sodium methyldithiocarbamate (24.5 percent), and dichlobenil, known as 2,6-dichlorobenzonitrile (1.77 percent), and inert ingredients containing grease emulsifiers, nonionic surfactants, and foaming agents if desired. When this chemical combination is applied in the sewer, the roots absorb the inhibitor and die away. Moreover, inorganic colloids and soil in the sewer joints and pipe breaks adsorb the inhibitor, permitting it to remain effective for 3 to 4 years.

The root inhibitor can be applied by either the soak or the foam methods. The first requires plugging the lower end of the line needing treatment, filling the line with a 1 percent solution and allowing it to remain for 1 hour or longer, and then releasing the solution, capturing it at the next pipe section to be treated.

The foam method requires that the root inhibitor be supplied with a foaming agent. The maintenance crew must first plug the sewer at the upstream end, using a plug that can resist a back pressure from the waste water of 30 pounds per square inch (206.8 kilopascals). The plug must have a connection that will receive a 1-inch (25.4-millimeter) pipe. The operators then connect a foam generator to the plug, and introduce the foam containing the fumigant until it completely fills the sewer and appears in the downstream manhole. Next they remove the plug, allowing the waste water to flow under the foam and compress it into the top portion of the sewer. The foam clings to the top of the sewer for 30 minutes or more, giving the roots ample opportunity to absorb the fumigant. To reduce the risk of having the foam enter the house connections, the operators can introduce the foam through a hose at the midpoint of the sewer being treated. Then, as foaming continues, they can pull the hose slowly back to the downstream manhole.

In large mains, the root inhibitor, known as Vaporooter, can be sprayed onto the upper portion of the sewer above the waste-water flow. However, the line should be thoroughly ventilated for this work. The root inhibitor can decompose and release irritating gases that can be troublesome in certain instances.

FLOW MEASUREMENT AND MONITORING

Today managers of waste-water systems must devote greater attention to the measurement and recording of flows within the collection system. No longer is it sufficient to measure and record flows entering the treatment plant or pumping stations. Monitoring flows within individual portions of the system, even for periods of a week or a month, yields valuable information that will help to calculate the reserve capacities of various sections of the system, estimate the abilities of the various sections in assuming new loads, and identify the infiltration and inflow of unwanted water that usurps the capacity of the sewers and the treatment plant.

Regulatory agencies, particularly the EPA, have become concerned with the degree of infiltration and inflow and require studies to identify this unwanted water and to show what is being done to reduce it to economically reasonable amounts before plans for improvements are approved or construction grants awarded.

Infiltration-prone Areas

Infiltration, or the entry of groundwater into the sewer system through defective and broken sewers, leaking joints, connections, and manholes, is particularly troublesome in areas where the groundwater table is high. A practical way to determine the groundwater level is to insert a slotted pipe horizontally into the ground above the sewer pipe, through the manhole wall. For convenience, the pipe should be placed close to the access steps mounted in the wall. An elbow should be connected with the slotted pipe, and a clear plastic pipe should be connected with the elbow. The plastic pipe should be mounted in a vertical position and secured to the manhole steps. The groundwater will rise in the plastic pipe to indicate the level of the water outside the manhole. By making a number of such installations in the system and observing them over an extended period one can determine the water table and learn how it varies.

However, these installations should be supplemented by observation wells elsewhere. The groundwater level adjacent to a manhole may not

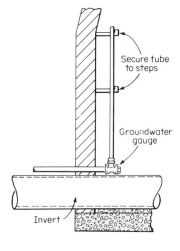

Secure tube
to steps

Groundwater
gauge

Invert

Figure 9-27 This device can be utilized to measure the level of groundwater near sewers. It consists of a clear plastic pipe mounted vertically and connected to an open metal pipe that extends through the manhole wall. [*American Pipe Services drawing*]

be representative of the level throughout the area, particularly if the manhole is subject to infiltration and leakage.

An ordinary thermometer offers a rough method of identifying infiltration in a sewer section. A drop in the temperature of the waste water below the normally expected level is evidence that cold infiltration water is entering the sewer at this point.

Effective Flow-monitoring Equipment

As indicated above, the flow monitoring of individual sewer sections should not be restricted to a momentary measurement but extend over a selected period, probably a week and possibly a month. Investigators making a study of sewer flows in Columbus, Ohio, first determined what they considered to be the characteristics of effective monitoring equipment:

1. The equipment must be able to make accurate flow measurements during both wet and dry weather even when the sewers surcharge.

2. The measuring equipment must be reasonably economical to purchase, install, and service.

3. The equipment must be reasonably vandal-proof since it must operate unattended.

4. It must be reusable at other monitoring sites.

5. It must create only a minimum head loss.

6. It must be able to operate automatically for at least 24 hours.[9]

A seventh requirement might also be listed. The equipment should be sturdy and dependable, able to operate reliably in the humid environment of a manhole, and capable of performing despite the conglomerate mixture of liquids and solids that characterizes waste water.

Measurement of Waste-Water Levels

In virtually all cases, flow monitoring requires continuous determination of the depth of water. A number of techniques that appear to serve well have been developed.

Floats attached to appropriate measuring and recording devices have the longest history of use and are the easiest to understand. Cylindrical or spherical floats are often placed in a stilling well in the manhole. Other floats are broad-based "scows" in the center of the channels being monitored. Since they float on the surface of the waste water, they need periodic inspection to remove any debris that may collect on them and interfere with the measurements.

---

[9] "Flow Monitoring Techniques in Sanitary Sewers," *Deeds and Data,* Water Pollution Control Federation, July 1974.

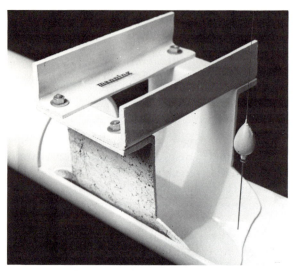

Figure 9-28 Flow measurements in sewers require some means of determining the depth of the flow. In this case, a weighted probe is used with a mechanism that lowers it to the surface at predetermined intervals. When the probe touches the surface, it completes a microampere circuit that causes it to retract. This probe is being used with a calibrated flume. [*Manning Environmental Corp. photo*]

Bubbler tubes employ a technique that commonly is used to measure liquid levels in tanks. They require accurate air or gas pressures introduced at the channel bottoms. The investigators at Columbus used these tubes, which are less affected by floating solids than floats are.

Ultrasonic monitoring employs sonar techniques to measure wastewater levels without contact with the water itself. To be effective this equipment requires precise placement.

Figure 9-29 The power and recording equipment used by the oscillating probe are contained in this unit, which can be clamped to the manhole ring by three setscrews. [*Manning Environmental Corp. photo*]

Oscillating probes can be constructed in a compact form that is easily mounted in the manhole.   A wire probe is lowered to touch the surface of the waste water at selected intervals.   This contact completes a microampere circuit that causes the lowering motor to stop and the instrument to record the level.   Then the motor retracts the probe until the next time interval.

A capacitance measuring probe can record waste-water levels directly by means of an electronic circuit.   The probe must be submerged in the waste water and for that reason often is mounted in a stilling well.

Use of the Sewer as a Flow-measuring Instrument

Rather than use flumes, weirs, or tubes to determine flow quantities, investigators can obtain reasonably accurate results by using the sewer pipe itself if conditions are favorable.   It will still be necessary to determine the depth of the waste water at the point of measurement. The quantity then can be calculated by measuring the velocity of flow or by using the old but highly respected Manning formula, which employs the n roughness coefficient.   This coefficient must be estimated but generally is placed at $n = .013$.   The Manning formula requires determining the slope of the waste water rather than that of the sewer. However, in practice the slope of the sewer is accurate enough. (For a graphic solution of the Manning formula, see Appendix, page A-1.)

To be used for measurement a sewer pipe should be smooth, providing nonturbulent flow for 200 feet (61 meters) or more upstream.   It should be free of abrupt dips, sudden contractions or expansions, and tributary inflows.

Velocity Measurements

If velocity is to be used to determine the volume of waste water carried in the sewer, the meter or technique must be able to measure and record the velocities over an extended period.   Few meters or techniques can meet this requirement.

Salts and radioactive tracers can meet it.   This technique requires two pairs of electrodes placed in the waste-water stream at known distances apart.   Salt or radioactive tracers then can be introduced at controlled intervals.   Galvanometers or other instruments record the passage of the tracers as well as the time, measuring the velocities at accuracies of better than plus or minus 2 percent.   Salt appears to be the preferred material, since many persons dislike placing radioactive material in the waste water.

Movable self-cleaning vanes placed at an angle to the flow measure and record the flow by measuring the angle that the waste water forces the vane to assume.

Techniques and meters that measure velocity but cannot record it for an extended period include dyes of potassium permanganate, fluorescein, and rhodamine. An observer is required to note the passage of the dye cloud; it must be recognized that this is a surface velocity rather than a mean velocity. Floats also can determine the velocity at the moment. Probably the best float is an orange that floats submerged close to the mean stream velocity. Utrasonic and electromagnetic probes also can be utilized to measure the flow at a given moment. The velocities so determined can be used in the Manning formula to calculate the actual n number.

Flumes for Flow Measurement

For a more precise measurement of flow, a scientifically prepared flume, weir, channel, or tube is required. These devices limit the uncertainty of velocity measurements and roughness coefficients. They are portable and rugged.

The Palmer-Bowlus type of flume is very effective. It has a round bottom, permitting it to be mounted in the channel of the manhole. It can be sealed to the channel either by mastic or by sandbags. This flume has demonstrated accuracies of plus or minus 3 percent of theoretical quantities even when the flow has equaled 90 percent of the pipe diameter. The throat of this type of flume should be equal to the length of one pipe diameter and never less than 60 percent of the pipe diameter. Depths should be measured at a point no more than half of the pipe diameter upstream from the entrance to the flume. The slope of the approach sewer should be no more than 2 percent.

The first Palmer-Bowlus flumes were designed in segments that could be assembled in manholes or at other points of flow measurement.

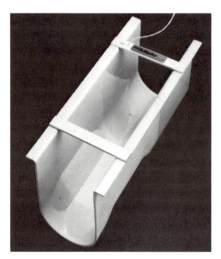

Figure 9-30 A Palmer-Bowlus type of flume can be used for flow measurements. This flume utilizes a sensing unit mounted in the wall to measure liquid levels. [*Universal Engineering Services photo*]

However, this required recalibration at every new point of measurement. The flumes are not prefabricated to fit specific pipe diameters.

The Leopold-Lagco flume is a proprietary type differing from the Palmer-Bowlus design. It has a rectangular throat section throughout the entire flow range, whereas the throat of the Palmer-Bowlus flume is trapezoidal at the bottom and rectangular at the top.

Weirs for the Measurement of Waste-Water Flow

Weirs also provide precision measurements without making assumptions of roughness and velocity. However, a weir, especially the popular 90-degree V-notch type, can measure only low flows. It can measure flows of 1 cubic foot per second (0.028 cubic meter per second) or less with precision and can measure flows as high as 10 cubic feet per second (0.28 cubic meter per second), but its special head requirements may rule out its use. For larger flows, the investigator can use the rectangular, the trapezoidal, or the Cipolletti weir.

The V-notch weir, which is most commonly used in this work, should meet these specifications:

1. Its upstream face should be smooth and perpendicular to the axes of the channel in both vertical and horizontal directions.

2. Its thickness should not exceed ⅛ inch (3.175 millimeters).

3. When installed, its crest should be at least 1 foot (0.3 meter) above the approach-channel bottom, and the minimum head should be at least 0.2 foot (0.06 meter).

4. The approach channel should have a cross-sectional area at least 8 times that of the nappe at the crest for an upstream distance of 15 to 20 times the height of the crest.

5. The crest should be thin and beveled, with the sharp edge upstream, and be placed so that the waste water flowing over it will not touch the weir structure but spring over it.

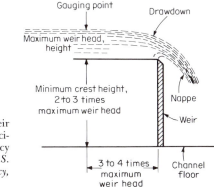

Figure 9-31 A measuring weir should be placed to these specifications to ensure accuracy [Sewer Flow Measurement, *U.S. Environmental Protection Agency, 1976*]

6. The weir crest should have a minimum height of at least 2 and preferably 3 times the maximum head expected over the weir.

7. The weir can be considered submerged if the water level beneath the nappe rises above the weir crest. Flow tables that will permit measurements can be obtained, but they require measuring the water levels both upstream and downstream.

8. Under normal conditions, the instrument measuring the water level should be located upstream of the weir crest for a distance of at least 3 and preferably 4 times the maximum head expected over the weir.

Factory-fabricated weirs are available, but weirs can also be constructed by shop mechanics. The factory-fabricated weirs are calibrated to provide direct flow readings in gallons per 24 hours.

To fabricate a weir, a mechanic should use either aluminum or stainless steel and mount it on marine plywood, employing nonferrous screws and a gasket. The metal edges should extend above the plywood for at least 1 inch (25.4 millimeters). The weir-supporting bulkhead should be braced accurately in a position at right angles to the vertical and horizontal directions. It should be sealed with mastic to ensure that all the flow will pass over the V notch.

SEWER INSPECTION AND TESTING

With the sewer cleaned and the flow measured, the maintenance crews can turn their attention to inspection of the lines for breaks in the pipe, leaking joints, and sources of unwanted inflow. Inspection also is required to ensure the integrity of newly laid sewers, but since new installations are only a minor part of a sewerage system, the responsibility of protecting and rehabilitating the existing system is far greater.

Testing and inspection of new and existing sewers can be placed in four general categories:

1. Smoke testing
2. Closed-circuit–television inspection of the pipe interior
3. Inspection by photography
4. Air testing

Smoke Testing

Smoke testing of sewers is a practical method. It can locate leaks in manholes that permit the entry of unwanted water; discover rodent passages that can do the same; and disclose connections, generally illegal, between roof and cellar drains and either the sanitary or the combined sewer that impose heavy peak loads on the system.

Production of the Smoke The sewer maintenance crew can use either smoke "candles" or smoke "bombs" that produce a zinc chloride mist for this detection work. They also can employ a generator that develops a smoke consisting of DOP (dioctylphthalate) aerosol containing particles 0.6 micron (0.6 micrometer; 0.00002 inch) in size and able to pass through relatively dense soil without difficulty. Suppliers can provide both types in colors varying from white to gray. They state that the smoke leaves no residue to stain building surfaces or clothing and that it is noncorrosive. Both types can be considered nontoxic, but if breathed in large amounts, they will cause coughing problems.

A smoke candle, bomb, or generator should not have to produce a smoke volume larger than 5 to 6 times that of the sewer section being inspected. A sewer run of 300 feet (91 meters) should need no more than a 3-minute bomb.

Preliminary Precautions   Before attempting a smoke test, the maintenance supervisor should notify the fire and police authorities that they will probably receive false alarms, particularly when the smoke emerges from a building. In addition, the supervisor should notify all residents connected to the sewer line being tested as well as those connected to sewers in adjoining sections since the smoke may work its way into them.

The crew should make a careful inspection of the area to locate any manholes that may have been carelessly asphalted over and spots where the smoke might appear. This precaution may prevent the necessity of looking into a forgotten manhole that the smoke may detect.

The supervisor should schedule a smoke test when the weather has been dry and both infiltration and inflow will be at a minimum. It can be conducted in cold weather provided the smoke can escape through the ground.

Choice of Test Lines   The supervisor can select a single sewer line connected by two manholes or two lines connected by three manholes if the total run is between 500 and 600 feet (between 152 and 183 meters). If a single line is selected, smoke can be introduced into either manhole. If two lines are to be inspected, the smoke can be applied through the center manhole.

Confining the Smoke   The test requires that the line be blocked sufficiently to confine the smoke but not necessarily to stop the flow of waste water. One method of accomplishing this so that personnel need not enter the sewer—and this is important as a safety measure—is to lower bags of large, coarse gravel into the manhole, placing them at the point where the sewer being tested enters. Then as many bags of sand as are required should be placed on the rock-filled bags to confine the smoke. The process should be repeated at the effluent manhole. This procedure will permit the waste water to flow through the rock-filled bags but confine the smoke to the line being tested and the two manholes. If the manholes are subject to infiltration or inflow, the smoke will detect this defect.

The maintenance crew should secure the sacks by tying the ropes to the top rung of the manhole access step or to a solid object at street level. This will prevent the possibility of the waste water's dislodging one of the bags and washing it into the sewer. If a bag is dislodged and the ropes are available, the crew can recover it easily from the ground level.

If the flow in the sewer is small, the crew can use a pneumatic plug to stop the sewer for the test, which rarely takes more than 15 or 20 minutes. However, the operators should not inflate the plugs completely until the smoke has reached them. Since the plugs seal the sewer tightly, the air pressure will prevent the smoke from reaching the ends of the line.

Introducing Smoke into the Sewer   To place the smoke in the sewer to be tested, the crew may use a plywood square ¾ inch (19 millimeters) thick and large enough to cover the manhole completely. The plywood can rest on a partially filled inner tube with two or three sandbags on it, or it can be provided with a sponge-rubber gasket pad. Either method will keep the smoke confined to the manhole. The plywood should have an opening with a diameter of 7⅞ inches (200 millimeters), to be used by the blower's flexible ductwork. A blower with a capacity of 1500 cubic feet per minute (0.71 cubic meter per second) will work well.

The smoke should be introduced by putting a candle or a bomb at the blower intake. As soon as the duct leading to the manhole starts receiving air and smoke, it will expand and make a tight connection as it passes through the hole in the plywood cover.

A blower of this capacity is normally part of the equipment of a sewer-maintenance crew. However, manufacturers can provide a gasoline engine–powered blower mounted on a suitable base that fits directly over the manhole opening. Smoke is introduced through a port in the base without the need for flexible tubing. Although this is a neat,

Figure 9-32 Smoke can be introduced by a specially designed blower placed directly over the manhole. [*Superior Signal Co. photo*]

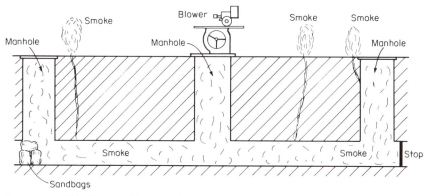

Figure 9-33 This diagram illustrates how one blower can introduce smoke into two connecting sewers and three manholes to detect flaws and illegal connections. [*Superior Signal Co. drawing*]

compact smoke applicator, it should not be mounted on the manhole until the gasoline engine has been started, since the process of starting the engine might ignite combustible gases emerging from the manhole.

Manufacturers also produce similar generators for DOP smoke. These, too, should not be started while in position on the manhole opening.

Procedure When the Smoke Appears   When the smoke fills the sewer and the manholes, crew members should be alert to locate its appearance

Figure 9-34 Smoke issuing from a downspout, as illustrated here, is clear evidence of an illegal connection to a sewer. [*Superior Signal Co. photo*]

on the ground surface and in other locations. Smoke appearing at a house vent pipe is normal and does not signify an illegal connection, but if smoke appears at a downspout or an outside drain, it indicates a violation. Smoke appearing through cracks in the pavement or in other nearby areas means trouble in the sewer, possibly a cracked barrel, a leaking joint, or poor manhole connections.

The supervisor should document all these appearances by notes and sketches and, in the case of illegal connections, by photographs so that appropriate action can be taken promptly. Reinspection should be scheduled promptly, within 90 days, to ensure compliance. Violators should be informed that the illegal connections pose harm not only to the sewerage system but also to their neighbors, whose basements may be flooded.

Sewer Inspection by Closed-Circuit Television

The application of closed-circuit television to sewer inspection has improved the quality and workmanship of sewer construction more than any other single development has. It provides visible evidence that the sewers have been placed in accordance with contract specifications, that the pipes are in alignment, that no infiltration exists, and that the laterals are connected tightly, preventing infiltration and root intrusion.

In the past the inspection of sewer installation unfortunately has been casual. Jointing has been poor, O rings have been omitted, and individual pipe sections have not been placed in alignment. Laterals have been connected simply by breaking an opening in the pipe and pushing the lateral through the opening, allowing it to intrude into the pipe interior, where it becomes an obstacle to cleaning operations and interferes with the flow by trapping rags and other floating solid material.

Contractors have learned that the television camera discloses bad workmanship. Other utilities making excavations in the roadway know

Figure 9-35 The television camera used to inspect sewers carries its own light source. [*Cues, Inc. photo*]

Figure 9-36 From the television control unit, the inspector can see clearly the condition of the sewer and locate flawed points with precision [*Cues, Inc. photo*]

that if they damage the sewer, the television camera will detect the damage. Contractors and builders are not so casual about blasting operations after a sewer has been installed.

At one time, sewer authorities relied on contract organizations to perform inspection work. But as the camera became more reliable and this type of inspection increased in popularity, a greater number of sewer organizations came to own and operate their own television-camera equipment.

Closed-circuit–television inspection equipment basically consists of these elements:

1. A camera mounted on skids able to pass through a pipe of 8 inches (203 millimeters) or more. Cameras have been assembled that can pass through smaller pipe.

2. A light source that will permit the camera to function.

3. A 1000-foot (305-meter) reel of television cable and steel conveying cable with footage-measuring recorders that permit the inspector to locate the camera accurately in the sewer.

4. A winch at one end, either hand-powered or electrically powered, to pull the camera through the sewer.

5. A control unit, generally housed in a truck or trailer body, containing the television monitoring screen and a Polaroid camera to photograph and record key locations in the sewer where trouble may be evident. A 16-millimeter videotape motion-picture camera also can be provided to make a permanent record of the inspection work for future reference.

Photographic Sewer Inspection

As an alternative to television viewing, inspectors can employ a water-tight camera, somewhat resembling the units used for underwater photography. The camera, generally 35-millimeter, also is pulled on skids by hand-operated winches with 500 to 700 feet (152 to 212 meters) of cable. The usual practice is to take a photograph, either in black and white or in color, every 2 to 5 feet (0.6 to 1.5 meters). One supplier offers a stereoscopic camera that provides a three-dimensional view of the interior.

Camera inspection is less costly than television, and the photographs in general provide a sharper reproduction than the television monitor does. However, the delay in developing and printing the pictures is a disadvantage, and the television monitor is very convincing.

Sewer Air Testing

Air testing of sewers provides an effective method of testing new work before it is backfilled. If the test shows that the joints or other points of workmanship are faulty, the contractor makes corrections immediately and need not reexcavate the trench. At one time, water was used to test the integrity of sewers, but water testing is difficult when a sewer is on a steep grade, and air pockets in house laterals and similar locations can weaken its accuracy. Air testing should be restricted to sewers having diameters of 18 inches (457.2 millimeters) or less. Some specifications require the inspector to conduct the air test immediately after backfilling and the contractor to make an air test before backfilling.

The test is based on the ability of the pipe to maintain an air pressure, when plugged, for a specified time period. At the start of the test, the pressure should be 3.5 pounds per square inch (24 kilopascals); at the end of the test, not less than 2.5 pounds per square inch (17 kilopascals). The time period can be calculated by the following formula, applied to a single pipe size:

$$\text{Test time } (t) = (0.085/q)d$$

where t = minimum time, in seconds, for the pressure to drop from 3.5 to 2.5 pounds per square inch

q = permissible air loss per square foot of internal pipe surface in cubic feet per minute

d = nominal inside pipe diameter in inches

The test time is based on an allowable air loss q of 0.003 cubic foot (0.000085 cubic meter) per minute with these limitations:

1. The minimum significant air loss shall be 2.0 cubic feet (0.056 cubic meter) per minute.

2. The total allowable air loss shall not exceed 3.5 cubic feet (0.099 cubic meter) per minute.

These limitations apply to any test section.   The formula is based on an air temperature of 68°F (20°C).   Air temperature stabilized between 43 and 96°F (between 6.1 and 35.5°C) introduces an error of less than 5 percent.   A nomograph that will provide these test times directly can be prepared.

After determining the test time, the inspector should add air to the test section until the internal pressure in the line has reached 4.0 pounds per square inch (27.6 kilopascals) and then allow the air in the line to be stabilized.   The pressure normally shows some drop.

When the pressure has been stabilized and is at or above 3.5 pounds per square inch (24 kilopascals), the inspector should commence the test, recording the drop in pressure for the test period.   If the pressure drops more than 1 pound per square inch (6.9 kilopascals) during the period, the line is presumed to have failed.   The test may be discontinued, and the test considered successful, when the time period has elapsed, even though a drop of 1 pound per square inch has not occurred.

The line being tested should be clean, and the interior should be wet. A wetted pipe surface produces more consistent results.   All pipe outlets, and especially pipe laterals, should be plugged.

No inspector should be allowed in the manhole during the test, and plugs should be installed and braced so that they will not blow out.   The sudden accidental expulsion of a plug that has not been solidly installed and is partially deflated before the pipe pressure is released can be dangerous.   Pressurizing equipment can include a regulator or relief valve set at 10 pounds per square inch (69 kilopascals) or some other recommended figure to avoid overpressurizing and damaging an otherwise-acceptable line.[10]

Pipe large enough to permit an inspector to enter it can be accepted by visual inspection.   The inspector can use a joint tester that isolates the joint and pressurizes it with either air or water so that the rate of loss can be measured.   In actual practice, the joint is either bottle-tight or sufficiently subject to leakage to require repair.

GROUTING OF LEAKING SEWER JOINTS OR CRACKS

If the sewer has been cleaned, its flow has been measured so that unwanted infiltration and inflow water can be identified, and the lines have been inspected to locate flawed portions, rehabilitation can begin. If the sewer has collapsed, the pipe should be replaced with stronger,

---

[10] *Proposed Recommended Practice for Low-Pressure Air Test of Clay Sewer Pipe,* Designation C 828-75T, American Society for Testing and Materials, Philadelphia, 1975.

infiltration-resistant pipe described earlier. If it is badly deteriorated but still is able to carry the water-water flow, it can be rehabilitated with plastic insertion pipe. If the flaws consist chiefly of leaking joints and transverse cracks, grouting offers the possibility of relatively inexpensive and nuisance-free rehabilitation.

Grouting is a new maintenance technique that is still subject to development, but results have been encouraging, and the cost savings as well as the avoidance of inconvenience for residents can be substantial when the work is performed well. As practiced today, sewer grouting is subject to these limitations:

1. It cannot repair a longitudinal crack unless the crack is short. The danger is that a longitudinal crack probably will grow and extend to two or three pipe lengths, since the pipe will be subject to some type of ground stresses.

2. It cannot produce a good grout seal on a broken or badly cracked sewer.

3. The inflatable sleeves on the packing unit must make firm contact with sound, unbroken pipe on each side of the joint or crack being grouted.

4. With one of the grouting materials, the presence of groundwater subject to strong movement may make the work difficult if the operator is unaware that this condition exists.

Two types of grouting material exist, and others are in the development stage. One developed type is an *acrylamide gel,* and the other is a *urethane foam.* The gel is generally known as AM-9 but is also marketed as Q-seal and as PWG. The foam is a liquid prepolymer that cures to form a flexible cellular-rubber gasket in the joint or crack. The gel stabilizes the soil surrounding the leaking joint or crack and also forms a barrier in the joint or crack. The urethane foam, in contrast, does not attempt to penetrate the soil but forms a gasket type of seal in the joint or crack itself.

Acrylamide Gel

The acrylamide gel is a combination of two organic monomers: acrylamide and n,n-methylene bisacrylamide. In a dilute aqueous solution, generally 10 percent by weight, and catalyzed, these will form the leak-stopping gel. The catalyst most often used is DMAPN, an abbreviation for the chemical name b-dimethylaminopropionitrile. No more than 0.5 to 1.5 percent by weight of the total solution is needed to start the reaction. A strong oxidizing salt, generally ammonium persulfate, initiates it. Between 0.5 and 3 percent by weight is required. The operator can vary the gel time from 1 to 500 seconds by adjusting the amount of DMAPN and ammonium persulfate used in the mix. For general work, a 20-second gel time is satisfactory, but if the gel is used to waterproof structures, a longer time is preferable.

The gel has demonstrated a capability of penetrating leaking joints and cracks even though water is flowing through them. According to the suppliers, a 10 percent solution of the acrylamide gel can withstand dilution to 3 times its volume and still react successfully. However, since the gel has a slightly greater specific gravity and viscosity than water, it tends to displace rather than mix with the water in most locations. Nevertheless, if the pipe is in coral sand, coarse rock, or gravel, the volume of water and its movement may be great enough to cause the gel to lose effectiveness. If these conditions exist, some suppliers suggest adding a fine, light filler, such as diatomaceous earth or fly ash, to the gel to increase its strength and viscosity.

To grout a leaking joint, the operating crew must first clean the pipe section and free it of obstructions, including intruding service connections (which should not have been allowed in the first place). This step is required to permit the sealing packer to operate. The packer is a hollow metal cylinder supplied with inflatable rubber sleeves at each end. By the use of closed-circuit television, the operator locates the packer on the joint or crack requiring sealing, then inflates the sleeves to form a tight seal against the pipe walls, and pumps the acrylamide gel into the annular space outside the cylinder and between the two inflated sleeves. The pressure of pumping forces the gel through the joint or crack and into the soil surrounding the pipe. After the selected lapse of time, the gel solidifies to produce a seal both outside the pipe and in the joint or crack. The packer sleeves can then be deflated and the equipment moved to the next trouble spot in the pipe.

The acrylamide powder is somewhat toxic; therefore, personnel should wear goggles, gloves, and respirators when mixing or handling

Figure 9-37 Grouting operations can be performed from a trailer unit such as this. Note the packer in the foreground. [*Cues, Inc. photo*]

Figure 9-38 Here the television camera and the packer have been drawn into the sewer to be positioned over a flawed point so that grout can be applied. [*Cues, Inc. photo*]

the grout. Some gel will remain in the sewer, but the waste water will carry it away without difficulty, and it is not solid enough to cause problems at the pumps or comminutors.

To seal small leaking service lines, the most practical way is to fill the entire line with gel, subjecting it to sufficient pressure to grout all the leaks at once. The excess grout must be cleaned from the line, but this is not difficult.

The gel can be made root-resistant by blending it with 200 parts per million of dichlobenil (see page 9-28, "Chemical Root Control"). The gel suppliers expect this treatment to make the grout root-resistant for 5 years.

Urethane Foam

In contrast to the acrylamide gel, the urethane foam forms a grout in the leaking joint or in the fractured pipe itself. It is a low-velocity pre-polymer with a viscosity that can vary from 300 to 350 centipoises (from 0.3 to 0.5 pascal second). Mixed with water, it foams and then turns to flexible cellular rubber.

To use urethane foam, the grouting crew must first clean the sewer thoroughly so that the packing mechanism can seat solidly on sound sewer pipe.   This mechanism is a hollow metal cylinder with three inflatable sleeves.   The sleeves must have coverings that will not adhere to the foam grouting, which has strong adhesive qualities.

Using a closed-circuit–television camera, the operator places the packer over the crack or joint to be repaired.   The two outer sleeves are then inflated so that the packer will be seated solidly.   Next the operator inserts the urethane prepolymer and water into the center space between the two inflated sleeves and allows them to react for the required period, generally about 35 seconds at 60°F (16.6°C).   When the material has foamed, the operator inflates the center sleeve and retains it on the crack or joint for approximately 5 minutes so that the grout will cure.   The operator then deflates the three sleeves and moves to the next point that requires grouting.   The grout requires an accelerator to hasten the cure time.   When added in a 0.3 percent concentration, the accelerator reduces the cure time as shown in the accompanying table.

Ambient temperature of the grout and water		Cure time (minutes)	
°F	°C	Water only	Water with 0.3 percent accelerator
40	4.4	15.0	7.8
70	21.1	8.2	4.6
100	37.7	4.6	2.8

SOURCE: Specification sheet of the Minnesota Mining and Manufacturing Company.

The supplier states that the cured grout has a density of 14 pounds per cubic foot (224 kilograms per cubic meter), a tensile strength of 90 pounds per square inch (620.5 kilopascals), and an ability to stretch to 8 times its original length.   It reportedly retains its characteristics regardless of whether the soil is wet or dry and is able to resist mild alkalis and acids as well as most organic solvents.

Since the grout is a cellular, spongelike material, it permits the entry of very small amounts of water, but not enough to be counted as true infiltration.   However, where moisture exists, roots also can enter; so the supplier will provide a root inhibitor if desired.

The record of the grout in checking infiltration seems best when used on concrete pipe at this stage of its development.   It appears to be less successful when used with vitrified-clay pipe, apparently because of the smooth, nonporous surface and the greasy film that can coat the joints, making adhesion more difficult.   Its ability to check infiltration through concrete over long periods is being demonstrated at Minnetonka, Minnesota, in a concrete lift station.   The foam grout has been able to check inflow through the wall amounting to 40,000 gallons (151 cubic meters) per day and is still demonstrating its effectiveness.

The ability of the grout to stay in place when the sewer has been subjected to vigorous cleaning remains to be demonstrated. The grout also presents something of a disposal problem when portions remain unused. The best practice apparently is to neutralize the grout by permitting it to react with water to form a foam and then disposing of it on a landfill or in an incinerator if this will not create an air-pollution problem.

Because of the urethane grout's strong adhesive qualities, special attention must be paid to cleaning the equipment. Acetone apparently is proving best for cleaning and purging the packing unit. For the rest of the equipment, the supplier provides a special cleaner that is both caustic and flammable. Those using it should protect themselves with suitable gloves and safety goggles.

The urethane-foam grout, like the acrylamide gel, should be considered for repairing leaking joints, minor bell shears, and circumferential pipe breaks only if the packer can be positioned against undamaged pipe. It is not intended to repair pipe that has suffered more serious structural damage.

SAFETY IN SEWERS

The need for greater safety of personnel working in and around sewers is more urgent than most people realize. In 1974 the Water Pollution Control Federation recorded 37.6 injuries and 0.15 deaths per 1000 person-hours in waste-water works. Industry in general experiences about 10 injuries.[11] The death rate for waste-water workers is higher than that of any other municipal classification, including the police.

Injuries and deaths in waste-water collection systems often also involve pedestrians and motorists. Aside from the sorrow and pain that they generate, the financial risk of costly damage suits for negligence must be considered. An accusation of negligence will be more difficult to refute if those bringing suit can show a failure to adhere to recognized safety standards.

Ground-Level Safety Measures

Since much of the work is carried out at street level, safety precautions should duplicate those recommended for street-repair work (see Chapter 14, section "Street Detours and Construction Warnings"). In view of the risk of loss of life and harm to persons and property, every street

[11] George W. Burke, *WPCF Releases 1974 Safety Survey Results,* Water Pollution Control Federation, Washington, 1975.

detour or warning system should be planned as carefully as the repair or maintenance work itself.

Belowground Safety Measures

Personnel assigned to work in manholes and sewers must be trained to realize that they will be in a potentially dangerous environment and that they should protect themselves accordingly.   Basic protective equipment should be as follows:

1. Safety harnesses, equipment to detect toxic and combustible gases, oxygen-deficiency–detecting equipment, portable blowers, first-aid kits, rescue breathing apparatus, and fire extinguishers.

2. Safety clothing, including hard hats meeting the American National Standards Institute requirement Z89.1-1969, rubber boots, safety goggles, foot protectors, and rubber gloves.

Precautions before Entering a Manhole

Before a manhole cover has been removed, the supervisor should test the air inside the manhole, using a combustible-gas indicator or an explosimeter with a detecting probe.   The probe can be inserted

Figure 9-39 Air in a manhole should be tested before the manhole cover is removed. [Journal of the Water Pollution Control Federation, *February 1970*]

Figure 9-40 Meters such as this, with an appropriate probe attached to the threaded outlet at right, can detect the presence of combustible gases. [*Mine Safety Appliance photo*]

Figure 9-41 An easily portable meter such as this one will disclose the atmospheric concentration of oxygen. [*Mine Safety Appliance photo*]

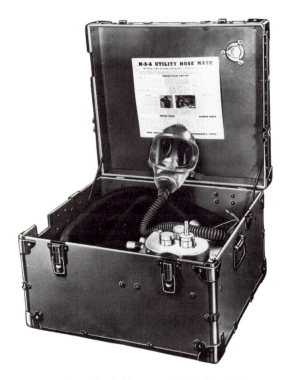

Figure 9-42 A mask of this type with 25 feet (7.62 meters) of hose will permit rescue work in atmospheres not immediately hazardous to life. [*Mine Safety Appliance photo*]

through a hole in the manhole cover.   If it indicates no danger, the cover can be removed, and the supervisor can then test the lower levels. The supervisor should test for gasoline vapors that are heavier than air and collect at the bottom and, in deep manholes, for carbon monoxide, hydrogen sulfide, and ammonia, all potentially lethal.   Preferably, tests should be conducted every 2 feet (0.6 meter) from top to bottom.

Manhole and Sewer Ventilation

Even if the tests disclose no dangerous gases, the manhole and sewer should be ventilated for at least 1 minute.   Any manhole more than shoulder-deep needs ventilation.   This procedure requires a blower with a capacity of 200 cubic feet per minute (0.09 cubic meter per second), equipped with a long, flexible ventilating tube about 8 inches (203 millimeters) in diameter that will extend well into the manhole. The blower should be located away from the manhole, preferably at a distance of about 10 feet (3 meters) and either downwind or crosswind to prevent troublesome combustible gases from reaching the engine or exhaust gases from being drawn into the manhole.

Breezes can be used to ventilate the manhole and sewer.   A metal or canvas hood that will deflect the breeze into the manhole can be mounted over the opening.   To encourage ventilation, the crew should remove adjacent manhole covers.

Potentially Dangerous Sewers

Sewers and manholes that can pose a risk to the life and health of personnel who work in them can be classified into four groups:

1. Any sewer laid to a grade of 0.4 percent or less.   This grade should produce a cleaning velocity in an 8-inch (203-millimeter) sewer when flowing half full.   More often than not, however, the flow will be less than this, and solids that decompose and generate troublesome gases will be deposited.

2. Sewers with runs of more than 300 feet (91 meters) between manholes and also those with inverted siphons.

3 Trunk sewers, particularly if they pass through industrial areas.

4. Sewers passing near gas mains or gasoline storage tanks.

Potentially Safe Sewers

Every manhole should be suspect, as should any pump wet well, sludge digestion tank, storage bin for incinerator refuse, or deep tank.   None of these should be entered without preliminary tests of the atmosphere in them.   However, if the sewer permits the waste water to flow freely, if there is no apparent evidence that the waste water has become septic, and if the holes in the manhole covers are open so that surface air can enter, aerobic conditions in the waste water probably exist, and no dangerous gases are present.

Safe Manhole and Sewer Illumination

If illumination is needed in a manhole or sewer, the lighting units should be explosion-proof as approved by the U.S. Bureau of Mines. On a sunny day, however, crews can use mirrors to reflect light into the manhole and even into the sewer itself, thus eliminating any chance of an explosive spark.

Safe Entry into a Manhole

Manholes generally are supplied with ladder rungs cast into the walls. However, the rungs often are made of steel that corrodes easily in the moist atmosphere. If this condition appears to exist, personnel should use a strong, sparkproof ladder.

Safety Belts

Safety belts should be required whenever workers enter a manhole with a depth greater than their shoulders. Use should not be made of a rope looped around a worker, since it can slip off and cause further harm to an injured worker who has dropped. The worker also may double up at the waist, making difficulties for the rescuers who attempt to pull the worker through the manhole opening.

The belt should be of a type that enables rescuers to lift the worker out in a vertical position. The supervisor should assign one worker at the surface for each worker in the manhole, instructing the one above

Figure 9-43 Personnel entering a manhole or a vault more than shoulder-deep should be equipped with a safety harness, and someone should be stationed at the surface to handle the safety rope. [Journal of the Water Pollution Control Federation, *February 1970*]

ground to hold the rescue rope and to see that the worker in the harness is in good condition.   One extra worker should be available at the surface in case help is needed.

Other Safety Guidelines

Atmospheric hazards are not the only safety factors involved in sewer work.   These guidelines should also be a part of the training program:

1. Instruct personnel not to raise their hands above the neck so as to eliminate the possibility of contamination entering the body through the mouth, nose, or eyes by way of the hands.

2. Provide workers with coveralls or similar outer garments to protect their regular clothes.   Supply them with rubber boots or nonsparking safety shoes.   Provide them with gloves, preferably rubberized to avoid scratches and abrasions.

3. If work involves a manhole in a remote location off the street, require all safety equipment to be transported to the manhole despite any inconvenience.   Workers often are tempted to enter manholes of this nature without safety equipment.   The result, unfortunately, has been injuries and deaths.

4. Insist that no smoking be permitted within the manhole or the sewer.

5. If high temperature and high humidity suddenly occur in a sewer or manhole, instruct personnel to leave at once.   Whenever the temperature rises above 100°F (37.7°C) in a humid atmosphere, oxygen deficiency starts to become a problem.   At 110°F (43.3°C) and 80 percent relative humidity, the oxygen will be depleted and workers can be expected to collapse if they are not removed promptly.[12]

6. If the atmosphere in the manhole can be combustible, do not use radio equipment in it.   Place a label on the radio equipment warning that it should not be used in a combustible atmosphere.

Rescue Work in a Manhole and Sewer

Despite all precautions, workers may be confronted with unexpected dangerous gases in sewers or manholes, and personnel must be trained to rescue the victims.   Rescuers must be equipped with safety hats, rubber or nonsparking footwear, nonsparking tools, and safety belts as well as respiratory equipment.

The *hose mask* is the most convenient to use and requires less training. It consists of a facepiece that fits snugly and a flexible hose leading to a good source of air.   The mask has a discharge valve that releases the respired breath.

---

[12] *Safety in Wastewater Works,* WPCF Manual of Practice No. 1, Water Pollution Control Federation, Washington, 1975.

If the atmosphere is not immediately hazardous to life and health, the mask will permit a rescue worker to operate within 25 feet (7.6 meters) of the source of air without the use of a blower or within 300 feet (91 meters) with a suitable blower.   When equipped with an *egress cylinder*, the rescue worker can operate in atmospheres that are immediately hazardous to life and health.   The air supply should be at least Grade D, ANSI Z86.1-1973, American National Standards Institute specifications for air.

An atmosphere that is not immediately hazardous to life and health will permit personnel to escape without the need for respiratory equipment.   Atmosphere that is immediately hazardous will not permit personnel to escape unaided.

Self-contained breathing apparatus should be preferred in any atmosphere that is immediately hazardous to life or health.   This equipment requires some training, and personnel should not do strenuous work when wearing it for more than a half hour.

Canister masks, gas masks, or similar filter respirators should *not* be used in manholes or sewers, especially in oxygen-deficient atmospheres. Such masks can block the entry of a specific gas, but they cannot provide oxygen if none is present.

The accompanying table lists and describes dangerous gases that may be encountered in sewers, manholes, pumping stations, and treatment plants.

RESTRICTIONS

Regulations on what should be carried in a sewer invariably place restrictions on liquid wastes contributed by industries connected to the sewer system.   At one time, such restrictions were basically a matter for decision by a particular industry and the local sewerage authority. Today, however, these industrial contributions are subject to federal law under the authority of EPA.   Since this is a relatively new agency trying to interpret and enforce laws passed by Congress, confusion gave rise to the impression that EPA did not wish industry to contribute anything to the public sewers and that industry would be better served by moving its plants out of cities, where a pool of skilled workers was available and goods and services, as well as transportation facilities, were conveniently located.

EPA has gone to a great deal of trouble to assure waste-water authorities that it endorses the contribution of industrial wastes to the public sewer system if the economics appear promising.[13]   It recom-

---

[13] *Pretreatment of Pollutants Introduced into Publicly Owned Treatment Works,* U.S. Environmental Protection Agency, October 1973, p. 7.

mends that industry attempt to reduce its in-plant water requirements, and thereby reduce its contribution to the public sewer system, and this suggestion has been beneficial to some localities. Steel mills have been heavy users of water and rather callous contributors of polluted wastewater containing troublesome amounts of suspended solids and iron and even small quantities of cyanide and phenol. The mills now recycle the water in a number of instances, presumably through EPA urging.[14]

Compatible and Incompatible Industrial Wastes

EPA requires pretreatment of an industrial waste if it contains "incompatible" pollutants. This means that the pollutants can damage the receiving waters but are not removed by normal treatment processes. A "compatible" pollutant is one that can be removed by a conventional plant; such pollutants are biochemical oxygen demand (BOD), fecal coliform bacteria, nitrates, phosphates, and possibly others.

EPA waives the need for pretreatment of incompatible industrial wastes if the authorities operating the sewerage system agree to provide special treatment that will remove these wastes sufficiently to leave their presence at acceptable levels. The city or sewerage authority is required by law to obtain from EPA a permit that acknowledges that these wastes exist in the waste water and that the treatment plant can remove them.

Major Contributing Industries

EPA restricts its concern with industrial wastes to what it classes as "major contributing industries." Such as industry is one connected to the sewer system that (1) contributes a flow of 50,000 gallons (189 cubic meters) or more per average day, or (2) has a flow greater than 5 percent of the flow in the collection system, or (3) contributes wastes containing certain toxic pollutants, or (4) imposes a significant impact on the quality of treatment that the plant can provide.

Prohibited Industrial Wastes

EPA has also established restrictions on certain wastes that it considers so incompatible that they should not be introduced into a sewer under any circumstances. The list includes:

1. Wastes that would create a fire or an explosive hazard either in the sewer or at the treatment plant.

2. Wastes that would cause corrosive damage at the treatment works. In no case should wastes with a pH of less than 5.0 be introduced unless the plant is specially designed to receive them safely.

[14] A. F. McClure, "Industrial Wastewater Recovery and Reuse," *Journal of the American Water Works Association,* April 1974, p. 240.

3. Solid or viscous wastes that will clog the sewer or interfere with the treatment process.

4. Wastes discharged on an excessively large batch basis.[15]

A city or a sewerage authority is entitled to adopt a more restrictive set of regulations if it so desires. Some restrictions suggest themselves.

Excessive temperatures in the wastes deserve restriction. Hot liquid wastes stimulate bacterial action in the sewer, where the atmosphere is dark and damp. This in turn makes the sewage septic and difficult to treat. It also can cause thermal stresses in the piping and loosen the joints in older pipe, inducing infiltration of groundwater. As related earlier, a high temperature and a humid atmosphere exhaust the oxygen in the air and make work in the sewer and manholes dangerous. A temperature restriction to a maximum of 150°F (65.5°C) as the waste water enters the sewer would seem logical. A temperature of 100°F (37.7°C) probably would be better for personnel who may have to work in the area.

EPA mentions restrictions on excessive acidity and names a minimum pH of 5.0. An alkalinity limit also would help prevent problems at the treatment works, and an upper limit of pH 9.5 should not be difficult to meet.

EPA makes general reference to the prohibition of wastes that would clog the sewer or interfere with the treatment process. Businesses and industries should be entitled to know what such wastes are. Common examples are cinders, sand, metal scrap, straw, glass, feathers, excessive amounts of eggshells as from a poultry house, oil, filling-station drainage, rags, petroleum products, waste synthetic rubber, bakery dough, and radioactive wastes.

Flammable and explosive materials generally are expensive, particularly now that energy costs have risen, and industry will not deliberately dispose of them through the sewers. Nevertheless, spills may occur, and to protect the community and its investment in its sewerage system and treatment plant, industry should be willing to install safety devices to ensure that these dangerous materials do not escape.

Toxic Materials

One must remember that almost any material is toxic or damaging if a person becomes exposed to too much of it. Toxic materials that should be kept out of the sewers are those that can be damaging at low concentrations. In this technologically innovative period, there are many new compounds whose toxicity must be appraised.

The toxicity of certain industrial wastes also relates to damage that the

---

[15] *Pretreatment of Pollutants Introduced into Publicly Owned Treatment Works*, U.S. Environmental Protection Agency, October 1973, Appendix A-3, pp. 128–131.

chemicals can do to the treatment process. Copper, for example, starts to inhibit or retard the aerobic metabolism when it is present in raw sewage in quantities greater than 1 milligram per liter. Lead becomes a problem at 0.1 milligram per liter. Boron, arsenic, chromium, nickel, and many others interfere with the healthy activity of aerobic and anaerobic bacteria.[16]

For the more familiar chemicals and compounds that should be prevented from entering the waste-water flow, limits probably should be established somewhat as follows:

Chemical Compound	Milligrams per Liter
Copper as Cu	0.5–1
Cyanide as HCN	0.1–2.0
Hexavalent chromium as Cr	1.0–3.0
Phenol	30

Each state or sewerage authority may have far more detailed and stringent standards. However, these may be considered a guide in understanding what should be allowed in the public sewer system and what should be restricted to avoid undue maintenance and costly problems at the treatment plant.

SEWER RODENT CONTROL

The most effective means of controlling rat populations is "source reduction," cutting off the rodents' supply of food, water, and places of harborage. If such a program can be pursued energetically and meticulously, it can completely eliminate the rodent population. However, for the sewer rat (*Rattus norvegicus*) this program is virtually impossible. The supply of food and water is continuous, and the places of harborage are many. So a bait program is the only alternative.

Rodent Characteristics

The sewer rat differs from its cousin, the roof rat (*Rattus rattus*), in several aspects. Both grow to lengths of 12 to 18 inches (305 to 457 millimeters) and are blackish brown. However, the roof rat spends its life aboveground, has large ears, a pointed nose, and a tail that is longer than its head and body. The sewer rat has small ears, a blunt nose, and a shorter tail. Sewer rats are generally heavier and more robust but less agile than the roof rats.

Both will live for 1 to 2½ years. At 4 months, the female will begin reproducing as many as six to ten litters per year, each with six to twelve offspring. Fortunately the mortality rate is high. Nevertheless, the overall population growth is substantial enough to force some of the

[16] Ibid., Appendix C.

rodents to seek food and living elsewhere.   As a consequence, they enter homes through the plumbing or by burrowing under foundations.   The damage they create not only is aesthetically objectionable but poses a health hazard through the spread of disease.

Poisoning Procedures

Obviously, an effective rodent control program depends on a careful poisoning attack that will keep the population low enough to prevent rats from feeling the need to leave the sewer environment.   Severe poisoning methods have been used.   One of the earlier methods made use of hamburger treated with sodium fluoracetate, known commercially as 1080, and required extremely careful supervision.   While the results were good, the bait tended to decompose rapidly and was effective for only a short period.   Its dangerous properties and its time-consuming factor made it ineffective in long-term control programs.

What is needed is a bait that is effective for an extended time after placement.   Also required are a bait station that cannot be flushed into the sewers and a bait that does not produce an immediate kill.   Rats are smart, and if the bait kills quickly, they will associate the bait with death.   If death is delayed, the rats will have difficulty in identifying it as the cause.   Bait placement should be altered periodically to help confuse the association.

Paraffin-impregnated Bait

A more effective and long-lasting bait program involves impregnating the bait in paraffin.   In 1958 Santa Clara, California, in conjunction with the county health department, developed a prepared bait containing 19 parts of whole rolled barley to 1 part of 0.5 percent Warfarin concentrate.[17]   A station using this type of bait requires a supply of prepared grain bait, some No. 10 cans, several pounds of paraffin, several 8- by 12-inch (203- by 279-millimeter) planks, a supply of wire, and a cooking unit.   For each station, approximately 2¾ pounds (1¼ kilograms) of the grain bait are mixed with approximately 1½ pounds (0.68 kilogram) of liquid paraffin and stirred in a No. 10 can.   To ensure a homogeneous mixture, the prepared grain and paraffin are added to the can in successive layers.   Each layer is allowed to solidify slightly before the next is added.

After the entire mixture has thoroughly solidified, the can is turned on its side and nailed to the rectangular plank; a length of wire is attached.   The station is then placed on the apron, or bench, in a manhole, and the loose wire is fastened to the wall with a concrete nail or

[17] Dean H. Ecke and S. M. Cristofano, "City-County Team Wins War on Rats," *The American City*, October 1959, pp. 104–105.

wound around one of the metal ladder rungs. A station of this type should make the bait supply available for several weeks. One should be sure to check the station for evidence of rodent activity before making the installation.

Commercial Bait

Because of the effectiveness of bait impregnated in paraffin, commercial suppliers now are ready to provide it.[18]   Currently it is available in blocks of several sizes. The large block is about 3½ by 6 by 1⅜ (89 by 152 by 35 millimeters) and weighs 1 pound (0.4536 kilogram). The bait can be produced in several flavors: fish, meat, and barley. Smaller blocks of prepared bait also are available.

These blocks have many advantages over stations prepared by the sewer-maintenance crews. They are uniform in concentration and are easily stored and transported. Moreover, they relieve crews of the time-consuming and tedious job of bait preparation.

---

[18] J. T. Eaton & Co., 10311 Meech Ave., Cleveland, Ohio 44105.

Characteristics of Common Gases Found in Sewers, Waste-water Pumping Stations,

Gas	Chemical formula	Common properties*	Specific gravity or vapor density (air = 1)	Physiological effect*
Carbon dioxide	CO_2	Colorless, odorless. When breathed in large quantities, may cause acid taste. Non-flammable. Not generally present in dangerous amounts unless an oxygen deficiency exists.	1.53	Cannot be endured at 10 percent for more than a few minutes, even if subject is at rest and oxygen content is normal. Acts on respiratory nerves.
Carbon monoxide	CO	Colorless, odorless, tasteless, flammable, Poisonous.	0.97	Combines with hemoglobin of blood. Unconsciousness in 30 minutes at 0.2 to 0.25 percent. Fatal in 4 hours at 0.1 percent. Headache in few hours at 0.02 percent.
Chlorine	Cl_2	Yellow-green color. Choking odor detectable in very low concentrations. Nonflammable.	2.49	Irritates respiratory tract. Kills most animals in very short time at 0.1 percent.
Gasoline	C_1H_{12} to C_1H_{20}	Colorless. Odor noticeable at 0.03 percent. Flammable.	3.0–4.0	Anesthetic effects when inhaled. Rapidly fatal at 2.4 percent. Dangerous for short exposure at 1.1 to 2.2 percent.
Hydrogen	H_2	Colorless, odorless, tasteless. Flammable.	0.07	Acts mechanically to deprive tissues of oxygen. Does not support life.
Hydrogen sulfide	H_2S	Rotten-egg odor in small concentrations. Exposure for 2 to 15 minutes at 0.01 percent impairs sense of smell. Odor not evident at high concentrations. Colorless. Flammable.	1.19	Impairs sense of smell rapidly as concentration increases. Death in few minutes at 0.2 percent. Exposure to 0.07 to 0.1 percent rapidly causes acute poisoning. Paralyzes respiratory center.
Methane	CH_4	Colorless, odorless, tasteless. Flammable.	0.55	Acts mechanically to deprive tissues of oxygen. Does not support life.
Nitrogen	N_1	Colorless, tasteless. Nonflammable. Principal constituent of air (about 79 percent).	0.97	Physiologically inert.
Oxygen (in air)	O_2	Colorless, odorless, tasteless. Supports combustion.	1.11	Normal air contains 20.8 percent. Man can tolerate down to 12 percent. Minimum safe 8-hour exposure, 14 to 16 percent. Below 10 percent dangerous to life. Below 5 to 7 percent probably fatal.
Sludge gas		May be practically odorless, colorless. Flammable.	Variable	Will not support life.

*Percentages shown represent volume of gas in air.
†Conforms to "Threshold Limit Values of Air-borne Contaminants for 1968," adopted at the Thirtieth Annual Meeting, American Conference of Governmental Industrial Hygienists, St. Louis, Mo., May 13, 1968.

Maximum safe 60-minute exposure (percent by volume in air)	Maximum safe 8-hour exposure (percent by volume in air)†	Explosive range (percent by volume in air)		Likely location of highest concentration	Most common sources
		Lower limit	Upper limit		
4.0–6.0	0.5			At bottom, when heated, may stratify at points above bottom.	Products of combustion sewer gas, sludge. Also issues from carbonaceous strata.
0.04	0.005	12.5	74.0	Near top, especially if present with illuminating gas.	Manufactured gas, flue gas, products of combustion, motor exhausts. Fires of almost any kind.
0.0004	0.0001			At bottom	Chlorine cylinder and feed-line leaks.
0.4–0.7	Varies,	1.3	6.0	At bottom.	Service stations, garages, storage tanks, houses.
		4.0	74.0	At top.	Manufactured gas, sludge digestion tank gas, electrolysis of water. Rarely from rock strata.
0.02–0.03	0.001	4.3	46.0	Near bottom, but may be above bottom if air is heated and highly humid.	Coal gas, petroleum, sewer gas. Fumes from blasting under some conditions. Sludge gas.
Probably no limit, provided oxygen percentage is sufficient for life.		5.0	15.0	At top, increasing to certain depth.	Natural gas, sludge gas, manufactured gas, sewer gas. Strata of sedimentary origin. Swamps or marshes.
				Near top, but may be found near bottom.	Sewer gas, sludge gas. Also issues from some rock strata.
				Variable at different levels.	Oxygen depletion from poor ventilation and absorption or chemical consumption of oxygen.
No data. Would vary widely with composition.		5.3	19.3	Near top of structure.	Digestion of sludge.

SOURCE: *Safety in Wastewater Works*, WPCF Manual of Practice No. 1, Water Pollution Control Federation, Washington, 1975.

Chapter Ten

Water-Distribution Maintenance

JOSEPH H. KURANZ

The primary purpose of a water utility, whether it is owned by the public or by private investors, is to supply water to the specific area served. While this purpose is basic, it is not complete. Those responding to the primary purpose, those managing and operating the water utility, perform their tasks to far more exacting specifications.

They provide a water that is bacteriologically and chemically safe, so

Figure 10-1 Water for public use, even when collected in beautiful mountain reservoirs like this one, still requires careful and often costly treatment before it is safe for distribution.

that an individual can drink it with confidence. They process the water to make it reasonably soft and also free from troublesome tastes and odors insofar as possible. And they make it available to their customers night and day, every day, under satisfactory and convenient pressures.

They provide the water in quantities that allow property holders to irrigate their lawns, fill their swimming pools, protect their homes and businesses from fire, and operate their businesses or industries. They perform this task at a very reasonable cost when it is compared with that of water supplied from other sources, such as bottled water or water in soft drinks, which still must be conveyed to the home.

Impact of the Water Utility on the Community

Some still argue that water is free, thinking of the easy access of water from a bubbling spring or the rain falling from the sky. But the water that the utility provides actually is a manufactured product. In the raw, untreated form, it is generally of unsafe and questionable quality and often is badly polluted. By scientific and skillfully designed methods the water utility removes these pollutants to exacting standards, and these methods continue to be improved to meet even more precise requirements.

On a volume basis, the water utility is the largest industry in a community. From the standpoint of maintaining the quality of life, it plays a restraining role in the urbanization of an area, since water resources have definite limitations that unfortunately are not recognized as widely as they should be.

Need for Good Distribution Maintenance

The water utility's distribution system accounts for 75 to 80 percent of its capital investment. Obviously, the utility will suffer costly waste at a time when resources need to be conserved if it produces water of high quality in ample volume, only to distribute it through a leaking and unreliable distribution system that can permit the entry of dangerous pollutants. A utility is wasteful if it spends money for chemicals to purify the water and for power to pump and transport it, only to learn that a substantial portion never reaches the customers but is lost as "unaccounted for" through leaks, badly maintained mains, and related defects.

Distribution-Maintenance Practices

This chapter should assist in preventing this unfortunate waste. In reviewing good practice, it will direct attention to the portions of the utility between the high-lift, or booster, pumps at the plant and the customers' service connections. All piping beyond these connections should be considered plumbing, and since they are on private property, the utility should not ordinarily trespass without full permission of the customers.

In most utilities, the distribution system involves these facilities:

- Pumping stations, including various high-lift pumps
- Storage tanks for the finished water
- Water mains
- Valves and hydrants
- Customer services, including meters

Maintenance requirements for each facility vary with the location of the utility, the topography, and other conditions evolving from local and state laws, codes, and regulations. Requirements for distribution-system maintenance are generally similar and can include construction methods and materials, weather conditions and ambient temperatures, pipeline surge, air, and water hammer, instrumentation and controls of pumping and pressures, the chemistry of the water, and soil conditions.

HIGH-LIFT PUMPING STATIONS

Most water utilities incorporate two separate and distinct pumping operations: low-lift pumping, from the source of supply to and through the treatment works; and high-lift pumping, which transports the treated water from the clear-water basin or well to the distribution system.

In the high-lift pumping station, a combination of pumps may be available to provide flows and pressures to separate high-service areas. Some systems may include high-lift pumping stations at a number of points in the distribution system where differences in elevation require repumping and separate storage capacity.

Depending on the thoroughness of the instrumentation, pumps may have automatic controls or be controlled from a central operating point. Frequently they have standby diesel or gasoline engines to provide continuity of service if the electric power fails.

Pumping-Station Buildings and Grounds

The water utility should give particular attention to the maintenance of the pumping-station buildings and grounds for two reasons. First, the public, the utility's customers, will have visible evidence of the competence of the operation and increased confidence in the utility's performance. Second, general thoroughness in housekeeping ensures the cleanliness of the pumps, motors, controls, and other appurtenances. This type of maintenance should not be left to chance; otherwise it will seldom be accomplished. A regularly scheduled procedure should be drawn up and assigned to appropriate personnel.

Figure 10-2 Pumping-station buildings and grounds that are attractive and show evidence of care give the public confidence in the reliability and safety of this important urban service.

Since high-lift pumping stations include a variety of equipment, such as pumps, piping networks including valves of various types, telemetering controls, meters, electrical control panels, electric substations, and similar items, the maintenance procedures associated with them are covered separately below.

Surge, Air, and Water-Hammer Problems

Many maintenance problems in distribution systems, particularly those concerned with surge, air, and water hammer, are traceable to high-lift pumps. For a pump to be operated and maintained efficiently, it must be installed to prudent and well-established engineering designs. Incorporated in these designs should be locations where maintenance personnel can have ready and convenient access for inspection and servicing.

Pump suction- and discharge-piping arrangements are primarily the responsibility of the design engineer. They should conform to good engineering practices, which require that piping networks be as simple and as short as is practicable. The accompanying drawings (Figures 10-3 and 10-4) indicate correct and incorrect methods of installing pump suction and discharge piping.

Pump alignment is also very important. It can easily be checked by placing a straightedge across the top and sides of the coupling. Parallel alignment can be determined by means of a set of feeler gauges. The pump is properly aligned when the measurement between the coupling faces is the same at all points and when the straightedge lies squarely

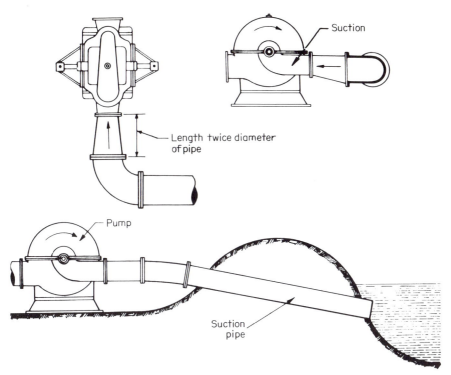

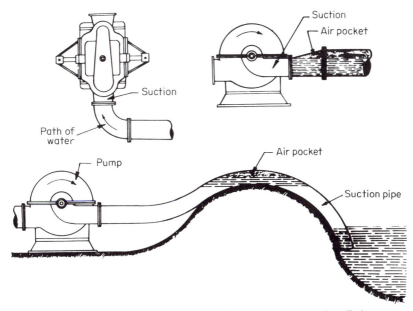

Figure 10-3 This drawing shows the essentials of correct pump installation that ensure good operation.

Figure 10-4 Common errors such as those in this incorrect pump installation cause faulty pump operation.

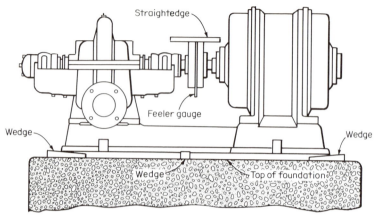

Figure 10-5 The pump and motor must be aligned perfectly for good operation. The alignment can be checked by a straightedge and a feeler gauge.

across the rims at any point (see Figure 10-5). Alignment must be rechecked after all the piping has been attached to the pump.

The design and installation must provide adequate and reliable support for the suction and discharge piping. This support will prevent straining the pump, thereby causing misalignment, hot bearings, worn couplings, and vibration.

Pump Air Problems

Suction lines must be sized correctly and installed properly to avoid air problems. Despite these and other precautions, however, it is necessary to provide some means of removing air from the suction and discharge outlets of the pumps.

If a pump operates under a suction head, care must be taken to assure that the air is vented from the top of the pump case. This can be accomplished manually or through an automatic vent valve.

If the pump operates with a suction lift, a satisfactory priming system must be provided. Such a system may utilize a foot valve on the suction line or, preferably, a vacuum pump system (see Figure 10-7). Since failure of a priming system could seriously damage a pump, regular checking by the operator is important.

Pump Packing and Bearing Maintenance

The rate of leakage through packing should be observed daily. Packing glands should never be tightened to the point at which there is no leakage, since this will cause premature packing wear and scored shaft sleeves.

New rings should be installed when the packing wears to the degree that the gland cannot be tightened further. The vendor's manual

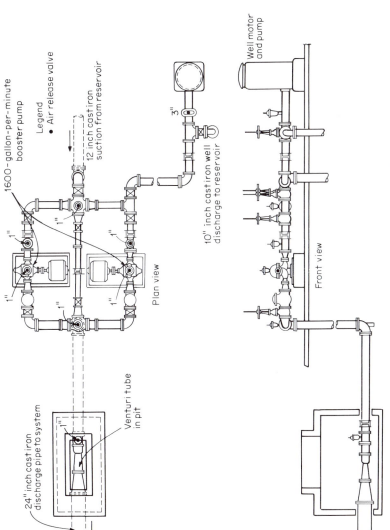

Figure 10-6 This drawing shows the proper location of air and vacuum release valves to remove air effectively on the suction and discharge lines of a typical booster pumping station.

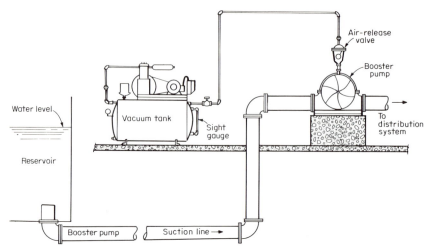

Figure 10-7 When a pump operates under a suction lift, trapped air can be vented by a vacuum system.

provides information on the proper size, material, and number of rings to be used. New rings should not be added on top of old ones.

Pump bearings should be adequately lubricated in accordance with the manufacturer's recommendations but should never be overlubricated. Excessive grease may cause overheating, and too much oil may generate foaming.

Water-Hammer Prevention

Most high-lift pump discharge-piping networks include a check valve and a gate valve near the pump discharge. These valves protect against backflow and provide a means of repairing the pump and controlling the rate of flow. The gate valve, of course, should not be used to control the flow rate. This type of valve is not suited to a throttling operation, since the velocity of flow against a partially opened wedge can cause chattering, damage to seating surfaces, and undesirable erosion effects called "cutting." If there is any possibility of creating high-pressure surge or water hammer, the discharge valve should be closed slowly before stopping the pump. The reverse sequence would be used when restarting the pump; that is, after the pump has been started, the valve should be slowly opened until the full flow is reached. This procedure may be accomplished by using butterfly, ball, or similar types of valves with appropriate controls.

Figure 10-8 shows a ruptured section of a 20-inch (508-millimeter) cast-iron water main. Air- and vacuum-release valves properly located and installed in the pump section and discharge piping and the distribution-system mains adjacent to the break, together with an

Figure 10-8 Water hammer must be controlled to prevent damage to pipelines.

automatically controlled butterfly-valve system, eliminate this serious air, surge, and water-hammer problem.

When high-lift pumps are properly installed, maintenance problems may be reduced, in their simplest terms, to lubrication, checking the packing, and cleaning.

STORAGE TANKS

High-lift pumps usually discharge into some type of elevated tank, standpipe, or reservoir. The number and type of tanks employed are functions of design and economics. For our purposes, it will be assumed that the two basic materials most commonly used in the erection of these tanks are concrete and steel. Each type of structure and material presents its own problems.

Concrete Tanks

A properly designed and constructed concrete tank generally presents fewer maintenance problems than does one of a comparable steel variety with its affinity for corrosion. Most concrete tanks are built to a prestressed design, and the more reliable types utilize a steel liner in the wall.

Despite this apparent advantage, however, concrete tanks are susceptible to damage from rapid and severe temperature fluctuations and thus occasionally require varying degrees of maintenance. Keeping a concrete tank free of leaks presents a challenge to those responsible for

Figure 10-9 Prestressed concrete tanks such as this reservoir that holds 1,500,000 gallons (5,678 cubic meters) can be made architecturally attractive and in harmony with the neighborhood.   Note the tennis court on the top.

distribution maintenance.   Such leaks not only are points of weakness but also create aesthetic problems not associated with steel.

Steel Tanks

The control of corrosion is a constant problem with steel tanks, but the use of cathodic protection equipment and techniques will reduce corrosion if the equipment is properly designed, installed, and maintained. The electrolytic anodes used may or may not be expendable.   If they

Figure 10-10 When built to attractive designs, elevated tanks can enhance the appearance of a community.

are expendable, a regular replacement program should be established. As a rule, in Northern states anodes are replaced each spring since they often are damaged by icing conditions in the tank.

Prevention of Freeze Damage

Long periods of subfreezing temperatures can create serious problems in elevated storage tanks. Most of these problems can be prevented simply by raising or lowering the water level of the tank, thus circulating the warmer distribution water through it. The risk associated with this practice is apparent. Not only does it lower the distribution-system pressure, creating the possible hazards of lack of pressure in the outer portions of the system and of introducing pollution through a negative pressure situation, but it also reduces the available storage at a time when the municipality is most vulnerable to fires. Consequently, raising and lowering the water level in the storage tank must be practiced cautiously.

Nevertheless, ignoring the ice in reservoirs may result in serious structural damage. Ice should not be permitted to form. Appropriate electrical heating devices may be used to prevent its formation, but they are costly to operate and maintain. In addition, crews can be assigned to break the ice.

Another practical method is to enlarge the distribution area served by the tank by means of valving, thus imposing a greater demand upon the storage facilities. This procedure requires higher pumping rates to maintain levels in the tank and the introduction of warmer water that melts the ice.

Painting Steel Tanks

Painting and repainting steel tanks, standpipes, and reservoirs should be scheduled in accordance with standards set by the American Water Works Association. A utility should be wary when selecting a contractor to perform this service. A number of unqualified operators advertise themselves as experts but more often than not fail to meet expert qualifications. If in doubt, it is a good idea to seek the advice and counsel of the firm that erected the storage facility.

Tanks should be overflowed occasionally to check the accuracy of the altitude-gauge system. Overflowing also removes surface films and provides a test of the network of overflow and drainage piping.

WATER-MAIN MAINTENANCE

As mentioned above, a utility's investment in its distribution system, and especially in its water mains, often represents a major portion of its capitalization. Nevertheless, many utilities cut corners to effect unreal savings. Although management should always be interested in econ-

Figure 10-11 Many water-main problems can be traced to faulty installation.

omy, this interest does not suggest that weak, inferior, and unreliable materials and construction practices should be tolerated merely to make an immediate saving.

Most water-main problems are traceable to main installation. To avoid these problems, many utilities favor force-account work, with the main being installed directly under the supervision of the utility's engineer and inspector. However, with proper designs and specifications and rigid inspection procedures, reputable contractors can accomplish the same results. Nevertheless, despite the care exercised, water-main failures remain one of the commonest problems of distribution systems.

Bedding

A survey covering forty water-main breaks in a city of medium size revealed that older pipe laid by hand digging and backfilling performed better than pipe installed in a similar manner but with machines. The best performance was obtained from pipe laid on a crushed-stone bed. From a study of these results, the utility specified that all future main construction follow these standards:

1. Bed and cover all pipe in crushed stone.
2. Avoid areas where cinder or slag fill exist.
3. Use compressed rubber joint material, such as the mechanical or slip type, rather than the lead-caulked variety.
4. Provide a qualified waterworks inspector on all new main construction projects to assure that the specifications are adhered to.

It is possible that soil conditions in other areas would dictate a revision of these standards, since more of the pipe in the survey was placed at a depth of 6 feet (1.8 meters) in heavy red clay. Nevertheless, the utility's experience emphasizes the importance of proper bedding of pipe to suit specific geological conditions.

Backfill Control by Nuclear Soil-Density Meter

Prevention of backfill settlement has always been a problem, generally solved by the use of granular backfill and by flooding the trenches. However, more convenient techniques are now available. The most promising involves a nuclear meter that is simple to use and remarkably accurate and that can measure both the soil density and the moisture quickly. All water utilities have recognized the importance of soil mechanics, but until this meter became available, soil-density determinations were laborious, time-consuming, and costly.

The method is simple. The soil density is determined before the trench is excavated. The backfill must then be placed in 1-foot (0.3-meter) lifts compacted to the equivalent of the preexcavation density or within 10 percent of it. Since the backfilled soil will now be comparable to the natural soil, settlement should not occur.[1]

Pressure and Weather Damage

A substantial increase in water-main failures recorded by a large municipal water utility was blamed in great measure on severe cold-weather conditions. Frost penetrated farther than expected, and the

[1] For a more detailed description of the nuclear soil-density meter, see Chapters 1 and 9.

Figure 10-12 Failures in water mains vary from pinholes to openings of half the circumference of the pipe.

frost caused the soil to heave.   However, failures of older mains were confined to deterioration, usually in the form of holes varying from the size of a pin to half the circumference of the pipe.   When several failures of this type occur at or about the same time, the cause usually can be traced to sharp pressure rises.   The condition of the pipe in the failure areas suggested the presence of electrolysis.

While a few of the deterioration-type failures were found in pipe less than 15 years old, the majority of the failures in the older mains were of the transverse type.   Where practical, this utility employed stainless-steel clamps, ductile clamps, and mechanical joint repair sleeves to restore these damaged pipes to service.   Failures of pipe in the 12-inch (204.8-millimeter) and 16-inch (406.4-millimeter) sizes were usually of the longitudinal type; replacement of at least 6 feet (1.8 meters) and, in some cases, of a full length of pipe was necessary.

Joint Damage

Joints made of sulfur compounds have caused this utility some concern. While joints of this type no longer are used, many still remain in older pipes.   A chemical action apparently causes the iron at the face of the joint and on the inside of some bells to deteriorate.   To correct this condition, the utility repoured some joints and caulked them with lead, applied bell-joint clamps to the pipes of larger sizes, and cut out the sulfur-compound joints in the smaller mains, replacing them with new bell-and-spigot pipes and sleeves and with lead joints.

Water-Hammer Correction

The most vexing problem encountered by a small municipally owned water utility is water-main breaks.   Most of them occur just after periods of unusually heavy demand; for example, six breaks occurred in the 10 days after a Thanksgiving weekend.   The utility's conclusion is that the breaks result from comparatively large fluctuations in pressure, leading to water hammer in the broad sense of the term.

Much of the distribution system in the utility consists of 4-inch (101.6-millimeter) pipe that experiences high friction head loss during periods of heavy demand, with resulting loss of pressure in much of the system.   Following the periods of heavy demand, the static line pressure rapidly returns to normal, and this rapid return undoubtedly creates the surge conditions, particularly at the undersize dead ends of the distribution system.   Little difficulty has been experienced in the portion of the distribution system consisting of water mains of 6 inches (152.4 millimeters) or more in diameter.

Water-Hammer Remedies

Although there is no simple way to prevent water hammer, measures can be taken to reduce and possibly to eliminate the problem.   One measure is to locate the high points within the larger trunk lines and distribution-system mains and to install appropriately sized air-release valves or air and vacuum valves, or both. Another is to install additional air-release valves at the pump discharge and in the proper locations within the piping network adjacent to the pumps. A third is to replace spring-loaded swing check valves with automatic units such as butterfly valves. Still another is to check the size of taps used. For example, the maximum permissible size in the pipe barrel of Class 150 Super de Lavaud cast-iron pipe, 6 inches (152.4 millimeters) in diameter, used without a saddle, is 1 inch (25.4 millimeters). If the maximum is exceeded in this class, failure can occur near such areas.

Hydrants located on these lines can aggravate the problem if they are closed rapidly after use. It is surprising to learn how few firemen, contractors, and city workers are aware of this fact.

Flushing

A water-distribution system should be flushed at least once a year. The most practical procedure is simply to open the hydrants, one at a time, throughout the distribution system until the water is clear.

To obtain optimum results, the utility should develop an organized procedure for flushing, and regardless of the procedure all programs should include the flushing of dead-end mains. An effective organized procedure, entailing more extensive planning and longer time, involves dividing the distribution system into a number of areas. Depending on

Flushing schedule hydrants

Observer _____

Date	Location	Make	Time Opened	Time Closed	Average pressure (lbs)	Diameter of opening (inches)	Discharge (gallons)	Remarks
10/9/77	Moreland north of Lindbergh	Darling	12:08	12:52	5	4 7/16	51,000	Brown
10/9/77	Motor east of Moreland	Darling	12:55	1:27	9	4 7/16	52,000	Brown
10/9/77	Washington north of Moreland	Darling	1:33	2:00	6	4 1/2	35,000	Light Brown
10/9/77	Motor west of Greenwood	Eddy	2:05	2:30	11	4 1/2	44,000	Light Brown
10/9/77	St. Paul west of Washington	Eddy	2:40	2:50	2	4 7/16	7,000	Clear
10/9/77	St. Paul east of Washington	Eddy	2:53	3:10	8	4 7/16	26,000	Fair
10/9/77	Motor west of Fairview	Eddy	3:15	3:30	23	2 3/8	10,000	Clear
10/9/77	Lindbergh and Hine	Darling	3:35	3:53	3	4 7/16	18,000	Light Brown
10/9/77	Washington south of Dopp	Darling	4:00	4:10	1	4 7/16	5,000	Clear
						Total:	248,000	

Figure 10-13 Work sheets of this type assist in main-flushing operations. For best results, flushing should reverse the normal flow in the main.

Main flushing plan

Section_____

Valves

Location	Size inch	Closed		Setting	
		Right	Left	Man-hole	Valve box
Lawndale east of Caldwell	6	20		x	
Fairview north of American	6	16		x	
American west of Fairview	6	20		x	
Greenwood north of Dopp	6	20		x	
Washington north of Dopp	6	20		x	
St Paul east of Fairview	6	22			x
Marshall east of State	6	22		x	

Hydrants

Location	No.
Moreland north of Lindbergh	428
Motor east of Moreland	429
Washington north of Motor	425
St Paul west of Washington	435
Motor west of Greenwood	424
State Street south of St Paul	436
St Paul east of Moreland	431

Industrial and commercial customers notified:
    Waukesha motor works
    Spring city foundry
    Waukesha memorial hospital

Note: Do not run Moreland station while flushing this section.

Figure 10-14 Knowing the sizes of the valves, their location, and the way in which they turn to close is important for water-main maintenance.

the particular distribution system, these areas could include from 1 to 3 miles (from 1.6 to 4.8 kilometers) of water mains.

The crew first isolates the area to be flushed from the rest of the distribution system by closing appropriate valves, leaving one open through which the water is to be supplied. Hydrants then are opened in a planned pattern so that water enters from a desired direction at a high velocity. The proper selection and opening of the hydrants provide a reversal of flow, which further agitates the solids in the mains and assures their removal. This procedure minimizes the possibility of disturbing areas other than the one being flushed.

One such section should be flushed each night until the entire distribution system has been covered. Daily newspaper and radio notices identifying the areas scheduled for a particular night should provide customers with sufficient information to meet their interests. The work sheets shown in Figures 10-13, 10-14, and 10-15 are typical of those that can be used advantageously by a flushing crew. The sheets should be turned in to the utility's office for recording at the completion of each night's work.

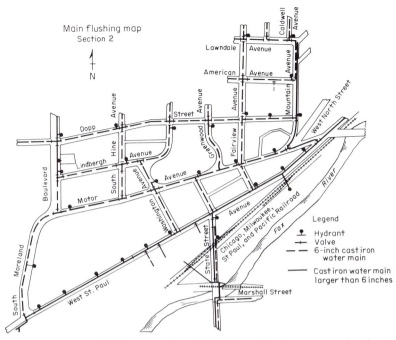

Figure 10-15 Flushing operations should be confined to areas embracing 1 to 3 miles (1.6 to 4.8 kilometers) of mains.

Types of Water Mains

Water utilities today can use pipe manufactured from many different materials and be assured that all will work well. Among the commonest materials in modern systems are cast and ductile iron, asbestos cement, steel, plain and reinforced concrete, and plastic, a relative newcomer to the field. Each pipe material has its advantages and disadvantages, and such factors as maximum water pressures to be encountered, trench loadings, aggressive soil conditions, and special installations in locations under streams, on bridges, and beneath highways or railroad beds will determine the most appropriate one.

Cast-Iron and Ductile-Iron Pipe Both types of iron pipe are very strong and have had a long history of reliable use. Ductile iron can absorb shocks and accept dents without fracture, while the cast-iron type and many other kinds of pipe cannot do so. However, both types are subject to electrolytic decomposition if they are placed in aggressive soils. Most utilities prefer iron pipe to be lined with cement mortar or a bituminous material.

Asbestos-Cement Pipe This type of pipe has a very smooth interior, giving it excellent flow characteristics. It should be placed and bedded carefully to prevent soil movement and consequent fracture of the pipe.

Steel Pipe   Steel pipe customarily is used in large-diameter transmission mains.   It is very strong, requires special couplings, and should be thoroughly protected with bituminous coatings both inside and out. Cement linings also can be used on the interior.

Concrete Pipe   This type of pipe also is customarily used in the larger sizes for transmission mains.   Plain concrete pipe, without prestressing, can be employed if it does not have to withstand excess pressures.   The prestressed type can be built to withstand very high pressures and is an excellent choice for this type of service.

Plastic Pipe   Plastic pipe does not have a particularly long service history.   If it is a single-wall pipe, it should be bedded and backfilled with care to prevent settlement and deformation of the pipe.   The plastic is relatively inert and should resist electrolytic decomposition. The interior should remain smooth and retain good flow characteristics.   If it can carry the imposed backfill loads and with stand some soil deformation, it should be very serviceable.

Repair and Maintenance

A certain amount of water-main repair and maintenance work is unavoidable, and a stock of repair items should be carried.   The maintenance and repair of water mains generally involve the following:

- Water-main breaks and emergency repairs
- Disinfection of water mains
- Pipe cleaning
- Cross-connection control
- Leak detection
- Corrosion control

Maintenance crews must be well organized and equipped with tools and repair items to cope with any of these situations.   The particular procedures and techniques to be followed are best learned through on-the-job experience, reading the various periodicals covering these subjects, studying manuals of practice issued by the professional associations and governmental agencies in the waterworks field, or attending appropriate short courses, seminars, and professional meetings of groups such as the American Water Works Association.

Cleaning   Cleaning is important in maintaining the flow capacity of water mains.   If the distribution system consists chiefly of cast-iron or ductile-iron pipes and the water is aggressive, tuberculation can take place, especially if the lining has lost its effectiveness.   Moreover, carbonate incrustation can occur with water high in carbonates.

Professional firms can be retained to remove tubercules and incrustations under contract.   Also a water utility can purchase the cleaning unit known as a "go-devil" or a "pig" and clean the mains with its own maintenance crew.

Figure 10-16 Tuberculation on the inner walls of water mains greatly reduces their capacity.

Cross-Connection Control   The control of cross-connections is a subject that haunts all conscientious water utilities. The distribution system ranges over a wide area, and the danger of cross-connections can be equally widespread.

The opportunities for cross-connections that involve the municipality itself probably are the easiest to control, but they must be watched. Sewer-maintenance crews may flush a sewer by connecting a fire hose to a hydrant and inserting the hose directly in the sewage flow. At the sewage-treatment plant, the pumps may be connected directly to the potable water supply for priming purposes, and the gate valve separating the flows may leak. Occasionally personnel at the treatment plant may drop a hose that is flowing into a settling tank. A drop in water pressure can siphon this waste water into the distribution system and create a hazardous condition.

On private property, the situation is more troublesome because the utility lacks easy access for inspection. Automatic car washes have occasionally pumped detergent solutions into the distribution system. Toilet facilities on the top floors of apartment houses and office buildings have occasionally contaminated the water supply through back siphonage. Incidents have occurred in hospitals and in asphalt mix plants in which recirculated water has been drawn into the potable supply through a drop in pressure.

Basic to the control of back siphonage are a legal enforcement document, good records, and knowledgeable personnel who can recognize danger points and also a list of backflow-prevention devices whose reliability can be guaranteed.

Leak Detection   The detection of leaks is a task that can be performed by an outside professional organization specializing in this type of work. Often such organizations can earn their fees simply by eliminating the sources of wasted water, since water pumped but not paid for by the customer represents lost revenue.

For the day-to-day detection of leaks, various types of audio equipment can be used to magnify the sound of running water when the equipment is placed on a hydrant, valve, or exposed pipeline. Evidence of leaks also can show on the surface, expecially in winter, in melted snow. However, not all water leaking from a main comes to the surface, nor does it always come to the surface directly above the leak. The water may follow a main for a considerable distance before flowing upward.

Figure 10-17 The detection of leaks can involve a variety of devices that listen for the sound of escaping water.

VALVES

In maintaining a distribution system, a utility crew often must stop or control the flow of water into, through, or from a pipeline. This is accomplished by valves. Because of the variety of conditions encountered, such as pressures and temperatures, valves vary greatly in design. Special purposes often require automatic valve control.

The *gate valve* is the type most commonly used. When open, it permits a straight-line flow without any throttling effect and with a minimum of pressure drop. A gate valve is known as a rising-stem type if it has been designed so that the stem does not turn but is threaded through the handwheel and is raised or lowered as the wheel operates. In a nonrising-stem valve, the stem rotates in the bonnet but is restrained from rising or falling and is threaded into the gate so that the gate goes up or down when the wheel is turned. Both types are used in waterworks operation, but the nonrising valve is more generally found in distribution systems.

The *butterfly valve* is supplanting the gate valve in many critical areas of a distribution system. The gate valve must force the gate down against the full pressure of the flowing water, and this can be very difficult. When larger mains are involved, the procedure requires "valving down" or closing upstream valves as much as possible to lower the pressure at the valve being closed. The butterfly valve uses a disc that rotates on an axis rather than a gate that must be forced down to stop the flow. Since the disc rotates, the water pressure balances and permits easy rotation. However, this type of valve puts an obstruction in the pipeline and causes some pressure drop. It also offers an obstacle to the easy cleaning of the line.

Distribution-System Valve Problems

Distribution-system valve problems include location, accessibility, and maintenance. The number and location of valves in a particular distribution system, while primarily a function of design, should nevertheless conform to the recommendations of the Insurance Services Office. A sufficient number should be provided so that no single casualty will necessitate shutting down a length of pipe in excess of 500 feet (152.4 meters) or affect the operation of a main trunk or transmission line.

This can usually be accomplished by installing at least three valves at each intersecting city street. However, the effectiveness of an adequate valve-distribution system is appreciably reduced when emergency and maintenance crews cannot locate the valves within a reasonable time. A good record of the location of all valves, coupled with a uniform policy of specifying their initial location such as property line, curb line, sidewalk line, and the like, reduces the time required to find them when emergencies arise.

Valve Accessibility   The necessity of being able to locate a valve when it is needed is apparent, but it is of little value to find a valve with the intention of using it and learn that it is inaccessible. Valves are enclosed in vaults or in valve boxes. The type of enclosure employed is a matter of preference and economics. While vaults are more accessible, considerable savings can be realized by employing boxes.

Perhaps the commonest frustrations in dealing with valve boxes occur when they have filled with dirt and debris or have shifted position. While one can usually clean a valve box with simple hand tools, a shifted box often must be exposed to facilitate its realignment. Under such circumstances, it is advisable to repack the valve at the same time. Manholes also are vulnerable to filling and flooding, but cleaning them is less difficult and would not, as a rule, restrict the operation of the valve.

Manhole covers often present problems, particularly when they must be raised or lowered slightly to meet changed pavement grades. Riser rings are used by some utilities, while others prefer to dig up and raise the entire frame to the new grade. In winter manhole covers often freeze in place, but an application of any antifreeze will usually free them.

Valve Inspection The problems of distribution-system maintenance are perhaps most acute in valves, but trouble can be avoided if a good inspection program is adopted. Scheduled routine inspections and preventive and corrective maintenance programs are major responsibilities. Such inspections should not be put off until other jobs have been completed or personnel are available; they should be done continuously to the exclusion of all other work except emergencies. Therefore, for a waterworks to initiate an inspection program, records should be prepared for every valve in the system.

Figure 10-18 is a suggested field form that can be used by crews conducting a valve survey. The information provided can be transferred to permanent records by others.

Valve Maintenance The most important procedure in valve maintenance is to operate each valve at least once a year. However, it is necessary to have good records that define the operating characteristics of particular valves, such as the number of turns and the direction to close. Without such information, one would not know whether a valve were performing correctly or not.

To facilitate operation, some utilities stencil this information on the underside of the cover. The arguments in favor of standardizing the direction of valve closure are strong, particularly for distribution valves. Carried one step farther, such standardization should be advocated on a national basis.

There are arguments both for and against the use of automatic valve operators. Units are available that can operate either pneumatically or electrically.

Since most distribution-system valves are seldom called upon to perform their function of control but still must be ready to perform it, it is imperative that a utility establish a definite inspection and maintenance program to ensure that the valves can function when they are needed.

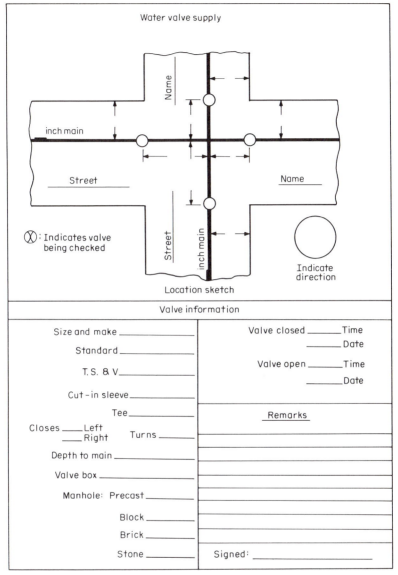

Figure 10-18 Valves should be inspected on a regular schedule and the results recorded on a form such as this.

HYDRANTS

One water-utility manager said lightheartedly but nonetheless accurately that hydrants have five prime functions:

    1. A focal point for every dog in the neighborhood

    2. A target for drunken drivers out after 2 A.M. on a cold Sunday morning

3. A convenient recreation center for ghetto children on a hot day
4. An outlet for water used to extinguish fires
5. The means of flushing the distribution system

All the utility's resources, both physical and economic, are ultimately directed to the fire hydrant. It stands as a constant reminder to the public that a water system is available to protect its families and properties.

Hydrants should be located in accordance with procedures established by the Insurance Services Office. The service main to the hydrant should be at least 4 inches (101.6 millimeters) in diameter and preferably a minimum of 6 inches (152.4 millimeters). A gate valve should be located on the lead-out to the hydrant so that if the hydrant is damaged or in need of repair, the valve can be closed while repairs are being accomplished and water service will not be interrupted.

Fire hydrants need occasional inspection. If properly maintained and inspected, they create little trouble, but they can become inoperative if

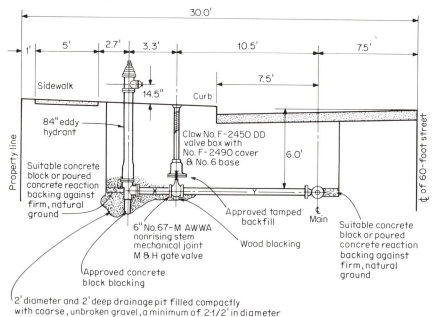

Standard cross section of 60-foot street shown

For 60 foot street
X = 2.5 foot plain ends
Y = 9.5 plain ends
For all other types of streets, cut X & Y to suit.

For 50 ft street
X = 2 foot plain ends
Y = 7.5 foot plain ends

The 14-1/2 inch clearance from the centerline of the steamer nozzle discharge to the ground must be within plus or minus 1 inch. X or Y may be deflected to obtain this distance. However, joint deflection must not exceed the AWWA standards. The hydrant must be plumb, and the 2- to 2-1/2 inch hose nozzle must be parallel to the street.

Figure 10-19 A typical hydrant installation should include a valve and be placed as in this general diagram.

they are allowed to go unattended. Many persons think that because a fire hydrant is used infrequently, it will always be ready to serve. This is not true, and any operator who justifies a poor maintenance and inspection program on this basis is performing a disservice. Moving parts need to be operated occasionally to keep them functioning.

A fire hydrant must be installed correctly if it is to provide trouble-free service. Figure 10-19 depicts a standard installation procedure. Each phase of the installation is important if reliable operation and maintenance are to be realized. The portion of the installation most often neglected is the provision of a good drainage bed. The procedure indicated in the diagram is one that works well in appropriate soils. However, each utility should establish its own standards to fit particular soil conditions.

If possible, a utility's hydrants should be standardized. This precaution will reduce the diversity of spare parts required and simplify the training of maintenance personnel.

Problems involving hydrants can be grouped under the following headings: (1) location, (2) authorized and unauthorized uses, (3) training in proper use, (4) identification, (5) snow removal, and (6) inspection and repair.

Location

No hydrant location seems satisfactory to all residents or all business and commercial areas. Experience seems to indicate that corner locations are vulnerable to traffic accidents and that locations in the middle of blocks create problems in public relations. One exasperated utility manager suggested that the ideal hydrant is one on wheels that can be placed close enough so that a resident can get favorable insurance rates and then be wheeled away so that it will not be in front of the resident's home.

Many utilities place hydrants on the property lines of adjacent lots. Despite the procedures used, conflicts of interest inevitably arise, particularly when private driveways are involved. Under these conditions, the property owner usually requests that the hydrant be moved. If the hydrant has been placed in accordance with an approved procedure meeting general public approval prior to the property owner's complaint, some utilities offer to move the hydrant if the complainant pays the cost of removal and offers no objection to the hydrant's being relocated in front of his or her property. The complainant usually withdraws the request upon learning of the cost involved.

Authorized and Unauthorized Uses

No one questions the authority of the appropriate fire department to use the hydrants, since fire protection is the hydrants' primary function.

However, others request permission to use this convenient source of water, and utilities must develop policies to govern this use.   Among those wishing to utilize water from fire hydrants are contractors, circuses, carnivals, and other organizations that promote public gatherings of various types.   Others include municipal departments such as parks, playgrounds, street cleaning, sewer maintenance, and, at times, road and street maintenance.   Such uses, while they should be discouraged, nevertheless should be permitted under controlled conditions.

Private groups such as circuses and carnivals should be required to pay a deposit covering the use of an appropriately sized meter, connections, and hydrant wrench.   When the engagement is over, the deposit can be returned, less an amount attributable to the water used, recorded through the meter, and to any required repairs on the meter, appurtenances, and hydrant.

Public groups such as city departments should be required to meter the water used or at least to measure it so that the utility can account for water pumped.   Fire departments also should have some means of measuring the water used, and in case of major fires someone from the water utility should be on hand.

Pranksters and others often are attracted to hydrants and find ways to open them and let them flow, even though this practice lowers the pressure and greatly increases the fire risk.   The smaller utilities are not often faced with this problem, but the larger ones in metropolitan areas frequently are plagued with general outbreaks of this type.   Some large utilities have tried to ease the situation by providing spray nozzles that reduce the loss of water while still providing local play activity.   Others have placed clamps over the hydrants that the firemen must cut off before using them.   For most utilities, however, more vigorous enforcement of the laws prohibiting this waste of water appears to be the best way to control the problem.

Training in Proper Use

Firemen should receive special training in how a hydrant functions and how it should be operated to avoid difficulties.   Even after the training, a prudent utility manager should discuss these procedures with the fire chief to reemphasize their importance, since hydrants that operate reliably are vital to the effective functioning of the fire department.

Qualified waterworks personnel should demonstrate the correct operating techniques to all who receive authority to use the hydrants. The instruction should emphasize the importance of closing them slowly.

Identification

Hydrants may be identified by their color.   Different color combinations may denote flow and pressure characteristics.   Hydrants should be painted regularly if for no other reason than to assure the public that the utility is not neglecting its responsibilities.   Repainting is a very inexpensive measure in public relations.

To protect and identify hydrants at night, it is good practice to use reflective paint or reflective stripes, or both.   Some utilities simply sprinkle reflective particles on newly painted hydrants.   This practice has the added advantage of refuting the arguments of motorists who park near hydrants and claim that they did not see them.

Snow Removal

The removal of snow from hydrants so that firemen can locate them easily often presents problems, particularly as to responsibility.   When plows clear the streets after a snowfall, they often cover the hydrants. To avoid legal complications and to assure the public that the water utility is responding to its responsibilities, utility crews should be assigned to this task.   However, many communities approach the problem in other ways.   Some place the responsibility on the property owners, who should have an interest in seeing that hydrants are accessible for their own protection.   Some assign the task to the fire or police departments, or to both, while others use unemployed or part-time workers or even Boy Scouts for this work.

Inspection and Repair

The importance of a regular hydrant inspection and maintenance program cannot be overemphasized.   Perhaps the most vital aspect of this program involves checking the opening and closing functions, the drainage operation, and the condition of the threads on the nozzles.   As the leather cap washers age, they often harden and can easily be cut and damaged by the nozzle, sometimes leaving small pieces on the lip that can foul the fire department's equipment.

Plastic washers that may reduce or eliminate this problem are available.   There are also new materials for repacking the operating stem gland.   Some utilities have been using braided plastic metallic packing, which they have found to retain its plasticity longer than does the older packing.   This material can easily be formed to suit almost any condition.

A detailed operator's guidebook, M-17, covering the installation, operation, and maintenance of fire hydrants is available through the American Water Works Association.[2]

CUSTOMER SERVICES

The water-service pipe leading from the utility's main to the customer's building should be large enough to permit a continuous, ample flow of

[2] American Water Works Association, Publications Order Department, 6666 West Quincy Avenue, Denver, Colo. 80235.

water under maximum, simultaneous use of all fixtures and points of service. This requirement should apply to residential customers but not to large industrial users. For the latter, a detailed hydraulic study of particular plumbing and water requirements should be made to serve the industries' best interests.

A ⅝- to ¾-inch (15.875- to 19.05-millimeter) service pipe should be ample for most situations in many homes. However, with the growing residential use of water as lot sizes increase and the need for water increases to irrigate lawns, shrubberies, and gardens and as the use of such water-demanding fixtures as washing machines, dishwashers, and garbage grinders also increases, there are many arguments in favor of a service pipe with a minimum diameter of 1 inch (25.4 millimeters). The adoption of such a standard would reduce the number of low-pressure and flow problems in many homes.

The utility can select one of many suitable materials for water-service piping. The choice is contingent upon local factors, including the chemistry of the water, soil conditions, and economics. While many types of material can convey water from the utility's distribution system to the customer's home or place of business, some may prove unsuitable in certain areas. For example, plastic or other nonmetallic service pipe or tubing is nonconductive and, if frozen, cannot be thawed out with an electric current. This type of pipe also is difficult, if not impossible, to locate with electronic pipe finders.

Customer Plumbing Deficiencies

One of the commonest complaints involves insufficient water pressures and flows on a customer's premises. More often than not, the trouble lies in the customer's plumbing system, but it is difficult to convince the customer of this. One of the best ways to overcome the customer's doubts is to remove the water meter and conduct a flow and pressure test. A recorder should be used to establish the time and rate of the maximum monetary demand. Comparing these data with information from the flow test will usually show the relationship between maximum flow and low pressures in critical trouble spots.

Frequently architects arbitrarily select the size of the service pipe without attempting to make even the most elementary calculations because, as one architect put it, "That size of pipe worked fine in our last job." Most often the architects' desired sizes are overoptimistic, but occasionally larger sizes are required than those indicated on their plans. As a general rule, one should not skimp on pipe size. If calculations show that the planned size is marginal, at least the next size larger should be selected, since the greatest cost in the majority of installations is labor. The additional cost attributable to labor when installing a larger pipe is only a nominal part of the total.

Curb Valves

Service curb valves and boxes often prove troublesome. The newer types of curb valves have O-ring seals and Teflon-coated plugs that assure easy turning and eliminate sticking or freezing even after prolonged idleness. The one disadvantage of these valves is that they cannot be drained.

Pipe joints around and on the curb valve are prone to failure, since curb boxes are sometimes driven down to meet existing grades and are vulnerable to other abuses. The easiest way to repair the joints is by the freezing method. Upon excavation, repairs can be effected simply by clamping off the inlet pipe and freezing it with a brine solution consisting of melting ice and salt. After the water is frozen, the clamped area can be cut off and a "pack joint coupling" installed. This coupling eliminates threading or flaring the pipe and provides a compression fitting between any combination of pipes.

Thawing Frozen Water Services

The most prevalent water-service problems encountered by many utilities in northern climates are associated with thawing frozen water services. The electric thawing machine, a direct-current welder, is the equipment most commonly used. A particular service may require several minutes or sometimes hours to thaw, depending upon the current employed. As a rule, 200 to 350 amperes should prove sufficient, but because of the lower resistance of copper higher currents are usually necessary.

All articles and comments about electric thawing stress the safety precautions required to prevent fires and other damage in homes and buildings. James B. Ramsey, director of standards of the American Water Works Association, has the following to say about safety precautions:

> I wish to repeat the most important precautions to be taken: of *removing a portion of the water service pipe* inside the house; and of *disconnecting the electrical ground wire* if it is connected to the water service pipe. If these two precautions are taken, the current cannot enter the house.
>
> Another check that should be made is to be sure that the *gas piping is not in contact with the water service line.* If there is contact, the current could enter the house through the gas-service pipe. These precautions should be taken on all service piping lead lines from the source of electric current.

Locating Installed Service Lines

The best and quickest way to determine the location of service lines that are installed and in use is by measurement. This of course requires up-to-date maps and records, and these are not always available, especially when a water utility inherits a distribution system in a fringe area without accurate records.

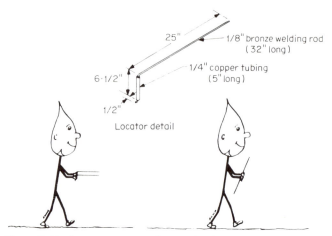

25" 1/8" bronze welding rod
(32" long)

1/4" copper tubing
(5" long)

6-1/2"

1/2"

Locator detail

Figure 10-20 Some persons can locate pipe by the use of a pair of bronze rods held as shown in this drawing of an underground pipe locator. When the rods pass over a buried pipe, they swing apart. The cartoon character shown is Willing Water, a service symbol of the American Water Works Association.

Several procedures may be used to locate these lost lines, the best known being the electronic pipe locator. However, this system does not work well when the service line is of plastic or other nonmetallic pipe.

Another simple system used by many utilities may be loosely classed as water witching, but not everyone is able to utilize it. Nevertheless, it has proved accurate with persons who do have the ability to use it. It consists of using two bronze welding rods, bent as shown in Figure 10-20, which the operator holds in two copper tubes. The rods are held about 10 to 12 inches (254 to 304.8 millimeters) apart with the ends pointing horizontally in front of the operator. The operator then proceeds to walk slowly at right angles to the area where the pipe should lie. When the operator crosses over it, the rods should swing out parallel to the direction of flow.

Service Repair Precautions

The maintenance and repair of services present many problems, not the least of which involves the utility's relations with its customers. No one enjoys seeing his or her street or property torn up. The problems are compounded in winter, when frozen ground makes the work even more difficult.

To thaw the frozen ground, many utilities use burning coal, bottled gas, and even corncobs, which create more smoke than heat, to thaw the ground. However, this procedure involves hazards that utility crews must recognize. Not only does it pose a fire hazard, but under some conditions the heat can create steam beneath the paving, giving rise to forces large enough to cause an explosion.

Other problems, particularly in winter, may involve one or more of the following: (1) flooding of streets and private property, (2) icing of streets, (3) frost penetration, (4) extra burdens placed upon machines and equipment, (5) uncomfortable working conditions for personnel, and (6) difficulty in providing emergency service.

Replacing Service Pipe

One does not always need to excavate to replace a deteriorating service pipe. Some old pipes are lead and should be replaced anyway because of the health risk. The procedure is to excavate at the main, disconnect the old service pipe where it connects with the customer's plumbing, and cut the pipe flush with the wall of the excavation. Next, a steel cable should be pushed carefully through the old pipe, starting at the customer's plumbing and extending to the curb valve box. Then the cable is threaded through a ½- by 3-inch (12.7- by 76.2-millimeter) eyebolt, looped back and secured with a ⅜-inch (9.525-millimeter) cable clamp. The eyebolt is inserted through a ¾-inch (19.05-millimeter) female iron-to-copper compression coupling with a hex nut added. The hex nut pulls against the collar inside the coupling but still leaves ample space to connect the ¾-inch plastic or copper replacement water-service pipe.

The other end of the cable should be connected to the bucket of a front-end loader by a chain and hook. Then the cable is pulled out by means of the tractor loader. The old pipe will come with the cable, and the new plastic or copper service pipe will be in place.

This method will not work well if the old pipe has been bent to go over another pipe. If this is the case, one can simply install a new pipe, using a pneumatic or hydraulic pipe pusher, and still avoid extensive excavation.

Service Piping and Appurtenances

A number of publications specifically discuss service piping requirements. In general, the primary objective is to remind the water-utility management of its responsibilities to its customers when it gives reasonable assurance, either direct or implied, that an adequate water supply will be available for their present and future needs. From these publications and discussions, it is apparent that a great variety of systems and procedures, many of which have been developed primarily to meet local requirements, are currently employed. However, each customer service usually consists of the following basic items:

1. The connection to the main, usually made by installing a corporation stop under pressure.

2. A section of pipe leading to the curb or parkway area.

3. A curb stop or shutoff valve.

4. A stop valve below the meter.

5. A water meter.

6. A stop valve above the meter. This could be a check valve if permitted by local plumbing codes. In some instances, a backflow-preventer valve would be necessary.

WATER-METER MAINTENANCE

The maintenance and repair of water meters are functions that directly affect the income of a water utility. With a good meter-maintenance program the utility receives payment for the water delivered to the customer, but this should not imply that good maintenance in other phases of waterworks operation is not equally important. Nevertheless, thorough and meticulous meter maintenance not only has immediate effects but provides long-range benefits in the development and use of the water resource that may be of greater value.

Since many types of meters are available, no attempt will be made here to discuss special meters regardless of their importance. We shall concentrate on the smaller sizes, ⅝ inch to 1 inch (15.875 to 25.4 millimeters), in cold-water displacement meters, or the commonest, the disc meter. This type accounts for more than 60 percent of all the water sold by most utilities. However, the same fundamental rules generally apply to all meters regardless of size or type. The basic items encountered in all meter-maintenance programs are (1) personnel, (2) layout of

Figure 10-21 Accurate water meters and a sound meter rate schedule are essential parts of a healthy water utility. Here four meters are being tested simultaneously.

the testing and maintenance shop, (3) reception and inventory of new meters, (4) testing of new meters, (5) setting meters, (6) reading meters, (7) removing meters, (8) repairing meters, (9) testing of repaired meters, and (10) records.

A trend that may have a bearing on future meter-handling practices has developed. When economic and other conditions so dictate, certain utilities have adopted the practice of returning meters needing repair and testing to the supplier or to others who will do the work for them. This practice relieves the utility of providing a meter-repair shop and offers the opportunity of economic savings. However, it makes the utility dependent on the ability of the supplier to provide prompt service. Many utilities have discovered to their chagrin that suppliers can experience delivery problems which can complicate the utilities' operations.

Inspection of New Meters

Little has been said or written about maintenance procedures for new meters. Most utilities are prone to assume that since the meters are new, they are ready for service. It is true that each new meter, when shipped from the supplier, has been thoroughly inspected and is accompanied by test data showing that it conforms not only to its own specifications for accuracy and reliability but also of those of the American Water Works Association.

Nevertheless, before a meter is put into service, the utility should make a few basic inspections. This procedure does not imply that the manufacturer cannot be trusted. On the contrary, it not only will prevent any difficulties that the utility may unexpectedly have to face with new meters but will actually protect the manufacturer's best interests as well.

What inspection and test procedures should be conducted on a new meter? No one has set formal standards for this all-important phase of the maintenance operation. The manufacturer's recommendations should be followed where applicable; depending on the individual requirements to be met, this will suffice in most cases. Some well-run utilities have adopted the following procedure:

1. After unpacking a new meter, place it on the workbench, remove the chamber and other parts, and inspect carefully to see that everything fits.

2. Reassemble the meter, making sure that all parts of a particular meter remain together. The meter is then ready for testing.

Meter Testing

It is true that manufacturers always test meters prior to shipment. However, as a minimum registration requirement, a utility should specify the accuracy standards set by the American Water Works Association. Many utilities have established more exacting specifications that they require manufacturers to meet. In these cases, the utilities usually emphasize registration at lower flows.

For example, a utility may require that all new meters must register a minimum accuracy of 97 percent at a flow of ¼ gallon (0.95 liter) per minute, and others specify an accuracy of at least 90 percent at ⅛ gallon (0.47 liter) per minute. Still others even require a sensitivity test of ¹⁄₁₆ gallon (0.24 liter) per minute or less. All these requirements represent a laudable desire to insist that small flows register on the meter. If a small flow does slip by each meter, the loss to the utility can be substantial.

Series testing of new meters is recommended except in small shops where only a very few meters are involved. Because of the many variables, no strict formula can be applied to assist the utility in determining the optimum number of meters that should be tested in this manner. This number can best be determined by experiment and, of course, will vary somewhat with each utility.

Setting Meters

As in many other phases of metering, this subject cannot be simply considered. One may feel that setting a meter entails nothing more than the physical effort expended by maintenance personnel while the meter is being connected to the customer's service line. On the contrary, careful consideration should be given to the study of setting meters. A meter that is set properly will measure flows more accurately and assure that the utility receives a fair and just payment for its service in obtaining the raw water, purifying it, pumping it, and delivering it to the customer.

Many questions must be answered before a utility decides on how its meters are to be set. Some utilities may be governed by state regulatory statutes as well as by local ordinances, codes, and laws. Probably the most important controlling factor may be the location of the utility and the attendant weather conditions. These will to a great degree determine the action required.

Such decisions as the merits and practicability of inside versus outside meter settings, location, type of mechanical settings, use of Copperhorns, yokes, Kornerhorns, ram's horns, tailpieces, and other details, and the location and number of stops, valves, and other appurtenances must be standardized by the utility. Many articles and papers have covered this phase of metering. Reference to them will enable a utility to formulate a program that embodies the best features of the programs already in effect.

Important as meter maintenance is, it actually may be said that this subject begins with the proper meter setting. Shortcuts and money-saving suggestions should be reviewed with great care. One should never jeopardize the accuracy or precision of the meter, which is the instrument that makes the utility financially viable.

Meter Retesting

Opinions diverge widely on the frequency of removing meters to retest their accuracy. Some states have laws specifying the limits in time or the total volume of water measured between tests. Unfortunately some of these regulations are vague and unrealistic. In the American Water Works Association standard specification for cold-water meters, the text recommends certain intervals between tests for average conditions but advises that the intervals must be governed largely by local conditions.

Many factors affect the frequency of meter testing, but all may be summarized by this simple economic statement: If a meter-maintenance program costs more than is gained in revenue, the period is too short; if the revenue lost is more than the cost of meter maintenance, the period is too long.

The regulations of some public-service commissions require that meters be removed and tested as often as warranted to comply with accuracy standards. Some utilities have adopted the following intervals as a standard:

Meter Size in Inches (Millimeters)	Years between Tests
⅝ (15.875)	7
1 (25.4)	3
1½ (38.1)	2
2 (50.8)	1
Larger	When needed

About 90 percent of all meters in use are of the ⅝-inch size. Accordingly, the following discussion of meter testing is limited to this particular size.

After a meter has been removed from the customer's service connection, it should be brought to the repair shop and given a superficial surface cleaning. The purpose of the cleaning is to avoid fouling the test equipment as well as to facilitate general good housekeeping.

When the meter has been cleaned, it should be placed on a test bench to be tested in series with other meters brought in for rehabilitation. Regardless of whether the meter meets the standards of accuracy or not, it should then be disassembled.

Meter Repair

This discussion cannot and should not offer a rigid, detailed meter-repair procedure. Each water utility must develop its own methods in its own way, since no one procedure will fulfill all requirements.

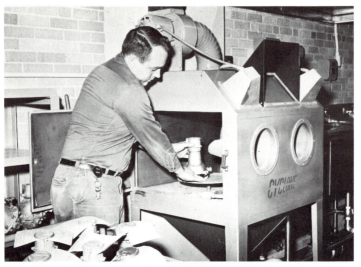

Figure 10-22 Water meters brought in for repair should be surface-cleaned, in this case by air-blast equipment.

However, there are certain dos and don'ts that can apply to most repair and rehabilitation programs.

To overhaul a meter, most manufacturers supply manuals that provide step-by-step instructions covering the more important points. Utility repair crews should follow these instructions as closely as conditions permit. A skilled mechanic can make changes that improve repair work, but an unskilled mechanic trying the same technique may damage the meter.

The following suggestions apply to the repair and rehabilitation of all meters in general:

1. Scrap immediately all old parts found to be worn or damaged.
2. Use only repair parts supplied by the manufacturer of the meter.
3. Do not use disc-ball shims made of absorbent materials.
4. Use the correct packing in stuffing boxes. Wrong packing wears spindles, distorts stuffing-box nuts, and by creating friction causes inaccuracies at low rates of flow.
5. Never use emery cloth or paper for cleaning chambers.
6. Use a prescribed grease for lubricating gear trains.
7. Store main-casing gaskets flat.
8. Store discs away from heat.
9. Seal meters following testing.
10. Store meters upside down in racks.

Each year new techniques are introduced to the meter-repair trade. Some of these concepts have not yet proved themselves, but from those that have, it appears that greater emphasis is being placed on the use of special tools and equipment.

Dial indicators are proving useful. The clearance between chamber seats and the disc assembly is measured by placing an indicator in contact with the disc spindle while the chamber is under mechanical pressure. The use of a dial indicator eliminates the cut-and-try methods that repair workers now must use. Another use for the dial indicator is to check the accuracy of the measurements of the half balls, which often are marked incorrectly.

Wear gauges also are proving useful. These show, by dial-indicator readings, the amount of wear in the chamber seats. This amount determines whether the chamber is out of round, the seat wear is eccentric with the chamber walls, or the chamber walls are worn.

The *disc-assembly gauge* is a useful instrument that has been developed to check the disc plate and its assembly by determining the accuracy of the disc-plate diameter and the correctness of the disc assembly. To determine the *freedom of motion* of the assembled meter, repair workers usually place the inlet side of the meter to their lips and blow; if the disc assembly rotates with a minimum of blowing, the meter is usually considered satisfactory. A *head-loss gauge* that measures the air pressure required at approximately the minimum flow to move the disc assembly can readily be substituted for the older and still more popular procedure of blowing.

Gear-train alignment and *seating gauges* may be used simultaneously to determine whether the gear train and its control block are seated correctly. If they are not, an *upper-and-lower alignment device* can be used to realign the gear-train seat.

Such special tools, jigs, and other devices should, if available, be acquired from the meter manufacturer. If they are not available through this source and an official of the utility has been delegated the responsibility of designing and procuring such equipment, the work should be assigned to the most competent machinist available. An improperly constructed and calibrated gauge is worse by far than none at all.

Retesting Repaired Meters

At this point, utility personnel are ready to prove the effectiveness of the repair work. Since the express purpose of meter repair is to ensure that the registration of flow through the meter is precise and reliable, retesting is an essential phase of the repair program. Because about 10 to 15 percent of all water required by a utility's customers is used at a rate of ¼ gallon (0.95 liter) per minute or less, it behooves the utility to see that a repaired meter can measure this flow at an accuracy of at least 95 percent. Some meter can give even more precise registration.

One cannot overemphasize the need for meters to be tested at rates of 10, 4, and 2 gallons (37.85, 15.14, and 7.57 liters) per minute and to record at 100 percent precision or nearly so. If the meter does not perform at this accuracy, it is not functioning as one has a right to expect, and the utility will be the loser. Such a meter will be an inefficient part of the water-utility equipment.

Meter Records

Most offices can profit by carefully examining the meter documents and records now in use. Some employ far too many forms; others could use the same number more effectively. There are two fundamental questions: Is the utility management actually using the information collected on the forms? Are all copies necessary? The utility management should appraise its system of meter documents and records in accordance with these criteria:

1. Purpose of the form (information required)
2. Purpose of copies, if any
3. Disposition of copies
4. Number of forms and copies required
5. Added administrative cost of the present system
6. Cost of filing, including the filing space required

The basic principle that should underlie any system covering meter documents and records is this: The system should provide a complete history of the use of each meter, and this history should be readily available. One should be able to refer to the meter records and trace the entire history of the meter from the moment that it was received until it was scrapped. Such pertinent information as is outlined in the following list will serve as a guide to the more salient features that should be included in meter records. If the utility wishes, headings can be combined or further subdivided. The basic list is as follows:

1. Meter serial number
2. Meter size
3. Manufacturer
4. Service location used
5. Dates set
6. Dates removed
7. Service and repair information
8. Amount of water measured
9. Time in service
10. Accuracy tests

The importance of keeping sufficient and accurate records cannot be overstressed. Such records are mandatory if the meter program is to succeed.

Manufacturer Repair and Maintenance

For various reasons, an increasing number of utilities simply rely on the manufacturer or other organizations to repair and modernize their meters. Some meters are not designed so that repairs consist simply of replacing the old chamber and other vital parts with new units. Some manufacturers now promote the throwaway concept, particularly as it applies to plastic components.

The success of this practice depends on the reliability of the manufacturer or other supplier and the prompt delivery of repaired and tested replacement meters. The system causes the utility to lose an important element of control over an important aspect of its operation, one that affects directly its financial viability. Nevertheless, if this trend is carried to its ultimate point, one can visualize a vanishing need for skilled meter-repair workers in the water-utility organizations.

OTHER DISTRIBUTION DEVELOPMENTS

Our discussion could include an unending number of subjects. Many developments, such as shop layout, repair-crew organization, and radio communication, should respond to local requirements rather than be analyzed generally. However, there are some general trends that can be expected to grow.

Remote-read meter registers that should permit the reader to determine the reading more conveniently, more accurately, and with less trouble for the customer are making their appearance. A variety of these registers are available, most with a readout feature that automatically records the reading on a tape which can be transferred to a computer for

Figure 10-23 Remote-read meter registers represent a new trend in water-utility management. The meter at left is equipped with a register that transmits reading by telephone to the central office. Its accuracy is being tested by comparison with a conventional meter.

automatic billing. This feature eliminates human error and speeds the work. Utilities can expect that such features will be expanded to telephone transmission of the meter registration, thus completely eliminating the need for meter readers. The technology is available now.

The provision of *dual water mains,* one for potable water and the other to supply water for sanitation, fire fighting, and lawn irrigation, has long been urged by some people in the waterworks field. Since the need for potable water is relatively small, this development should simplify water-treatment problems. However, the great danger of cross-connections between the potable and nonpotable supplies is enough to concern any conscientious waterworks manager.

Reduction in the customer's water requirements is a trend that must be faced. This is difficult for those who have made a lifework of water supply and distribution. For years the policy has been to provide the volume of water that the customer feels is needed and is willing to pay for. With the urbanization of the nation, however, water resources have developed surprising limitations. Many restrictions, such as those placed on lawn irrigation by limiting it to certain alternate days of the week and to a few hours of the day, already have been used and have lowered the peak demands that have created low pressures periodically even though the supply has been ample.

Building code changes requiring the use of toilet fixtures that need only 3 gallons (11.4 liters) instead of the usual 5 or 6 gallons (19 or 23 liters) and shower-head fixtures that reduce the pressure and thereby also the volume of water are among other significant trends. Ordinances limiting the amount of grass that requires irrigation have been proposed, as have shrubs that do not require excessive watering.

Chapter Eleven

Snow and Ice Control

WILLIAM S. FOSTER

A snowfall, an ice storm, or a combination of the two on any roadway, urban or rural, is at best an emergency and at worst a disaster. However, the problem becomes more critical on an urban roadway network than on rural roads. An urban society exists on the movement of traffic, whether between urban centers or within a community's own borders. Nations have fought wars to disrupt traffic patterns or to gain control of a critical traffic and transportation point. Nations have been lost when they have been denied the use of vital transportation arteries.

An intense snow or ice storm can deny the use of these traffic arteries and disrupt traffic patterns completely. Within an urban complex, such storms can create great problems in maintaining essential public health and safety by interfering seriously with the deployment of fire and police services. They can cause suffering and loss of life by impeding the travel of ambulances and other rescue equipment. There may be vehicular accidents that result in painful injuries and loss of life as well as in property damage.

Public Demand for Snow and Ice Control

In snow-belt areas of the United States, snow and ice emergencies occur frequently. Consequently, governmental jurisdictions, both urban and rural, organize and equip themselves to keep trafficways open for the protection of health and safety.

In this era of rising expectations, people want this service to be increasingly thorough, to the point that they will object to any inconvenience despite the intensity of a storm. They have become so confident that the work of controlling snow and ice will be thorough that they do not even dress for storm conditions. Such a practice can be dangerous if

Figure 11-1 At one time snow clearance was concentrated in the downtown areas of municipalities and depended primarily on manpower. Here work is in progress to remove a 13-inch (330-millimeter) snowfall in Burlington, Vermont, in the 1930s. [The American City & County]

lightly dressed people become involved in an accident or if their vehicle is immobilized by snow. This conduct is a frailty of human nature, and those in charge of snow and ice control must reckon with it as diplomatically as possible.

Bad snowstorms can occur as far south as Alabama and Georgia. Ice storms occur on occasion in northern Florida. In these areas, the difficulties are intensified because the public does not know how to cope with snow and ice conditions.

Storm Characteristics

Snow and ice storms have generally predictable characteristics. Yet each storm can be sufficiently different to pose problems of adaptibility for those responsible for combating it. High winds can cause drifting that quickly negates the effectiveness of plowing. Snow can be dry and fluffy or wet and heavy. Temperatures can vary sharply and unpredictably and change a rainstorm to snow and ice without much warning.

The public has difficulty in appreciating the volume of material that must be handled during a snowstorm. A 10-inch (254-millimeter) snowfall, for example, can deposit 5000 cubic yards (3800 cubic meters) of snow per mile (1.6 kilometers) on a 30-foot-wide (9-meter-wide) street. And all 5000 cubic yards must be moved.

Ice control involves one technique, and snow removal another; yet both generally must work in combination. Ice frozen solidly on a roadway surface creates a very dangerous condition, particularly when the air temperature is only slightly below freezing and the ice is in its most slippery condition. Snow that has been allowed to pack and bond to the pavement is difficult to remove.

TACTICAL ORGANIZATION FOR SNOW AND ICE CONTROL

Since a snow or ice storm is at best an emergency and at worst a disaster and since such storms occur in snow-belt areas rather frequently, tactical plans must be prepared. The first and most important step is to establish a command organization. The diagram in Figure 11-2 shows a typical organizational plan; this one was developed for Des Moines, Iowa.

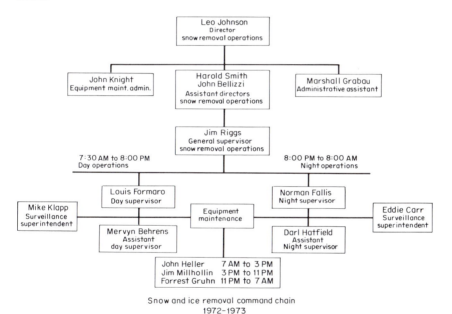

Figure 11-2 Snow and ice control requires a well-developed tactical organization, such as this one in use in Des Moines. [*Des Moines, Iowa, Department of Public Works,* Snow and Ice Removal Program: Administrative Manual]

Routes for Snow and Ice Control

Familiarity with duties is important. Well before winter, routes for snow and ice control must be established, and crews should arrange to make dry runs over them to uncover any weaknesses. The routes should be mapped clearly, with trouble spots identified. It is important to establish priority routes, which normally would include arterial ways, streets in the vicinity of schools, hospitals, fire stations, and police stations, and streets used for fire and public safety. Business and commercial areas also rate good priorities.

Weather Information

Snow and ice control can be expensive if crews are called to prepare for work when no actual need develops. Consequently, provision of as precise weather information as possible is mandatory. Conventional sources include the National Weather Service, weather-forecasting facilities at nearby airports, newspapers, and radio and television stations.

However, these sources have general weather information or information directed to the needs of aviation. Because of the sensitivity of the proper time to start control work and the costliness of errors, many well-managed municipalities call on the services of private weather consultants with documented records of accuracy. These forecasters attempt to provide weather information designed to meet the special needs of urban snow and ice control. They can give more accurate guidance on the possibility of ice formation, on the time when the snow will be deep enough to require the dispatching of equipment, on the possibility of winds that will cause drifting, and on whether the temperature is expected to rise or fall and when the change will take place.

These private forecasters should be capable of providing forecasts that are between 80 and 90 percent accurate for the purposes of urban snow removal and ice control. Some administrators feel that skillful forecasters earn their fees in the amount that they save municipalities in the cost of snow and ice control.

Chain of Command

Since the decision to begin the work of snow and ice control involves considerable cost, the tactical organization should indicate clearly the person with the responsibility of initiating the program. In the Des Moines diagram, the responsibility lies with one of four administrators: the director of public works, who should be responsible if available; the general supervisor of snow-removal operations; the day supervisor; and the night supervisor. If someone other than the director of public works initiates the program, that official notifies the director, stating the starting time and the extent of operations.

Mustering Personnel

To expedite calling crews into action, a list of all personnel, complete with their names, home addresses, and home and work telephone numbers, must be prepared. Key persons in the organization should have lists of those reporting to them with this information. Then, when the appropriate supervisor authorizes a decision to combat a snow and ice storm after a normal working day, the official initiating the order notifies these key personnel, who in turn notify those for whom they are responsible.

Since this work is of an emergency nature, it should be organized in two 12-hour shifts. If the emergency starts during the normal working day, the day crew should be held for the added 4 hours of overtime. This arrangement should be clearly set forth in any work agreement between the governmental jurisdiction and the work force.

Preliminary Work

While the crews are reporting to the maintenance depots, personnel at the depots should load the salt and abrasive spreaders. Before loading, they should run the spreaders empty for a short period to see that everything is functioning properly. A loaded spreader that refuses to function is difficult to unload.

The maintenance personnel also should prepare the trucks and other rolling stock to see that they are ready to operate. If the equipment is stored outside, special measures should be taken to ensure that the vehicles can be warmed up and made operational quickly. One method is to place electrical connections on the head bolts of the engines to warm them. Another is to provide a piping system at the yard where the equipment is stored. The system should be connected to a pump and a source of heat so that it can circulate warmed antifreeze through the engines and radiators.

SALT AND ABRASIVE SPREADERS

Salt and abrasive spreaders should be the first equipment to go out in either a snow or an ice storm. They should be directed to known

Figure 11-3 Salt and abrasive spreaders should be dispatched first to locations where traffic problems are known to occur. [The American City & County]

trouble spots where traffic tie-ups can cause dangerous conditions and accidents. These spots should be identified on clear, easy-to-read maps for the guidance of the spreader crews. Trouble spots in general are high-traffic areas, hilly areas, and sharp curves in the roadways.

Use of Sodium Chloride, Calcium Chloride, and Abrasives

The material that has proved most effective in eliminating a glaze of ice on roadways and preventing snow from bonding to the pavement and making it difficult to remove is salt, in the form of sodium chloride, NaCl, or calcium chloride, $CaCl_2$, or a combination of both. Chemically, both are salts, but for convenience the term "salt" usually refers to sodium chloride and will be so used in this discussion.

Because of its lower cost, salt has become the principal agent for melting. By itself it can reduce a snowfall of 1 or 2 inches (25.4 or 50.8 millimeters) to slush that will flow away as runoff without the need for plowing. It appears to perform best when the air temperature is between 20 and 32°F (between −6.7 and 0°C). Below 20°F its melting action becomes slower, and at 6°F (−14.4°C) it reacts scarcely at all. When temperatures are expected in the lower ranges, good practice dictates mixing the salt with calcium chloride at a ratio of 3:1, with the calcium chloride content increased at the colder temperatures. The combination permits the calcium chloride to start to work immediately, while the salt will continue its effectiveness over an extended period.[1]

Some prefer to use sand, rock chips, or cinders to eliminate icy conditions on roadways and to provide greater traction for vehicles. For best results, the abrasive should be mixed with salt at a ratio of about 200 pounds of salt per cubic yard of sand (119 kilograms per cubic meter). The salt helps the sand to embed itself in the icy surface. The abrasive must be removed in the spring. Some abrasive remains on the roadways, and some enters the catch basins and sewers, where removal is difficult.[2]

Rate of Salt Application

The lowest recommended rate of application, quoted by various highway departments, is 500 pounds of salt per mile (142 kilograms per kilometer) of 24-foot (7.3-meter) roadway width. However, most urban requirements will at least double and possibly triple this figure. In any case, the use of salt should be dictated by the character of the roadway.

---

[1] Thad Nosek, "Sand, Salt and Calcium Chloride," *The American City,* December 1967, p. 82.

[2] R. R. Fleming, "More Plows and Better Plans," *The American City,* November 1968, p. 69.

Straight roadways on flat grades can receive a very light application of salt or none at all in some instances. Critical points should receive heavier applications. A city in a hilly terrain probably will be a heavy user of salt. Colder weather also will dictate that the salt application be increased.

Salt Particle Size

Recent studies conducted by the Shuman Laboratory in Battle Ground, Indiana, showed that a deicing salt mixture with a larger percentage of fine grades of rock salt would melt snow and ice more quickly than coarse grades would.[3] Salt particle gradations ran as shown in the accompanying table.

	Percentage passing	
Sieve size	Coarse crushed	Fine mixture
⅜ inch		
(9.5 millimeters)	100.0	100.0
No. 4	73.1	79.7
No. 8	23.9	42.1
No. 30	0.9	10.0

The fine mixture, identified as "highway-tested salt," consisted of 25 percent fine salt and 75 percent coarse salt. The tests showed that the fine mixture worked faster than the salt applied to a control roadway 50 percent of the time and as well as the control roadway 25 percent of the time. For the remaining periods, no comparisons were made.

Advantages of Salt and Calcium Chloride for Deicing

Enough records now are available to show that the use of these deicing chemicals reduces the incidence of accidents. Although records are difficult to document precisely, one survey of fourteen Northern cities suggested an average of 4 times as many accidents on unsalted roadways as on the salted ones.[4] In Ann Arbor, Michigan (not included in this survey), police records showed a drop of more than 40 percent in accidents after a salt program was instituted. The Ann Arbor Fire Department also praised the work. During the winter months, fire and rescue runs are more frequent, and the advantage of having streets free of snow and ice to the bare pavement is real.[5] Moreover, as mentioned above, the use of deicing salts reduces the cost and labor of spring cleanup.

[3] "Salt Particle Size," *Urban & Rural Roads,* June 1974, p. 50.
[4] "Salt Deicing Cuts Accidents," *The American City,* January 1973, p. 19.
[5] F. A. Mammel, "We Are Using Salt Smarter," *The American City,* January 1972, p. 54.

Disadvantages of Salt and Calcium Chloride for Deicing

Environmentalists have spearheaded most of the opposition to the use of deicing salts. Many persons have presented evidence to show that the salt can damage trees, shrubs, and grass. Other evidence shows that it can pollute shallow wells, particularly when the salt is stored in the open where rains can dissolve away much of it. No one disputes the fact that salt can damage certain types of trees, shrubs, and grass. However, as noted in Chapter 4, salt-resistant types are available. Moreover, if salt brine enters a shallow well through surface runoff, other pollutants also can enter the well, making it suspect from a health standpoint. Thus one could argue that the salt brine from the surface runoff identifies a dangerously unsanitary well. These are problems that should be resolved by better practice in storing the salt, as explained below, and by restricted application of the salt, which should be adopted as an economy measure in any case.

The aggravated corrosion of automobile bodies has long been an argument against the use of salt. However, more careful undercoating of the bodies, the use of corrosion-resistant metal in them, and regular washing of cars in winter should reduce this source of damage.

Legal Considerations

Legal decisions have been unanimous that a governing body cannot be held liable for accidents caused by snow and ice. However, with consumer interests of increasing concern, if a number of accidents and possibly deaths could be traced to snow and ice conditions that would have been eliminated with good practice in snow and ice control, especially the use of salt, new legal decisions could readily result.

Salt Storage

Many of the problems associated with the use of deicing salts can be traced to storing them in the open. These salts should be stored under some type of cover to eliminate waste, if for no other reason. A wooden bin mounted so that the trucks can be loaded by gravity eliminates much loss of salt and reduces the danger of runoff.

Some communities store the salt in glass-lined steel tanks such as those customarily used for grain storage. These silos will store 150 tons (136,100 kilograms) of salt in only 350 square feet (32.5 square meters) of area. The silo is 32 feet (9.8 meters) high and 14 feet (4.3 meters) in diameter. It has a ground-level receiving hopper and an elevating loader for use by trucks delivering the salt. The elevator also supplies salt to the spreader trucks. Filling a 5-yard (4.6-meter) truck requires about 5 minutes. Unloading 23 tons (20,865 kilograms) of salt from a

Figure 11-4 Salt should not be stored in the open, as it is here. Such a practice is wasteful, resulting in the loss of salt, and it creates pollution damage as the salt dissolves and brine enters freshwater supplies. [The American City & County]

Figure 11-5 Glass-lined silos are proving effective for storing salt. They are easy to fill and to use for loading trucks. [*Baltimore, Maryland, Department of Public Works*]

Figure 11-6   Some type of cover should be provided for salt.   It can be of the igloo type or a variation, as shown here, or the salt can be stored in an existing building.   [*Boston Salt Company, Boston, Massachusetts*]

semitrailer requires only a half hour.   Both tasks can be performed by one person.[6]

To store large quantities of salt, igloo-type structures can be used. These were developed by the Ontario, Canada, Department of Highways.   The structures are 100 feet (30.5 meters) in diameter and about 50 feet (15.2 meters) high, designed to conform to the angle of repose of moist sand, or roughly 45 degrees.   The structure is formed of plywood panels and generally rests on a concrete footing of varying height.   The igloo storage structure is designed to support a snow load of 80 pounds per square foot (391 kilograms per square meter) and resist a wind velocity of 120 miles (193 kilometers) per hour.[7]

Deicing Salt-Distribution Equipment

Deicing salt spreaders and abrasive spreaders can be divided roughly between those that operate from the tailgate of a dump truck and those that are self-contained, having their own hoppers and a conveyor system that delivers the salt or abrasive to the spreader mechanism.   The first type is generally less costly.   The second type can be built to carry a large load, and since there is no dump box, it is somewhat easier on the truck frame.   A raised dump box that is loaded can impose twisting stresses that can damage a truck frame.

Most spreaders distribute the salt or abrasives by a spinning mechanism that has the advantage of making the application to varying widths. A few apply the material through a trough to a fixed width.   Most can

---

[6] "A Salt Silo for Speed, Economy and Convenience," *The American City*, October 1968, p. 60.

[7] J. R. Fitzpatrick, "Beehives Protect Snow-Removal Salt, Prevent Water Pollution," *The American City*, September 1970 p. 81.

Figure 11-7 Most salt and abrasive spreaders use some type of spinner mechanism to distribute the material. [*Highway Equipment Co., Cedar Rapids, Iowa*]

be provided with controls in the truck cab that permit the operator to vary the amount of material applied and the width of the application. Controls that apply a consistent amount of material regardless of the speed of the truck, within limitations, can also be provided. Suppliers state that the accuracy of application is within plus or minus 2 percent.

The self-contained spreaders can be large-capacity units mounted on heavy-duty trucks, or they can be provided as small units on pickup trucks or even as small units on tricycle-type motor-scooter bodies. The smaller units are useful in deicing trouble spots early in a storm.

Figure 11-8 Some spreaders are operated from the tailgate of a dump truck. Here the spreader is operated through a gearbox powered by the traction of the wheels. [*Epoke Spreader photo*]

Intersection Deicing

Without precise, cab-controlled operation, intersections will generally be salted excessively as trucks make a double application, running up the salting costs and disturbing environmentalists in the community. This waste can be avoided by a "crossover" method that depends on careful operation.

The approach lanes of an intersection are the ones most in need of deicing. The spreader operator therefore should begin a salt application about 100 feet (300 meters) from the intersection in the right-hand lane. Then, as the truck with its spreader reaches the intersection, the driver should cross over to the left-hand lane, moving against traffic for 100 feet, and continue the salt application. The driver repeats the crossover application on the intersecting roadway.

With this method, motorists are provided with control of their vehicles in the approach area, and the vehicles tend to draw the salt across the intersection without doubling the application. It has been determined that this procedure reduces salt requirements by one-half, to 150 pounds (68 kilograms) per intersection, while placing the salt where it is needed most, in the approach lanes. The work requires extreme caution, with all flashing lights operational, and a helper to warn oncoming vehicles when the truck crosses over to proceed against traffic in the left-hand lane.[8]

Prewetting Salt with Liquid Calcium Chloride

An innovative method of chemical deicing developed by the Iowa Highway Commission, which involves prewetting the salt as it is applied with liquid calcium chloride as the prewetting agent, is showing ability to reduce the amount of salt applied by about 40 percent. Its developers assert that it increases roadway safety and reduces the potential for salt pollution of the roadside environment.

Prewetting the salt in this manner enables it to be effective at temperatures approaching 0°F(-17.8°C), whereas salt loses its effectiveness when the temperature drops below 20°F (-6.7°C). At milder temperatures, the snow and ice will melt more rapidly because the time interval of 30 to 45 minutes normally required for the salt brine to form has been eliminated. This speedier action also reduces salt waste, since the salt will not be so readily removed by traffic action.

The Iowa tests included several wetting agents, among them water, methanol, and ethylene glycol, but liquid calcium chloride appeared best on a cost-effective basis. Applying the liquid calcium chloride over the top of the hopper loads proved unsatisfactory. It was awkward, wasteful, and lacked uniformity. Moreover, many of the hopper boxes suffered from accelerated rusting and deterioration. However, the Iowa tests showed that the salt could be prewetted satisfactorily by the use of a small spray bar placed in the spreader discharge chute and fed by a supply tank of chloride liquid and a small positive-displacement pump. Approximately 8 gallons (30 liters) of liquid calcium chloride appear to

[8] "Cuts Salt Needs by 50%," *The American City,* January 1974 p. 12.

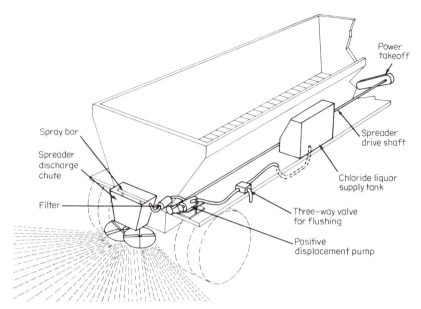

Figure 11-9 Liquid calcium chloride applied to salt as shown in this drawing greatly improves the effectiveness of the salt and reduces the amount required. [Bulletin 73-2, *U.S. Department of Transportation, Federal Highway Administration, April 1973*]

be required to dampen completely 1 ton (907 kilograms) of salt, using salt that meets the grading specifications of the American Association of State Highway and Transportation Officials (AASHTO).

The applicator kit developed by Iowa Highway Commission investigators cost approximately $150 in 1973. It consists of a fiberglass tank with a capacity of 55 to 63 gallons (208 to 239 liters) to hold the liquid calcium chloride plus a positive-displacement pump and spray bar for delivery of the liquid chemical to the discharge chute. The pump is driven from a V-belt pulley assembly off the spreader drive shaft. The pulley size and the adjustable sheave width of the pulley control the delivery rate of the pump.

An itemized list of materials used to assemble the liquid calcium chloride applicator, as shown in Figure 11-9, includes the following:

1	55–63 gallon (208–239 liter) fiberglass tank
1	¼-inch (6.35-millimeter) brass line filter
1	pump, Viking model G32-B
1	three-way ½-inch (12.7-millimeter) brass valve
1	3-inch (76.2-millimeter) pulley
1	1¼-inch (31.75-millimeter) bushing
1	⅝-inch (15.875-millimeter) bushing
30 feet	⅝-inch (15.875-millimeter) heater hose
1	4-inch (101.6-millimeter) butt hinge
2	⅛-inch (3.175-millimeter) WF 5/5 50-degree Delavan nozzles
2 feet	1-inch (25.4-millimeter) hard plastic pipe
1	V belt to drive pump
	Miscellaneous items such as elbows and nipples

The liquid calcium chloride used in the Iowa deicing program is specified to be clear and free from suspended matter and to meet these requirements:

	Total Percentage by Weight
Calcium and magnesium chlorides	Not less than 31
Calcium chloride	Not less than 21
Alkali chlorides, as NaCl	Not more than 4

Since the prewetted salt will have less tendency to bounce and scatter, the operator may have to readjust the spinner deflection shields to obtain the required spreads.   After spreading is completed, the operator should turn the three-way valve so that the pump can draw from an auxiliary line connected to a fuel-oil reservoir.   One gallon (3.785 liters) of the oil should be pumped through the system to flush out the remaining liquid calcium chloride and to lubricate the pump for its next application.

The process was developed and implemented by Charles L. Huisman, maintenance area engineer of the Iowa Highway Commission.   Iowa officials believe the system to be extremely beneficial on urban streets, giving quicker melting with reduced rates of salt application.   It is adaptable to most tailgate spreaders, a single basic requirement being that there be a power source (auger shaft, hydraulic-drive motor, and so on) to drive the small pump rated at 2½ gallons (9.46 liters) per minute to deliver the liquid calcium chloride to the spray bar.[9]

Airport Deicing Practices

In most cases airports must avoid the use of salt and calcium chloride, which can damage planes and delicate aeronautical equipment.   Some airports employ pellet urea, a chemical synthesized from ammonia and carbon dioxide that is used normally as a fertilizer and in resins.   Others use ethylene glycol.   Still others heat the sand to help it become embedded in the ice and snow.

The urea is generally effective at an air temperature of 15 to 32°F (−9.4 to 0°C) and performs well on either concrete or asphalt.   It provides the most desirable results when moisture is present on the runways.

The Buffalo, New York, airport applies urea at a rate of 1 pound (0.45 kilogram) per 300 square feet (27.9 square meters) of runway surface.   The Buffalo practice is to broom the water and slush resulting from the application of urea off the runway and to apply a light cover of grit to provide the needed traction for good braking action.

The ethylene glycol is essentially the product used as an antifreeze in motor vehicles.   The general practice is to mix it with equal parts of water and pour the mixture over sand used for antiskid purposes.

[9] *Use of Liquid Calcium Chloride to Improve Deicing and Snow Removal Operations*, Bulletin 73-2, U. S. Department of Transportation, Federal Highway Administration, April 1973.

At the Buffalo airport, crews apply heated sand without the urea when temperatures drop well below freezing. The sand is stored in a separate closed area and kept warm with heating coils in the floor and infrared lights mounted in the ceiling. The temperature of the sand is kept at 75 to 80°F (23.9 to 26.7°C) so that it can easily embed itself in the snow and ice.[10]

PLOWING

Although deicing salts and abrasives can solve snow and ice problems completely in favorable instances, conditions requiring the more positive action of plows constantly arise. As a general rule, plows should be ready to start operating when 2 inches (50.8 millimeters) of snow is on the ground and forecasts warn that more is coming and that the air temperature will remain at its present level or drop.

If no more than 6 inches (152.4 millimeters) of snow is anticipated, plowing can be limited primarily to arterial streets, bus routes, business districts, and similar critical areas. If more is expected, a full-scale plowing attack must be initiated.

Figure 11-10 Plows should normally be in operation when 2 inches (50.8 millimeters) of snow is on the ground, when forecasts warn that more snow is on the way, and when the air temperature will remain at its present level or drop. [The American City & County]

Plowing Routes

Like operators of trucks carrying deicing salts, the operators of plowing trucks should be provided with instructions and maps that designate not only the plowing routes but also routes that must receive special con-

[10] "Chemical Prevents Runway Icing, Is Not Corrosive," *The American City,* January 1974, p. 12; "Treated Sand Keeps 'Em Flying," *The American City,* December 1968, p. 34.

sideration such as emergency routes for fire and police and hospital areas. A good policy is to assign one truck and plow to hospital duty, moving it from location to location until all hospital entrances have been cleared and will remain so.

Plowing Start

Plowing is more effective if it is started in the evening after traffic loads have dropped. Each truck should have a driver and a helper. Wherever possible, trucks should operate in pairs at a tandem offset to enlarge the plowed width.

If plowing must start during the daytime hours, the most productive policy is to keep the center lanes open and neglect the parking lanes, which probably will be occupied by cars. Toward evening, most of the cars will have been moved, particularly if the municipality has an ordinance requiring them to do so. At that time, the full width of the streets can be opened.

Plowing to the Center of the Street

Communities with wide streets, especially those that have good control over on-street parking, can plow the snow to the center of the streets and allow the traffic to circulate on each side of the snow median strip. This procedure is very convenient when loaders and trucks follow shortly thereafter to remove the windrowed snow.

Older cities with narrow streets are not so fortunate. Curb space is rarely available for traffic passage, and a center lane is about all that can be opened during a heavy snowfall.

Figure 11-11 If the street is wide enough, plowing can windrow the snow to the center of the street, where it can be conveniently picked up. [The American City & County]

Alley Plowing

Many cities have alleys, especially in downtown areas, that fire departments want kept clear and open. For these assignments, a heavy truck, a tractor, or a grader, each equipped with a V plow, works best.

Automatic Transmissions and Power Steering

If possible, trucks should be supplied with automatic or power-shift transmissions and power steering. Clearing snow from streets is arduous in any case. Automatic transmissions and power features are easier on drivers and equipment. The torque converter permits a vehicle to start quickly and smoothly, yet the vehicle does not move so quickly that it breaks traction on the snow or ice. The driver can control the action by the throttle alone and need not accelerate the engine or balance engine torque to the wheels by slipping the clutch. Specialized pieces of equipment such as snow blowers frequently are equipped at the factory with automatic transmissions or power shifts.

Plowing without Deicing Salts

Today local or state laws may prevent or sharply reduce the use of salt on urban streets. In such cases plowing tactics must be revised. The snow must be moved before traffic has had an opportunity to pack and bond it to the pavement and create a heavy layer of ice. Such layers can attain depths of 4 to 6 inches (102 to 152 millimeters) and often require pneumatic hammers to break them loose.

Plows must be scheduled to go out early, almost at the same time that the snow starts, particularly if forecasts predict that the snow will continue. The shoes must be removed from the plow assembly so that the blades reach closer to the pavement surface. This procedure requires careful inspection of the roadway in summer to find and lower any projections more than 1 inch (25 millimeters) high, such as manholes and valve boxes. Projections less than 1 inch high can be protected by providing bituminous ramps around them.

Graders will have to be used more frequently to plow the snow. These heavy units with their powerful blades can cut into packed snow and break it loose when standard plows generally are ineffective.[11]

Plowing Semirural Roadways

Often a municipality has semirural outlying districts within its political boundaries. Generally the roadways serving such areas have neither curbs nor gutters; most have drainage ditches running alongside the roadway.

[11] D. O. Blood, "Snow Removal Tailored to Reduce Salt Pollution," *The American City,* January 1973, p. 16.

Figure 11-12   In semirural areas, wing plows can widen the cleared roadway without great difficulty. [The American City & County]

Clearing these roadways is a task for plows with wing-plow attachments. These provide extra cleared width on a single pass, permitting
parking and easier mail delivery. Wing plows can also be attached to
graders.

PUBLIC COOPERATION

The designation of certain urban arterial roads and streets as snow
routes is useful not only in concentrating work on vital traffic arteries
but also in emphasizing to motorists that they have an obligation to cooperate in this emergency community work. The more frequently that
citizens can be reminded that a free democratic society entails responsibilities as well as rights, the more effective that society will be.

An ordinance establishing snow routes should ban parking on the
routes whenever the governing body establishes the existence of a snow
emergency. If the public is ready to accept additional restrictions that
will aid in snow and ice control, the ordinance can be enlarged to prohibit all on-street parking during a snow emergency. Appropriate signs
should designate streets selected by ordinance as snow routes. Master
maps indicating these routes and all other routes subject to snow clearance and ice control should be available at operating centers.

In the interests of general safety for motorists who must travel during
these emergencies, prudent judgment on the part of the governing body
dictates that the motorists should be required by ordinance to use snow
tires or tire chains or to arrange for their cars to be equipped with non-
slip differentials to ensure that both driving wheels operate under
slippery conditions. If a vehicle impedes traffic on snow routes and is
not equipped as the ordinance requires, the driver should be subject to
arrest.

Appeals to the public for cooperation in reducing traffic during a
snow or ice emergency also can help. These can be made through the
press, radio, and television, by insertions in water bills, and by public-

address systems on cars or trucks traveling through the streets. The appeals can ask the public to (1) refrain from driving unless this is absolutely necessary, (2) park cars off the street in all areas, (3) use public transportation when available, (4) drive in car pools whenever possible, and (5) be sure that cars and trucks are completely equipped for winter driving. Some municipalities remind the public of the need for support by placing signs on snow-plowing equipment which state that the equipment represents a tax investment and that it can be effective only with public cooperation.

EQUIPMENT

Various types of reversible, tripping, straight moldboard plows are the most practical plows for general urban snow-clearing service. The plow blades vary in width from 8 to 12 feet (from 2.4 to 3.7 meters) and in height from 30 to 60 inches (from 762 to 1524 millimeters). The blades are curved to assist in throwing the snow off the roadway. The tripping arrangement consists of heavy springs that form a part of the connection between the frame and the plow. The springs allow the plow blade to trip over obstacles in the pavement such as manholes, valve boxes, and catch-basin frames and possibly even over faults in the pavement.

The plows can be positioned either manually or by power, with the angle varying from 0 degrees (straight across, bulldozer fashion) to 42 to 45 degrees. The blades can be straight, with the top parallel to the bottom, or tapered with the large end forming the discharge portion. The tapered plows can be supplied with a reversible feature, but most are used for one-way duty, with the truck traveling in the direction of traffic.

The frames that support the plows and connect them to the truck generally ride on skid shoes, although if the pavement is very smooth, as

Figure 11-13 Reversible tripping-type plows with straight moldboards are used most frequently for this work. [The American City & County]

Figure 11-14   For airport clearance, a heavy truck traveling at high speeds and carrying a 60-inch (1.524-meter) plow can throw snow in an effective manner.   [The American City & County]

on airport runways or on well-maintained arterial highways, casters can be used instead.   The plow blades can be adjusted to ride as closely to the pavement surface as desired.

The height of a plow blade should vary with the amount of snow that can be expected in the area and with the speed of operating the truck or tractor.   A 30-inch (762-millimeter) blade is satisfactory in areas with light snows and should be used at a minimum truck speed of 8 to 10 miles (13 to 16 kilometers) per hour.   The 60-inch (1524-millimeter) blade is used to clear airport runways and should operate at a minimum speed of 40 miles (64 kilometers) per hour.   At this speed, it should do a rather spectacular job of throwing the snow in the direction desired.

The larger blades require the truck operator to be at a higher vantage point in order to see how the work is progressing.   Generally, the driver's seat should be elevated at least 1 foot (0.3 meter) above the top of the moldboard.

Rubber Blades

In an increasing number of organizations charged with snow and ice control, plows are equipped with rubber blades.   These cost somewhat more than steel blades but resist wear much better.   The rubber also has the effect of producing a "squeegee" finish on the pavement surface. At one airport using large plows that operate at high speeds, the rubber blades are 10 inches (254 millimeters) wide and 1½ inches (38.1 millimeters) thick and weigh 7¾ pounds per foot of length (11.53 kilograms per meter).

Among those who have chosen to retain steel blades, some have expressed interest in a model that is heavier than those conventionally used.   Standard blades are 6 inches (152.4 millimeters) wide and ½ inch (12.7 millimeters) thick.   By selecting blades that are eight inches (203.2 millimeters) wide and ⅝ inch (15.875 millimeters) thick, operators have been able to record service records twice as long as those of conventional blades. The cost increase is about 30 percent.[12] Special, tungsten carbide–edged snowplow blades also show a substantial increase in service life. Similar inserts on snowplow shoes increase the life of these units.

V Plows

In heavy drifts, large V plows can be used to force open a lane of traffic. These plows generally are mounted on heavy four-wheel–drive trucks, patrol graders, or the front of heavier front-end loaders, where they replace loader buckets. This last combination has the advantage of allowing the operator to raise the plow to whatever height seems advantageous, permitting the operator to open a lane in two or more passes.

A V plow mounted on a truck should be somewhat different from one mounted on a patrol grader, since the truck will travel at a minimum speed of 20 miles (32 kilometers) per hour and the grader is restricted to about 12 miles (19 kilometers) per hour. The truck type has a cutting width of 8 to 9 feet (2.4 to 2.7 meters), a nose height of about 3 feet (0.9 meter), and a rear height of about 5 feet (1.5 meters). The curve of the plow is designed to cast the snow as far as possible off the road during operations.

The grader-mounted V plow is designed to move drifts rather than to throw or cast them to one side. The cutting edge will open a lane of

[12] R. P. Wolsfeld, "Wider, Thicker Snow Plow Blades Pay Dividends," *Public Works,* August 1973, p. 64.

Figure 11-15 V plows on heavy four-wheel–drive trucks or partol graders are useful in forcing an opening in heavy drifts. [The American City & County]

Figure 11-16   A V plow replacing the bucket of a front-end loader has certain advantages over other equipment because of its ability to control the height of the plow.   [The American City & County]

about 9½ feet (2.9 meters) at the roadway level and will push the snow about 12 feet (3.7 meters) at the upper wings of the plow, thus giving the grader wheels a cleared roadway surface with little opportunity for snow to fall back under the wheels.   The plow can be provided with a fin about 8 inches (203 millimeters) high at the plow nose that tapers to a stop at the top point of the plow.   This fin is helpful when the plow widens the roadway with only one side of the plow in use by reducing the possibility of snow spilling over to the opposite side.

Number of Plows in Use

A survey of plow usage, recorded in the accompanying table, shows that local governments in snow areas averaging 50 inches (1270 millimeters) of snow or more per year own an average of more than ten plows per 100 miles (161 kilometers) of streets.   Almost seven plows per 100 miles of streets are in use in areas of 20 inches or less per year in what the author of the report classed as a snow-belt area.

On the basis of each 100,000 people served, a municipality will use almost twenty-eight plows in areas with 50 inches of snow per year and almost twelve plows in areas with less than 20 inches.   These averages do not take into account the fact that many urban areas are densely populated through apartment developments and consequently have fewer miles of streets to serve them.[13]

Graders

Most municipalities own graders, and these can be useful in snow and ice control.   The articulated units work especially well in downtown areas

[13] Fleming, op. cit.

Figure 11-17 Although graders cannot travel at high speeds, they are surefooted and powerful. [The American City & County]

because of their added flexibility.   The sensitive blade control permits their use in intersections and around obstructions such as parked cars.

Graders also are more surefooted on streets with steep grades. Trucks generally must depend on speed, but graders have enough reserve power to provide clearing action without high speed, which often can be dangerous.   Moreover, graders can be equipped with many attachments that increase their usefulness in this type of work.   Among these attachments are bulldozer-type blades, snow blowers, moldboard extensions, wing blades, and, of course, V plows.

Trucks for Plowing Work

For general plowing work, heavy trucks rated at 5 tons (4536 kilograms) or more offer many advantages when working under these difficult con-

Figure 11-18 Jeep-mounted plows often are used for sidewalk plowing as well as for clearing drives and culs-de-sac that would be different to open up with conventional equipment. [The American City & County]

Equipment and Techniques

Item	Annual snowfall rate (in inches)		
	Over 50	20–50	Under 20
Average number of plows per 100 miles of street	10.4	9.0	6.8
Average number of plows per 100,000 population	27.5	14.6	11.6
Average number of graders per 100 miles of street	2.0	1.8	2.1
Average number of graders per 100,000 population	3.9	2.1	4.9
Average number of loaders per 100 miles of street	3.7	3.2	2.7
Average number of loaders per 100,000 population	9.6	6.2	5.4
Popularity by type of loader (percent):			
Front-end	53	63	84
Blower	31	22	9
Conveyor	16	15	7
Percentage of streets plowed	97	86	75
Percentage of streets, snow hauled away	11	7	8
Contractor's equipment rented (percent):			
Always	20	16	6
Often	27	28	15
Seldom	37	40	48
Never	16	16	31
Plows work (percent):			
In tandem	13	27	36
Independently	30	40	49
Both	57	33	15
Percentage of vehicles with two-way radios	46	38	23
Percentage of cities that have tried rubber cutting edges	47	40	21
Opinions of rubber edges (percent):			
Good	62	53	50
Fair	8	26	0
Bad	15	9	36
Undecided	15	12	14
Percentage of cities using:			
Salt	97	97	86
Calcium chloride	60	48	30
Sand	28	48	47
Cinders	0	8	11
Percentage of cities plowing some or all sidewalks	73	60	27
Average number of sidewalk plows per 100 miles of street	3.1	2.7	2.2
Number of snow-belt cities replying to questionnaire	30	92	70

SOURCE: R. R. Fleming, "More Plows and Better Plans," *The American City,* November 1968, p. 69.

Figure 11-19 For heavy work, a large four-wheel–drive truck capable of relatively high speeds and equipped with a plow that can cast the snow to one side is very useful. [The American City & County]

ditions. However, every urban area has culs-de-sac and similar street areas that often are difficult to clear with heavy equipment. For these areas, small four-wheel–drive jeep-type vehicles serve well. They also can clear parking areas, driveways, and wider sidewalks and walkways.

For very heavy work, in areas where snow drifts, large four-wheel–drive trucks carrying either a one-way or a V plow are almost indispensable. This equipment also can carry a rotary snow blower capable of clearing a roadway and also of loading the snow.

Equipment for Sidewalk Plowing

Clearing snow from heavily traveled pedestrian walkways has become an increasingly significant responsibility in any snow-removal program. Sidewalks requiring clearing normally include (1) crosswalks in business districts and other locations experiencing heavy pedestrian traffic, (2) sidewalks within parks and pedestrian malls, and (3) sidewalks along streets that can expect large numbers of schoolchildren. Among other walks that may have to be kept clear of snow are those at hospitals, bus stops, and school properties. In certain prosperous suburban areas, the local government clears all sidewalks that adjoin residences. In some locations, sidewalk plowing includes walks in all business districts. As public aspirations rise, the demand for more sidewalk plowing will increase along with insistence on more urban services.

Equipment used in clearing sidewalks can include a small walking plow, a small tractor with either a bulldozer blade or a loader bucket, and occasionally plows attached to mowing equipment. Small rotary blowers also are being used. More specialized equipment has appeared in areas where snowfall is heavy. Montreal, Canada, where snowfalls can average nearly 140 inches (3556 millimeters) annually, is an example. For sidewalk plowing, this municipality makes use of a rubber-tracked unit with steel cleats. In most cases, the little tractors carry one-

Figure 11-20 A small walking plow is frequently used to clear sidewalks and parking areas. [*Gravely Motor Plow & Cultivator Co.*]

way reversible plow blades, but they can be supplied with V plows if desired. The tractor, called a Bombadier, has an enclosed cab for operator convenience. Operating speeds range from 5 to 10 miles (from 8 to 16 kilometers) per hour. While the unit is designed for specialized duty, it has been employed for light bulldozing and grading during summer months in parks and playgrounds.

Figure 11-21 This rubber-tracked sidewalk plow is proving popular in Canadian cities. [The American City & County]

Montreal officials report that two such units can clear from 55 to 60 miles (from 88 to 97 kilometers) of sidewalks in a day. Officials in the city of Quebec report even better results, with 50 miles (80 kilometers) of sidewalks cleared in a day with only one unit. Of course, much depends on the condition of the sidewalks and the depth and density of the snow being cleared.[14,15]

Plow-Blade Waxing

To prevent accumulations of snow from sticking to the faces of the plow blades when they are in use, various wax formulations can be applied. The wax must be reapplied after each snow-clearing operation.

As an alternative that reduces labor requirements, a silicone paint can be applied to the face of the plow to give it an especially smooth finish. This finish has proved more permanent than waxing; normally it can last for a full season. One typical silicone product carries the trade name Sno-Flo (Meyer Products, Inc., Cleveland, Ohio).[16]

SNOW LOADING, BLOWING, AND DISPOSAL

After the plows have opened the traffic lanes so that vehicles can move in a limited fashion, the task of removing the windrowed snow remains. Except in unusual situations, removal should be started in the evening after traffic loads have disappeared or at least have been reduced. Loading should begin in the portions of the street system where the traffic is heaviest and the need for all lanes to be cleared is greatest.

Front-End Loaders

In all urban maintenance tasks, equipment that can perform more than one assignment and be active all year is especially desirable. The most popular such piece of equipment is the versatile front-end tractor loader mounted on rubber tires. Units of this type have been used for everything from snow plowing to changing street lights and to rescuing people trapped in flooded areas.

In areas of light snow, under 20 inches (508 millimeters) annually, front-end loaders represent nearly 85 percent of the snow-loading equipment. The balance generally is divided among snow blowers, which are specialized units, conveyor loaders, designed primarily to load sand and gravel but drafted for this emergency work, and miscellaneous other equipment.

In areas of greater snowfall, averaging 50 inches (1270 millimeters) or

---

[14] J. McFeggan, "Why We Began Plowing Sidewalks," *The American City*, January 1970, p. 70.

[15] J. V. Arpin, "Contract Snowfighting," *The American City*, December 1969, p. 98.

[16] R. A. Bartholomew, "Snow Need Not Be a Sticky Business," *The American City*, March 1969, p. 28.

Figure 11-22   The useful and versatile tractor-mounted front-end loader performs well in snow-loading operations.   [The American City & County]

more per year, dependence on front-end loaders declines, but they still account for about half of the snow-loading equipment.   The share of blowers rises to about one-third, and conveyor loaders represent most of the balance.   During heavy snows, draglines and power shovels also have been called into service.

The effectiveness of the front-end tractor loader can be enhanced if it is equipped with an oversize snow bucket for loading.   The normal bucket has been designed to lift material much heavier than snow and consequently is underutilized in snow-loading work.   The usefulness of the tractor loader can be increased still more if the bucket can be emptied at the side rather than from the front.   This feature permits the operator to pick up a bucket of snow and dump it directly into a truck awaiting beside the windrow of snow without time-consuming maneuvering by the tractor.

Figure 11-23   In some instances, oversize "snow buckets" enhance the usefulness of a loader.   [The American City & County]

A further advantage of the tractor loader is that it can be used to plow during the day.   At night the plow can be removed and the bucket attached.   A snow-blower unit also can be attached to this tractor if desired.

Snow Blowers

As the volume of snow increases and the need for quick snow clearance is intensified, a unit faster than the front-end loader becomes necessary. The equipment used most often is the high-capacity snow blower. Snow blowers range from extremely large units with the cab mounted

Figure 11-24   Snow blowers can be obtained in many sizes and types. Here a walking blower clears a pedestrian pathway on a bridge.   [The American City & County]

Figure 11-25   Snow blowers also can be mounted as an attachment on a jeep-type vehicle.   [The American City & County]

Figure 11-26   Blower-loaders work well as tractor attachments.   [The American City & County]

over the rotary unit and the discharge chute in back of the cab so that the driver's vision always is as clear as possible to small, walking-type blowers for clearing sidewalks and driveways.   The blowers may be mounted on large four-wheel–drive trucks, on smaller trucks, on tractors or graders, or even on power lawn mowers that are put into service for snow work.

The large units frequently have directional discharge chutes so that they can throw the snow into vacant fields or direct it into waiting trucks,

Figure 11-27   Heavy-duty blower-loaders with directional chutes have proved able to load quickly and pack snow into a truck firmly.   [The American City & County]

Figure 11-28   Although extra-heavy snow blowers are not designed to load, they can do a powerful job of casting snow and are especially useful at airports. Note that the discharge chute is behind the cab, giving the operator good visibility at all times. [The American City & County]

where they are able to pack the snow very tightly. To permit easier dumping of a blower-loaded truck the operator frequently removes the tailgate and depends on the packed density of the snow to hold the load in place.

Snow Disposal

The problem of where to put the snow after it has been loaded into trucks can be challenging. Early in the year, the supervisors should try to select dumping areas large enough to accept the expected accumulations of snow.

If a river or other body of water is nearby, it can be a convenient disposal location, provided that environmentalists do not challenge the practice as a pollution threat, since polluting material is on the streets. Carefully selected open fields can be used if enough are available. In a few cases it may be possible to discharge some of the snow into the storm drainage system through snow chutes, although this practice also may come under environmental challenge.

Snow-Melting Pits

Certain Canadian cities such as Toronto and Quebec, where snowfalls are heavy and the weather offers little opportunity for melting, make use of artificially heated snow-melting pits. Most use direct-firing, fuel-oil–

Figure 11-29 Snow-melting pits or channels are used to dispose of snow in areas where snowfall is excessive and disposal points are difficult to locate. [The American City & County]

fed burners. The Canadian melting pits are designed to accept snow at 10°F (−12.2°C) weighing 35 pounds per cubic foot (561 kilograms per cubic meter). Snow introduced to the pit at these standards requires about 165 British thermal units per pound (383,790 joules per kilogram) to be transformed into water at 42°F (5.6°C).

Pits need a continuous grit-removal mechanism and also a reliable method of moving the semimelted material to the exit end of the pit. The burners fire vertically downward 18 inches (457 millimeters) below the surface through tubes 20 inches (508 millimeters) in diameter. Each tube has a baffle plate 1½ inches (38.1 millimeters) from the end. These heat the water sufficiently to generate hot bubbles that in turn develop turbulence in the melting pond. Turbulence appears to be highly important. Even in warm water, a stationary mass of snow soon builds up a layer of cold water that insulates the remaining mass from the surrounding warmth.

Since melting takes place principally near the tubes, the snow dumped into the pits must be moved toward them. Water jets protected by cover plates and discharging from the side of the pit where the dumping occurs move the snow to the melting tubes.

The walls of the pit should be at a 60-degree angle from the horizontal. The pits should be supplied with a chain-and-flight grit-removal mechanism 4 feet (1.2 meters) wide at the bottom. The water depth should be about 6½ feet (19.8 meters) with an overall pit depth of 9 feet (2.7 meters).[17]

[17] "Snow Melting at 64¢ per Ton," *The American City,* November 1966, p. 34.

Melting by Radiant Heat

Snow also can be melted by radiant heat, which avoids the necessity of plowing or removal as well as the need for deicing salts. However, the first cost of the installation is high, and its use has been limited. In downtown areas of high value, merchants have occasionally employed radiant heat to keep the sidewalks clear at all times. It also has found use at key access points in heavily traveled areas that must be kept constantly open and at strategic locations such as the driveways of fire stations subject to frequent calls.

In most cases, radiant heat uses pipes embedded in the concrete base of the pavement. It rarely has been employed in a pavement made of asphaltic concrete, although it probably could be used with the correct selection of asphalt.

Generally, an ethylene glycol solution that has been warmed by a fuel-fired heat exchanger circulates through the pipe. The pipe, which may be 1½ inches (38.1 millimeters) in diameter, should be placed in the concrete slab at least 2½ inches (63.5 millimeters) below the surface. In other designs the piping system consists of two headers 2 inches (50.8 millimeters) in diameter at each side of the slab, with ¾-inch (19.05-millimeter) pipe connecting the headers in grid fashion.[18]

One radiant-heating application that makes use of electric heating cables is employed on a steep grade reaching to Holyrood Palace in Edinburgh, Scotland. The cables are placed in panels of half-carriageway width. A bituminous surfacing covers the cables to a 2-inch (50.8-millimeter) depth.[19]

[18] "Melting System Clears Fire House Drives," *The American City,* February 1968, p. 44; "Snow Melting on a Serpentine Street," *The American City,* January 1969, p. 40.
[19] "Try Radiant Heat for Snow Removal," *The American City,* January 1972, p. 36.

Figure 11-30   Where the need for continuous and reliable snow removal is essential, radiant heat has proved its worth. This installation is in the driveway of a fire station in Maywood, New Jersey. [The American City & County]

RENTAL OF EQUIPMENT
AND CONTRACT SERVICES

The rental of reserve snow-removal equipment and contracts with appropriate firms for both personnel and equipment are essential parts of any program for snow and ice control.   Although municipalities must be ready to contend with snow and ice situations of an emergency magnitude, it is not economically feasible for them to own all the equipment that would be needed for critical periods that may occur infrequently. Moreover, contractors and other suppliers whose work is normally suspended during winter months have usable equipment and normally welcome this opportunity to put the units to constructive use.

As is the case in all other aspects of snow and ice control, the rental of equipment and the preparation of contracts for personnel and equipment deserve careful planning before a snow or ice emergency arrives. The preliminary work normally will include (1) a survey of all contractors and equipment suppliers to see whether they have equipment that can be adapted to this type of work at a reasonable cost and whether they wish to participate and (2) a tabulation of supporting equipment needed to convert the contractor-owned vehicles for snow and ice control.

Equipment Needed from Renting Suppliers

Equipment available from contracting firms generally includes heavy dump trucks to haul snow, front-end loaders and loaders of other types, graders, bulldozers, and, possibly, ready-mix–concrete transport trucks to be used for snow plowing.   The supporting equipment that the municipality probably must provide usually consists of plows and the push frames that hold the plows to the trucks.   If the municipality is in an area of heavy snowfall and the contractors feel that they can depend on plowing as a reliable source of supplemental income, they may be persuaded to purchase their own plows and push frames.   Otherwise the municipality must acquire them and make sure that they will fit the greatest number of available trucks.

Equipment Not Available for Rent

In general, salt and abrasive spreaders are not available for rent because of the specialized hydraulic equipment involved.   V plows and snow-blower attachments, especially those that can be used on front-end loaders and graders, also rarely are available on a rental basis.   When loaders and graders are rented, the contractors, anticipating that they will be used with snow-blowing equipment, probably will ask that the municipality meet the cost of incorporating the hydraulic systems of the contractors' equipment into the blowers or loaders.   This is a point that must be resolved early in the season.

Rental crawler tractors should be supplied with street pads by the contractors. Crawler tractors operating without pads can do great damage to streets, especially asphalt streets.

While graders are excellent units for snow-clearance work, unless the municipality is fortunate, rental equipment will not be as useful as its own graders, since they will not ordinarily be able to use the attachments that increase the graders' snow-fighting potential. Among such attachments are V plows, bulldozer-type blades, snow blowers, moldboard extensions, and wing blades.

Contract Terms

The simplest contract arrangement is on a cost-per-hour basis. In arranging contracts, the municipality must realize that it will have to compete with others who also want snow-removal service. These can include the operators of shopping centers, industrial parking lots, owners of private roadways and drives, and adjoining municipalities.

The contractors generally will find an agreement more attractive if the municipality offers a minimum annual payment that will reimburse them for an agreed minimum number of rental hours. If the contractors' services are required beyond this minimum, their rental payment will be at the agreed contract price per hour.

Contract Details

In any rental agreement, a number of small but important items must not be overlooked. Representative terms are as follows:

1. Fuel, lubricants, and hydraulic oil are to be supplied by the contractors.

2. Public-liability and property-damage insurance are to be provided by the contractors in accordance with the municipality's specifications.

3. Tire chains are provided by the contractors if the municipality feels that they are needed.

4. Downtime, spare parts, and transportation to and from the points of snow-removal work are to be specified in advance.

The contract also should specify precisely when payment starts and when it stops. Legal counsel should review the agreement as carefully as it reviews any other contract.

Two-Way Radio on Rental Equipment

Under the most effective conditions, all equipment should be provided with two-way radio to ensure that it is utilized to its greatest advantage. The importance of good radio equipment in emergencies cannot be overemphasized.

Many contractors already have radio equipment. Consequently, the municipality should investigate ways of incorporating this equipment into its own system.   It can provide a telephone tie-in between its dispatcher and the contractors' dispatcher, obtain approval from the Federal Communications Commission to place the contractors' frequency on that of the municipal communications system, or require the contractors to provide a base or portable unit on their frequency at the municipality's operational headquarters.   The municipality can also provide a radio unit on its frequency at the contractors' base station. If the contractors do not have two-way radio, the municipality can provide portable units on as many of their vehicles as are available.

Rental Contractor Assignments

To make the most effective use of contractors who agree to supply rental equipment and personnel, those administering the snow-control program should try to assign each contractor the same route each year so that the contractor's workers will be familiar with it.   Contractors also should be given some level of responsibility for their equipment while they are on call.   Some agreed liaison between the contractors and the municipal snow-control organization must be established in advance.   Options that have been successful include the following:

1. In the contract with the supplying firm, a complete crew should be requested for a specific area.   Provision of the crew would include trucks, loaders, graders, and any other needed equipment.   The contractor supervises the crew as an operating subsection of the public agency.

2. In the contract, the supplier is requested to provide a specified group of equipment units and vehicles.   The contractor reports to a district superintendent with the vehicles for assignment.[20]

SUPPORTING SERVICES

During an emergency such as a snowstorm when trucks and other mobile equipment must operate for long hours, supporting equipment must be provided.   Trucks break down or become immobilized in snowdrifts.   Fuel is required.

To respond to this need, utility crews must be organized to go to the aid of immobilized equipment or to move equipment from one location to another if needed.   Each crew should be equipped with a wrecker truck, preferably with a boom and winch, and with two-way radio equipment to provide constant contact with the dispatcher's office.   The truck should have a two-person crew.

[20] A. F. Jungers, "How to Use Contractors for Snow Removal," *The American City,* October 1970, p. 70.

Service repair facilities also should be provided. Trucks used to provide this service must be stocked with parts, supplies, and other equipment needed for field repairs. Each truck should have two mechanics assigned to it.

Tank trucks should be provided to keep the trucks assigned to plowing supplied with fuel. They should be stationed at convenient locations known to the plowing crews. Arrangements also can be made for the trucks to obtain fuel at fire stations throughout the community.

SNOW FENCES

Of all the tools available to the administrator responsible for snow and ice control, none has been used with less effectiveness than snow fences to control drifting. Some people dismiss them as unimportant because "they just fill up and drift over anyway." When snow fences are placed according to rational principles, however, they can keep a roadway clear of drifting and thus eliminate costly plowing. They also can improve visibility during a storm by trapping the snow that normally would blow across the roadway. At the same time, they reduce the possibility of ice formation caused by snow on a roadway.

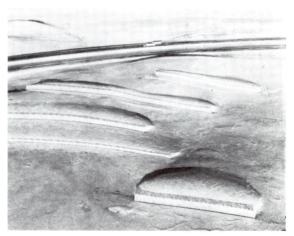

Figure 11-31 Scientifically placed snow fences located on this stretch of Wyoming highway completely stopped drifting by capturing snow that would have traveled across the roadway. Four are 12-foot (3.6-meter) fences, and one is a 6-foot (1.8-meter) fence. [*U.S. Forest Service*]

Effect of the Snow Transport Distance

One of the concepts that few recognize is that blowing and drifting snow travels only for a well-defined distance. It does not travel for miles, as most people believe, coming to rest when the wind ceases. Studies by

Dr. R. A. Schmidt, Jr., of the Rocky Mountain Forest and Range Experiment Station, Fort Collins, Colorado, have shown that the snow particles undergo evaporation or, more properly, sublimation until they finally disappear.[21]   The rate of sublimation depends primarily on solar radiation, ambient temperatures, relative humidity, and the size of the snow particles.   In Wyoming, at an elevation of 8000 feet (2438 meters) where some of the tests were conducted, a snow particle will travel an average of 4000 feet (1219 meters) before disappearing through sublimation.   For every 18°F (32.4°C) increase in temperature, the sublimation rate approximately doubles.

Tests conducted by Dr. Ronald D. Tabler, principal Forest Service research hydrologist of the U.S. Department of Agriculture, have shown that blowing snow tends to concentrate at a level close to the ground. About 95 percent of the snow transported in the first 15 feet (4.6 meters) above the ground is contained in the first 3 feet (0.9 meters).

Rules for Placing Snow Fences

Dr. Tabler has developed a scientific and technically sound method of calculating where a fence should be placed to be effective in preventing drifting.   And he has used this method to control drifting on troublesome sections of Interstate 80 as it passes through Wyoming.[22] The fences have allowed these sections to remain open throughout bad winter seasons, whereas in the past they had to be closed for much of the winter.   However, Dr. Tabler also has established practical rules that will enable urban administrators to reexamine their use of snow fences and, by experimentation, to enable their crews to place the fences at points of maximum effectiveness.   His guidelines are as follows:

1. Place the fence at a distance from the road right-of-way at least 25 times the height of the fence from ground level.

2. Place the bottom of the fence between 6 and 18 inches (between 152.4 and 457.2 millimeters) above the ground.

3. Maintain a porosity of fence of about 50 percent (the distance between fence boards or slats should be equal to the width of the individual boards or slats).

4. Place the fence perpendicular to the prevailing wind.

With regard to the first point, the fence should be sufficiently far from the roadway so that the developed drift will not reach it.   Normally the drift will extend from 20 to 25 times the height of the fence.   The height should be measured from the top of the fence to the ground and include the distance that the fence is above the ground.

[21] R. A. Schmidt, Jr., *Sublimation of Wind-transported Snow: A Model*, Forest Service Research Paper RM-90, U.S. Department of Agriculture, May 1972.

[22] R. D. Tabler, *Evaluation of the First-Year Performance of the Interstate-80 Snow-Fence System*, Wyoming Highway Department, Aug. 15, 1972.

The second point recognizes that wind velocities at ground level are minor. Consequently the snow at ground level will be less subject to drifting. The gap helps to keep the drift from burying the fence and causing it to lose effectiveness.[23,24]

Rows of Fences

The number of rows of fences and the fence height depend on the amount of snow expected to fall within the distance that the snow will travel before being sublimated, that is, within the transport distance. Dr. Tabler has developed methods of calculating this figure on a theoretical basis. He also suggests that a good method of determining the required snow storage is to measure the largest drifts that can be found in the particular area, either in road cuts or in natural accumulation areas. If the amount expected in the transport area is greater than the quantity that a single row of snow fence can capture, then either another row is required or a taller fence should be used to capture a greater amount.

Height of Fences

Dr. Tabler's tests indicate that tall fences are more efficient in trapping snow than short ones are. However, his most convincing conclusion is that construction costs per unit of snow storage when using a 12-foot (3.7-meter) snow fence are about two-thirds less than when using 6-foot (1.8-meter) fences with equal storage capacity.

Increase in Water Resources

Although water resources are far removed from this chapter's subject, their importance is great enough to make them worth mentioning. Many areas depend on melting snow for their water supplies and often refer to their "snow crop" as their supplemental reservoir. Much moisture can be lost on these watersheds through in-transit sublimation. Snow fences located on the brows of valleys can capture and hold snow that would sublimate and be lost if the fences were not there. In the high plains of Wyoming, where Dr. Tabler developed this method of increasing the potential of water resources, about one-third of the winter's total precipitation is lost through sublimation. Dr. Tabler's experiments showed an increase in the snowpack on a test area of 133 percent through the use of a single row of fence.

[23] R. D. Tabler and D. L. Veal, "Effect of Snow Fence Height on Wind Speed," *Bulletin of the International Association of Scientific Hydrology*, vol. XVI, no. 4, December 1971, pp. 49–56.

[24] *New Snow-Fence Design Controls Drifts, Improves Visibility, Reduces Road Ice*, Annual Transportation Engineering Conference, University of Colorado, February 1973.

The ability of a fence to capture snow diminishes as the accumulation of snow increases. Therefore, to maintain high snow-trapping capabilities, fences that are higher than those normally used to control drifting are required.[25]

---

[25] R. D. Tabler, "Design of a Watershed Snow-Fence System," *Western Snow Conference Proceedings,* vol. 39, pp. 50–55, April, 1971.

Chapter Twelve

Urban-Park Maintenance

WILLIAM S. FOSTER

HOW PARKS ORIGINATE

No one has yet developed a satisfactory standard park, although many have tried. Parks come into being by responding to the desires of the people to be served and also to the characteristics of the parkland itself. If the proposed area has natural physical traits that make it of special interest, such as waterfalls, an attractive grouping of hills, wetlands, or a historic center, the design of the park facilities can take advantage of them. But most parks in urban areas must make use of land obtained where it is accessible and, it is hoped, where conflicting land uses are small.

Often such potential urban parkland results from property given to

Figure 12-1 Parks like this, one of several in St. Petersburg, Florida, can create peaceful environments.

Figure 12-2 This Sacramento, California, park adds to the interest and pleasure of young people. [*U.S. Bureau of Reclamation photo*]

the municipality. In other cases, the land is not particularly good for other purposes and is not difficult to acquire. Occasionally it is land that does not fit into other urban planning and development. Los Angeles has a small and charming park in its downtown area that the planners have lightheartedly called "Sloip," an acronym meaning "space left over in planning." Seattle has developed small neighborhood park spaces, called "street triangles," out of unused areas left in street-improvement programs.

Central Park in New York also came into being by taking advantage of available land that at the time had virtually no conflicting land uses. The land, acquired prior to the Civil War, was in a remote location, a tangle of swamps, low hills, and rocks unused except by a few squatters. However, the great urban planner Frederick Law Olmsted eventually created a magnificent park complex out of it. This park has been a vital part of New York life ever since.

Phoenix, Arizona, likewise took advantage of available land that did not have conflicting uses. Phoenix acquired an entire mountain as a

Figure 12-3   Small unused parcels of land can be developed into charming park areas like this.

park resource and developed its many challenging qualities into a tremendously valuable urban recreational asset.

However, conflicting land uses commonly arise to create troublesome problems if the best interests of the community are to be served. The beautiful Chicago lakefront, probably the most attractive urban development in the United States, had to overcome the belligerent and aggressive opposition of commercial interests occupying the area before it could come into being. The opposition frequently bordered on violence.

Jones Beach, located on what was once a windswept sandy island off the south shore of Long Island, New York, and in the New York City metropolitan area, has brought great pleasure to millions through its imaginative design and development. Nevertheless, it had to overcome angry opposition, even from the New York Regional Plan Association. Some are still reluctant to recognize the tremendous benefits of this magnificent park complex.

In the case of neighborhood parks and the acquisition of park space,

Figure 12-4   This is the way the area in Figure 12-3 looked prior to improvement.

Figure 12-5   Central Park in New York faced no conflicting land uses when planner Frederick Law Olmsted created it more than a century ago out of land that at that time was remote, swampy, full of large rocks, and largely unused.   [*City of New York Department of Parks and Recreation*]

Figure 12-6 Jones Beach, on the south shore of Long Island, New York, faced angry opposition, which was overcome by the determination of the park creator, Robert Moses. [*Triborough Bridge and Tunnel Authority, New York*]

the problems are not always so great or conflicting land uses so significant. Land devoted to such purposes would otherwise be used for housing. Planners can insist, particularly in the case of a new subdivision, that a park in a strategically favorable location would be profitable for the developer and would better serve the interests of potential residents.

HOW TO MEASURE PARK UTILIZATION[1]

The advice to place parks where the people are has degenerated almost into a cliché and is far easier to say than to activate. A well-planned, well-maintained park with good recreation facilities will attract people and often will add to the value of adjoining property, especially if the design of the park can insulate adjacent neighbors from undue noise and activity. Nevertheless, if a municipality creates a park that no one uses, it has wasted its investment. Some type of measurement is needed to appraise park use and the benefits that the park brings.

Some simple and logical coefficients that will help in this appraisal can be developed. These coefficients are suggestive rather than conclusive. Each makes use of readily available data and is addressed to a particular characteristic of the park and its utilization.

[1] The section "How to Measure Park Utilization" is a contribution of Prof. William S. Hendon, Department of Urban Studies, University of Akron.

Intensity-of-Use Coefficient

The first of these coefficients, the intensity-of-use (I-U) coefficient, provides a measure of the current use of the park. To make the evaluation, samples of use must be taken at given points in time. More specifically, these samples should be head counts by activity groupings over a series of hours of the day, over a series of days, and through the seasons of use of the park. The counts can be averaged "horizontally" for the entire park or separated "vertically" by activities and then averaged.

To determine the intensity-of-use coefficient, the average use per point in time should be divided by an estimated capacity of the park facilities. For example, if a park bench is designed to seat 4 people and the park has 12 benches, the maximum capacity of this feature is 48 at any point in time. Other features of the park facilities can be subjected to similar analysis. A swimming pool can hold a maximum safe limit by health standards; each table-tennis unit can accommodate a maximum of four people; and swings, picnic tables, and other equipment have measurable maximum limits that can yield use coefficients. The system is particularly valuable when analyzing the use-type parks that have a variety of activities. From these calculations and estimates, the intensity-of-use coefficient then becomes

$$\text{I-U coefficient} = \frac{\text{actual average use per point in time}}{\text{estimated present capacity}}$$

If the ratio falls at unity, or 1, then presumably the park, on the average, is being used to capacity. If the ratio is greater than 1, the park could be considered overcrowded or overutilized. If it is less than 1, the park could be considered underutilized.

In any estimate such as this, the result must be reasonable. If it does not appear so, the estimating techniques should be scrutinized. However, if they prove sound, a more searching examination is required to discover why the calculations produce an unreasonable I-U coefficient. Has the park been designed for peak rather than average loadings? A community would not be well served by designing a park able on a year-round basis to accommodate a Fourth-of-July crowd.

When the I-U coefficient is applied to all urban parks of similar types, the results can be challenging. Why, for example, do the coefficients vary widely among playgrounds? Is the park governing body operating under unsound planning criteria?

When the capacity of a park is being approximated, an approximation must be made for open space. The only effective means of estimating open-space capacity would be on the basis of head counts. Actual observed open-space estimates would be somewhat conservative, biased downward, but there appears to be no better way to make the estimates.

Design Coefficient

The design coefficient is the second useful calculation for park analysis. From it, one should be able to estimate how the usefulness of the park can be enhanced and the capacity increased by redesigning it to newer quality standards.   An evaluation team consisting of professional park administrators, landscape architects, and professors of art, along with affected local citizens, could evaluate the present park system and recommend additions or deletions of facilities or programs.   Since most parks have developed over a long period, severe design failures may have occurred without notice.

The purpose of the design coefficient is a comparison of current with potential capacity; it can help uncover the reason why certain parks are underutilized.   In simple terms the design coefficient is as follows:

$$\text{Design coefficient} = \frac{\text{estimated present capacity}}{\text{redesigned capacity}}$$

Optimal-Use Coefficient

The optimal-use (O-U) coefficient is another factor that can aid in analyzing a park system.   It relates the actual use of the park at a specific point in time to the park's redesigned capacity.   As another check on current park-design standards, this coefficient effectively indicates any disparity between current and maximum use.   As a formula, the optimal-use coefficient is as follows:

$$\text{O-U coefficient} = \frac{\text{actual average use per point in time}}{\text{redesigned capacity}}$$

When the O-U coefficient is 1, the park capacity can be considered at maximum use.   If the ratio is a fraction of 1, the park is underutilized; and if it is greater than 1, park use is excessive.

Spatial-Distribution Coefficient

The spatial-distribution (S-D) coefficient is the fourth factor that will assist in urban-park analysis.   By gathering regular samples of park attendance as well as the residences of the users and plotting these on maps, it is possible to develop a park service zone or area of use.   And although the procedure is somewhat difficult, estimates of the actual user population can be ascertained.   These estimates can be matched with the population that the design anticipates would be served by the park.   If, for example, a park is designed to serve 1000 people but the survey shows only 100 users, the coefficient would be .10.   The S-D coefficient is as follows:

$$\text{S-D coefficient} = \frac{\text{estimated population in actual user zone}}{\text{population anticipated in design}}$$

Park-Size Coefficient

The park-size (P-S) coefficient permits evaluating the actual acreage in a park and comparing it with what the design standard suggests is desirable for the particular type of park.

$$\text{P-S coefficient} = \frac{\text{actual size of the park (in acres or hectares)}}{\text{recommended size (in acres or hectares)}}$$

Other Coefficients and Usefulness of the Method

A few other coefficients could be developed. They might include coefficients of lighting, of the quality of supervision, of neighborhood identification with the park, and of user satisfaction. All will help to provide a more thorough understanding of the individual park units serving a designated urban area.

An analysis of the park potential in a large city shows the usefulness of the coefficient method. The results for one of the city's parks are as shown in the accompanying table. These results document the conclusions that the park is too large, serves too great a population in too large an area, and while well designed, lacks sufficient intensity of use.

Coefficient	Value	Interpretation
Intensity of use	.116	Seriously underutilized with significant idle capacity
Design	.918	Designed well with little need for change of physical facilities
Optimal use	.108	Seriously underutilized on the basis of redesigned capacity
Spatial distribution	1.63	Poor spatial allocation; too distant from other parks and serving too large a population
Park size	1.59	Too large for recommended service zone based on population

CITIZEN PARTICIPATION IN PARK SURVEYS

Periodic surveys of the people served by park facilities will provide guidance on the effectiveness of the parks for different citizen groups. The greater the citizen input and the greater the response to that input, the surer of success the park program will be.

A manual prepared by the Urban Institute of Washington and published by the U.S. Government Printing Office describes how a government might go about collecting citizen feedback in this area.[2] Two tests of the procedures, one in Washington and the other in Rockford, Illinois, disclosed that despite highly publicized urban crime problems, fear or concern for safety evidently plays a minor part in the public's

[2] *How Effective Are Your Community Recreation Services?* U.S. Department of the Interior, Bureau of Outdoor Recreation, April 1973.

decision to use or not to use park and recreation facilities. About half of the people within range of the facilities in the two cities did not use them for reasons that could be attributed partly to management itself. Roughly half of the reasons cited reflected lack of publicity or information about the facilities; another 25 percent of the respondents gave location as the reason why they did not use the facilities. Potential danger at the park amounted to no more than 6 percent of the reasons.[3]

Citizen involvement is basic to good park administration or, for that matter, to the administration of any municipal service. No professional is sufficiently skilled to anticipate the park and recreation needs which the people of a community actually feel that they want.

Joseph J. Bannon, chief of recreation and park resources of the University of Illinois, has offered a fifteen-point list of suggestions to help win citizens' support for a park program that would involve their community or neighborhood:[4]

1. Don't expect people to agree and rubber-stamp all the programs and policies of your park program.

2. Don't underestimate the people's ability to make rational decisions.

3. Do make every effort to explain to the people involved what your own problems and anxieties are about the proposals so that they will be able to give more substantial support to the proposals that they like and approve of.

4. Do understand that the citizens involved will use a value system different from yours.

5. Do understand that inner-city residents, especially ghetto communities, are already skeptical of your concern for citizen involvement.

6. Don't overcommit yourself. Make clear what you can and cannot do under existing laws and ordinances. Don't let yourself be trapped into an accusation that you "didn't produce as you said you would."

7. Do encourage involved citizens to explore your programs and your park administration. Be confident that this will strengthen your work.

8. Do encourage involved people to speak freely.

9. Do initiate a program of involvement for citizens before a crisis hits and their involvement will be too late to do any good.

10. Be a good listener. Involved citizens generally have worthwhile things to say.

[3] "Survey Citizens to Assess Park and Recreation Needs," *The American City,* November 1973, p. 122.

[4] Joseph J. Bannon, "Do's and Don'ts of Citizen Involvement in Good Park and Recreation Programs," *The American City,* February 1971, p. 20.

11. Offer involved citizens some control over policies and fiscal arrangements.

12. Be sure that involved citizens actually are representative of the community. Frequently those with established communitywide reputations do not necessarily represent a neighborhood's interests.

13. Give involved citizens opportunities to discuss all items, including administration and finance. You may lose time at the start, but you will get a better program eventually.

14. Encourage involved citizens to present formal written reports on programs and policy recommendations. This will help special-interest groups and disgruntled minorities.

15. Help involved citizens to realize that you consider them allies, not a threat.

Community recreation facilities not under the direct control of the community park and recreation department should be incorporated into the overall recreation program. Such facilities can include neighborhood athletic clubs, men's and women's groups, church clubs, veterans' halls, and other groups with strong local identity.

With constructive approaches, it is possible to enlist volunteers and often to get the use of sports equipment, costumes, musical instruments, and meeting rooms that can supplement those provided by the community. If this cooperative work is planned well, it can strengthen the overall recreation program.

Schools and universities also have facilities that can be used in a recreation program; generally their administrators are anxious to cooperate with the local community. Military installations near the community also offer resources that can be incorporated into the local recreation program.[5]

PARK-MAINTENANCE EQUIPMENT

Although park maintenance requires a wide range of equipment, mowers of various types appear to be the largest classification, understandably so since about half of the park acreage is devoted to grassland. And this grass needs cutting at least thirty times a year and possibly forty times in the extreme southern areas of the nation.

Other types of equipment commonly used include seeders and spreaders, for both fertilizers and insecticides; sprayers and foggers; stump cutters; leaf loaders of various types; leaf mulchers; lawn sweepers; lawn and hedge trimmers; landscape rakes; chain saws; tractors and attachments, other than mowers; and transportation vehicles of various

---

[5] Joseph E. Curtis, "Park Programs on a Bare-Bones Budget," *The American City*, December 1971, p. 51.

Figure 12-7   Mowers of various types represent the largest single classification of park-maintenance equipment.

types such as cars, pickup trucks, scooter-type "trucksters," and trucks with dump bodies.[6]

The three-wheeled scooter type of vehicle equipped to carry limited loads and some personnel is demonstrating great usefulness in park maintenance because of its flexibility and adaptability to many duties. When a pickup box is provided at the rear and the personnel seat doubles as a toolbox, one man can perform such diverse duties as picking up litter baskets, hauling hose and sprinkler attachments, pulling a drag mesh to renew a baseball diamond or other playing fields, and transporting sprayer accessories for the application of fungicides and insecticides. The unit is especially useful in maintaining golf courses and is relatively inexpensive to operate. It materially extends the effectiveness of human power and reduces labor costs.[7]

[6] John B. Scott, *Survey of Park Maintenance Equipment, The American City,* Research Department, Pittsfield, Mass., 1974.

[7] "Three-Wheelers Influence Park Care," *The American City,* August 1972, p. 71.

Figure 12-8   Stump cutters like these have simplified a difficult maintenance task. [The American City]

Figure 12-9   The collection of leaves is a continuing assignment in any park system well supplied with trees.   Vacuum
loaders like this one help to carry it out.   [The American
City]

Figure 12-10   Chippers of this type greatly simplify brush collection and
also provide a continuous supply of chips for mulch.   [*Wayne Products photo*]

Figure 12-11   The three-wheeled scooter type of vehicle pulling a trailer has proved valuable for its flexibility and maneuverability.   [*Allegheny County, Pennsylvania, Department of Works photo*]

When a number of parks are maintained with one crew, a pickup truck with a large cab is proving to be worth its investment.   Both the mobility and the comfort of the crew are important, and a truck of this type can carry four persons easily.   The truck should be supplied with a trailer to transport equipment such as a riding mower and trim mowers. The truck itself should carry supporting equipment and be provided with a two-way radio to avoid backtracking as the crew moves from one assignment to another.[8]

PARK MOWING

Efficient mowing techniques as well as park design details that help make mowing faster and more effective are important means of controlling maintenance costs while not sacrificing maintenance quality.   In virtually all parks, grass occupies the largest part of the area, and the cost of mowing can get badly out of hand without proper attention to some rather simple details.

The first is the selection of mowing equipment.   *Reel mowers* appear to be best for maintaining areas that are programmed for regular cutting, while *rotary mowers* are more effective in tall grass, weeds, or brush. The small, walking type of *sickle-bar mower* can be effective in land areas that may have stones, discarded cans, or other litter which pose problems for mowers of other types.   If a municipality has a weed-control ordinance requiring that lots be mowed and that the governing body will mow them and charge the property owners, this type of mower will work well in that rather rough duty.

Park design details that permit larger equipment to perform mowing will help raise efficiency and keep costs under control.   One tractor

[8] Dennis Showalter, "Park Maintenance Operation," *The American City,* March 1970, p. 84.

powering a five-gang or a seven-gang hydraulic-lift, out-front mowing unit generally outperforms as many as three tractors, each towing a three-gang unit, covering the same area.

Mowing efficiency will be increased if park areas can be designed according to these general principles:

1. Provide a continuous mowing pattern by eliminating sharp corners around buildings, retaining walls, fences, plant beds, and other above-grade landscape features.

2. Use paved mowing strips against walls and buildings and under fences to eliminate costly hand trimming.

3. Keep grass surfaces flush with paved areas such as walks, parking lots, terraces, roads, and playgrounds to prevent unnecessary trimming and to facilitate the movement of equipment from one area to another.

4. Space groups of trees or shrubberies sufficiently far apart to accommodate the mowing equipment.

5. Eliminate costly hand trimming around trees by using grass barriers such as flush metal edging.

6. Use flush paving around lawn obstructions such as light poles, fire hydrants, and drinking fountains.

7. Use low-maintenance ground cover on steep slopes and bumpy areas and other terrain that is difficult to mow.

8. In areas with sharp differences in elevation, provide ramps so that equipment can gain access easily under its own power.

9. Plan roads, walks, and entrances with sufficient widths to accommodate passage of mowing equipment easily and efficiently.

10. Keep lawn areas clear of unnecessary obstructions. Avoid locating flower beds and shrub planting where they will obstruct mowing patterns and thereby increase maintenance costs.[9]

LEAF COLLECTION AND COMPOSTING

Leaf collection and removal from a park area can be costly and time-consuming. Nevertheless, it is necessary for the healthy maintenance of the grassed surfaces.

One way to reduce the labor costs is to equip personnel with walking-type "air brooms." By taking advantage of prevailing winds, an experienced worker can windrow the leaves at the rate of about 15 acres (6 hectares) per day. These air brooms can clear leaves from corners and from shrubbery plantings so well that hand raking is virtually eliminated. They can also blow accumulated grass clippings off turf if the accumulation is heavy.

Once the leaves have been windrowed, a leaf vacuum unit such as that

[9] Walter F. Bruning, "How to Control Park Mowing Costs," *The American City*, February 1972, p. 57.

used to collect leaves from streets can pick them up handily. Other leaf-collection equipment can be used, and occasionally a park crew will bale the leaves for removal at their convenience. A bale weighs from 50 to 60 pounds (from 22.7 to 27.2 kilograms) and will reduce the volume of leaves by about 35:1. Baling operations can receive either wet or dry leaves. In Canton, Ohio, where leaf baling is practiced, garden-oriented citizens immediately pick up the bales for their own use, thus relieving the park department of a disposal expense.[10]

Composting

Leaf composting is a disposal method that should win new adherents in an ecology-minded age. It represents an activity that the municipality can undertake to restore an element in nature's cycle that in the past has been wasted, often burned. Leaves contribute to the enrichment of the soil. When they are gathered and hauled away, that link in nature's chain has been broken in the affected area. The soil deteriorates and must be renewed artificially if grasses and plants are to thrive.

One of the best-established and most successful municipal composting systems is at Maplewood, New Jersey, where it has been in operation since 1931. Leaves present difficulties in composting, but the park-maintenance personnel in this community have resolved most of them.

The first important step is to select a good site for the composting operation. It should be well drained and on a slight slope to prevent stagnant water from accumulating. It also should be hard-surfaced, either naturally or with suitable pavement, so that trucks and tractors can operate under adverse weather conditions. Furthermore, the site should be insulated from residential areas, either by distance or by plantings.

The site should be ample. To help estimate the size, Maplewood, a community with about 20,000 shade trees lining 60 miles (97 kilometers) of streets and with additional trees on property occupied by 6400 homes, uses a 2-acre (0.8-hectare) site, which provides room to compost approximately two-thirds of the collected volume of leaves, or some 12,000 cubic yards (10,973 cubic meters).

The next step is to stack the leaves carefully. The stacking should gently fluff any compacted leaves to eliminate compression points. The width of the stack should be as narrow as possible, no more than 8 to 10 feet (2.4 to 3 meters), to permit good air penetration. The height should be the operating height of the tractor bucket, generally about 12 feet (3.6 meters). Air normally will penetrate the pile through the sides of the stack to depths of 2 to 3 feet (0.6 to 0.9 meter).

Stacking should begin as soon as leaves are delivered to the site; a delay of a few days can generate odor problems. When stacking is

---

[10] "Blow Your Leaves and Bale Them," *The American City,* October 1970, p. 38.

Figure 12-12 Composting leaves is a useful method of recycling them to enrich the soil. These stacks are in the process of being built. The valley between the windrows will be cleaned and widened. [*Garden City, New York, photo*]

complete, the aisles between stacked rows should be cleaned, and the rows trimmed as nearly vertically as possible. Before stacking, the leaves should be watered thoroughly; thus a hydrant or other source of water is needed at the site. Later the tops of the leaf rows can be cupped to help add water and to receive rainfall. Normally, rain adds enough water for the composting operation.

Nitrate of soda or ammonium nitrate can be added to the stacked leaves to introduce nitrogen and enhance their fertilizer qualities. Maplewood limits this supplement to approximately 1 pound per cubic yard (0.49 kilogram per cubic meter) of stacked leaves.

Within one year decomposition will penetrate the stacks for a distance of about 3 feet (0.9 meter) from an exposed side. The leaves should then be trimmed from the initial windrow and moved to the point of final processing. Transfer and restacking mix and aerate the composted leaves and hasten the process so that it can be completed within the second year. If the compost site is sufficiently far removed so that odor is not a problem, the leaves then can be turned and restacked frequently, thus hastening the decomposition process.

Processing the compost so that it can be used for topdressing, seeding, planting, or mulching requires that it be shredded and cleaned of debris. Maplewood uses a Royer 362 soil shredder for this processing. The unit not only can shred the compost but also can fluff it, separate it from any trash, and load it into a truck.

The biggest compost users are the parks, athletic fields, and school grounds of Maplewood. A York rake spreads the compost and works it to a depth of about ½ inch (12.7 millimeters) for topdressing purposes.

One application will serve for almost four years.   Unshredded leaf compost can be used directly if it is to be plowed or rototilled into the soil.[11]

BEACH MAINTENANCE

Beach maintenance is a responsibility that a park department must assume, and keeping a beach free from debris is never-ending.   It has become particularly difficult during a period when so-called convenience packaging (not convenient for those who have to clear away the litter) and a general social philosophy of permissiveness have resulted in an explosive growth of cans, bottles, and plastic packaging on the beaches, making the task of keeping sand areas clean increasingly costly and complex.

Mechanical beach cleaners that can ease the task of clearing the debris have been developed.   One successful unit, the Barber Surf-Rake, has a cleaning width of 6 feet (1.8 meters) and a cleaning depth of 4 inches (101.6 millimeters).   The unit uses spring-steel torsion tines to pick up the debris.   (Other cleaners pick up a quantity of sand and run it through a vibrating screen, and this has caused excessive maintenance problems.)   The unit also has been able to remove broken sharp-edged shells from sand that has been freshly dredged into the beach to replace sand that ocean currents have eroded away.[12]

[11] Richard Walter, "How to Compost Leaves," *The American City,* June 1971, p. 115.

[12] LeRoy Riggs, "A Mechanized Beach Rake," *The American City,* October 1972, p. 81.

Figure 12-13   Various mechanical beach cleaners have been used over the years to improve beach sanitation.

Erosion Control

The control of beach erosion is a persistent problem associated with shifting sand that is caused by the power and persistence of ocean currents and by strong winds. Storms can make massive changes in the shoreline, and when these changes affect a popular beach area, they can disrupt the recreation and pleasure of many people.

Public demand requires park-maintenance personnel to restore the beach front and to protect it from further damage. To accomplish this, many municipalities have resorted to groins of various types, with which they have experienced varying degrees of success. A convenient and easily assembled groin can be produced by using heavy, mass-produced, three-legged Sta-Pods, which can be placed so that the legs interlock and develop a great deal of stability. These can be produced in a variety of weights, the 2-ton (1814-kilogram) and 5-ton (4536-kilogram) models being popular choices.

At the beaches maintained by the Long Island town of Hempstead, five double rows of these pods were used to construct five groins to reduce wave action that was threatening cabanas at the town park. The groins extended 100 feet (30.5 meters) from the shoreline and were reinforced with rubble placed between the double rows. The advantage of the pods is that they can be removed and reused. When the Hempstead beach appeared to have attained stability, park-maintenance personnel removed them and placed them in other areas where erosion problems were then appearing.

However, establishing natural sand dunes stabilized with beach grass and protected with sand fences has proved to be more effective in protecting and stopping beach erosion at the Hempstead parks than groins of any size or length. These fences are the familiar snow fences adapted

Figure 12-14 Groins offer some help in stabilizing a beach, and portable three-legged units like these, interlocked for strength, have shown their usefulness. [*Town of Hempstead, New York, photo*]

Figure 12-15 Sand fences often have proved even more successful than groins. They are an adaptation of the familiar snow fences. [*Town of Hempstead, New York, photo*]

to a new duty. They reduce the tendency of the sand to drift and retain it on desired areas.

Artificial headlands are a device that apparently has proved successful in Australia and Singapore but has not yet been tried in the United States. They are placed about 200 feet (61 meters) seaward from the proposed edge of the area to be reclaimed or protected and are spaced about 800 feet (244 meters) apart. They can be formed by the random dumping of rock, by the use of gabions (stone-filled containers of steel mesh coated with plastic), or by riprap over an earth fill. The headlands apparently impede the flow of sand and cause it to form crescent-shaped harborlike sandbars.[13]

Floating Piers

Floating piers for marinas that park departments must place in bodies of water where the water level varies substantially are proving their utility. They reduce maintenance costs, provide a stable elevation between the boat and the pier, are less costly to anchor, and do not require high-strength foundation soils.

Park officials can select from a number of commercially available floating-pier designs. One type uses cellular polystyrene for flotation. It employs galvanized structural components with welded connections at all points except the joints between pier sections, which are bolted together for easier maintenance and repair. Treated wood customarily forms the pier decks.

Floating piers require an anchorage system suited to the site conditions. An underwater system of galvanized mooring cables and anchors can be used to hold the floating piers in position, or spuds or piles can

[13] Richard Silvester and Siew-Koon Ho, "New Approach to Coastal Defense," *Civil Engineering,* September 1974, p. 66.

Figure 12-16 Floating piers for marinas provide a stable elevation between the boat and the pier regardless of the water level. Note the hinged ramp connecting the pier to the walkway. [The American City]

be employed to position them where appropriate. Winches can pre-tension the cables to permit adjustment of the pier position to the changing water levels.

These floating piers appear able to resist winter ice and storms rather effectively.[14]

[14] R. H. Anderson and Fred W. Reusswig, "A Gale-tested Marina," *The American City*, April 1971, p. 130.

Figure 12-17 This close-up shows how the floats support the piers. [The American City]

PLAYGROUNDS

Playground concepts appear to be changing. In the past, playground designs tended to become stereotyped into what some chose to call the SST pattern (slides, swings, and teeter-totters), and youngsters, not

Figure 12-18 Treated logs innovatively assembled provide an enjoyable play area for active youngsters.

Figure 12-19 An old airplane helps to add interest to this play area. [*Miami-Metro photo*]

surprisingly, often found them boring. One young subteenager, when interviewed about his family's move from the inner city to the "more wholesome" environment of the suburbs, said: "There aren't any alleys, and there aren't any fences to climb and walk on." This complaint showed his desire for something more imaginative in a park than a piece of grass with the conventional play equipment on it.

Many innovative park administrators are responding to this desire by equipping play areas to emphasize themes that challenge and attract youngsters. Some adopt a theme such as Frontierland and provide the playground with Indian tepees, stagecoaches, and similar equipment. A play area emphasizing a space-age theme may have rocket rides, flying saucers, and possibly a model of a space capsule. Still other park administrators have developed unusual child-related play equipment using wood poles, posts, and lumber.

Play Sites

An unusual play site often appeals to children more than a conventional one, especially if the site had been denied to them previously. For example, most urban administrators consider that the space below an elevated expressway is "dead" or unusable, except possibly for parking or storage. Yet it invariably is located in an area that is short of playground space, and it always is liberally supplied with "No Trespassing" signs.

Nevertheless, a few park administrators are taking advantage of it. For example, in Miami, Florida, this type of space now provides room for basketball courts and tennis as well as swings and merry-go-rounds. It is supervised, protected by chain link fences, and provided with outdoor lighting.[15] Even more innovative was the resolution of a highway-park conflict at Manchester, Connecticut. By preliminary conferences when the highway was being considered, the town was able to acquire added athletic fields, to obtain help in developing the recreational resources of a brook for pedestrian and equestrian uses, and to improve outdoor skating facilities.

Still other park administrators have been able to get the cooperation of their water utilities and to transform space used for water storage into playground areas. Most water-storage tanks are unimaginative, warehouse types of structures with a single function and forbidding fences around them. By placing the tanks underground, a municipality is able to provide needed water storage and at the same time to obtain space for play areas of various types. The recreation activities should be those that lend themselves to the use of a concrete surface, such as tennis, basketball, handball, and shuffleboard. With them, less disruption of the entire recreational facility occurs if the reservoir needs maintenance.

[15] "Under-Expressway Playgrounds," *The American City,* October 1969, p. 46.

Garden Grove, California, has a reservoir and recreation facility that has performed satisfactorily. Nevertheless, its developers offer a few precautionary points that should be helpful in park maintenance:

1. Do not place heavy objects on the reservoir top unless you are absolutely sure that it has been designed to receive them. Such objects would include trees and other plantings in boxes.

2. Do not operate heavy vehicles or equipment on the reservoir top.

3. Avoid using fertilizers around the reservoir top if there is any possibility of seepage.

4. Any effort to grow grass on the reservoir top will probably run into difficulties because of drainage problems and because concrete is the hardest of hardpans.[16]

Movable and Temporary Play Areas

Movable play areas represent an imaginative solution to the problem of putting parks where the people are, or play areas where the children are and where no conventional play areas are available.

Some have enjoyed success in responding to this need by using traveling show wagons, each equipped with a sound system and a stage, hinged so that two persons can raise and lower it. One such wagon, in Greensboro, North Carolina, carries a number of cages with animals native to the area. A supervisor gives instructive talks about the animals and allows the children to handle those tame enough to be held safely. The wagon does not require much space and can be placed on an off-street parking lot or on a vacant lot when available. The show wagon also puts on programs using local talent from each neighborhood. At the end of the season, a final show combines the best acts of the season.

[16] Richard O. Rafanovic, "Bury the Water Reservoir," *The American City,* April 1972, p. 63.

Figure 12-20 Trailer-type vehicles like this one have been used to bring small animals to children in areas where it is difficult for them to visit zoos. [*Greensboro, North Carolina, photo*]

Greensboro also assembles a mobile athletic unit with a portable basketball goal. The supervisor of this unit generally is the coach of the local professional basketball team or one of the team's players.

Still another unit developed at Greensboro is a "playmobile" that contains enough play equipment to provide amusement for a small playground. This unit visits neighborhoods that do not have supervised play areas and provides this missing ingredient.[17]

Temporary street play areas have proved popular in densely populated sections of many cities. A relatively lightly used cross street in the central city can be closed to traffic, and an assortment of games can be arranged with striping that outlines courts for basketball, hopscotch, stickball (youngsters' imaginative adaptation of baseball to inner-city limitations), and possibly volleyball.

Play Fountains

Play fountains respond to an inner-city summer need. Rare is the large municipality that is able to prevent the casual opening of fire hydrants for inner-city play purposes during extremely hot weather. Both water

[17] Oka T. Hester, "Try Mobile Recreation Units," *The American City,* February 1971, p. 70.

Figure 12-21 Water "sculpture" such as this arrangement of piping can provide inner-city children with relief from heat without excessive use of water from fire hydrants. [*Anita Margill*]

Figure 12-22   A popular water-sculpture play area. [*Anita Margill*]

and fire department officials have tried many devices to prevent these unauthorized hydrant openings because of the dangerously heavy load that they place on the water system, critically reducing the amount of water available for fire fighting.   However, the ingenuity of the local residents has always seemed to find a way to circumvent these preventive techniques.   So, as an alternative, some have placed sprays on the hydrants.   These give a great deal of pleasure to the youngsters and do not make such excessive use of the water.

A few cities have carried this idea further to prepare more imaginative water-play fountains.   In New York the artist Anita Margill has designed what she terms "water sculpture" to provide this cooling recreation.   One of her creations, made from yellow-painted pipe, forms an X shape.   It sends out plumes of fine spray that converge into a mist so that the children can climb onto the crossarms or run through the spray.   Other examples of her water sculpture are squares set flat on the street so that children can jump through a hoop of water.   She has created about fifty of such play-type art forms for use by the city of New York.   All are portable.[18]

Permanent spray play areas also have been built into park areas. Scottsdale, Arizona, commissioned a San Francisco architect to create "dragons" of concrete in the park playgrounds.   These spout streams of water instead of fire and bring pleasure and relief to children on hot days.

[18] "Make Play Fountains in an Art form," *The American City*, April 1972, p. 10.

Skating Rinks

Temporary ice-skating rinks not equipped with freezing coils and other expensive equipment can provide the public with 8 or 9 weeks of winter pleasure at relatively low cost.   Richfield, Minnesota, offers its citizens pleasure skating and hockey on twenty-nine such outdoor rinks that are open and available starting with the school Christmas vacation period. It tries to place a rink within about 2000 feet (610 meters) of every home. Each rink is located in an area, about 150 feet (45.7 meters) wide and 200 feet (61 meters long, that does not require crossing a major street. The site must be fairly level, with a maximum grade of 0.05 percent.

These rinks receive six light spray coats of water as soon as the outdoor temperature consistently remains at or below 25°F (−3.9°C).   These $\frac{1}{16}$-inch (1.6-millimeter) coats serve to seal the cracks in the ground and provide a proper base for further flooding.   Next, coats of water $\frac{1}{4}$ inch (6.35 millimeters) in depth are placed and allowed to freeze until an average ice thickness of 3 inches (76.2 millimeters) is achieved.   For this work the park department uses the city's three 2100-gallon (7.9-cubic-meter) street flushers.

Richfield maintains the rinks on a daily basis according to weather conditions.   In case of snow, the hockey rinks are cleared by a snow blower attached to a 37-horsepower (27.6-kilowatt) tractor and then swept with a 5-foot (1.5-meter) power broom attached to a similar tractor.   All general rinks receive a daily sweeping with the power broom. When a snowfall is 2 inches (50.8 millimeters) or more, all rinks are plowed with a 7½-foot (2.3-meter) angle blade attached to a four-wheel–

Figure 12-23   Skating rinks without freezing coils can provide 8 or 9 weeks of pleasure to people in most northern areas.   [The American City]

drive pickup truck. If no snow plowing is required, all rinks receive a fresh ¼-inch (6.35-millimeter) coat of water daily to reseal the skating surface. Labor and equipment to maintain the twenty-nine rinks are assigned as follows:

Hockey Rinks		*General Skating Rinks*	
2	snow blowers	1	snow blower
2	¾-ton (680.4-kilogram) plow trucks	1	¾-ton (680.4-kilogram) plow truck
2	power brooms	2	power brooms
2	hand shovelers; no vehicle	2	maintenance personnel; a truck
1	flusher truck	2	flusher trucks

TRANSPLANTING TREES AND SHRUBBERIES [19]

Tree replacement is a continuing task. Trees die, become damaged, or do not grow well where they are. A 5 percent annual loss of trees is normal and should be anticipated. If a municipality is sufficiently large, it should maintain a tree nursery and grow most of its replacement stock. If not, it should pick a reliable supplier.

To transplant a tree successfully, these simple rules should be followed:

1. To discourage vandalism, plant trees with trunks having diameters (calipers) of 2 to 2½ inches (50.8 to 63.5 millimeters) and wrap the trunks.

[19] The section "Transplanting Trees and Shrubberies" is a contribution of Ruth S. Foster, landscape consultant, Boston, Massachusetts.

Figure 12-24 The transplanting of trees can be expedited with the use of a common truck-mounted crane. [The American City]

Figure 12-25 Trees can also be transplanted with more specialized equipment such as this. [The American City]

2. Protect the root ball of a tree that you plan to transplant. Keep it moist during transport, and do not allow it to stand in the hot sun or to wilt while awaiting planting. Bare-rooted trees should be moved while dormant.

3. Prepare a good-size hole, large enough to give the roots an opportunity to get started in enriched soil. When transplanting, fill the hole with a good loam mixed well with leaf mulch, peat moss, or other organic material. Add sand if the soil is heavy. Fertilize with an organic nitrogen fertilizer according to the directions on the fertilizer package.

4. Set the tree at the depth at which it had been growing. Cut the burlap and tuck it under the ball.

5. Soak and tamp the soil around the roots to remove air pockets while backfilling the hole. When the backfilling is completed, leave a saucer depression around the tree to catch any rainwater and help irrigate the new planting.

Figure 12-26 Winter is the most appropriate time to inspect trees and remove those that have not survived. A loss of about 5 percent is normal. [*Caterpillar Tractor photo*]

Figure 12-27   Flowering trees, such as this hardy flowering cherry, add much to a community.   The tree reaches a height of about 15 feet (4.6 meters) and a spread of 12 feet (3.6 meters).   [The American City]

6. Stake bare-rooted trees and evergreens against heavy winds. Most heavily balled trees do not need staking.

7. Prune the trees back sufficiently to compensate for root loss but no more than one-third.   Be sure to prune out double leaders, weak crotches, and cut-back branches that are too long or rub together, are unevenly spaced, or are at bad angles with the trunk.

8. For the first two years after transplanting, water the trees regularly when dry.   If a tree is surrounded by concrete, be meticulous in watering it.   Enlist the help of neighbors or community groups if you can.

The lesson of the Dutch elm blight that virtually wiped out all the American elms in many communities shows the necessity for a variety of trees.   With a variety, a park supervisor can add interest to the community and reduce the hazard of massive loss from disease or insects that can be so harmful to a community's appearance.   On wide streets and in parks, one can select large trees, while on narrow streets or beneath power lines smaller varieties should be selected.

When transplanting shrubberies, the procedure depends on the type being moved.   Most evergreen shrubs should be balled and burlapped according to the directions given above for trees.   Deciduous shrubs can

Figure 12-28   The pyramidal London plane tree is an excellent choice for industrial and commercial areas.   [The American City]

be moved bare-rooted in the spring or fall and should be trimmed back at planting time.   Evergreens should not be trimmed when they are moved.

Before shrubs are selected, their mature size and growth habit should be checked.   A bush with a normal 8-foot (2.4-meter) mature growth planted in a 3-foot (0.9-meter) space will require yearly pruning maintenance.   For hedges, shrubberies of the desired height (3, 6, or 12 feet; 0.9, 1.8, or 3.7 meters) should be used to minimize shearing.

To save labor, reduce costs, and help ensure the survival of transplanted material, the holes and the soil should be prepared before the transplant work is started.   Large trees, 2½ inches (63.5 millimeters) in diameter and more, are heavy and should be transplanted with the help of a truck and a mechanical lift.   Survival depends mostly on (1) careful digging, (2) careful planting, (3) good soil, and (4) watering all summer during the first year.

Most new-tree failures result from drought.   Most other deaths of trees in urban areas can be attributed to the aftereffects of construction around them.

Pruning is often the last task to be attended to.   The prompt removal of weak branches, dangerous V crotches, and dead trees saves complaints and accidents.   High-branch pruning or work near a utility line

Figure 12-29   High-branch pruning, especially near a utility line, should be entrusted to a registered arborist. [The American City]

should be left to a registered aborist if the community does not have one on its staff.

Young trees benefit from structural pruning to prevent future accidents. Trees showing Dutch elm disease should be pruned or removed immediately if the disease appears. Sometimes immediate branch pruning can stop the spread of the disease in a newly infected tree, but a badly infected tree cannot be saved. Pruning tools should be sterilized in alcohol between uses on branches and trees when disease is suspected.

Mechanical brush shredders used with a truck on the site can save labor and provide a supply of wood chips for mulch. Also useful is a mechanical stump remover that shreds a stump to several inches below the surrounding ground surface. The area may then be covered with loam and seeded so that evidence of the stump will be completely gone.

Pruning should be done early in the spring except when pruning "bleeder" trees (elms, maples, and birches). These trees should be pruned after the leaves are out. Winter, when other tree work is minimal, is a convenient time to remove dead trees.

Chapter Thirteen

Refuse-Collection Practices

WILLIAM S. FOSTER

One of the principal differences between the present urban environment and the past environment that people like Shelley and Thomas Jefferson denounced so colorfully is that wastes, both solid and liquid, do get removed, with a constructive impact on urban life. One must recognize that as the United States becomes more intensively urbanized, the standards of solid-waste removal and disposal become more exacting. Nevertheless, an objective observer would conclude that the nation's urban areas have the capability of meeting these exacting requirements and of making the entire service more efficient, less costly, and more productive to society in general.

Impact of Solid Wastes on the Urban Environment

The quantity of refuse is substantial, and its generation is continuous. A study made by the U.S. Environmental Protection Agency (EPA) discloses that solid wastes generated in urban residences, businesses, and commercial areas amount to 135 million tons (122 million metric tons) per year, and the flow to a little more than 3½ pounds (1.6 kilograms) per person per day.[1] Those who have followed this aspect of urbanization will recognize that these figures are not as great as those that have been published in the past, but more accurate methods of reporting and analysis are becoming available and provide a more exact measure of refuse removal.

---

[1] F. A. Smith, "Quantity and Composition of Post-Consumer Solid Waste: Material Flow Estimates for 1973 and Baseline Future Projections," *Waste Age*, vol. 7, no. 4, April 1976, pp. 2–10.

Solid-waste management involves more than a substantial, impersonal, and continuous volume. Community emotions also must be taken into account. In 1974 the National League of Cities named solid wastes the most troublesome problem facing mayors and councilmen. It was not the problem that generated the greatest number of citizen complaints. Dogs, cats, and other pet-control measures were easily first in this dubious contest. But in ranking major urban problems, solid waste was at the top of the list, well ahead of law enforcement.[2]

CONSTITUENTS OF SOLID WASTES

Solid wastes consist of the goods and products which society finds that it cannot use productively. A more pertinent definition might be that they represent resources that the public seems reluctant to learn how to reuse. As matters stand today, less than 10 percent of the wastes are reclaimed for productive use, but as raw materials become scarcer, wastes become more attractive.

Tables 13-1 and 13-2, drawn from the EPA study cited above, analyze solid-waste constituents. It is noteworthy that nearly two-thirds are nonfood products and that roughly one-third is paper. About one-

[2] Raymond L. Bancroft, *American Mayors and Councilmen: Their Problems and Frustrations,* National League of Cities, Washington, 1974.

Figure 13-1 Solid waste, or refuse, includes all the solid material that an urban society can no longer use constructively or economically and must discard in some manner so that it will not harm the environment. [The American City & County]

TABLE 13-1 Estimates of Residential and Commercial Solid-Waste Collection and Disposal Volumes, 1973

Kinds of materials	Product source categories (10 million tons as generated weight basis)							Total as generated	
	Newspapers, books, magazines	Containers and packaging	Major home appliances	Furniture and furnishings	Clothing and footwear	Food products	Other	Million tons	Percent
Paper	11.3	23.3	...	Trace	Trace	...	9.6	44.2	32.8
Glass	...	12.1	Trace	Trace	...	...	1.1	13.2	9.9
Metals*	...	6.5	1.9	0.1	Trace	...	4.0	12.5	9.3
Plastics	Trace	3.1	0.1	0.1	0.2	...	1.6	5.0	3.7
Rubber and leather	...	Trace	...	Trace	0.5	...	3.0	3.6	2.7
Textiles	Trace	Trace	...	0.6	0.6	...	0.7	1.9	1.4
Wood	...	1.9	...	2.5	Trace	...	0.5	4.9	3.6
Total, nonfood solid wastes	11.3	46.9	2.0	3.4	1.3	...	20.5	85.4	63.5
Food wastes						22.4		22.4	16.6
Total	11.3	46.9	2.0	3.4	1.3	22.4	20.5	107.8	80.1
Yard wastes								25.0	18.5
Miscellaneous inorganic wastes								1.9	1.4
Total, solid wastes								134.8	100.0

*Metals are approximately 88 percent ferrous, 8 percent aluminum, and 4 percent other.

TABLE 13-2   Solid Waste Composition and Quantity, 1971 and 1973

Materials and products	1971 (million tons)	1973 (million tons)	Growth, 1971–1973	
			(million tons)	Percent change
Material composition:				
Paper	39.1	44.2	5.1	13.0
Glass	12.0	13.2	1.2	10.0
Metal:	11.8	12.5	0.7	5.9
Ferrous	10.6	11.0	0.4	3.8
Aluminum	0.8	1.0	0.2	25.0
Other	0.4	0.4	0.0	0.0
Plastics	4.2	5.0	0.8	19.0
Rubber and leather	3.3	3.6	0.3	9.0
Textiles	1.8	1.9	0.1	5.5
Wood	4.6	4.9	0.3	6.5
Subtotal, nonfood	76.9	85.4	8.5	11.1
Food waste	22.0	22.4	0.4	1.8
Subtotal	98.9	107.8	8.9	9.0
Yard waste	24.1	25.0	0.9	3.7
Miscellaneous inorganics	1.8	1.9	0.1	5.6
Total material	124.8	134.8	10.0	9.0
Product source composition:				
Newspapers, books, magazines	10.3	11.3	1.0	9.7
Containers and packaging	41.7	46.9	5.2	12.5
Major home appliances	2.1	2.1	0.0	0.0
Furniture and furnishings	3.2	3.4	0.2	6.3
Clothing and footwear	1.2	1.3	0.1	8.3
Other products	18.4	20.5	2.1	11.4
Subtotal, nonfood	76.9	85.4	8.5	11.1
Food waste	22.0	22.4	0.4	1.8
Total product waste	98.9	107.8	8.9	9.0
Yard waste and miscellaneous inorganics	25.9	26.9	1.0	3.9
Total	124.8	134.8	10.0	8.0

sixth is food wastes, and roughly the same amount is yard wastes. Whether the volume of refuse grows or shrinks depends to some extent on the nation's economic health. Metals amount to about 10 percent of the total, and most of these can be reused. Aluminum is only a small portion of the total, but at the time of the survey it showed the greatest rate of growth.

Most quote the heat value of solid wastes at 4500 to 5000 British thermal units per pound (10,467,000 to 11,630,000 joules per kilogram) on a dry basis. This figure approaches the heat value of oil shale, and if the plastic and paper content should rise, the value could increase. In fact, a number of innovative communities, electric utilities, and other organizations are making use of refuse as a fuel for the generation of power. Florida recently made a study of solid wastes as a source of energy and discovered that the wastes collected there had a heat value of 5000 British thermal units per pound.[3]

Classification of Refuse Components

The solid wastes that must be collected by the community and placed in a suitable disposal point which will be in harmony with the community's environmental standards can be defined in the practical terms used by those performing the work. They also can be defined in legal terms, used in the preparation of ordinances.

"Solid wastes" is a term that those doing the work have adopted only recently to distinguish wastes of this type from liquid wastes, more generally known as sewage, and from air-borne wastes, which are exhaust gases, stack gases, and other sources of air pollution. Curiously, the treatment of liquid wastes and airborne wastes so that they will not degrade the environment aggravates the solid-waste problem, because both produce solids that operators of solid-waste programs frequently must dispose of.

Refuse, Garbage, and Rubbish   "Refuse" is an all-inclusive term that is older than "solid wastes." It embraces all the solid wastes that the community must collect and includes some semisolids such as doughs, slurries, and sludges. Refuse also includes "garbage," which is organic in nature and is connected with food handling. Garbage is putrescible and can generate offensive odors and attract rats and other vermin, as well as flies, all known as disease vectors. The storage of organic food wastes on household premises often has been identified as the weak point in home environmental protection. "Rubbish" is the general classification of solid wastes except for organic food wastes. It includes the bulky wastes that must be classified separately because they require special collection arrangements.

Industrial Wastes   Normally industrial wastes are the responsibility of the particular industries that produce them, and many industries maintain their own disposal areas. Nevertheless, disposal of these wastes must be subject to municipal control. Leachings from the wastes can pollute streams as well as groundwater. Disposal areas can become fire hazards, and if organic wastes are deposited in them, they can be breeding places for rats, flies, and other potentially dangerous nuisances.

However, as disposal areas become more difficult to find, industries turn to municipalities to provide this service. In a few instances, municipalities have erected incinerators solely for the purpose of disposing of troublesome industrial wastes.[4]

[3] *Energy Recovery from Solid Waste,* Florida Resource Recovery Council, 2562 Executive Center Circle East, Tallahassee, Fla. 32301, 1976.

[4] "Will Incinerate Liquid Industrial Wastes," *The American City,* January 1972, p. 30; "Separate Plant for Industrial Wastes," *The American City,* March 1972, p. 24.

Construction and Demolition Wastes   These wastes are chiefly building materials of brick, concrete, wood, metal, plaster, and similar items. Delivering them to the point of disposal or processing is the responsibility of those doing the work.   The material itself rarely poses a health or environmental problem.

Market and Street Refuse   Market refuse is generated by the handling, storing, and selling of food.   It includes a high percentage of putrescible material and consequently must be collected frequently, preferably daily.   Street refuse or debris results from the cleaning action of street sweepers, from the cleaning of catch basins, and from litter from public waste receptacles.   Many cities combine street cleaning with refuse collection, but the collection of these wastes is the responsibility of the street-cleaning forces.

Animals and Vehicles   Dead animals abandoned in an urban environment require prompt handling.   Many municipalities assign this work to the police department.   Special equipment may be needed if the animal is large.

Abandoned vehicles generally must be handled with police cooperation because of the risk that the owner may appear and claim the vehicle after it has been moved.   Actual movement of the vehicle from the street generally is the responsibility of the department of public works or streets.

Sludges   Sewage-treatment sludges frequently can be used as top-dressings on golf courses, rights-of-way, and other properties.   Farmers often can be persuaded to use the sludge on their lands, and some innovative uses of the sludge to reclaim run-down agricultural properties have been developed in various parts of the United States.   However, the sludge frequently is simply brought to the municipality's disposal area, especially if this area is a sanitary fill.   Many sanitary authorities object strenuously to the disposal on these fills of undigested sludge even though it has been dewatered on a vacuum filter.

Sludges almost always have gone through the digestion process, which reduces the volume and transforms the material into a product that emits an earthy, peaty odor.   They can be applied most easily by tank truck in liquid form; this is useful since the liquid contains many soil-nutritive products.   A well-known exception is the Milwaukee sewage treatment plant, which markets an undigested, heat-dried activated sludge under the name Milorganite.

Air-Pollution Particles   Collected in scrubbers and electrostatic precipitators used with various fuel-burning equipment and incinerators, these particles can pose an annoying disposal problem.   The particles are fine and abrasive and will flow almost like a liquid.   They are stable, however, and do not decompose.   Some have tried to use the waste particles in building construction, but these efforts have not met with great success.

Legal Classifications

No one has made standard definitions of solid-waste components, but each municipality must prepare definitions for its regulatory ordinance. The Milwaukee, Wisconsin, definition reflects much thought and appears to have withstood enough court challenges to make it authoritative. The city's ordinance defines solid wastes as follows:

Solid waste consists of the following categories:

(1) *Bulky waste* is discarded articles of such dimensions as are not normally collected with domestic waste, including, but not limited to, items such as furniture, appliances and stoves.

(2) *Commercial waste* is garbage, rubbish, tree waste, and nauseous or offensive materials resulting from the operation of business enterprises including, but not limited to, factories, offices, stores and restaurants.

(3) *Construction waste* is waste resulting from building fires, construction or demolition, alteration or repair, including excavated material.

(4) *Domestic waste* is garbage, rubbish, tree waste, and certain liquid waste and nauseous or offensive materials resulting from human habitation and the usual routine of housekeeping of residential units, churches, charitable educational institutions, charitable organizations and residence buildings used by such charitable organizations incident to their operation.

(5) *Garbage* is all waste, animal, fish, fowl, fruit, or vegetable matter incident to and resulting from the use, preparation, and storage of food for human consumption, including spoiled food.

(6) *Manufacturing waste* is waste resulting from manufacturing or industrial processes, but shall not include waste generated by human habitation on the manufacturing or industrial premises.

(7) *Rubbish* is miscellaneous waste material resulting from housekeeping and ordinary mercantile enterprises, including boxes, cartons, excelsior, paper, ashes, cinders, tin cans, bottles, broken glass, metals, rubber, plastics, lawn and garden waste and similar materials.

(8) *Tree waste* is domestic or commercial waste resulting from the removal, pruning or trimming of trees and shrubs, including branches, limbs, trunks and stumps.[5]

Solid-Waste Unit Weights

Knowledge of the weight of solid waste per cubic foot or cubic yard (or cubic meter) is helpful in determining the sizes of containers for bulk storage of waste. It also aids in selecting the most effective size of truck bodies for general collection.

Local authorities in charge of this work should have no difficulty in making this type of determination for the community involved. Garbage may weigh as much as 1000 pounds per cubic yard (593 kilograms per cubic meter). Mixed refuse in a compactor truck can weigh from 350 to 800 pounds per cubic yard (from 208 to 475 kilograms per cubic meter), 500 pounds per cubic yard (297 kilograms per cubic meter) being a common average.

[5] City of Milwaukee, Wis., Ordinance No. 160, Aug. 13, 1971.

DISPOSAL METHODS

Methods of disposal of the collected refuse can be grouped under the following headings:

1. Sanitary landfills, the ultimate disposal points.

2. Milling and shredding, a processing method with disposal adjacent to or near the plant.

3. Baling, a processing method that can take place at a distance from the disposal point since the refuse bales are easily transported.

4. Incineration, also a processing method. The ash or residue still needs to be placed in a disposal area.

5. Pyrolysis, a processing method that should yield oil or gas for a fuel. It also leaves a residue for disposal.

6. Processing the refuse into a fuel that can be used to generate power, which still leaves some residue for disposal.

Figure 13-2 Sanitary landfills have become popular as a method of disposing of solid waste and of providing a limited amount of improvement to the land. In the Los Angeles area, shown here, fills reclaim out-of-city wasteland. [The American City & County]

Figure 13-3 To provide more thorough compaction of waste, some municipalities use this heavy equipment with steel compacting wheels and knifelike lugs. [The American City & County]

Sanitary Landfills

The use of sanitary landfills is the commonest disposal method because the cost of operation is the lowest among methods that meet the requirements of public-health authorities. The fills can receive a wide variety of wastes and accommodate refuse contributions of varying sizes without great difficulty. However, sanitary landfills require substantial amounts of land, which has only limited use when the fills are complete because of subsequent settling and the occasional development of combustible gases generated by the decomposition of organic matter.

A good sanitary fill contains refuse that has been compacted to a dense, stable mass and then covered with sufficient earth to prevent rats and other rodents from penetrating it. This process requires at

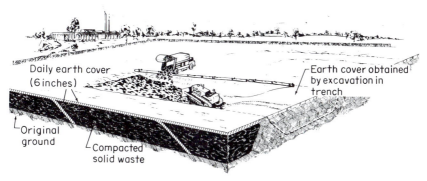

Daily earth cover
(6 inches)

Earth cover obtained
by excavation in
trench

Original
ground

Compacted
solid waste

Figure 13-4 The trench method of sanitary fills, shown here, is best applied on level ground. The tractor obtains the earth cover material as it excavates for the trench. [*Dirk R. Brunner and Daniel J. Keller,* Sanitary Landfill Design and Operation, *U.S. Environmental Protection Agency, p. 28, 1972*]

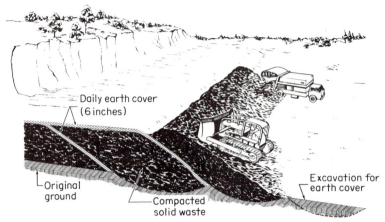

Figure 13-5 The progressive slope method can be adapted to more irregular terrain than can the trench method. The tractor compacts the refuse and then covers it with earth obtained from the front of the slope. [*Dirk R. Brunner and Daniel J. Keller,* Sanitary Landfill Design and Operation, *U.S. Environmental Protection Agency, p. 28, 1972*]

least 6 inches (152.4 millimeters) of earth cover at the end of each day and 2 feet (0.6 meter) more when the fill has been completed.

In the past, the conventional crawler tractor has been used to compact the refuse and cover it with earth, but the broad tractor treads have not been as effective as desired in producing a firm refuse mass. Manufacturers now provide heavier equipment that uses wheels with knifelike lugs to increase the degree of compaction and reduce subsequent settlement.

Fills are built by the trench method, the ramp method, and the area method. Under the first method, which is useful on level ground, the tractor obtains the earth cover by excavating for a future trench. Under

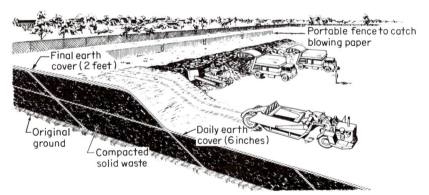

Figure 13-6 The area method, used on irregular ground, frequently requires that the earth be transported to the site for cover. [*Dirk R. Brunner and Daniel J. Keller,* Sanitary Landfill Design and Operation, *U.S. Environmental Protection Agency, p. 28, 1972*]

the second, the cover can be obtained by excavating in front of the working face.   Under the third, the cover material generally must be transported to the site.

The fills have been used to create ski slopes, amphitheaters, athletic fields, golf courses, and parklands.   They cannot be relied on to support buildings that impose heavy loads.

Milling and Shredding

This is a relatively new process that responds to the nationwide need to recover salvable material from refuse.   The method requires capital investment in a plant designed to reject metals from the refuse and to pass the remainder through shredding equipment for disposal on the land.   Heavy, bulky material such as engine blocks, concrete, rocks, and rubble must be removed manually before the refuse goes to the shredder.

In the shredding process, the food wastes become sufficiently intermixed with the other refuse that the final product apparently does not attract rats and flies.   The principal installation is at Madison, Wisconsin.   Although the refuse can be covered with earth for cosmetic purposes, this installation suggests that health and environmental considerations do not require such a cover.

Baling

Baling is a relatively new process that has enjoyed only limited acceptance.   The principal installation is in St. Paul, Minnesota.   This method also requires capital investment in baling equipment.   However, the

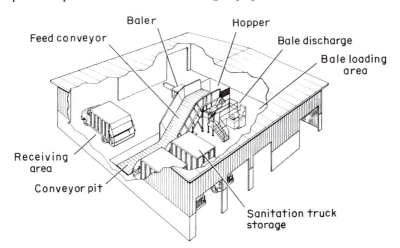

Figure 13-7 The baling of refuse encourages the reclamation of salvageable material and facilitates mechanically compacting the refuse into easily handled packages that can be placed for disposal with a minimum of nuisance.   This drawing shows the baling plant designed for Chadron, Nebraska.   [*American Solid Waste Systems, St. Paul, Minnesota*]

bales undergo heavy compaction and consequently experience little settling. The bales can easily be stacked in the disposal area and subsequently be covered with earth.

Incineration

Incineration is one of the oldest disposal processes, distinctive for its ability to reduce the volume of the refuse and produce a residue that should be free from organic, decomposable material and make a stable fill. Incineration also generates heat, which is of growing interest to power producers. Many oils and coals have high contents of sulfur, but refuse is virtually sulfur-free. As indicated above, refuse has a fairly good heat value, around 5000 British thermal units per pound (10,467,000 joules per kilogram) on a dry basis, and this heat content probably will rise as the content of plastics and paper increases.

Incinerators have suffered in recent years because of their inability to meet increasingly strict air-purity codes. Nevertheless, a growing number of American and Canadian cities are utilizing the waste heat for constructive purposes. Nashville uses it to heat the downtown area in

Figure 13-8 European cities make more constructuve use of their incinerators than do those in the United States. This Dutch incinerator, capable of receiving 700,000 tons (635 million kilograms) of mixed refuse per year, generates electricity and desalts water with the waste heat. [The American City & County]

winter and to air-condition it in summer.   Chicago and Quebec generate electricity from the incinerator waste heat.   For more than a quarter of a century Atlanta generated steam from its incinerator and sold it to the local utility for use in the downtown area.

Pyrolysis

Pyrolysis is still another new process that holds much promise.   Essentially it is the destructive distillation of the carbonaceous material in the solid wastes to produce a flammable oil or gas, either of which can be used directly in power-producing boilers.   The most promising installation currently is in Baltimore, although many other cities are considering its adoption.

Refuse Processing

Processing refuse to transform it into a usable fuel for boilers also is new and is demonstrating its practicality.   Here again, the refuse must be shredded and the metallic portion removed for salvage.   The process appears to be practical only when the refuse is used in boilers that are designed for coal and are able to discharge the ash.   The electric utility serving the St. Louis area has been able to use the refuse to good advantage.   The little city of Ames, Iowa, also is processing refuse for this purpose and is demonstrating that the process can be used in relatively small plants.

COSTS AND EFFICIENCIES

Despite the sophisticated processes of refuse disposal, collection represents 80 percent of the more than $4.5 billion that the people of the United States must invest annually in solid-waste management.   And of this collection cost, probably 70 percent represents labor.[6]   Consequently any saving that can be made in collection procedures will help

[6] David H. Marks and Jon C. Liebman, *Mathematical Analysis of Solid Waste Collection*, SW-5re.1, U.S. Environmental Protection Agency, 1972.

Figure 13-9   Collection costs, which amount to at least 80 percent of the entire refuse management program, offer great opportunities for savings. [The American City & County]

substantially to lower costs for the entire management program. Lynn, Massachusetts, for example, revised its collection procedures, purchased new equipment, and still was able to provide the service of solid-waste management at a reduction of 25 percent from the budgeted figure.[7] However, changes must be introduced diplomatically. The public dislikes change, particularly if the change requires a little extra effort by the householder.

Public versus Private Collection Services

On a purely theoretical basis, with all factors equal, a municipally operated refuse service should operate more economically than one under private management. The difference, of course, is the profit that the private firm must earn to remain viable.

However, all factors are never equal, and they tend to change unpredictably. The most recent change is that of the rising militancy of municipal employees, making them strike-prone even when laws prohibit strikes by public employees. This trend has forced costs upward sufficiently so that, wherever possible, urban administrators have entered into contracts with private firms to perform many of the services that at one time were the responsibility of municipal crews. Solid-waste management has not been the only municipal service affected by this trend.

[7] D. L. Phillips, "Revised Refuse Procedure Cuts Budget More Than 25%," *The American City*, April 1971, p. 66.

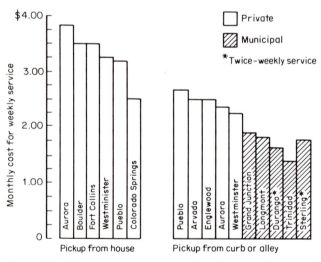

Figure 13-10 Although many persons believe that the collection of refuse by private contractors is more economical than that by municipal forces, some evidence supports municipal collection, as this survey of Colorado cities shows. [The American City & County]

Because of its labor-intensive character, refuse collection has been strongly affected. New York City was quickly forced into crisis conditions by a strike of its refuse-collection forces. The assassination of Dr. Martin Luther King, Jr., came about during labor difficulties that the city of Memphis had with its refuse-collection workers.

Because of these rising labor costs and, in many cities, lowered productivity of municipal forces, many municipalities have switched to private firms for the performance of this service. Large companies known as agglomerates have been organized to assume this service, taking advantage of the improved management techniques that a large organization can adopt.

Whether this trend will continue is not clear. Strikes and employee militancy can occur in the private sector as well as in the public one. Moreover, innovative administrators in the public sector can develop techniques that are equally productive.

Comparing costs among municipalities always has been difficult because of differing methods of cost accounting. However, in 1970 Robert C. Westdyke, director of solid wastes in Boulder, Colorado, made a study of collection and disposal costs in seventeen cities in his state, all of over 10,000 population but not including Denver. His study showed that without exception the total cost of operating the municipal systems was less than that of private organizations.[8]

Improved Collection Efficiencies

Measures that a community can take to obtain the greatest dollar effectiveness and at the same time maintain a high service standard can be grouped under seven main headings. Four require the cooperation of the resident or business establishment, and three require study and analysis by those administering the program:

1. Better and more effective storage of refuse at the site (requires cooperation of the resident).

2. Placement of the container at the curb or the alley line (requires cooperation of the resident).

3. Use of plastic or paper bags to hold the refuse and to make collection more efficient (requires cooperation of the resident).

4. Binding yard waste into convenient bundles if it cannot be placed in containers (requires cooperation of the resident).

5. Development of more efficient routes for collection (requires administrative study).

6. Adoption of improved equipment that will utilize human power more effectively (requires administrative study).

[8] Robert C. Westdyke, "Municipal Collection and Disposal Cost Less in Colorado Cities of 10,000 or More," *The American City*, July 1970, p. 16.

Figure 13-11   Refuse placed in plastic bags at the curb for collection can substantially reduce collection costs.   [The American City & County]

7. Development of refuse-transfer facilities to prevent the costly transport of relatively small loads of solid waste to distant disposal points (requires administrative study).

RESIDENTIAL SOLID-WASTE CONTAINERS
AND COLLECTION METHODS

The requirements for containers used in residential collections are simple and well known.   A container, unaccountably and illogically called a "can," should have a capacity of about 30 gallons (0.114 cubic meter).   It should be tapered with the larger end at the top to facilitate emptying.   The container should be made of galvanized steel with fluted sides or of appropriately strong plastic.   It should have a tight cover designed so that dogs, raccoons, and other animals cannot dislodge it easily.   If the container is of galvanized steel, it should have handles, and if it is of plastic, it should have handholds.

Plastic containers have the advantage of lightness and ease of handling, but some become brittle at low temperatures and break easily. Since they are light, they tend to blow away when empty if the wind is high.

Residential containers should not consist of empty 55-gallon (0.208-cubic-meter) drums, which generally have jagged edges and can cut collectors' hands.   They should not be cardboard boxes that can break and make collection difficult.   Residential containers should not be of a type that is stored underground with a covering lid.   These are difficult to pick up, and frequently solid waste drops into them, interfering with their use.   The containers are generally small and inadequate, and the underground location may cause rust and deterioration.

Galvanized-metal containers, while strong, do rust when placed di-

Figure 13-12 Containers can be supported on specially designed brackets such as this, thus preventing them from being rusted on the bottom and from being tipped over by dogs, raccoons, and other animals. Supports of this type frequently are used in parks and recreation areas. [The American City & County]

rectly on the ground, although rusting can be minimized to some extent if the lower rim of the container extends below the bottom.   If collection is made at the alley, the container can be placed on a small wood platform or be hung by the handle on a special support designed for this purpose.   Such supports have been especially useful for holding litter containers in parks and playgrounds, where the service can be rough and the possibility of overturning by animals is great.

Either plastic or waterproof paper bags are acceptable to store refuse at the household.   These have the advantage of ease of handling by the collection crew. However, they should not be stored outdoors overnight because of the danger of damage from dogs and other animals.

A few households have purchased kitchen compactors which seal the wastes in waterproof paper bags that are easily stored and handled.   If the compaction follows the manufacturer's instructions, the containers will be flyproof and odorproof.

Many homes have garbage grinders mounted in kitchen sinks.   These eliminate waste food by transforming it into sewage, but they do not eliminate the need for collection of other refuse.   Ordinances should require food wastes to be drained and wrapped before being placed in refuse containers.

Automatic Container Collection

For many years, commentators on this phase of urban sanitation have stated that while automation and process improvements have reached other urban services, the only real difference in refuse collection has been the substitution of the truck for the horse and wagon.   Until recently, despite the work of inventive minds, this was true.   Some have tried to convey refuse in packages propelled in tubes by air pressure to the point of disposal.   Some have proposed macerating all refuse and conveying it by water carriage in the sewer system.   None of the proposals has proved practical for community-wide collection, although the air-transport method has worked in specialized locations like Disney World in Florida, where all operations are directed by a single management.

Nevertheless, resourceful people have developed ways to make the collection less laborious and less conducive to injuries.   The injury rate in refuse collection is sufficiently high to cause concern among urban managers.

Use of a *wheeled container* is one of the methods.   The householder is given an 80-gallon (0.303-cubic-meter) container on wheels, which is large enough to meet the weekly storage requirements of most families. The householder wheels it to the curb, and the collector fits the container to a hoisting mechanism that discharges the load automatically. The container is plastic and can easily be kept clean by the householder.

A *mechanical arm* operated by the driver of the truck has been developed and is in successful use in limited parts of the United States.   First produced in Scottsdale, Arizona, and named Godzilla (a subsequent model is called Son of Godzilla), the unit picks up specially designed containers and empties them into the truck body.

A variation of the mechanical arm, *MBR* (mechanical bag retrieval), was developed by the Gulf Chemical Company.   It depends on the uni-

Figure 13-13 One innovative improvement has been the adoption of a mechanical lifting arm.   The driver-operator can pick up a specially designed plastic container and empty the contents into the truck without leaving the cab.   [The American City & County]

Figure 13-14 A device somewhat similar to the mechanical lifting arm is designed to pick up bagged refuse and place it in a conveyor that transfers it to the truck. [The American City & County]

versal use of plastic or paper bags for collection. The unit has a light, basket-type bag retriever that transports the bags to a conveyor, which in turn puts them into the truck.

An experimental *jumping-bean unit* appears to be operationally successful but requires a great deal of householder cooperation and to an extent interferes with roadway traffic. The householder must place the plastic

Figure 13-15 The "jumping bean" collector has a set of elastic bands that capture the bags and snap them up onto the conveyor. [The American City & County]

or paper bag about 3 feet (0.9 meter) from the curb at a location identified by a mark on the pavement.   The collection unit has a belt conveyor
that transfers the bagged refuse to the collection truck.   To put the bags
on the conveyor requires the use of a resourceful mechanism that gives
the jumping-bean unit its name.   Mounted in front of the conveyor is a
pair of standard automobile wheels, spaced about 15 inches (381 millimeters) apart and supplied with strong elastic bands that stretch from
one wheel to the other.   The elastics capture the bags and thrust them
against the conveyor belt.   As the elastic pressure is released, the bags
jump upward onto the conveyor.   The system, which was developed
in Covina, California, relies on the use of strong bags, well fastened at
the opening, to prevent the tearing or scattering of waste.

A *rail-loading system* that appears to be an ultimate step in fast, mechanized waste collection is now available.   However, it requires much

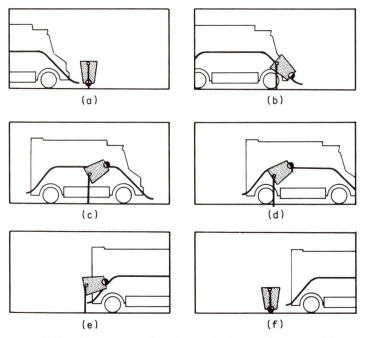

(a)   (b)

(c)   (d)

(e)   (f)

Figure 13-16 The rail type of continuous loader requires a special container held by a post mounted at the curb or alley.   The container has a
sheave wheel on the street or alley side and near the base of the container
(*a*).   The truck has a collecting rail mounted on its side and a receiving
compartment that accepts the refuse and transfers it to the truck body (*b*).
The rail engages the sheave wheel, lifting the bottom of the container to
discharge the refuse (*c, d*).   As the truck advances, the rail lowers the
container to the upright position (*e, f*).   [Mechanized, Non-Stop Residential Solid Waste Collection, *Report G06-EC-00328, U.S. Environmental
Protection Agency, August 1973*]

householder cooperation as well as a certain amount of relaxation in city ordinances. The rail, in the form of an inverted but very flat U, is mounted on the side of the truck over a special refuse-receiving mechanism. The containers are modified 55-gallon (0.208-cubic-meter) drums with a pair of holders mounted on one side and a sheave wheel on the other side, close to the bottom of the container. A vertical pipe framework mounted in the street close to the curb receives the two holders on the container. A lug on the pipe permits the upper holder to support the container off the ground. As the collection truck proceeds down the street, the rail connects with the sheave wheel, and as the truck moves forward, it lifts the container, tipping it up and back into the truck's receiving hopper. As the truck proceeds, the rail, still engaged with the sheave, returns the container to an upright position, hanging on the pipe support.

The *rapid-rail system* is still another type of mechanical collection. It is based on the use of a side-loading compaction-type body to which are affixed a pair of rails and a hydraulically powered lifting device. This system has been designed to use 90- or 300-gallon (0.341- or 1.136-cubic-meter) plastic containers. The smaller size is used at residences, and the larger one at most commercial locations. The driver aligns his truck beside the container, brakes it so that it will not move, and then activates the lifting device, which can extend as much as 3 feet (0.9 meter) from the truck to secure and pick up the container. The hydraulic elevator lifts the container and empties the contents into the truck.

Figure 13-17 The "rapid rail" mechanical collector uses an elevator mechanism with a side-loading compactor body. [*Government Innovators, Inc., Phoenix, Arizona*]

Then the elevator returns the container to the curbside position. The system requires that each solid-waste contributor be supplied with an appropriate container for the rapid-rail operation. When the operator moves the truck to the next container, the compacting blade clears the receiving hopper and compacts the refuse. In one Nebraska city the rapid-rail system operated successfully in a blizzard.

All these systems eliminate the need for common labor to make the collection and permit the operator to be more than simply a truck driver. They allow the driver to operate in an air-conditioned cab in summer and a heated cab in winter. Most of them should be able to function even with snow on the ground. However, two of the systems require that the street be free of parked vehicles, a condition that often is difficult to attain.

Acceptance of Improved Collection Methods

Any of the foregoing methods that has shown an ability to make refuse collection less costly and more efficient nevertheless must win the support of the public before it can be successful. The change cannot be produced by the simple passage of an ordinance. People generally will accept a new regulation or a change in collection methods if they understand it and believe that it is in their best interests. In general, simple, easily understood instructions that are carefully worded to avoid seeming overbearing will win cooperation. These instructions can be printed on cards so that they can be conveniently displayed in households. Cartoons or other devices can add to the cards' attractiveness and acceptability.

For a general change in collection procedures, especially a major change, a technique that has been used with encouragingly good results is the experimental district. Solid-waste administrators try the new technique for a test period, measure collection efficiency, calculate costs, and then poll the residents of the district, showing them the results of the study, and ask for their opinions. If the residents react well, the experiment can be expanded to the entire municipality for a trial period and then be adopted as a permanent measure if public reaction continues to be favorable. This method enables the public to participate in the decision and eventually to play the role of decision maker.[9,10]

COLLECTION PROCEDURE AND ROUTES

The frequency of refuse collection should depend on the length of time that wastes can be stored at the site without attracting flies and insects and creating putrefaction odors. If the containers have good, tight-

[9] Kenneth E. Smith, "The People Choose Sacks over Cans," *The American City*, June 1970, p. 82.
[10] Phillips, op. cit.

fitting covers, collections can be made twice a week and, in many cases, once a week for most residences. Because food wastes constitute a relatively small portion of today's refuse, the longer period probably will serve well in most instances. Even in warm areas a great many municipalities collect refuse only once a week.

Nevertheless, a study by Dean H. Ecke and Linsdale[11] showed that refuse stored in household metal containers with weekly collections produced high fly populations in 67 percent of the containers. With twice-weekly collections, only 10 percent of the containers were affected. If either paper or plastic bags were used, the fly problem was greatly diminished. With weekly collections only 20 to 25 percent of the bags had high fly counts, and on a twice-weekly schedule none had fly problems.

Market, restaurant, and hotel wastes, all containing greater amounts of organic matter, need to be collected daily and sometimes more often. Industrial and construction wastes, having no organic matter, can be collected at the convenience of the industry or the contractor unless the accumulation begins to constitute a nuisance.

Backdoor Collection Methods

Some communities insist on backdoor collection despite the increased cost. If the public is thoroughly aware of this cost and is willing to pay for it, the solid-waste administrator must be ready to adjust collections accordingly.

The cost of collection from backyards is about double that of collection at the curb or alley and may be more as the cost of labor continues to rise. The principal methods of controlling this cost are (1) to speed the collection process to make more effective use of the equipment and (2) to reduce the number of trips from the backs of houses to the collection vehicles.

Collection speed can be increased by the use of "set-out crews." In most cases, this procedure requires workers to precede the truck and move the containers to the curb, other workers at the truck to serve as loaders, and still others to follow the truck to return the containers to the rear of the house. The method is labor-intensive but may be preferred in wealthy communities where cost is not a consideration.

To reduce the number of trips from the truck to the backyard, various simple devices can be employed. Some communities use large burlap squares that can hold the solid wastes from two or three houses. Collectors empty the containers into a square and immediately replace them, then pick the square up and carry it to the adjoining house to obtain its contribution of solid wastes.

Other municipalities equip collectors with large plastic tubs that can

[11] *California Vector News*, April 1969.

Figure 13-18 "Truckster"-type motor scooters help speed backyard collections. [The American City & County]

hold wastes from more than one house. These tubs can be provided with handholds and an indentation to fit the collector's shoulder so that they can be transported easily.

Still other communities utilize three-wheeled motor scooters with dump boxes. These units permit the collector to motor up the driveway, collect the container contents, replace the container, and quickly travel to the next dwelling. When the scooter dump box is full, the operator travels to the collection truck and unloads the solid wastes into its hopper.

Certain precautions should be required in the use of these satellite vehicles. They weigh from 1200 to 2600 pounds (from 544 to 1179 kilograms), and their dump boxes hold from 1 to 3 cubic yards (from 0.76 to 2.29 cubic meters). The boxes normally should be equipped with hydraulic lifts for unloading into the collection truck. The vehicles work best in residential areas of low to medium density where single-family houses predominate. The hoppers should not be loaded above their tops because of the risk of spillage. Similarly, the driving speed should be slow enough to keep the waste from blowing out of the hopper. The receiving truck should have a hopper with a capacity of at least 2 cubic yards (1.53 cubic meters) to accept the load of one vehicle for the compaction cycle.

Increasing the Efficiency of Collection Routes

Many persons expressed confidence that the analytical capabilities of the computer could produce refuse-collection routes with maximum efficiencies and the lowest possible operating costs. Some computer experts attempted to assemble models to provide solutions. However, the many variables and the difficulty of determining their values soon made the computer approach impractical.

The alternative is to study routings with the municipality's administrators, using the knowledge and experience of those who have performed the tasks.   This, according to a recent EPA report, is known as "heuristic routing," which is defined as "a logical, commonsense thought process learned through experience that helps organize ideas, concepts, and information into a useful form or solution."[12]   It acknowledges that those responsible for the work are in the best position to improve routes if they follow a few logical rules and guidelines.

Those making these studies use terms such as "macrorouting" and "microrouting."   The first refers to the areas or districts that the collection routes cover, and the second to the actual route within a particular district that an individual truck and crew follow.   Macrorouting also can embrace the assignment of routes to the collection crews on a daily basis. If the community's policy is to make one collection a week, and many communities do operate on this frequency, one crew is assigned to a different route for each working day of the week.

For microrouting, the EPA's heuristic rules can provide constructive guidance to the solid-waste administrator.   Reworded slightly, they are as follows:

1. Confine each route to an area that is as compact as possible.   Do not fragment or overlap routes.

2. Equalize the workload so that the collection and haul time for each route are reasonably equal.

3. Start the collection route as close to the maintenance garage as possible, taking into account heavily traveled and one-way streets.

4. Avoid collections on heavily traveled streets during hours of heavy traffic.

5. If the area has predominantly one-way streets, start the route at the upper end of the area, looping around the cross streets as shown in Figure 3-19.

6. Include dead-end streets in the collection area of the streets that they intersect.   Schedule collections on them so that the truck turns to the right when entering the street.

7. If possible, start the collection in a hilly area at the point of highest elevation.   Collect on both sides of the street while the vehicle is moving downhill.   This procedure aids safety, reduces wear on the vehicle, and conserves gas and oil.

8. If practicable, start all routes at the highest elevation in the macrodistrict.

9. As far as possible, schedule route turns in a right-hand direction. This is especially important for one-person trucks with the driver at the right-hand side.

10. For collection from both sides of the street at the same time,

[12] Kenneth A. Shuster and Dennis Schur, *Heuristic Routing for Solid Waste Collection Vehicles*, Publication SW-113, U.S. Environmental Protection Agency, 1974.

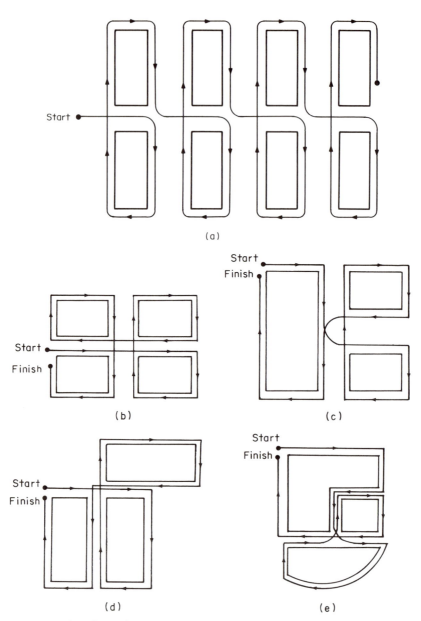

Figure 13-19 Sample routings such as these illustrate how heuristic analysis can improve collection performance. (*a*) Specific routing pattern for a one-way street, one-side-of-the-street collection. In this pattern, collection is made from both sides of the one-way street during the pass. For wide or busy one-way streets, it is necessary to loop back to the upper end and make a straight pass down the other side. (*b*) A four-block configuration applicable wherever four blocks are positioned as shown. (*c*) A three-block configuration. (*d*) A variation of the three-block configuration. (*e*) Another variation of the three-block configuration. [*Kenneth A. Shuster and Dennis A. Schur,* Heuristic Routing for Solid Waste Collection Vehicles, *Publication SW-113, U.S. Environmental Protection Agency, 1974*]

schedule the routes with long, straight paths across the grids before looping back, generally with clockwise turns.

These general rules apply best to old grid-type street systems. Few new streets follow this pattern as consistently as they did in the past, and with curved streets administrator and operators must pay greater individual attention to routing.

Yard Waste and Bulky Waste

The most economical policy is to collect all wastes at once rather than make separate collections for fractions of the refuse contribution. If salvage drives are in progress, collection depots can be established and the public encouraged to bring salvageable material to them.

Yard wastes should be bundled and tied in packages small enough so that collectors can place them in the trucks handily. Yard wastes can be a seasonal problem in areas where the climate is warm and rainfall is frequent.

For collection of bulky wastes, such as discarded refrigerators and old davenports and chairs, the most economical policy is to require the householder to deliver them to selected disposal areas or to ask private haulers to transport them. However, many communities pick such items up in a separate collection when they are notified by the householder and a date is selected that meets the collection routine of the refuse administrator.

For the inner-city portions of large municipalities, the removal of bulky wastes may have to be handled on a more highly organized basis.

Figure 3-20 At times special collections and equipment are required for yard waste. [The American City & County]

Residents in such areas have less opportunity to transport wastes to disposal points. Moreover, low-income residents often lack resources to move the waste themselves. Frequently, because of their circumstances, they have learned to accept such wastes without great objection. However, such objects as discarded refrigerators can pose great danger for children, who may become locked inside them with no way of escape.

Collection Scheduling

The public wants regularity and neatness in collection schedules. The householder wants collectors to appear on specified days and preferably at a certain time of the day. The householder also does not want litter to remain after the collection crew performs its task. This requirement for regularity can interfere with a high degree of efficiency, since refuse quantities vary and the trucks may be partially filled or filled to capacity before completion of the route. Nevertheless, techniques can be adopted to alleviate this problem.

The *task system* is undoubtedly the most popular technique. A crew is assigned a specified route that normally requires a working day to complete. When the crew has completed the route, the workers return to the garage, clean their truck, and are permitted to leave. This method encourages promptness, which pleases householders and rewards workers. However, it may also encourage the workers to be careless in their performance and prone to accidents as well as sloppy in emptying the containers.

The *large-route method* can be used if the public insists on backyard collections and does not insist on regularity in the collection work. The route is designed to provide work for a single crew for an entire week. The crew starts on Monday, collects for the entire working day, and then returns the following day to the point where it left off. If the crew finds that volumes are so great that it cannot complete the week's assignment, a swing crew may be assigned to assist it, although this procedure tends to be inefficient and expensive.

A *variable crew size* can compensate for larger or smaller refuse volumes on the routes. By careful attention to collection quantities, the administrator can anticipate the increased amount of refuse and provide personnel to collect it.

The *interroute relief method* provides a way to accommodate variations in refuse contributions. A route driver radios or telephones the superior when the route has been completed and the truck is only partially loaded. The driver can then be assigned to the end of an uncollected route and instructed to work backward on the route to meet the regular crew. Similarly, a driver who finds that there is so much refuse that the truck will be filled before the route is completed can request assistance.

The *reservoir-route method* is still another way to utilize equipment effectively. The administrator selects three to five routes surrounding a center route and considers them a single unit. Each crew works its own route, moving constantly toward the center, and then all collect the center route to complete the task.

These are not all the methods of scheduling crews. Some variation probably will perform efficiently and still provide the public with the reliability and regularity of collection service that constitute the ultimate goal. Time and motion studies of the individual routes, careful records showing the amount of refuse collected, and the introduction of work incentives all should help improve this service.

COLLECTION EQUIPMENT

Collection equipment must be sturdy enough to absorb a great deal of punishment. Vehicles must travel over good roads and bad; if they must deliver refuse to a sanitary fill, they can expect rough roads that create a great deal of tire damage as well as twisting of their frames. They must be maintained in good condition so that they can operate in hilly terrain, and if the community is subject to snow, they frequently must help in the plowing.

During periods of inflation, good management dictates that equipment be acquired and maintained to ensure long service life. Policies should aim at ensuring that the equipment works reliably and at as low a cost as is practicable and that employees assigned to it can have confidence in its performance.

Engines should be provided with enough horsepower to perform the work efficiently. The choice between gasoline-powered and diesel-powered engines must be made locally. Diesel engines use less fuel, and the fuel is somewhat less expensive. However, the first cost is greater, and mechanics must be familiar with the engines. Diesel exhausts have fewer dangerous pollutants than gasoline-powered engines have, but they can be odorous if the engines are not kept in good operating condition.

Automatic transmissions should be specified in most cases for the assistance of the operators, especially when one-person operation is contemplated. The transmission should be matched to the engine to ensure maximum efficiency of engine power. Shift points should be matched to the power peak of the engine. With the hydraulic torque converter supporting the gear train, the engine will not experience "lugging" or stalling and thus will need repair less frequently.

It is generally recommended that truck frames be heavy-duty for this type of service. They should be straight rather than tapered and be reinforced. The reinforcement should be of the inverted-L type and provide a section modulus of at least 20. Reinforcement should run from the front spring hanger to the end of the frame section; it should not start from behind the cab and extend only to the first spring hanger. It should reduce bending and twisting that causes problems to packing controls and hydraulic systems generally.

If possible, hydraulic cylinders and lines should be located so that they will not be damaged accidentally if the truck is backing and hits some object. Because of the danger of hitting children or unexpected objects, trucks should not be required to back for an extended distance while making collections if this can be avoided. In general, trucks should have reliable braking, conspicuous stop, backup, and turn signals, good vision in all directions, and a balanced distribution of weight.

Refuse Bodies

The volume of the refuse body placed on the truck chassis is a decision that also must be made locally. The size should depend on (1) the amount of refuse that will be collected on the route which will ensure a full or nearly full load on an average day, (2) the size of the crew making the collection, and (3) street or alley widths.

For communities fortunate enough to have the convenience of curb or alley collection, with no need for personnel to go to backyards for containers, a truck and body designed for one-person operation can show great efficiency. Some have claimed that, with containers placed at the curbs, one-person operation with a truck designed for this type of service can come within 70 percent of the productive figures of a more conventional truck with a driver and a two-person collection crew. This type of equipment, which puts the driver in complete charge of a district or route, can produce a sense of personal responsibility.

Figure 3-21 One-person collection trucks have been remarkably effective in reducing costs. The driver also loads the truck, using a right-hand–drive vehicle to save steps. [*Maxon Industries, Inc., photo*]

Figure 13-22 This hopper type of truck body uses a swinging panel to transfer the refuse to the truck interior and to provide compacting action. [The American City & County]

The truck can be supplied with a right-hand drive so that the operator can easily move out of the driving seat, pick up the container at the curb, empty it quickly, return it, and move along the route. This type of equipment is designed to be loaded at the side with the opening at a conveniently low elevation. It also can be provided with various types of compaction equipment.

However, collection requirements in many communities make the use of this type of truck impractical, and the conventional driver and collection crew still appear to be the combination needed. The most popular equipment for conventional collection is the unit that can be loaded at the rear, the body generally having a capacity of about 20 cubic yards (15.3 cubic meters). This type is a *batch loader*. Refuse is dumped into a hopper at an elevation that makes loading relatively easy. The hopper is able to receive contributions from several households. When filled, it utilizes a panel hinged horizontally to transfer the refuse into the body, the force of the panel providing the compacting action. Most of these units discharge their loads by hoists that operate like conventional dump trucks. This action can induce stresses in the truck frame if the dumping area is rough and uneven and the body, when in the hoisted position, tends to tilt.

Another type with a body that operates on the dump-truck principle can be classed as a *trough loader*. A trough with a capacity of about 1

Figure 13-23 This trough type of truck body has four side-mounted loading units. Note that the trough can become the top of the truck body. [The American City & County]

cubic yard (0.76 cubic meter) is suspended by a hoisting mechanism at the rear of the truck.   The collection crew fills it with refuse, and the truck operator activates the hoisting mechanism to lift the refuse to the top of the truck and discharge it into an appropriate opening.   The trough can be mounted on the side of the truck if desired; in this case, it is lifted by cables.   The truck body can also be provided with compaction equipment.

Still another dump-truck type is the *continuous loader.* This also loads from the rear, using a hopper that feeds into a conveyor. The conveyor transfers the refuse to the truck body continuously, avoiding the

Figure 13-24 This continuous loader has a smaller hopper with a conveyor that moves the refuse to the interior constantly, thus eliminating the packing cycle. This truck was designed to operate in narrow alley-type streets. [The American City & County]

Figure 13-25 A movable-bulkhead truck body of this type loads from the side. When the truck reaches its disposal point, the moving bulkhead forces the refuse out of the truck body. [The American City & County]

delay experienced in activating the swinging panel or the hoisting apparatus in trucks of other types. This type of equipment has proved popular in large cities with concentrated populations and substantial amounts of refuse.

A *movable-bulkhead type* of truck body eliminates the need to lift the body to discharge the collected refuse. This type of truck is loaded from the side and may require loaders to lift the refuse container somewhat higher. The truck-body cross section may be cylindrical or square. The movable bulkhead compresses the refuse as it is collected, and it pushes the refuse out of the body when the truck arrives at the disposal point. This method of emptying the truck eliminates the need to raise the body and induce stresses in the truck frame.

Another type of collection body is the *revolving-drum compactor*. The collection crew loads the refuse from the rear into a hopper with a rotating screw-type crusher. The helical blades of the compactor move the refuse forward, packing it solidly into the truck and providing a continuous, instead of a batch-loading, operation. Compaction can proceed as the truck moves to new collection points, thus making collection somewhat faster. To discharge the refuse, the operator raises the loading hopper and reverses the compactor mechanism. The crushing action of the helical blades has occasionally forced broken glass outward, thus endangering the collectors. A piece of burlap hanging loosely over the opening provides protection against these glass particles.

Bodies of these types keep the refuse out of sight, prevent blowing and littering, ease the problem of loading the trucks, and prevent water in the refuse from dripping onto the pavement. The one disadvantage is that loaders may bring the truck to the disposal point before it is completely full so as to avoid some of the arduousness of the work. This

Figure 13-26 The revolving-drum collector can be loaded continuously. [The American City & County]

practice can be stopped by establishing a weighing station at the disposal area (such a station should be provided in any case to obtain an accurate record of quantities).   Weighing will quickly identify trucks with light loads.   Automatic weighing and recording equipment will prevent a weighmaster from weighing loads incorrectly to protect the operators of trucks that arrive only partially filled.

Large-Container Collection

Many areas within a community generate refuse in quantities that are too large to be collected in a 30-gallon (0.114-cubic-meter) container.   These

Figure 13-27 One common type of large container, used in multifamily-dwelling complexes and other locations, has caster-type wheels for transport to the refuse truck.   [The American City & County]

Figure 13-28 Trucks with lifting arms empty the large container and return it immediately. [*Dempster Brothers photo*]

can include public areas such as parks, schools, hospitals, auditoriums, and marinas. They can also include commercial areas, hotels, industries, and markets of various types. Most communities require commercial areas to pay for refuse removal or to engage a private hauler. Public areas become the responsibility of the community. Charges against commercial and industrial areas are justified by the reasoning that generation of refuse is a part of business and industrial activity and should not be subsidized from tax funds. Some municipalities will collect refuse only from multifamily dwellings with a limited number of dwelling units; a limit of four units is often used. Larger multifamily

Figure 13-29 Trucks can be provided with special hydraulic loading mechanism. [The American City & County]

Figure 13-30 Large containers like this one originally required a special truck for transport. [The American City & County]

dwellings are considered business ventures and are excluded by the same reasoning that applies to commercial and industrial activities.

The large containers vary widely in size. The early models were designed to be picked up by a truck with hoisting arms and carried individually to the point of disposal. Later, the trucks were provided with large bodies, with openings at the top so that the trucks' lifting arms could pick up large containers and place the refuse in the body immediately, thus reducing the number of trips to the disposal point. Some of the large containers can be provided with independent compacting mechanisms, and some are designed to be towed away separately. In the case of commercial and industrial refuse, concerns are frequently

Figure 13-31 Improvements produced trucks of this type, which empty the container directly into a large body. [The American City & County]

Figure 13-32 Some trucks have adapted a forklift to empty the container into a movable-bulkhead body such as this. [The American City & County]

Figure 13-33 Refuse trucks with front-end loading mechanisms can empty the large containers directly into the compactor truck bodies and thus return them to their designated sites. [*Maxon Industries photo*]

Figure 13-34 Scooters with dump boxes can deliver refuse to the large container. The truck lifting arms can then place the refuse in the body. [The American City & County]

Figure 13-35 Very large containers, of 40 cubic yards (30.6 cubic meters) or more, may have independent compacting mechanisms. They require a special truck for pickup and delivery. This one is located at the Houston Astrodome. [The American City & County]

required to purchase their own containers and maintain them in good condition.

Large containers have done much to improve conditions around areas where excessive volumes of refuse are generated. In the past, the refuse would spill over and litter the entire ground, encouraging rats, flies, stray dogs, and other nuisances.

TRANSFER STATIONS

The solid-waste administrator always has had difficulty in finding a disposal facility that will not cause neighborhood opposition. The general advice used in locating incinerators, landfills, and other disposal facilities has been to take any site to which opposition is minimal and utilize it.

The result of this trend has been a long dead haul from the collection route to the disposal point. This, in turn, has stimulated interest in transfer stations that receive refuse from the collection vehicles and place it in large trailer bodies. Tractor units are connected to the trailers and convey the refuse from several collection trucks to the dis-

Figure 13-36 Transfer stations may have a simple form like this. [The American City & County]

Figure 13-37 Transfer stations may be complex. This one has a receiving bin and a bridge crane that places the refuse in the compacting and loading hopper. [The American City & County]

tant disposal point.   Not only does this procedure reduce hauling costs, but it also lowers the number of vehicles on the highway.

Transfer stations can be simple affairs, consisting of a ramp that allows a truck to back to the loading point and a hopper to receive the discharged refuse.   If the transfer truck is positioned below the hopper, it can receive the refuse immediately.   The transfer unit should have ample capacity and consist of a truck or tractor-trailer with a body as large as 75 cubic yards (57.3 cubic meters).

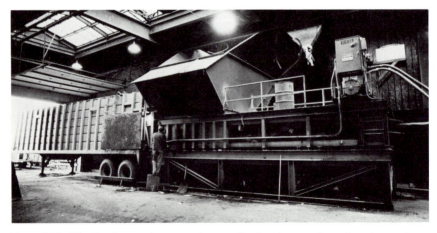

Figure 3-38 The loading and compacting mechanism inserts the refuse into a large trailer. When the trailer is full, a tractor is connected to it to haul the refuse away to the distant disposal site. [The American City & County]

Figure 13-39 Here is a large transfer station.   The route-collection trucks deliver their loads to the storage bin at right, while individual residents bring trash by private car to the bin at left.   [*Dempster Brothers photo*]

The stations may also be sophisticated. Such a station may consist of a separate building that can serve as a district headquarters for the refuse operation or as the primary headquarters in a small community. The building can be equipped with a weigh station to record the quantities of refuse received. It should have an upper level that permits discharging the vehicles into a transition hopper, which in turn releases the refuse to a permanently mounted transfer-station packer, located at the lower level.   A bay at the lower level provides room for the truck or tractor-trailer to receive the compacted refuse.   The compaction runs to about 650 pounds per cubic foot (10,412 kilograms per cubic meter).

Good programming permits one tractor to move a loaded trailer to the disposal point while the transfer station is filling a second trailer

Figure 13-40 Three tractor trailers are ready to transport refuse to the point of disposal. [*Dempster Brothers photo*]

Figure 13-41 In some locations the refuse must be transported by barge to the disposal facilities.   These barges are delivering refuse to the Rotterdam incinerator.   [The American City & County]

placed in the loading bay.   This scheduling depends on the time and distance to the disposal point and the selected size of the trailer.   Larger transfer stations need to provide a more detailed arrangement with more numerous bays, trailers, and tractors.

In very large cities, the transfer may have to take place by barge. New York is an example.   It has appropriately large transfer stations on the riverfront that for many years loaded barges and moved the refuse to landfill sites on Staten Island.

Many have proposed transferring the refuse to a distant disposal site by rail, reasoning that in lightly populated locations the negative impact of a disposal operation would be less severe and savings in the cost of the transport would be substantial.   Theoretically, the reasoning is sound, but in practice people in lightly populated areas resent importing "foreign" wastes and pass ordinances that prevent it.   Communities on the rail route may also enact ordinances forbidding the transport of refuse through their municipal limits.

A study by EPA investigators of the Baltimore solid-waste collection system disclosed the importance of the travel speed of transporting vehicles.   If the vehicles could increase their travel speed from 16 to 30 miles (from 26 to 48 kilometers) per hour, costs would drop by 7.5 percent.[13]

Transfer stations and other solid-waste–handling facilities must be operated with as little nuisance as possible.   Litter and dust should not escape.   Cleanliness should be thorough to prevent the escape of odors.

[13] David H. Marks and Jon C. Liebman, *Mathematical Analysis of Solid Waste Collection,* SW-5rd.-1, U.S. Environmental Protection Agency, 1972.

The structure should be functional and attractive and made of concrete or brick to avoid maintenance problems.

COLLECTION PERSONNEL

Collection crews can no longer be recruited from the least effective members of the labor force, especially if the highly successful one-person collection system is employed. Personnel should pass rigid physical tests, have a chauffeur's license, and preferably be motivated to rise to other technical positions within the local government. Some recommend limiting recruiting to those with an average age of 27, but this policy may present legal problems because of age discrimination.

Productivity

The tendency most visible among municipal employees is increased militancy and demands for collective bargaining. Another trend not so generally publicized is an increase by urban administrators in requirements for productivity. A benefit of collective bargaining is that administrators have been forced to calculate all costs of providing services in the municipal sector.

Flint, Michigan, is an example of the use of productivity requirements. A few years ago it developed a plan aimed at measuring employee performance quantitatively and objectively. The purpose was (1) to cope with increased wage demands, (2) to reduce excessive usage of expensive overtime, and (3) to respond to a large number of complaints about failure to collect residents' refuse. The plan that Flint developed embraced shared savings for increased productivity, contingent on cutting total overtime by 25 percent. It also included a modified task system that released a crew after 6 hours of work if the route collections had been completed. It also required redrawing routes so that each would have between 500 and 585 stops. In 2 years the system reduced overtime by nearly 50 percent. In 1974–1975 the employees received a productivity bonus of $26,600.

The Flint system is not without problems. Garage mechanics and supervisors who feel that they contribute to collection productivity argue that they should be included. However, the city has not yet been able to devise a plan that would embrace them.[14]

RURAL SOLID-WASTE COLLECTION

With the continued urbanization of the United States, former rural areas have acquired solid-waste problems. In the past, when the population

[14] A. W. DeBlaise, "Municipal Engineering," *American Public Works Association Reporter,* April 1976, p. 15.

was too thinly scattered to justify house-to-house collection, most governmental units simply established dump sites where householders could dispose of their refuse.   This system was never particularly satisfactory. Unsightly litter was common, as were rats, insects, and fires that posed dangerous hazards.

In many cases, the solution to these problems is the replacement of open dumps with strategically located large containers that can be collected and emptied on an established basis, such as once a week.   The size of container best fitted for the work must be carefully selected.   An analysis made by Humboldt County, California, bordering the Pacific Ocean about 300 miles (480 kilometers) north of San Francisco, illustrates the sort of study that would be helpful.   Of the county's 106,000 residents, 14,000 are in widely scattered locations in rugged mountain terrain away from the ocean.   The study showed that large roll-on containers which can be loaded on a trailer and transported by the tractor unit to be the most practical selection.   Each container has a capacity of 40 cubic yards (30.6 cubic meters).   These containers were compared with containers holding 8 cubic yards (6.1 cubic meters) each and capable of being lifted and loaded into transfer trucks with compacting mechanisms.   The trucks were to be equipped with the usual front-end loading arms.   The 40-cubic-yard containers showed less tendency to be associated with litter at the site.   They also seemed able to hold more refuse than five 8-cubic-yard containers.   They could accept a wider variety of waste products, waste lumber being of special importance in the mountain areas.   In addition, collection costs per ton were somewhat lower for the larger containers.

At each collection point, a dumping ramp and platform, similar to the usual loading ramp, had to be provided so that trucks could deliver the waste to the containers.   It was found that the tops of the containers should be approximately 18 inches (457 millimeters) above the dumping platform to minimize the wall height and to permit direct dumping from a pickup truck.

Some vandalism can be expected at the container sites, but the units are sturdy enough so that their functional reliability is not affected. The container lids can protect the refuse from the entry of an undue amount of rainfall.[15]

GENERAL FINANCING CONSIDERATIONS

The financing of a solid-waste collection and disposal service can draw revenues either from the community's general fund or from service charges that should make the collection self-supporting and not a drain

[15] T. R. Leslie, *Containerized Storage and Collection of Solid Waste in Humboldt County, Calif.*, Sixth Annual Western Regional Solid Waste Symposium, 1974.

on the general tax fund.   The first alternative assumes that refuse collection and disposal protect the health, welfare, and safety of the community, as do other services such as fire and police.   It also requires the solid-waste administrator to compete for revenues with other municipal services supported by the general tax fund.   The second alternative assumes that refuse collection and disposal constitute a utility like water, electricity, and telephone service.   It gives the administrator a source of revenue independent of the general fund but requires bookkeeping, billing, and collection of delinquent accounts.

If capital costs are involved, the first alternative will use the familiar general-obligation bonds, which are supported by the faith and credit of the community and generally command a somewhat lower rate of interest.   These bonds, however, need to be approved by popular vote, which can be troublesome.   Moreover, the amount of bonded indebtedness is generally restricted by state law.   In contrast, the second method permits the issuance of revenue bonds, which are guaranteed by the financial integrity of the refuse service itself and therefore need no referendum.   They also are not restricted by state law since they are not part of the community's bonded indebtedness.

Service charges should be based on the amount of service that the refuse contributor requires.   They may be based on time studies made at the premises of each contributor, on the number of 30-gallon (0.114-cubic-meter) containers set out or their equivalent, or on some other consideration.   If the people in a community have become accustomed to refuse collection financed from the general fund without special charges, a change to service charges will be extremely difficult, occasionally producing a change in the political administration of the community.   Some municipalities have financed refuse service with funds from both service charges and general taxes.   This procedure makes administrators' work difficult and impairs their ability to compete with other departments for funds.

Chapter Fourteen

Traffic Control
and Street Lighting

WILLIAM S. FOSTER

Traffic control should have three primary purposes: (1) it should seek to prevent injuries and loss of life; (2) it should strive to reduce damage to vehicles and other property; and (3) it should enhance the economic strength and social qualities of the community by expediting the movement of people, goods, and services.

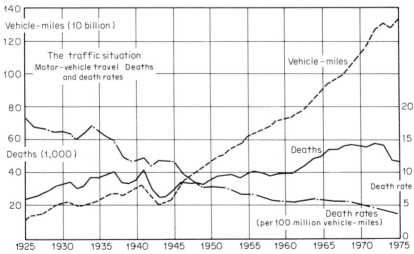

Figure 14-1 This graph, prepared by the National Safety Council, shows the spectacular rise in vehicle-miles traveled and the equally impressive drop in the death rate. Note that the actual number of traffic deaths has increased only modestly and that it showed a distinct drop when the 55-mile-per-hour (88-kilometer-per-hour) speed limit was initiated. [Accident Facts, *National Safety Council, Chicago, 1976*]

Figure 14-2 Sound principles of traffic control, intelligently applied, have reduced traffic fatalities to 4.7 percent of the level prevailing in the 1920s. Here is an offset intersection at Little Rock, Arkansas, with signals and traffic lanes carefully channeled for the protection of motorists. [The American City & County]

That the efforts of those responsible for traffic control have been successful and beneficial to the public can be seen in the substantial drop in the death rate associated with traffic accidents. The National Safety Council records that from 1913–1917 to 1975 motor-vehicle deaths per 10,000 registered vehicles in the United States were reduced by 87 percent, from 24 to 3. Between 1925 and 1975 total vehicle-miles traveled rose spectacularly, from about 12×10 billion vehicle-miles (12×16 billion vehicle-kilometers), to about 133×10 billion vehicle-miles (133×16 billion vehicle-kilometers). In the same period the death rate per 100 million vehicle-miles (161 million vehicle-kilometers) traveled fell from about 75 to less than 3.5.[1]

Although achievement of the purposes of traffic control will assist in improving the quality of life within a community or region, the public frequently opposes the measures that protect life and property and strengthen the community's economic and social bases because of its instinctive distrust of change. This is a facet of human nature that those who have been assigned the responsibility for traffic control cannot ignore.

As discussed in Chapter 1, urban roads and streets can be grouped

[1] *Accident Facts,* National Safety Council, Chicago, 1976, p. 40.

into (1) rural, nonfarm roadways; (2) local streets, both residential and business-industrial; (3) semiarterial or feeder streets; and (4) arterial roads, including limited-access expressways or freeways.

RURAL, NONFARM ROADWAYS

The class of rural, nonfarm roadways is probably the most dangerous in terms of accident rates based on vehicular miles traveled. Since traffic is generally light, the accident frequency will seem low, and the public will be lulled into a false sense of security.

This classification, which is relatively new for urban analysis, reflects the insistence of the public on building homes in predominantly rural areas because the cost of the land and taxes are low and because it feels that it will enjoy a more attractive, noncitified environment. The roadways generally are dangerously substandard in design, often are indifferently maintained, and frequently include portions where the driver's ability to see oncoming traffic is hazardously limited.

Since vehicular traffic is relatively low and tax funds are limited, the traffic-control administrator is forced to limit protective improvements to the installation of stop and yield signs at appropriate locations, thus establishing an arterial system within the rural roadway network. Warning signs also should be placed where there are dangerous conditions, such as side entryways that are not clearly visible. All signs should conform to the *Manual on Uniform Traffic Control Devices for Streets and Highways,* prepared by the U.S. Department of Transportation with the support and cooperation of a number of authoritative technical groups. This manual represents the most authoritative thinking of responsible traffic-control officials. The placement of signs in accordance with its recommendations will be of great help if an accident occurs and those involved claim that the traffic signs were misleading.

Trees and shrubberies should be trimmed to aid motorists in observing oncoming traffic. When one road enters another at an acute angle, the traffic administrator should insist, if at all possible, that the intersection be rebuilt so that the roads intersect at right angles and visibility is good.

For safety even the most rural roadways should have traffic-line markers to designate both the center line and the edges of the roadway. The center line should be marked to indicate no-passing zones at curves, over hills, and at certain intersections, as recommended by the *Manual on Uniform Traffic Control Devices for Streets and Highways.*

Street lighting will be opposed vigorously by those who have chosen this rural environment. However, the traffic administrator should consider lighting potentially dangerous intersections, probably with high-pressure sodium lamps because of their low power requirements for

Figure 14-3 Traffic safety on lightly traveled rural-type roads requires clearly marked traffic lines.

equal amounts of illumination.   (For a discussion of street-lighting lamps, see below, "Street-lighting Maintenance.")

The traffic administrator should encourage making simple vehicle counts to disclose conditions on the roadways.   These will enable the administrator to anticipate urbanization of the area and to plan for more detailed control measures if such a change takes place.

The administrator must confer with appropriate school officials to select well-protected locations where school buses can pick up and return students without creating danger.   The record at protected school crossings and similar locations is excellent.   However, 1 out of every 4 children killed in a traffic accident is on the way to school or returning from school.[2]

RESIDENTIAL STREETS

The second group of urban streets and roads, residential streets, provides service to the greater portion of most communities.   Since streets in this group are of the kind that serve as the origin and destination of most vehicular trips, they must provide space for the storage of vehicles after they have arrived.

Parking Prohibitions

In most residential areas, the residents consider it one of their rights to park their vehicles overnight on the street.   Nevertheless, some parking bans must be instituted if the traffic administrator is to protect the safety of the people.

Periodic parking bans on alternate sides of the street facilitate the operation of street-cleaning equipment.   In snow-belt areas, a winter on-street parking ban aids snowplows in clearing the streets more quickly and allowing traffic to move normally.   If a street is narrow, and many residential streets are, on-street parking bans on one side of the street or

[2] M. B. Snyder and R. L. Knoblauch, *Pedestrian Safety: The Identification of Precipitating Factors and Possible Countermeasures*, Operations Research, Inc., Silver Spring, Md., January 1971.

both may be required to ensure that parked cars do not obstruct the entry of emergency vehicles such as those operated by the police, the fire department, and ambulance services. Dead-end streets should be studied to ensure that these vehicles can maneuver in and out freely.

Traffic-Control Function

Traffic control in residential neighborhoods should concentrate on protecting the area from intrusion by arterial or through traffic. Motorists are innovative and will search out routes through quiet neighborhoods if these appear to save time and distance, regardless of the disruption of this portion of the community.

Stop signs and traffic signals should be able to guide motorists around these areas. If traffic insists on intruding, more vigorous efforts can be used to block its entry. One-way streets can be established. Frequent stop signs can be used to impede the traffic, and certain streets can be closed to traffic if this is practical.

BUSINESS AND INDUSTRIAL STREETS

Local business and industrial areas also are the origin and destination of many motorists, and they too must have places to store vehicles once they arrive. Motorists who do arrive will be understandably annoyed if they find no suitable locations for their vehicles. A lack of parking places does not enhance a community's status either economically or socially.

Space allotted for off-street parking must be based on the activity that generates the need. Guidelines must never be used for definite rules, and any study of parking needs must be based on an analysis of the specific area. Nevertheless, general figures such as these can help to initiate a specific study:[3]

Facility Generating Off-Street Parking Needs	One Stall Needed for Each
Multifamily dwellings	Two-thirds of a family
Theaters, auditoriums, etc.	5 to 10 seats
Hotels	2 to 6 rooms
Retail stores and office buildings	Gross area of 200 to 1000 square feet (18.6 to 93 square meters)
Hospitals	2 to 5 beds
Industrial plants	2 to 5 employees
Wholesale businesses	2 to 5 employees
Restaurants	3 to 10 seats
Colleges and high schools	2 to 5 students

[3] *Design Guide for Permanent Parking Areas*, National Crushed Stone Association, Washington, June 1972, p. 5.

The need for vehicular parking spaces appears greatest in small communities. However, even there off-street parking spaces constitute the majority of the spaces available for use, as shown in the table appearing on page 14-10.

Parking-Lot Designs

Off-street parking areas require from 300 to 500 square feet (from 27.9 to 46.5 square meters) of space per car accommodated, which includes space for the vehicle to circulate within the area. Actual stall space is at least 9 feet (2.7 meters) wide by 19 feet (5.8 meters) long. To accommodate as many vehicles as possible, the designer should restrict traffic to one-way movement.

If there is a choice, the designer should select a rectangular design for the lot. With this it is possible to provide stalls at an angle of 90 degrees from the edge of the parking area and have little waste space.

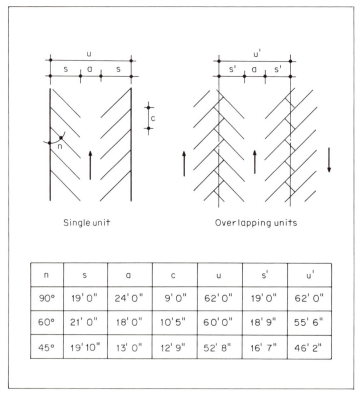

Single unit   Overlapping units

n	s	a	c	u	s'	u'
90°	19' 0"	24' 0"	9' 0"	62' 0"	19' 0"	62' 0"
60°	21' 0"	18' 0"	10' 5"	60' 0"	18' 9"	55' 6"
45°	19' 10"	13' 0"	12' 9"	52' 8"	16' 7"	46' 2"

Figure 14-4 This general parking-lot layout suggests the dimensions that can be applied to three types of parking-stall arrangements. [*National Crushed Stone Association drawing*]

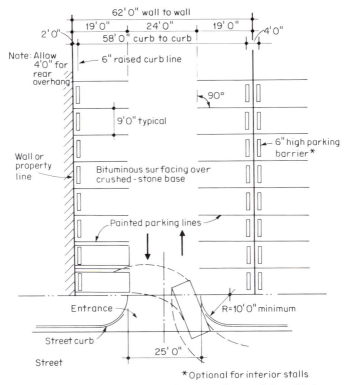

Figure 14-5 Parking stalls at 90-degree angles can follow this layout. [*National Crushed Stone Association drawing*]

However, the motorist often has difficulty in maneuvering into a 90-degree parking stall. The lane for the moving vehicles should be from 24 to 25 feet (from 7.3 to 7.6 meters) wide to permit this maneuvering, as Figure 14-5 shows, and this is wide enough to permit two-way traffic. A 60-degree stall angle permits the motorist to park a car much more easily, and a 45-degree stall angle is even more convenient, but its use tends to restrict the capacity of the parking lot.

If parking lots are designed for one-way traffic, they must have clearly marked entrance and exit points. Parking stalls should be defined by lines or stripes of at least 4-inch (101.6-millimeter) width and maintained in good, clearly visible condition. Stops should be supplied to confine the entry of the vehicle into the parking-lot stall. These may be made of asphaltic concrete, precast portland-cement concrete, or timbers of various types staked into the ground. To protect fire hydrants, utility poles, and other fixed objects, steel bumper posts should be set firmly around them, preferably anchored in concrete.

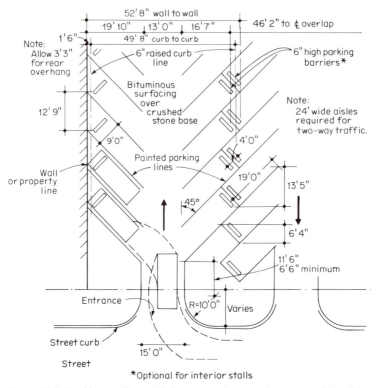

Figure 14-6 Parking stalls at 45-degree angles can be arranged in this manner. [*National Crushed Stone Association drawing*]

Parking Garages

In a central business district, where the cost of land can be high, space for ground-level parking often is restricted. Consequently an economic appraisal of off-street parking in these areas, especially where the need is great, will disclose the value of a multistory garage structure erected on a limited site. Such a garage will provide parking where needed and will not negate the economic usefulness of other downtown land areas.

Since the detailed design of a parking-garage structure should be executed by architects familiar with these needs, it will not be explored here. Nevertheless, some general guidelines can be useful.

Ramps Ramps provide entrance to and exit from a parking garage and also access to the various floors. If the site of the garage is on a slope, the designer can provide access and exit at relatively low cost from the natural ground level. If the site is flat, the designer must select a ramp from a variety of types. The ramp may be straight, leading to the various floor levels; or it may be helical, leading the motorist

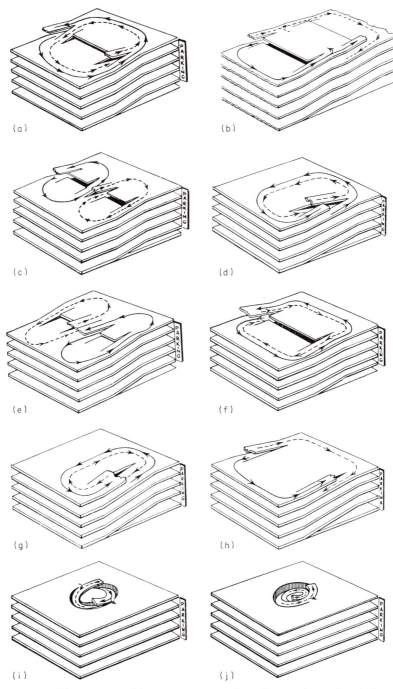

Figure 14-7 These suggested layouts are among those that can be used to design off-street parking structures: (*a*) double-width undivided ramp; (*b*) double staggered ramp; (*c*) twin-circle opposed-plane ramp; (*d*) full-floor ramp; (*e*) twin-circle same-plane ramp; (*f*) concentric divided opposed-plane ramp; (*g*) straight-ramp system; (*h*) opposed straight ramp; (*i*) double-threaded–screw ramp; (*j*) circular concentric opposed-plane ramp. [*National Parking Association*]

in rising, circular fashion to the floor level desired. The floors themselves may form the ramp, causing the motorist to park at a slope.

If the floor itself is ramped, the slope should not exceed 4 percent, and the stalls should preferably be at an angle of 60 degrees to minimize the danger of a car's rolling out of the parking stall. Ramps used solely for access and exit and not for parking should be built to slopes not greater than 10 percent, but if attendants park the cars, the slopes may be as much as 15 to 20 percent.

Traffic Lanes   Lanes on the ramps should be from 14 to 18 feet (from 4.3 to 5.5 meters) wide with straight runs of 12 or more feet (3.7 or more meters). Helical ramps should have a minimum outside radius of 32 feet (9.8 meters), a radius of 35 to 37 feet (10.7 to 11.3 meters) being desirable.

Parking Spaces per 1000 Population

Community size (in thousands)	Spaces per 1000 population	Parking spaces (percent)		
		At curb	Off-street	Garage
10–25	150	43	57	. . .
25–50	120	38	59	3
50–100	70	35	60	5
100–250	50	27	62	11
250–500	30	20	64	16
500–1000	30	14	56	30
Over 1000	20	14	55	31

SOURCE: *Parking Principles,* Special Report No. 125, Highway Research Board, Washington, 1971.

Clear Interior Spans   A structure that can be built with clear interior spans, not cluttered with columns, is of substantial aid to the motorist, who must maneuver in this limited and unfamiliar area. It will also accommodate a somewhat larger number of vehicles, but the cost will be from 5 to 10 percent greater.

Traffic Directional Signs and Lighting   Directional instructions within the garage should be given by signs that duplicate those used on the open street. The driver is familiar with these signs and will respond to them with less confusion. If the garage is very large and is equipped with sophisticated controls, it may have lighted signs that direct the motorist to the appropriate parking stall.

Lighting should be ample, from 8 to 15 footcandles (from 86 to 161 lux) over the driving aisles and from 3 to 10 footcandles (from 32 to 108 lux) over the parked vehicles. Lighting at the entrance should range from 50 to 100 footcandles (from 538 to 1076 lux).

Safety from Violence and Robbery   Safety from assaults, particularly on women, should be a prime consideration in the design of parking garages. Motorists generally must take long walks before emerging from the garage, and the opportunity for violence-prone individuals to hide between cars waiting for a victim is troublesome.

Lighting is an important safety measure. In addition, the designer should consider an exterior stairwell of transparent fire-resistant glass, thus making it difficult for violence-prone people to hide. Stairwells located in this manner also are useful as fire exits.

Generally, these garages are equipped with elevators. These should be provided with controls that will keep the elevator door open until the passenger is inside and has pressed the button for the floor desired. Such an arrangement makes it difficult for anyone to hide in the elevator and pull a victim inside.

Protection against Other Hazards Violence is not the only risk in a parking garage. Closed garages should have alarms sensitive to dangerous levels of carbon monoxide and also to the presence of smoke. Automatic sprinklers should be supplied for fire protection.

Revenue Control For garages to approach a self-sustaining financial condition, they must have a sound revenue-control system. In general, a metered arrangement does not work especially well. Every vehicle entering the garage should leave a transaction record at the exit. A common type makes use of a swinging gate that issues an entrance ticket, stamped with the time of entrance, when the vehicle approaches the access way. The gate can be actuated by an electric eye or other means; the driver picks up the ticket as it emerges from the column that supports the swinging gate. Thus the only attendant needed will be stationed in the exit area. In other arrangements the attendant issues the ticket at the entrance and collects the ticket and the parking fee as the vehicle makes its exit.

Attendant Parking Most drivers prefer to park their own cars, lock them, and carry the keys. If an attendant does the parking, this eliminates the chance of violence for the driver. Nevertheless, most drivers feel that attendants tend to be careless. Labor costs for attendants also can increase the cost of parking operations by as much as 40 percent.

Variety in Parking Structures Parking garages have been built completely underground. Frequently they form a part of a structure that has other functions, such as an office building or an apartment or hotel. Occasionally they have been built to cross a street. Some are composed of prefabricated members that reportedly can be disassembled and re-erected elsewhere. Exteriors frequently are made more attractive by the skillful use of anodized aluminum siding in various forms and colors. Other architectural treatments and landscaping can add attractiveness to this type of utilitarian structure, which nevertheless contributes economic strength to a central business district.[4]

[4] Institute of Traffic Engineers, *Transportation and Traffic Engineering Handbook*, Prentice-Hall, Inc., Englewood Cliffs, N.J., 1975, pp. 685–691; "How to Get Off-Street Parking," *The American City*, January 1970, p. 91.

Parking-Meter Use

The parking meter is a device that originally was designed to relieve crowded and congested situations in central business districts and similar locations. Its purpose is to provide parking space for the shopper for a restricted period, thus making the space available to other shoppers. Often, unthinking businessmen and their employees have usurped the space required by shoppers, thus forcing them to go to competitive areas such as shopping plazas with ample off-street parking.

The installation of parking meters also is a means of raising some revenue. However, fees should be low enough to prevent shoppers from feeling that they are being imposed upon, yet large enough to finance the meters and pay for their operation and upkeep.

A 1967 survey of parking-meter use by the National League of Cities showed that the total number of meters in use varied from 120 in communities of 2500 or less to more than 23,000 in cities of 1 million or more.[5] Of these meters, nearly 90 percent were located in central business districts in communities of less than 2500. This percentage dropped to 43 percent for cities from 500,000 to 1 million. In the category of great cities, with populations of 1 million or more and high densities and with parking generally at a premium, no more than 10 percent of the meters were in what those cities classed as their central business districts.

Parking-Meter Revenues   The same study showed that annual revenues per meter varied from $45 for the communities under 2500 to nearly $112 for cities of 1 million or more. Average maintenance cost per meter varied from $3.23 for the small communities to $17.81 for the cities of 1 million or more. Average collection costs ranged from $3.54 for the small communities to $7.59 for the great cities. This resulted in net earnings per meter per year of about $38 for the small communities and $86 to $88 for the great cities.

Vandal-Proof Meters   Although no individual meter holds a great deal of money at any one time, vandals have broken meter heads off the posts, taken them to a hidden place, and broken into them. This kind of vandalism became virtually endemic a few years ago, particularly in the larger cities. To thwart the trend, the manufacturers produced vault-type coin-storage boxes for the meters that were strong enough to discourage those who would like to rob them. These stronger boxes have largely solved the problem.

Types of Meters   Meters can operate automatically or manually. In automatic meters, a clockwork spring activates the mechanism that sets the timing device when the money is inserted. In manually operated

---

[5] W. D. Heath, J. M. Hunnicutt, M. A. Neale, and L. A. Williams, *Parking in the United States: A Survey of Local Government Action,* National League of Cities, Washington, 1967, pp. 66–87.

meters the motorist must insert the money and then turn a handle to set the timing mechanism. Either type works satisfactorily, and the choice is a matter of personal preference.

Meters can be provided with open coin boxes that can be emptied directly into the collection unit, or they can be supplied with sealed boxes that are removed from the meters to be replaced by empty sealed boxes. Personnel making collections deliver the boxes to a central point where they can be opened under supervision, thus removing temptation from the collectors.

Pedestrian Traffic Control

Within the central business districts, good traffic-control principles require greater attention to the convenience of the pedestrian. Arthur D. Bird, director of public works of Cincinnati, has observed that the pedestrian is a humble man, pushed around first by a man on horseback, then by a man in a carriage, and now by others in cars and trucks. Yet the municipality's business districts cannot live without him or, more properly, her. People reach downtown areas as drivers or passengers but become pedestrians at the ends of their trips. Bird suggests four measures that will aid the pedestrian without making major changes in the downtown area:

1. Coordinate traffic signals to favor the pedestrian instead of the motorist.

2. Place traffic signals at midblock, giving the pedestrian a protected crossing. Time the signals to be convenient to the pedestrian instead of the motorist.

3. Widen sidewalks at intersections to give the pedestrian more room and to discourage traffic from entering the block. Casual traffic need not enter a business district.

4. Make traffic one-way in the downtown grid, thus enabling the pedestrian to watch for traffic traveling in only one direction.

Pedestrian Characteristics   Pedestrians generally walk a path that is the shortest distance between two points if at all possible. They make midblock crossings and resist staying in established crosswalks. They use underpasses and overpasses most unwillingly, and they generally express annoyance with traffic regulations that involve them, making enforcement of these regulations difficult.[6]

Pedestrian Crosswalks   Despite pedestrian reluctance, crosswalks must be marked clearly. Some cities have passed ordinances requiring vehicular traffic to stop whenever a pedestrian steps into a crosswalk located at midblock.

Ramps are now gaining popularity at crosswalks for the assistance of handicapped citizens (see Chapter 4 for details of ramp construction).

[6] Arthur D. Bird, "How to Plan for the Pedestrian," *The American City*, July 1969, p. 76.

Figure 14-8 Pedestrians generally use underpasses and overpasses unwillingly.   Here is one under construction, designed to carry foot traffic over a traffic interchange.   [The American City & County]

Since a sizable percentage of the population is about 60 years of age and since this percentage appears to be growing, traffic lights must be bright enough to be seen and recognized easily by those whose vision is less acute.   Occasionally someone proposes a series of bell signals to indicate a change in traffic direction to these older citizens and others with impaired vision.

Pedestrian Malls   To make central business districts more popular and useful to shoppers, a number of communities have redesigned

Figure 14-9 This attractive crosswalk and traffic-signal arrangement has been designed primarily for pedestrian convenience.   [*Rohm & Haas photo*]

Figure 14-10 Pedestrian mails such as the Lincoln Mall, Miami Beach, Florida, have become increasingly popular. [*Miami Beach News Bureau*]

and rebuilt the downtown area, transforming a portion of it into a pedestrian plaza with no vehicular traffic except that of an emergency nature.

Grand Rapids, Michigan, was one of the first cities to establish this concept. Miami Beach followed with its Lincoln Mall, capitalizing on a roadway that was not essential to the free flow of traffic in this resort city. Fresno, California, went to a great deal of trouble to create perhaps the most attractive pedestrian mall in use in the nation. All the malls are carefully landscaped and lighted to add to the attractiveness of the area. Most provide some sort of informal transit through the mall.

Semipedestrian Malls An alternative is the semipedestrian mall, which allows limited vehicular circulation through the area so that there is only minimal interference with pedestrian circulation. The usual practice is to rebuild the street on a serpentine routing and to prohibit all parking.

Curves are preferred by nature and add a touch of beauty and interest by varying the point of vision of the driver. The curved route should be enhanced by landscaping and appropriately chosen street furniture in the form of benches, water fountains, telephone booths in uncon-

Figure   14-11 Semipedestrian malls built to a serpentine pattern allow the passage of traffic but no on-street parking.

ventional shapes, and kiosks for newspapers and magazines.   Examples of semipedestrian malls can be found in the smaller cities, such as Grand Junction, Colorado, Atchison, Kansas, and Fort Myers, Florida.

Covered Sidewalks   Short of major surgery in the central business district, other aids to the pedestrians are available.   One is the covered sidewalk, which can be used if the street is wide.   The canopies over the sidewalk protect the pedestrian from the weather and make the adjoining stores more inviting.

Another method, which arcades the sidewalk into the building, is useful if the street is narrow.   This method is used in many of the older European cities and adds a great deal of charm to shopping areas.

Arcading requires the city to negotiate suitable financial arrangements with the property owners and their lessees to cover costs of remodeling, loss of sales or display space, inconvenience, and other irritations. Moreover, the city must acquire from each owner a ground-floor easement for the width of the arcade.   This easement is three-dimensional, abutting the public sidewalk and extending across the frontage of the property, one story in height and with depths varying from 7 to 12 feet (from 2.1 to 3.7 meters).

Allentown, Pennsylvania, makes use of canopies over the sidewalks in shopping areas.   Cincinnati has employed the arcade principle.

Figure 14-12 These bronze-tinted acrylic-plastic sidewalk canopies add to the attractiveness of the downtown area and provide pedestrians with protection from snow, rain, and intense sun. [The American City & County]

Moving Sidewalks   Moving sidewalks occasionally have been suggested as a means of encouraging pedestrian circulation. Their chief advantage is that they save pedestrian energy rather than time. They travel at a rate slower than that at which most pedestrians can walk, and for this reason some will prefer not to use them. However, they are useful in business districts that are hilly, with differences in elevation that make access from one level to another laborious.

Pedestrian Intersection Extenders   Communities with wide streets that have four or more lanes of traffic can assist pedestrians with what some choose to call "intersection extenders."   These consist of a sidewalk platform at the intersection that extends into the street for a distance of about 10 to 12 feet (3 to 3.7 meters) on a quarter-circle pattern.

Pedestrians can walk safely to the edge of the extension, where they can see and be seen by oncoming traffic. The extender shortens the walking distance across the intersection, thus making the crossing safer. Its platform has a 20-foot (6.1-meter) radius that causes no problems for mechanical street sweepers. The extender can provide a space for shrubs and flowers that add beauty to the area. Traffic signals and street signs also can be located there.

One of the earliest cities to adopt the pedestrian intersection extender was Enid, Oklahoma, which is located in an area where wide streets were popular among pioneeer town planners. A typical drawing of the design used in this city is shown in Figure 14-13.

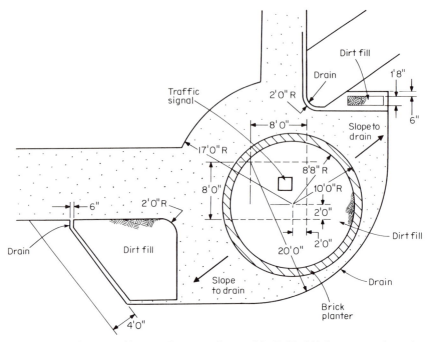

Figure 14-13   The type of intersection extension used in Enid, Oklahoma, to assist pedestrian traffic.   [The American City & County]

Parking Studies

The traffic-control administrator has the responsibility of making studies of parking in any areas where traffic volume can be considered high and availability of parking spaces may be a problem.   Among such

Figure 14-14   Arterial roadways through urban areas often generate substantial commercial roadside development and complicate the work of the traffic director.

areas are central business districts, the vicinity of schools, auditoriums, sports centers, and parks, and other areas that attract vehicular traffic.

One convenient procedure in making such a study is to record the license numbers and other identifying information about parked cars in the area. The surveyor can compile the record on some convenient time interval such as each 15 to 30 minutes or longer.

This information will disclose the occupancy of parking space in the block studied and the time that the vehicle remains there. An analysis of the information should disclose the need for added parking spaces, if required, and the possible need for parking meters to prevent drivers from monopolizing parking space in areas better suited to shopper convenience.

ARTERIAL STREETS

Arterial streets demand the greatest of attention from those charged with traffic control, since they carry the greatest volume of moving vehicles. Most arterial streets primarily move traffic and secondarily provide access to abutting property. Since the volume of traffic is substantial, business concerns are attracted to the abutting property, and this complicates the problems of the traffic administrator.

Traffic-Lane Markings for Arterial Streets

The late Henry Barnes, probably the most accomplished and knowledgeable traffic-control expert of this age, once stated that the most useful traffic-control device was a paintbrush and a pail of paint. This was his way of stating that the intelligent use of clearly marked traffic lanes is the most effective way of bringing order out of a confusing and dangerous traffic situation.

The lines may be painted, they may be thermoplastic, they may be tape with adhesive backing for temporary use, or they may be raised markers. Each type has its specific use and limitations.

Figure 14-15 Painted traffic lines applied by modern methods dry instantly and should last at least 6 months. [The American City & County]

Painted traffic lines should be able to serve for at least 6 months and preferably 1 year. The paint should produce a film thickness of 15 mils (0.38 millimeter) and should dry rapidly. To increase visibility at night, beads with a standard refractive index of 1.50+ can be applied at the rate of 6 pounds per gallon (0.72 kilogram per liter) of paint.

Thermoplastic traffic lines can be cold-rolled into place or glued down with adhesive backing. They work best as markings for crosswalks and stop lines on bituminous pavements in high-density urban areas. Thermoplastic lines can be used for lane marking for new asphalt if the stripes can be rolled into the asphalt with the last pass of the roller. Thermoplastic lane markings have proved to be more durable on bituminous pavement than on concrete, with the least success on recently placed concrete. The plastic is subject to damage by snowplows, but when traffic volumes are high, the plastic lane markings can prove to be more economical.

Raised markers can be used in areas that experience virtually no snowfall. They have reflectors mounted in them and extend above the surface of the pavement by as much as 1 inch (25.4 millimeters). Motorists prefer these markers especially for night driving during a rain.

Traffic paint will fail for a number of reasons. Among them are insufficiently cleaned pavements, overthinned paint, damp or wet pavements, application on windy days or in temperatures below 40°F (4.4°C), the presence of limestone or other alkaline materials that break down the paint, and application of an insufficient paint film.[7]

Median Types

A median strip of some type should be mandatory on most arterial roadways. Medians can be raised or painted. They can be narrow barriers

[7] Institute of Traffic Engineers, op. cit., p. 772.

Figure 14-16 Painted medians are enlargements of the customary center stripe. This one has been designed to accommodate a left-turn bay at the traffic light. It also requires that the roadway be widened at this point.

4½ feet (1.4 meters) wide to prevent head-on collisions. They can be wide enough for left-turn bays, or at least 14 feet (4.3 meters). Or they can be 20 feet (6.1 meters) or more in width. All provide safety for pedestrians trying to cross arterial streets.

Painted medians are essentially an enlargement of the familiar center-line stripe. They cannot physically deter head-on collisions or prevent left turns between intersections, but they can help to expedite traffic movements and separate conflicting traffic lanes. When sufficiently wide, they provide room for left-turn movements. Widths are generally from 8 to 14 feet (from 2.4 to 4.3 meters).

Left-Turn Bays

Left-turn bays are of great assistance in the smooth control of traffic. They permit traffic wishing to turn to the left to pull out of the main traffic stream and wait until an opportunity presents itself to make the left turn safely.

Although bays differ in design principles, most feel that a bay should be designed so that the motorist can recognize it easily and not slip into it without being aware of the location. As shown in Figure 14-17 and the

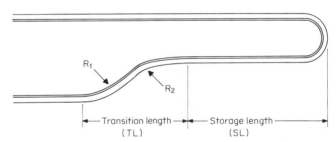

Figure 14-17 Design standards for left-turn bays in medians vary from city to city, as this diagram shows. [Arterial Design Standards, *American Public Works Association, 1969*]

accompanying table, transition lengths can vary from less than 50 feet (15.2 meters) to more than 200 feet (61 meters). The transition consists of a compound curve with radii varying from 10 feet (3 meters) to more than 300 feet (91.4 meters). The 10-foot radius requires a short length of tangent to connect the two curves. The storage slot can vary from 50 to 250 feet (from 15.2 to 76.2 meters), depending on the amount of traffic anticipated.[8]

[8] *A Survey of Urban Arterial Design Standards,* American Public Works Association, Chicago, 1969, pp. 31–42.

Left-Turn Bays in Various Cities

Jurisdiction	Turn-bay dimensions (feet)			
	R^a	R^b	Transition length	Storage length
Baltimore, Maryland	200	200	. . .	. . .
Chicago, Illinois	. . .	. . .	100	100
Cincinnati, Ohio	. . .	. . .	. . .^{a}	50 minimum
Dade County, Florida	150	200	121	50 minimum
Denver, Colorado	50–287	50–287	44–100	150–200
Detroit, Michigan^b	. . .	. . .	. . .	. . .
Fort Worth, Texas	280 or 1000	280	210–215	. . .
Los Angeles, California	. . .	. . .	80	100–250
Middletown, Ohio	300–600	300–600	. . .	. . .^{c}
Pasadena, California	. . .	. . .	60 minimum	various
Phoenix, Arizona	. . .	. . .	100	100–200
Portland, Oregon	. . .	. . .	. . .^{d}	. . .
Salem, Oregon	. . .	. . .	75	. . .
Skokie, Illinois	. . .	. . .	. . .^{e}	. . .
Toronto, Ontario	. . .	. . .	250	. . .^{f}
Washington, D.C.	10^g	10^g	. . .	. . .

^{a} 2 times lane width.
^{b} U-turn slots constructed on the near side of intersections.
^{c} Three-car length minimum.
^{d} 20 times offset minimum.
^{e} 20:1 ratio tapered to turning lane.
^{f} $N/30$ times 25 feet (N = number of turning vehicles), or 75 to 200 feet.
^{g} Connected by tangent sections.

Right Turns on Red

Permission for a vehicle to make a right turn when the traffic signal shows red, the vehicle is in the right-hand lane, and no cross traffic is present has many supporters. It helps to remove from the arterial-street traffic vehicles that do not want to be there, thereby benefiting

Figure 14-18 An exclusive right-turn lane can assist drivers making right turns against a red traffic signal when this is permitted.

the vehicles traveling on the arterial road.   And it benefits the motorist making the right turn by eliminating a certain amount of delay.   If space permits, an exclusive right-turn lane can be provided that will make the movement more rapid and will not force a driver wishing to turn right to queue up behind a vehicle that will not turn right and thereby slow the process.

Left Turns on Arterials without a Left-Turn Bay

If no left-turn bay can be provided on the arterial road, the safest procedure would be to prohibit left turns.   However, this prohibition generally meets with strong opposition from motorists, who argue that they are willing to assume the risk for the convenience of the left turn. Nevertheless, motorists making a left turn without provision of a left-turn bay invariably block traffic and create congestion.

MEASUREMENT OF TRAFFIC VOLUMES

Traffic control must be based on studies of traffic volumes as well as accident incidents.   Traffic measurements, to be thorough, should include not only vehicles but also pedestrians.

Since the installation of traffic signals on any intersection is relatively expensive, the investment will be better justified by traffic counts, preferably made manually, with the counters noting the direction that the vehicles take at the intersection.   Occasional origin and destination counts at a typical intersection can produce evidence to justify a traffic signal or give guidance on whether it is unwarranted.

Cordon Survey

The traffic administrator also can arrange for a study of a specific area rather than of individual intersections.   To accomplish this, the surveyors determine the number of vehicles entering or leaving the area selected. The survey establishes a boundary around the area and then counts the number of vehicles passing over each street that provides entrance to or exit from it.   This is frequently called a cordon-line survey.

Vehicle-Speed Survey

A study of vehicle speeds on critical arteries helps to establish safe maximum and minimum speed limits.   It also aids in guiding the location of regulatory and warning signs.   The survey can make use of road tubes set at fixed distances apart.   However, the visibility of the tubes has an inhibiting effect on drivers and does not always give reliable information.   Radar speed meters are accurate, but they are highly visible.

A simple way to make the survey while being undetected is to mark the pavement in a selected multiple of 88 feet (26.8 meters).   If the predominant speed is below 25 miles (40 kilometers) per hour, the distance can be set at 88 feet. If the speeds are between 25 and 40 miles (64 kilometers) per hour, 176 feet (53.6 meters) should be selected. If the predominant speeds are over 40 miles per hour, a distance of 264 feet (80.4 meters) will be needed. The surveyor, who is placed halfway between the two markers, with a stopwatch records the number of seconds t that each vehicle requires to pass the two markers. The determination of the vehicle velocity is very simple:

For the 88-foot distance

$$\text{Miles per hour} = \frac{60}{t}$$

For the 176-foot distance

$$\text{Miles per hour} = \frac{120}{t}$$

For the 264-foot distance

$$\text{Miles per hour} = \frac{264}{t}$$

The calculation is based on the determination that 88 feet is the distance that a vehicle traveling at 60 miles per hour will cover in 1 second. If speeds in metric units are needed, the survey length should be 27.8 meters (91.2 feet) and the velocity in kilometers per hours can be determined by the formula

$$\text{Kilometers per hour} = \frac{100}{t}$$

This calculation is based on a velocity of 100 kilometers per hour, which is roughly equivalent to 60 miles per hour. In this case, 27.8 meters represents the distance that a vehicle will travel at 100 kilometers per hour in 1 second. The stopwatches should be able to measure in tenths of a second.

To avoid difficulty in determining the exact time that the vehicle crosses the marks measuring the distance and to eliminate the use of the marks if desired, the surveyor can use a periscopelike mirror arrangement called an enoscope at each end of the measured distance. With it the observer can see accurately when the vehicle passes each base line. To determine speeds at night, the surveyor can place a light on the side of the road opposite the enoscope and observe the time by the disappearance of the light as the vehicle passes by.[9]

[9] Institute of Traffic Engineers, op. cit., pp. 419–420.

Vehicle-Delay Studies

Congestion also can be a symptom that the traffic administrator must analyze. It can be determined best by measuring the delay in traffic rather than simply by measuring traffic volume. Vehicles that queue up in attempting either to enter an intersection or to pass through it represent time lost and community economic value damaged.

The amount of vehicle delay can be measured by a surveyor with a stopwatch who records the arrival and departure time of vehicles at the intersection being studied. The surveyor can note the time delay on a work form such as the one illustrated in Figure 14-19 or by a tape recorder, with the data to be transcribed at the office.

If the intersection is subject to a large number of vehicles experiencing delay, two surveyors may be required. One will note the time at which the vehicle arrives at the queue. The second will note the departure time. The surveyors must be supplied with coordinated timepieces. The recorder enters the time observed in the "in" and "out" columns of the vehicle-delay field-count sheets. Others can compute the time delay in seconds. Those making the computations also can calculate the information shown in the "Delay Interval" table. From this, they can prepare the delay-interval graph disclosing the accumulation of delay incidents.

At this time, no one has established standards to indicate how much delay will justify traffic signals that will eliminate or at least reduce the amount of this delay congestion. However, the studies will document the fact that congestion exists and will enable the traffic administrator to document existing conditions objectively. The policy has been in use for several years in the Rochester area of Monroe County, New York.[10]

Accident Surveys

Accident reports represent a convincing and often an emotional way to justify improvements in traffic flow. The reports must document what happened and carry information such as incidents of fatalities, personal injuries, and property damage. Records obtained from the police and from the drivers of the vehicles involved can be considered accurate. Newspaper reports of accidents or reports from casual observers must be confirmed before being recorded.

For the traffic administrator, an accident report should give the following information:

1. Date, time, and location of the accident
2. Weather conditions
3. Condition of the road surface

[10] R. R. Smith, "A Simple Technique Helps Locate New Traffic Signals," *The American City,* June 1972, pp. 140–141.

Vehicle delay field count

Location: Clifford and Woodman St   Date: Wed. 2/4/70
Conditions: Clear, wet, 15°   Time: 4:15 – 5:15

In	Out	Second delay	In	Out	Second delay	In	Out	Second delay
0:15	0:20	5	25:00	25:10	10	39:20	39:55	35
2:40	2:43	3	27:05	27:01	2	39:50	40:00	10
4:25	4:29	4	27:30	27:50	20	39:55	40:05	10
5:10	5:15	5	27:35	27:55	20	40:20	40:35	15
5:10	5:15	5	28:10	28:13	3	42:20	42:35	15
5:35	5:38	3	28:10	28:15	5	42:25	42:55	30
6:35	6:50	15	28:30	28:32	2	42:55	43:00	5
9:25	9:38	13	28:55	29:20	25	43:30	43:33	3
9:50	9:55	5	28:55	29:25	30	44:50	44:55	5
9:55	9:59	4	30:05	30:40	35	44:55	45:05	10
11:25	11:30	5	30:35	30:50	15	46:10	46:14	4

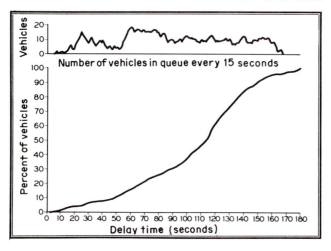

Number of vehicles in queue every 15 seconds

Delay intervals

Seconds	Number vehicles	Accumulation	Percent accumulation
0-5	42	42	50
6-10	12	54	64
11-15	9	63	75
16-20	7	70	83
21-25	3	73	85
26-30	3	76	90
31-35	3	79	94
36-40	1	80	95
41-45	3	83	99
46-50	1	84	100

Figure 14-19 A traffic surveyor can use a form like the one shown at the top to make a field record of the traffic delays. The delays can then be plotted as a graph, shown immediately below, and the occurrence of delay intervals can be tabulated as shown at left. [The American City & County]

4. Description of the accident with an estimate of its severity
5. Probable cause of the accident
6. Make and type of the vehicles involved
7. A diagram to show how the accident happened

The administrator will find that this information is useful when appraising a section of the roadway for changes in traffic signals, signs, or markings or when adopting other traffic-control measures.

In addition to the pain and anguish involved in accidents, the administrator can place an economic cost on accidents. A study made in 1972 estimated that each fatality represented a cost of \$82,000; each disabling injury, \$3400; and each incident involving property damage only, \$480. The costs undoubtedly have risen since then.[11]

Floating-Car Survey

The traffic administrator also can obtain useful and factual information by driving in the traffic stream and recording travel time, delays, interruptions, and the effectiveness of existing traffic-control devices. Personal observation of the visibility and ability of the devices to attract attention and command obedience will enable the administrator to detect weakness that otherwise would be overlooked.

Prohibition of Curb Parking

The prohibition of parking at the curb when the evidence shows that it interferes markedly with traffic flow is a useful technique. However, the institution of such a prohibition will be greeted with hostility and therefore should be accompanied by a program providing off-street parking in areas convenient to the motorist.

Curb parking robs an arterial roadway of one lane, and double parking drastically reduces the traffic volume and generates congestion. If the traffic on the artery is largely of the commuter type, the ban may be adopted solely for the period of peak traffic, but such a limitation requires meticulous enforcement.

Reversible Traffic Lanes

Reversible lanes have proved successful in coping with commuter-type traffic, although they require careful signing and signaling. The lane change can be made by overhead traffic signals that designate the lane, by the use of traffic cones, and, on occasion, by hydraulically raised and lowered lane delineators.

---

[11] *Estimating the Cost of Accidents*, Traffic Safety Memo No. 113, National Safety Council, Chicago, 1973.

TRAFFIC SIGNS

The policies of traffic signs have been thoroughly established in an authoritative manner by a manual issued by the U.S. Department of Transportation.[12]   This manual has the support of a number of professional organizations active in traffic control.

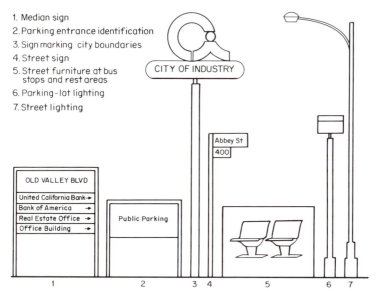

1. Median sign
2. Parking entrance identification
3. Sign marking city boundaries
4. Street sign
5. Street furniture at bus stops and rest areas
6. Parking-lot lighting
7. Street lighting

CITY OF INDUSTRY

Abbey St
400

OLD VALLEY BLVD

United California Bank→
Bank of America   →
Real Estate Office →
Office Building   →

Public Parking

1   2   3 4   5   6   7

Figure 14-20 Distinctive signs and street furniture were proposed for the city of Industry, California, by consultants, Gruen Associates.   [*Gruen Associates drawings*]

Special Signs

Within a community's business districts, especially districts whose appearance the community has made some effort to improve, supplemental information signs can be provided.   These can be prepared with special attention to their architectural and artistic character, making them a little more distinctive than those used solely for traffic control in nonurban areas.

All signs must command attention and convey their meanings quickly and unmistakably.   As motorists enter a business district, they need much more information than that on the types supplied in rural settings. Moreover, entrance into a central business district provides the opportunity to identify the particular character and purpose of the community.

[12] *Manual on Uniform Traffic Control Devices for Streets and Highways,* U.S. Department of Transportation, 1971.

Stop Signs

The familiar stop sign is a simple traffic-control device and for that reason probably tends to be overused. In this period of fuel conservation, the most efficient condition is one in which traffic moves at an even, consistent rate without stops. Each passenger-car stop-and-go cycle requires roughly an extra 0.02 gallon (0.07 liter) of gasoline to return the vehicle to a speed of 60 miles (97 kilometers) an hour.[13]

A stop sign should be used when a preponderantly local road intersects one that is arterial or semiarterial, particularly when the intersection has no traffic signal and the arterial roadway has traffic signals at other intersections. It also should be used at the intersection of local roadways if accident records show the intersection to be dangerous. A stop sign should never be placed at an intersection equipped with traffic signals since this would give motorists conflicting and confusing instructions.

Four-Way–Stop Intersections

Four-way–stop intersections, or multiple-way stops, can be adopted at intersections where no predominant traffic flow can be established but where the flow of traffic is sufficiently high to require some type of control. In general, such a condition indicates a need for traffic signals, but in the interests of economy or of local objections to traffic signals as symbols of urbanization the traffic-control administrator often will find it necessary to use the four-way–stop method.

Figure 14-21   Four-way–stop intersections can be adopted when the volume of traffic is moderately high and there is no predominant traffic flow.

Four-way stops should be considered if (1) the intersection is accident-prone, with five or more accidents per year; (2) traffic at the intersection exceeds 500 vehicles for any 8-hour period; and (3) total pedestrian and vehicular movements exceed 200 units per hour from the minor roadway for the same 8-hour period, with an average delay to vehicles on

[13] P. J. Claffey, "Running Costs of Motor Vehicles as Affected by Road Design and Traffic," in *Costs and Benefits of Transportation Planning*, National Research Council, Highway Research Board, Washington, 1971, p. 17.

the minor street of at least 30 seconds per vehicle during the maximum hour. If 85 percent of the traffic approaches the intersection at speeds exceeding 40 miles (64 kilometers) per hour, the minimum vehicular volumes may be reduced to 70 percent of these figures.[14]

Yield Signs

Yield signs are a convenience for motorists and implement a method of clearing a traffic lane where a queue might otherwise develop. They may be used to assign the right-of-way from a minor road to an arterial roadway where an examination shows that a full stop is not necessary and the safe approach speed can exceed 10 miles (16 kilometers) per hour. Frequently they are used on entrance ramps at expressways when the ramps lack acceleration lanes. They can be used on an intersection with a separate, channelized right-turn lane without an adequate acceleration lane, and they can also be used at any intersection with special problems susceptible to solution by this type of sign.[15]

Overhead Traffic-Control Signs

Overhead traffic-control signs can be used where traffic is heavy and instructional signs at the curb cannot attract sufficient attention to give the drivers the necessary guidance. They also should be used where the traffic speed is sufficiently high to make it difficult for motorists to see roadside signs. Complex intersections often benefit by their use. If the roadway carries a substantial amount of truck traffic, overhead signs can be helpful.

Breakaway Supports for Overhead Signs

Overhead signs or any other signs with a width of 48 inches (1219.2 millimeters) or more must be supported on posts, and these can create

[14] *Manual on Uniform Traffic Control Devices for Streets and Highways*, p. 2 B-6.
[15] Ibid., p. 2 B-8.

Figure 14-22 Overhead traffic signs give the motorist guidance directly over the traffic lanes and away from distraction by roadside billboards.

danger for vehicles that are momentarily out of control. To reduce this danger, the traffic administrator can mount such signs on supports that yield or break on impact.

If the signs are supported by posts of Douglas fir or structural pine, with cross sections of 4 by 4 inches (101.6 by 101.6 millimeters) or 4 by 6 inches (101.6 by 152.4 millimeters) and with the longer dimension perpendicular to the roadway, the supports should break on contact. If the signs require support posts of 6 by 6 inches (152.2 by 152.4 millimeters), they should be weakened by placing two holes in the posts. The holes should be 1½ inches (38.1 millimeters) in diameter, drilled in the center of the post parallel to the face of the sign. One should be 6 inches (152.4 millimeters) above the ground level, and the other 18 inches (457.2 millimeters). If the support posts must be 6 by 8 inches (152.4 by 203.2 millimeters) with the longer side perpendicular to the roadway, the holes should be 2½ inches (63.5 millimeters) in diameter and placed in the same manner.

Steel breakaway support posts can be provided with a variety of designs that will reduce the possibility of a damaging impact with a vehicle.[16]

Truck Height Detector

Many older bridges and overpasses spanning arterial roadways provide only limited headroom. Despite clear instructions from prominently located signs warning of limited headroom, trucks continue to try passing under such a structure, damaging the vehicles as well as the overpass or bridge.

A height detector and warning system can prevent or at least reduce this source of damage. The detector consists of a photoelectric device with a light source and receiver mounted at a height corresponding to the clearance. An overheight truck triggers the photoelectric alarm, which in turn activates special warning bells and lights loud and intensive enough to command the attention of the driver. Representative installations have reduced this type of accident, at times by as much as 90 percent.[17]

Protection from Vandals

Overhead structures with pedestrian sidewalks appear to offer attractions to the violence-prone. Irresponsible pedestrians throw rocks and other heavy objects onto cars passing beneath the structure, causing property damage and often physical injuries. In typical installations

[16] Institute of Traffic Engineers, op. cit., pp. 748–749; "Breakaway Sign Posts Reduce Hazards," *The American City,* January 1969, p. 112.

[17] "Height Detector Forewarns Trucks of Decapitation," *The American City,* September 1973, p. 150.

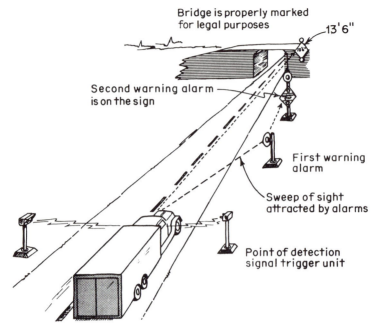

Bridge is properly marked
for legal purposes

13'6"

Second warning alarm
is on the sign

First warning
alarm

Sweep of sight
attracted by alarms

Point of detection
signal trigger unit

Figure 14-23 An overheight truck receives three warnings before it can collide with a bridge deck. These are enough to prevent most accidents. [The American City & County]

over the Dan Ryan and Eisenhower Expressways in Chicago, chain link fences 12 feet (3.7 meters) high have reduced this hazard by making a vandal's efforts more difficult and more visible.[18]

Crash Cushions

The traffic-control administrator must be alert to the danger of concrete or steel piers supporting structures passing over arterial roadways. These constitute traffic risks that create more than their share of accidents.

An effective way of reducing this source of accidents is the use of an energy-absorbing cushion. One successful example, known as the Texas crash cushion, consists of thirty to forty steel barrels of 55-gallon (208-liter) capacity welded together in triangle form and held in place by a wire cable.

Another, developed by the Port Authority of New York and New Jersey, consists of water-filled plastic cylinders, each 6 inches (152.4 millimeters) in diameter and from 36 to 41 inches (from 914.4 to 1041.4 millimeters) in height. The cylinders have a wall thickness of ¼ inch (6.35 millimeter). Each cylinder has a molded plastic cap that

[18] "Blocks Rock Throwers," *The American City,* July 1969, p. 130.

Figure 14-24 Steel barrels secured in front of an overpass pier provide protection for out-of-control vehicles. [The American City & County]

is forced open if a vehicle hits the cylinder barrier. If the predominant top speed of vehicles passing under the structure is 50 miles (80 kilometers) per hour, the cushion consists of a group of cylinders six cells wide and twelve cells across. If a vehicle hits the cushion, all that is required is to refill the cylinders and replace the caps. An addition of 12 pounds (5.4 kilograms) of flake calcium chloride to each cylinder prevents the water in the cells from freezing in all but exceptionally cold weather.[19]

[19] "Steel Drum Crash Cushions," *The American City*, December 1970, p. 78; "Water-cushioned Gore Areas Reduce Deadly Vehicle Impacts," *The American City*, May 1973, p. 90.

Figure 14-25 Here is the cushion in Figure 14-24 after it absorbed the shock of a vehicle. [The American City & County]

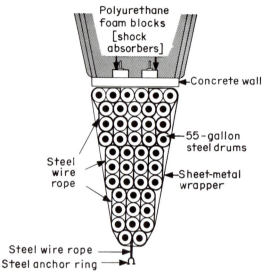

Figure 14-26 The steel-drum shock cushion is assembled in this manner by the Texas Highway Department. [The American City & County]

Large Street Signs

Oversize street signs, preferably reflective, aid traffic in downtown areas and along urbanized arterial roadways. Since motorists must find their way to specific addresses while guiding their vehicles in heavy traffic, anything that can provide them with the information they need quickly and easily will simplify their problems, allowing them to drive more safely and to avoid creating traffic problems.

In crowded areas of Los Angeles, street name signs are 18 inches (0.46 meter) wide and from 4 to 6 feet (from 1.2 to 1.8 meters) long, with reflectorized silver lettering on a blue background. The signs need no artificial lighting and can be seen well in advance of the intersection.

Another sign that can assist the motorist is a midblock number plate. Many businesses do not list their address numbers, and this causes problems to motorists unfamiliar with the area. Midblock number signs give them the information they need and allow them to concentrate on driving safely.[20]

TRAFFIC SIGNALS

Traffic-control signals, often called traffic lights, offer great opportunities to improve the regulation of traffic. Since they represent a

[20] "Big Street Signs Make City Driving Safer," *The American City*, April 1976, p. 102.

Figure 14-27 Oversize street signs help orient motorists in busy and often-distracting downtown areas. [The American City & County]

substantial investment in both capital cost and operation, they must be placed only after careful traffic studies have demonstrated their value. They can be pretimed to intervals that appear to serve traffic needs; they can be traffic-actuated; and, if traffic-actuated, they can be programmed by computer to vary the signal timing to accommodate greater traffic flow over the length of the street or highway where traffic problems exist.

"Platooning" the Traffic

A single traffic-control signal can control traffic at a single intersection or at midblock if a signal appears to be needed there.   However, with computer control a series of signals can move traffic at a safe speed over the length of the roadway under control.   The action of the computer tends to group the traffic into platoons, thus providing clear openings between the platoons so that cross traffic can pass with the aid of an appropriately timed signal.

Light Arrangement

A signal should have at least three and no more than five lights.   The three are the conventional green, yellow, and red, indicating that traffic may proceed, that movement is about to be terminated, and that traffic is ordered to stop.   Additional lights will give instruction to the motorist

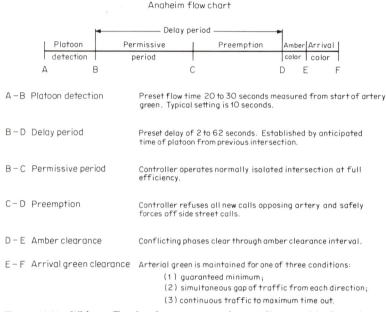

Anaheim flow chart

A–B Platoon detection   Preset flow time 20 to 30 seconds measured from start of artery green. Typical setting is 10 seconds.

B–D Delay period   Preset delay of 2 to 62 seconds. Established by anticipated time of platoon from previous intersection.

B–C Permissive period   Controller operates normally isolated intersection at full efficiency.

C–D Preemption   Controller refuses all new calls opposing artery and safely forces off side street calls.

D–E Amber clearance   Conflicting phases clear through amber clearance interval.

E–F Arrival green clearance   Arterial green is maintained for one of three conditions:
(1) guaranteed minimum;
(2) simultaneous gap of traffic from each direction;
(3) continuous traffic to maximum time out.

Figure 14-28 With traffic signals programmed according to this flow chart, a larger traffic platoon can preempt time sufficiently to allow it to flow smoothly and increase the carrying capacity of an arterial roadway. [The American City & County]

for left turns and any other special information that the traffic administrator feels is needed. A light may be provided to inform pedestrians that they are allowed to cross at indicated times.

Lens Size

Lenses for the signals are 8 or 12 inches (203.2 or 304.8 millimeters) in diameter. At intersections where 85 percent of the traffic travels at speeds in excess of 40 miles (64 kilometers) per hour, the larger lens should normally be used. At lesser speeds, the smaller lens is adequate.

Under most conditions, lenses should be arranged in either vertical or horizontal lines. They should be equipped with visors to help direct the signal instruction to the oncoming traffic and eliminate false signals created by the sun's rays at certain times of the day. If "tunnel" visors 12 inches (304.8 millimeters) in length are required, the signal should be placed on a rigid mounting and not be free-swinging.

Observation of Signals by Motorists

The existence of a traffic signal should be apparent to motorists for at least a quarter of a mile (two-fifths of a kilometer). They should be able to distinguish the instructional signal of the light for distances varying with the speed of 85 percent of the traffic. This distance should be at least 700 feet (213 meters) if the traffic moves at 60 miles (97 kilometers) per hour. The distance can be reduced by 75 feet (22.9 meters) for each lowering of the speed by 5 miles (8 kilometers) per hour until it reaches a minimum of 100 feet (30.5 meters) for traffic moving at 20 miles (32 kilometers) per hour.

Signal Maintenance

The maintenance of traffic-signal controllers should be handled on a thorough and detailed basis to guarantee the continuing performance of the signals and the safety of motorists and pedestrians. Timers in the signals either operate on a fixed-time basis or are traffic-actuated. Both types must be cleaned and inspected for wear and malfunctioning. The time cycles should be checked by a stopwatch. If the timer has remote controls, the fuses should be removed and all functions checked from the controller side of the fuses. If the signal has a traffic-actuated control, timing circuits should again be checked with a stopwatch, and all circuits should be inspected.

Flashers should be cleaned and in some cases lubricated. The flashings should be checked by stopwatch to show from 50 to 60 flashes per minute.

The following traffic-signal maintenance checklist was developed by the Los Angeles Department of Traffic. Its rating symbols are especially useful in appraising the condition of the signals.

ELECTRICIAN TRAFFIC-SIGNAL MAINTENANCE CHECKLIST

Intersection _____

Date completed _____ Total person-hours _____

Electrician _____ Crew No. _____

Symbols:
V: No work required; equipment up to specifications.
X: Equipment brought up to specifications.
R: Replaced.
W: Filled out unsatisfactory condition request.
F: Referred to foreman in writing.
   Fill in number of units for appropriate symbol box.

Instructions:
Replacements or repairs that are solid-blocked in the symbol boxes will have work detail cards made out for them, and the appropriate box will be circled.

A. Timer

V	X	R	W	F

1. Fixed time controller
    a. Clean timer and related components.

    b. Visual inspection for evidence of wear and/or malfunction of timer and related components.

    c. Check all dials for correct placement of keys according to the signal controller chart.

    d. Check total cycle length and coordination with stopwatch.

    e. Check sequence of signal indications through at least one drum revolution.

    f. If timer is controlled remotely, remove fuses and check all remote functions from the controller side of fuses.

2. Actuated controller—all of item *A*1 when applicable plus:
    a. Check all timing circuits with stopwatch.

    b. On volume density, check minimum initial, clearance, and maximum circuits.

B. Panel

Check securement of terminals, all screws, nuts, etc. Tighten when necessary.

	■			

C. Fuse
1. Check fuses for correct current rating:
Service _____ Controller _____

2. Take current reading at main controller fuse. Record reading: _____ Compare with last reading: _____

3. Record line voltage: _____

D. Flasher
1. Clean and lubricate flasher mechanisms (Eagle and Automatic signals only).

2. Check flashings per minute with stopwatch (50 to 60 per minute). Replace if fewer. Also check contact conditions.

E. NAB timer switch

Check timer through the NAB time switch for proper dials and/or offsets functions. Check riders and cutout settings.

F. Relays
1. Clean relays and run a piece of paper under armature until paper comes out clean.

2. Check contacts for pits and metal buildups, clearance, and proper function.

3. Check timing with stopwatch.

G. Coordinators

Check zero point.

H. Auxiliary equipment (preemption)

V	X	R	W	F

An operational check of the special equipment shall be made at intersections where special control equipment is coordinated with traffic signals, that is, fire station control, railroad preempt, etc.

■	■			

I. Schematics

Check schematics legibility (box print and "as built"). If they are missing or are not legible, notify the maintenance foreman in writing and give all pertinent information.

J. Auxiliary time equipment (P.T.1., Minor, etc.)
   1. P.T.1. timer
      a. Check "Walk" and flashing "Don't Walk" time with stopwatch.

	■			

      b. Clean inside of timer and check for wear on points and relays.

	■			

   2. Minor movement; check with stopwatch the following circuits:
      a. Initial interval.
      b. Vehicle interval.
      c. Maximum intervals.
      d. Stop timing to parent controller.

		■		
		■		
		■		
		■		

K. Detectors
   1. Pressure pads
      a. Place controller on recall one phase at a time.

      b. Remove leads from panel terminal and use triplet meter to check pad condition.

		■		

      c. Replace wire on panel and check controller operation when vehicles run over pad.

   2. Loop detectors
      a. Retune sensor for peak setting.
      b. Check sensor and controller operation.

		■		
		■		

      c. Check resistance of groups of loops with megger and record readings here: _____

_____

_____

_____

L. Heads

Repair or replace damaged visors and backplates.

	■			

M. Pedestrian heads
   1. Clean inside of protection glass on pedestrian heads. Clean high voltage insulator and neon tubes (green "Walk" tube excepted).
   2. Make visual inspection of all parts of heads.

		■		

   3. Tighten all screws on heads (transformer, terminal screw), etc.
   4. Replace faded-out tubes.

		■		

N. Remote disconnect cabinet
   1. Tighten all screws and/or nuts.
   2. Check terminal board for burn spots.
   3. Route cable and wires in an orderly fashion.
O. Cascade
   1. Tighten all screws and/or nuts.
   2. Check terminal board for burn spots.
   3. Route cable and wires in an orderly fashion.
   4. Clean relays and run a piece of paper under armature until paper comes out clean.
   5. Check contact for proper clearances, pits, and metal buildups and proper functions.
P. RFL equipment
   Use Form No. 100.
Q. Motorola receiver/decoder
   1. Check antenna alignment for strongest signal and coaxial fittings.
   2. Use dummy reeds and check out all functions.
   3. Use form No. 400.
R. Audio tone interconnect equipment
   1. Encoder
      a. Check audio tones on telephone line.
      b. Check summing amplifier level.
      c. Check encoder board level.
      d. Check relay output functions.
   2. Decoder
      a. Check audio tones on the telephone line.
      b. Check line amplifier level.
      c. Check decoder board level.
      d. Check relay output functions.
S. Econolite AC telephone equipment
   1. Encoder
      a. Check AC and/or DC voltages on telephone.

      Line 1 voltage [   ]   Line 2 voltage [   ]

      b. Check all functions.
   2. Decoder
      a. Check AC and/or DC voltages on telephone.

      Line 1 voltage [   ]   Line 2 voltage [   ]
      b. Check relay output functions.
      c. Check interrupter operation.
T. Telemetry system
   Use form No. 700.
Comments and/or abnormal corrective work for which a work detail card was made out:

Computer Traffic Control

As mentioned above, computerized traffic control is one of the aids that increase the ability of an arterial street to carry large volumes of traffic when required. Traffic signals have long been coordinated with an established speed of the vehicles, and this system works well when the artery does not have to carry peak loads. Whenever traffic lights turn red to admit cross traffic, they deny the use of the artery to the main bulk of the traffic.

Utilization of the Platoon Effect   If the traffic signals are successful in grouping the traffic into platoons with sufficient distance between them so that the signal can allow cross traffic to pass unimpeded, the system is working well. Under a computerized system, the green-light period will be extended during peak traffic periods to increase the size of the traffic platoon and maintain the size of the gaps between platoons. Traffic detectors or sensors detect and measure the volume of traffic, transmitting the information to the computer, which in turn adjusts the lighting sequence of the traffic signals to enlarge the size of the platoons.

Use in Small as Well as Large Cities   The platoon concept was first developed in large urban centers with serious traffic problems. However, as developments continued, it was applied successfully in smaller centers such as Renton, Washington (population 25,000), and Chula Vista, California (population 68,000). In Hamden, Connecticut, a master control system increased the capacity of a heavily traveled 4.3-mile (6.9-kilometer) stretch from 21,000 to 26,000 vehicles per day and reduced the average travel time from 17 to 9 minutes.[21]

STREET DETOURS AND CONSTRUCTION WARNINGS

Detours around construction and maintenance work in urban streets and warnings that such work is in progress are two of the most neglected parts of traffic control, probably because responsibility is split between those in charge of road and street maintenance and those administering traffic control. In any case, planning for any work in the streets that will interfere with traffic flow should begin by providing adequate advance notification of the work to other concerned agencies. These agencies should include the following:

1. Police department, especially if it has responsibility for traffic control

2. Fire department, in case fire trucks must be dispatched to the area

[21] E. F. Granow, "A Mickey Mouse Traffic Signal Interconnect," *The American City*, August 1971, p. 55; "Travel Time Cut 45%," *The American City*, August 1974, p. 41; "Turn Congested Streets into 'Green Wave' Arterials," *The American City*, February 1976, p. 50.

3. Traffic department, if it is separate from the police department
4. Bus and other transit services, including taxi companies
5. Water and sewer departments
6. Other public utilities such as gas, electricity, telephone service, and cable television, generally not publicly owned

All utilities that plan work for the area where traffic will be interrupted by repair and maintenance work in the street should coordinate their work so that it will commence before rather than after resurfacing and repair.   The public rightfully is scornful of any municipal administration that schedules street maintenance, only to have it followed by fresh cuts in the repaved street.

Role of Construction Warnings and Detours

Planning for construction warnings and detours must meet at least three general specifications:

Figure 14-29 Detours of any temporary change in traffic flow should receive the same sort of care and attention as the design of the improvement itself receives.   This was a detour designed to implement construction work at the George Washington Bridge between New York and New Jersey. [*Port Authority of New York and New Jersey photo*]

1. Motorists should receive ample advance warnings, but these warnings should not be so far in advance of the work that they will forget them or see no evidence of work.

2. A detour should be clearly marked so that motorists will have no difficulty in following it. If possible, it should not slow traffic more than 10 miles (16 kilometers) per hour.

3. Warnings and detours should be designed to give every consideration to the safety of motorists, pedestrians, and work personnel.

Standards and Guidelines

Standards now exist for the control of traffic both during normal conditions and during periods of construction and maintenance of the road and street system. The most authoritative compilation is the manual adopted by the Federal Highway Administration of the U.S. Department of Transportation.[22] This discussion centers on the use of these standards, especially as applied to the maintenance of urban-type roads and streets.

Types of Signs

Signs used to warn of maintenance and repair operations in the road and street traffic lanes fall into three categories: traffic regulatory signs, warning signs, and guide signs. The warning signs are of the greatest importance in this protective work. They must have distinctive colors, a black legend on an orange background, a color combination not used in any other type of sign. This difference will call motorists' attention to the existence of something unusual ahead.

The signs must be simple, with nothing that distracts from their messages. They may carry orange flags or yellow flashing lights to help call attention to them if these do not interfere with the motorists' view of the sign face.

The signs normally should be on the right-hand side of the road and be well raised so that motorists can see them. Under special conditions, when maintenance work is difficult or extensive, the signs may have to be placed on both sides of the roadway for emphasis.

Sign Visibility Aids

The signs may be lighted or reflectorized to assist the motorists in seeing them. They should not be lighted by flaming torches or by the familiar kerosine "bomb." These devices are easily extinguished by wind and can be dangerous in case of an accident that ruptures a gasoline tank. Nor should one depend on street or highway lighting to illuminate the signs.

[22] *Manual on Uniform Traffic Control Devices for Streets and Highways,* U.S. Department of Transportation, 1971.

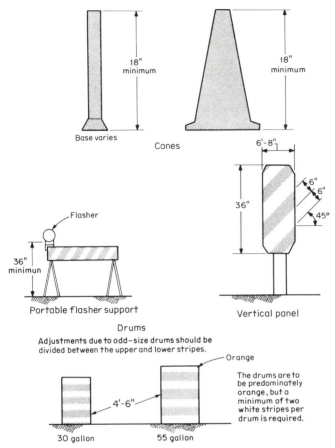

Figure 14-30   Equipment such as these units can be used to channel traffic away from construction and repair work in the street safely. [Manual on Uniform Traffic Control Devices for Streets and Highways, *U.S. Department of Transportation, 1971*]

Warning signs should generally measure 48 by 48 inches (1219 by 1219 millimeters) except in areas with low traffic counts and speeds. In these cases, a warning sign measuring 36 by 36 inches (914 by 914 millimeters) will serve.

Detour Lane Widths and Transition Calculations

If possible, detours should have the same traffic-lane widths as those used by the finished roadway in the area. If the work requires usurping a traffic lane and traffic must be moved from one lane to another, motorists must be provided with ample transition lengths.

The minimum transition taper can be calculated by multiplying the width of the traffic lane by the roadway speed limit or by the estimated speed of 85 percent of the traffic, whichever is higher.   For example, if the speed is 50 miles (80 kilometers) per hour and the lane width is 10 feet (3.1 meters), the transition taper should be 500 feet (152.4 meters), changing at the rate of 1 foot per 50 feet (0.3 meter per 15.2 meters) of roadway length.

Barricades

Barricades should conform to the three types shown in the accompanying table.   The horizontal bars should be provided with diagonal stripes. If a detour is indicated, the stripes should slope downward in the direction that the traffic must travel.   If the detour is intended to direct traffic to both right and left, the striping may slope downward in both directions, starting from the center of the barricade.

Supplementing barricades are semibarricades, consisting of traffic cones or tubes that are large enough to be seen easily, can indicate the edge of a traffic lane or the boundary of an area under repair, can

Figure 14-31 Warning flags and signs such as this assembly aid motorists and protect workers. [*International Plastics, Inc., photo*]

Figure 14-32 Traffic cones move vehicles out of a lane that will be used for repair work. Note the barricade, with stripes slanted downward in the direction in which the traffic must move. [*International Plastics, Inc., photo*]

withstand damage if hit by a vehicle, and will not damage the vehicle itself. These semibarricades should be reflectorized and colored orange. If they are not reflectorized and must be used at night, they should be equipped with lights. They should be at least 18 inches (457 millimeters) high and larger in areas of relatively high traffic speed or in areas where one may need excess visibility for safety. Generally the cones or tubes channel traffic around an area under repair. However, they can be used as barricades in certain low-traffic areas.

The cones are easy to stack and store. In the case of high winds or traffic-induced air eddies, it may be helpful to double the cones to provide extra stability. Sometimes the cones are provided with weights formed by reinforcing rods that have been bent to be dropped over the cone. However, these may damage motorists' vehicles if they are hit.

Barricade Types

	Type I	Type II	Type III
Width of rail	8 inches minimum, 12 inches maximum	8 inches minimum, 12 inches maximum	8 inches minimum, 12 inches maximum
Length of rail	6–8 feet	3 feet minimum, 4 feet maximum	3 feet minimum
Width of stripes	6 inches	6 inches	6 inches
Height	3 feet minimum	3 feet minimum	5 feet minimum
Type of frame	Demountable or heavy A frame	Light A frame	Post or skids
Flexibility	Movable	Portable	Permanent

Drums for Barricades   Drums are another popular form of barricade. These familiar 55-gallon (0.21-cubic-meter) containers are easily visible and are not difficult to obtain. They are portable and give an appearance of solidity that drivers respect, but they do not create great damage when hit.

The drums should be painted orange and white, in horizontal stripes 4 to 6 inches (101.6 to 152.4 millimeters) wide. They should be reflectorized if used at night. A warning sign should caution motorists when the drums are used. If a single drum is used alone, it should have the aid of a flashing warning light. If drums are used to channel traffic, they should be equipped with steady warning lights.

Directional Panels and Reflective Delineators

Simple vertical panels, post-mounted, also can be used to channel traffic. The panel should be 6 to 8 inches (152.4 to 203.2 millimeters) wide, 24 inches (609.6 millimeters) high, and mounted on a post so that it stands a minimum of about 3 feet (0.9 meter) from the ground. These, too, should be painted orange and white, in stripes 6 inches (152.4 millimeters) wide at a 45-degree angle. They are useful to separate traffic or to provide other warnings when space is at a premium.

Reflective delineators also are useful in maintenance and repair zones. They provide guiding illumination from motorists' headlights. The delineators should be used to support other control devices and be spaced sufficiently close to outline the roadway clearly.

Temporary Pavement Lane Marking

Pavement traffic-lane markings must be considered if a street or roadway is to be detoured because of the repair work. If the detour is to be for a short, temporary period, the lanes can be indicated by pressure-sensitive traffic marking tape. Longtime detours, such as those supplied when bridgework is involved, deserve the more conventional types of lane markings.

Lighting

Lighting should be at least as bright as it is on the adjacent roadway and preferably somewhat brighter to call attention to the construction zone. However, the lighting, especially if supplied by floodlights, should not create a glare in the eyes of the motorists.

At points of special danger, a flashing yellow signal at least 8 inches (203.2 millimeters) in diameter should call attention to the danger spot. These signals, generally termed "hazard-identification beacons," should operate 24 hours a day. They are useful in heavily traveled areas where traffic-lane changes are required or in the temporary dead-ending of a well-traveled roadway. They may operate singly or in groups.

As an alternative, low-watt yellow electric lamps that burn steadily can provide the means of attracting attention, although they are not as effective. They can be used on barricades to denote traffic lanes through a construction area or on barricades where a portion of the pavement has been removed.

Barricade Warning Lights

The *Manual on Uniform Traffic Control Devices for Streets and Highways* classifies barricade warning lights into Types A, B, and C. These lights are portable, the illumination being directed by lenses and emitting a yellow color.

Type A: Low-Intensity Flashing Lights   These, which are generally mounted on separate portable supports, are designed to warn motorists that they are in a hazardous area. The lights emit 55 to 75 flashes per second, with a minimum effective intensity of 4.0 candelas. They are expected to operate from dusk to dawn.

Type B: High-Intensity Flashing Lights   These lights, which are generally supported independently or on advance warning signs, denote extremely hazardous conditions. They also emit from 55 to 75 flashes per minute but have an effective minimum intensity of 35 candelas. Since they are used in dangerous areas, they operate around the clock.

Type C: Steady-Burn Lights   These lights form the edge of the traveled way on detour curves, lane changes, lane closures, and other locations. They operate from dusk to dawn at a minimum beam of 2 candlepower. Flashing lights should not be used for these delineations, since they have a tendency to obscure the vehicle path. If the lights are mounted on barricades, the lens should be at least 36 inches (914 millimeters) from the ground.

Construction Traffic Directors

Personnel assigned to direct traffic may be needed if traffic must move through a work area. They should be equipped with orange vests, preferably reflectorized. These directors should be alert, with a good sense of responsibility, be in good physical condition, with good sight and hearing, and be able to direct traffic with confidence and courtesy.

The flag should measure at least 24 by 24 inches (609.6 by 609.6 millimeters) on a 3-foot (0.9-meter) pole. It should be weighted to hang clearly in a wind. In some cases it may be preferable for the construction traffic director to use sign paddles with one side carrying the word "Stop" and the other "Slow." The faces of the signs should be at least 24 inches in diameter. The "Stop" side should be red, preferably reflectorized for use in the night, with white letters. The "Slow" side should be reflectorized orange with black letters and a black border. The lettering should be at least 6 inches (152.4 millimeters) high.

The traffic director should stand alone, with no work personnel around, so that motorists can see the director clearly. While easily visible to approaching traffic, the director should not be in the lane of traffic itself. If the traffic travels normally at a relatively high speed, the director should be posted about 200 to 300 feet (61 to 91 meters) ahead of the work area.

Figure 14-33 Personnel directing traffic can use either a properly designed flag or a stop paddle like this one. The traffic director should wear a reflective vest and stand facing traffic and out of the traffic lane. [*International Plastics, Inc., photo*]

Advance warning signs should notify motorists of the traffic director, who should use standardized signals taken from the *Manual on Uniform Traffic Control Devices for Streets and Highways,* shown in Figure 14-34.

Personal Check of Detour Routes and Warnings

In preparing detour routes and warnings to protect a work area that must occupy a lane of traffic and possibly more, the person in charge should check the routes by driving through them, particularly at night. This will ensure that the warnings actually give motorists the necessary guidance. At times, lights can be misleading. A carefully prepared lighting system can appear to be a maze of purposeless blinkings. Barricade lights occasionally produce the illusion that the hazard is from 10 to 15 feet (from 3 to 4.6 meters) farther than it actually is.

When detours are needed and no street system is available for the detour route, a temporary road must be built. The designers of such a road should try to limit the curvature to at least a 50-foot (15.2-meter) radius. The roadway should be as smooth as possible for the convenience of motorists rather than that of the maintenance crew or the contractor.

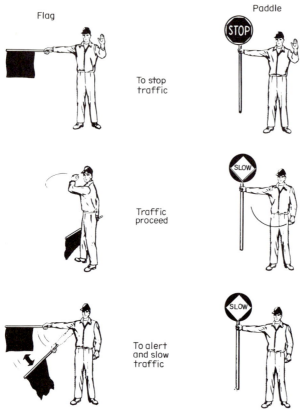

Figure 14-34 To ensure that motorists understand directions clearly, the traffic director should use these signaling procedures. [Manual on Uniform Traffic Control Devices for Streets and Highways, *U.S. Department of Transportation, 1971*]

BICYCLE TRAFFICWAYS

The public's reawakened interest in bicycling is a recent phenomenon, probably stimulated by, or at least coinciding with, the increased cost of gasoline. At present, bicycling can be considered a form of outdoor recreation more than simply a means of transportation. However, if the cost of gasoline continues to increase, as it apparently seems destined to do, then many more people will depend on the bicycle for transportation within their neighborhoods or to close-by business and shopping districts.

Moreover, the public's interest in bicycles as a means of transportation will be increased by the introduction of small motors that enable riders to be transported without the effort of pedaling and are of a size which requires neither licensing nor insurance in a number of states. These motorized bicycles ordinarily have a top speed of about 25 miles (40 kilometers) per hour. However, a strong rider on a ten-speed bicycle can attain speeds faster than this.

Bike-Path Location

In view of the growth of bicycle use by adults and the impact of this growth on urban transportation, an economic cost-benefit study would appear to play a basic role in bike-path location. Apparently it does not do so.

Frank E. Terpin, location engineer of the Oregon State Highway Division, has discovered that bikeways are planned locally, generally through bicycle committees that determine individual community needs based on commuter and recreational interests. Their decisions seem to be independent of economic parameters. Nevertheless, the highway division has identified some of these parameters, which can be useful for their supporting evidence. Pertinent among them are the following:

1. If the bicycle path can convert 500 to 700 business commuters from cars to bicycles, it can justify an expenditure of $40,000 for a path 4 miles (6.4 kilometers) long or less.

2. If the proposed path can convert no more than 100 business commuters, it can justify no more than $6000 to $8000 per mile for a pathway of 3 to 4 miles (4.8 to 6.4 kilometers).

3. In the interests of safety, bike paths designed for schoolchildren would justify an expenditure of $10,000 to $15,000 for a 2-mile (3.2-kilometer) path. If the route would obviously reduce the number of accidents, greater expenditures seem reasonable.

4. For a trip of 7 miles (11.3 kilometers), which should take the average bicyclist about 30 minutes, the cost to the cyclist should be no more than 2 cents per mile (1.6 kilometer). The cost to operate an automobile ranges from 11 to 15 cents per mile.

In 1960 fewer than 4 million bicycles were sold in the United States, and less than 12 percent were used by adults. In 1973 sales amounted to some 15 million cycles, with about 60 percent being purchased by adults. More than 75 million bicycles are currently in use, or well over 3 times the number used in 1960.[23,24]

Current Bicycle-Path Practice

The American Public Works Association (APWA), through its Institute of Municipal Engineering, has conducted a review of current bicycle-path practice by a questionnaire mailed to 136 cities and counties

---

[23] *So You Want a Bikeway*, Robert Cleckner, Bicycle Manufacturers Association of America, New York, 1976.

[24] *Bikeway Design Manual*, Oregon State Highway Division, Salem, Oreg. 97301, January 1974.

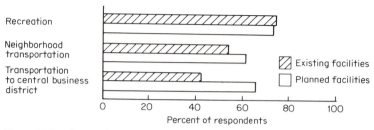

Recreation

Neighborhood transportation

Transportation to central business district

Existing facilities
Planned facilities

Percent of respondents

Figure 14-35 A sample survey of communities across the United States conducted by the American Public Works Association indicates that bicycle routes are being used and probably will be used as shown. *[American Public Works Association]*

throughout the United States.   Of these, 6 percent had populations of less than 10,000; 9 percent, between 10,000 and 25,000; 35 percent, between 25,000 and 100,000; and 50 percent, over 100,000.   Of those responding, more than half allowed the use of bicycles on existing sidewalks, although many did not allow them in areas of heavy pedestrian traffic, such as business districts.   Communities with populations of less than 25,000 were more often inclined to prohibit the use of bicycles on sidewalks than were larger urban centers.   This practice undoubtedly reflects the lesser amount of vehicular traffic in the streets of the smaller communities and the reduced danger to bicycles traveling in these streets.

Types of Paths or Routes

The APWA survey disclosed five different types of bicycle trafficways: (1) trafficways sharing moving lanes of traffic with other vehicles, with no specific path designated but with street signs indicating that the

Figure 14-36 This bicycle path in a small Southern community is located off the roadway.

streets are also bicycle routes; (2) exclusive bicycle lanes on the streets, using space normally required by on-street vehicular parking: (3) exclusive bicycle lanes in the street roadways other than the parking lanes; (4) bicycle lanes in the street rights-of-way not on the streets or on the sidewalks; (5) other bicycle routes away from the street pattern, on areas such as railroad rights-of-way, flood-control districts, utility rights-of-way, and parks.

If an interstate throughway or other expressway passes near or through the urban government's boundaries and if the rights-of-way of the highway are generous enough to permit it, occasionally a local government will arrange for bicycle paths on these rights-of-way, often with the cooperation of the appropriate highway authority.

Widths of Paths

The APWA survey disclosed that bicycle-path widths can vary from 5 feet (1.5 meters) when traffic is in one direction to 8 feet (2.4 meters) or more if the path carries two-way traffic. Bicycle trafficways on the street, occupying space adjacent to the curb, are almost always one-way.

Pavement Surfaces

The bicycles used today are much lighter than those of the past. The most popular are equipped with small-diameter tires that must be inflated to pressures of 50 to 60 pounds per square inch (from 345 to 414 kilopascals). As a result, these bicycles are more comfortable when ridden on a smooth surface such as that provided by a dense-graded asphalt. As a minimum, the thickness of the surface should correspond to that needed for sidewalks.

However, successful paths have been created with material such as crushed granite or cinders. When the soil is favorable, some routes are in use without formal surfacing.

Maximum Grades

Gears on most bicycles now permit climbing hills that were difficult in the past. However, a grade of 8 to 10 percent appears to be today's maximum, and only for short distances. The APWA survey indicates that a 6 percent limit is more general.

Miscellaneous Guidelines

Some municipalities restrict the turns in a bicycle route to at least a 15-foot (4.6-meter) radius. For safety, a number of authorities require that the bicycle path must have a solid white stripe 8 inches (203.2 millimeters) wide to designate each side of the pathway.

At signalized intersections, some municipalities provide push buttons at traffic lights to permit cyclists to cross safely. Others extend the yellow phase of the traffic signal for the convenience of cyclists. Some provide bicycle parking stands at selected locations such as shopping centers, the city hall, parks, and libraries.

Apparently there is little demand for lighting off-street bicycle paths, but some communities require bicycles to be equipped with lights, reflectors, and a bell or horn if cyclists travel at night.

Accidents

Accident prevention undoubtedly will improve as urban governments become more familiar with bicycles and learn how to control them for their safety. One municipality noted an increase of 17 percent in bicycle accidents after bike paths were established. However, it also noted an increase in the number of cyclists of 50 percent, indicating that safety for the individual cyclist had improved.

Bicycle-proofed Catch-Basin Gratings

One problem that has arisen with the popularity of the new high-speed bicycles is the risk of accident when they pass over the drainage gratings that direct storm water to catch basins. In the past the most useful gratings have been those with openings parallel to the line of traffic, giving the water the greatest opportunity of flowing into the basin. However, some bicycles have narrow tires inflated to pressures of 60 to 80 pounds per square inch (414 to 552 kilopascals). Bicycles formerly used wider tires that could ride over the gratings safely, but the new tires can slip through the grating openings even when these are as narrow as 1 inch (25.4 millimeters). This can cause some painful falls and can damage the bicycle.

Some safety-minded city officials have taken the protective step of welding flat bars across the openings. While this procedure aids cyclists, it interferes with the entry of storm water and can aggravate flooding of the street system. A better solution, introduced and then forgotten nearly two decades ago, is to use gratings that have openings perpendicular with the line of traffic, but with the grating bars shaped approxi-

Figure 14-37 Catch-basin gratings with bars that are shaped in this manner encourage the flow of storm water into the basin and cause no harm to a bicycle passing over them. [*Neenah Foundry Co., Neenah, Wisconsin*]

Figure 14-38 Gratings with diagonal bars can support bicycles safely and have the added advantage of being self-cleaning. [*Neenah Foundry Co., Neenah, Wisconsin*]

mately to the form of the free fall of the water. With this shape, the bars provide effective openings of 3 inches (76.2 millimeters) or more from the leading edge of one bar to the leading edge of the succeeding bar (see Figure 14-38). The bars also can be cast at a 45-degree angle, making the grating self-cleaning. In both cases, the bicycle should be able to pass over the grating without any danger of accident (see Figure 14-39).

The grating bar sloped to conform to the fall of the water was a concept introduced in 1949, based on research at the St. Anthony Falls Hydraulic Laboratory of the University of Minnesota. The same research suggested the concept of diagonal bars, which have been used to a limited extent for the past 15 years.

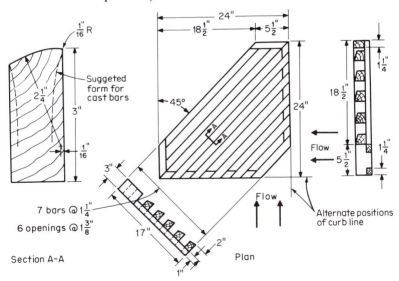

Figure 14-39 The concept of diagonal grating bars and of bars with surfaces shaped to conform to the free flow of water originated with hydraulic research by the University of Minnesota. This drawing shows one of the early designs. [*Curtis L. Larson and Lorenz G. Straub, Grate Inlets for Surface Drainage of Streets and Highways, University of Minnesota, St. Anthony Falls Hydraulic Laboratory, Minneapolis, 1949*]

STREET-LIGHTING MAINTENANCE

A street-lighting program provides two important benefits for a community. It allows the street system to be used more effectively and safely for longer periods, and it deters violence and robbery in the streets.

The amount of light needed at street levels can vary with the type of people in the locality served. Young people have much better visual perception than their elders. One frequently quoted figure states that a 60-year-old person needs 7 times the illumination to equal the visual perception at night of a 20-year-old.[25]

Lighting standards established by the *American National Standard Practice for Roadway Lighting,* sponsored by the Illuminating Engineering Society and approved by the American National Standards Institute, have much general support. While, as shown in the accompanying table, they list minimum illumination levels, they do not make recommendations for standards and other hardware to be used.

As noted earlier, the nonfarm rural areas of an urban complex generally confine street lighting to danger points in the traffic pattern and provide sufficient illumination so that vehicles can be stopped or controlled within the potentially hazardous location. In most urban areas deterrence from crime and vandalism plays a more important role. In certain troubled portions of Washington, D.C., an intensified lighting program was successful in lowering the nighttime crime rate by 54 percent.[26]

[25] J. S. Lapporte, "How Much Lighting Is Enough?" *The American City,* January 1976, p. 50.

[26] J. E. Hartley, "Lighting Reinforces D.C. Crime Fight," *The American City,* August 1974, p. 59.

Horizontal Footcandles Recommended for Roadway Lighting

Roadway and walkway classification	Commercial areas		Intermediate areas		Residential areas	
	Foot-candle	Lux	Foot-candle	Lux	Foot-candle	Lux
Vehicular roads						
Freeways	0.6	6	0.6	6	0.6	6
Major roads and						
expressways	2.0	22	1.4	15	1.0	11
Collector street	1.2	13	0.9	10	0.6	6
Local street	0.9	10	0.6	6	0.4	4
Alleys	0.6	6	0.4	4	0.2	2
Pedestrian walkways						
Sidewalks	0.9	10	0.6	6	0.2	2
Pedestrian ways	2.0	22	1.0	11	0.5	5

SOURCE: *American National Standard Practice for Roadway Lighting,* Illuminating Engineering Society and American National Standards Institute, New York, 1972.

Lighting Efficiency

Lighting standards and other hardware are a part of what is known as "street furniture" and as such command the attention of those who want to develop a more aesthetic appearance in the central business district. Fixtures that have been used in the past and still appeal to many of these people provide no optical distribution of the lighting, only about 11 percent of the light being distributed to the street.

Street-lighting luminaires now available utilize at least two-thirds of the illumination developed by the lamp. This efficiency has been made possible by reflectors that direct light toward the roadway and by the glass refractor on the bottom of the fixture, which bends the light rays along the roadway.

Lighting Control

Street-lighting fixtures today almost always make use of photoelectric cells or astronomical clocks to energize the system at sunset and to shut it off at sunrise. Controllers that probably will be available soon should be able to dim the light intensity or to deactivate portions of it during selected hours of the night.

Maintenance Practices

Normal maintenance should consist of cleaning the internal parts of the luminaire, especially the reflector and the glassware, and replacing lamps, preferably on a group-replacement basis. The replacement of obsolete and inefficient facilities also should be a part of the program.

Dirt and dust have been shown to reduce the effectiveness of new fixtures by more than one-third. Aging of the lamps reduces the effectiveness by nearly one-fourth.

Strategic tree trimming also is necessary in a good lighting-maintenance program. If done well, it will allow the illumination to reach the street level without harming the appearance of street trees.

High-Pressure Sodium Lamps

As shown in the accompanying table, high-pressure sodium lamps appear to provide the greatest amount of illumination per watt of power required. Moreover, sodium lighting does not have damaging effects on trees and shrubberies, as shown in observations in Chicago, Cleveland, and Milwaukee and reports from sixteen other cities.[27]

Trees and shrubberies growing in the immediate vicinity of high-pressure sodium lighting do not require special treatment such as trim-

[27] J. W. Andresen, "Street Trees Are Safe with Sodium Lighting," *The American City*, December 1975, p. 53.

ming other than to permit maximum light distribution at ground level. No extra precautions are required when transplanting, and recent transplants may remain in place.

Lighting Outputs for Various Types of Lamps

Lamp type	Lumens per watt
Incandescent	20–30
Mercury	40–55
Fluorescent	60–80
High-pressure sodium	100–140

Energy-saving Street Lighting

Since lighting is obvious, in times of energy crises the public tends to think immediately that one easy solution is to extinguish the lighting. Lighting the streets is not a significant user of energy, accounting for no more than 0.75 percent of all energy used on a national basis.   Recommendations made by responsible national agencies suggest these power-conservation measures:

1. Do not deactivate street lights indiscriminately without consideration of alternative measures and discussion with police officials and other affected parties.

2. Utilize efficient light sources.

3. Convert older and obsolete systems so as to utilize modern equipment.

4. Maintain uniformity of lighting along roadways.

5. Provide good maintenance to secure maximum lighting from the energy used by existing systems.[28]

Street-Light Poles

Street-light poles fall into the general classification of street furniture. They perform a utilitarian function, yet their appearance should harmonize with and enhance the urban environment.   Most of them can be included in one of the following categories:

- Prestressed concrete
- Stainless steel, including stainless-clad steel
- Aluminum, both spun and cast
- Glass fiber
- Carbon steel
- Low-alloy steel
- Wood
- Cast iron

[28] J. S. Lapporte, "Municipal Street Lighting," *American Public Works Association Reporter*, Chicago, December 1975, p. 10.

Prestressed-Concrete Poles   These poles, constructed by the spinning process, have many advantages. They are strong and attractive and require practically no maintenance. In the manufacture, marble or granite chips can be added to the concrete. In the spinning process, the chips move to the perimeter of the pole, and subsequent sandblasting exposes them, adding to the pole's attractiveness. Although the poles tend to be costly as well as heavy and somewhat difficult to install, their advantages make them a prudent long-term investment.

Figure 14-40 Prestressed concrete poles have been demonstrated to have long service lives with low maintenance costs. [The American City & County]

Stainless-Steel Poles   These poles also are attractive and highly free from maintenance problems. They can resist corrosion, abrasion, and minor dents. Weather does not harm them. In fact, rainfall provides a cleaning action that preserves the normal sheen and attractiveness of the poles without other care or attention.

Stainless-steel–clad poles are fabricated with an outer layer of stainless steel and an inner layer of carbon steel. They are produced in most cases by the heat-and-pressure process, often called roll bonding, although other methods are available. In this method, sheets of both types of steel are heated to temperatures approaching the molten stage and then rolled or pressed, bonding the two together.

Figure 14-41 Stainless-steel poles can be produced in shapes that are attractive and graceful. [The American City & County]

Aluminum Poles   Poles made of aluminum, generally produced by the spinning process, also are attractive and require little maintenance. They are light and therefore are easy to place, and they are not difficult to repair if damaged. (Most other poles must be replaced if subject to a motor-vehicle accident.)   Cast-aluminum poles can be used in specialized applications, generally when poles of small diameter are to be installed.

Glass-Fiber Poles   The street-lighting field has only recently expressed an interest in glass fiber as a pole material.   Poles of this type are formed by winding glass-fiber sheets in both a circular and a longitudinal pattern around a mandrel, combining them with pigmented polyester resins.   They utilize a protective layer consisting of a sprayed, light-stabilized, pigmented isophthalic gel coat and a baked surface coating.

These poles are relatively light.   In most locations they can be installed without concrete foundations if the poles are placed at least 4 feet (1.2 meters) in the ground, and the height aboveground is between 19 and 20 feet (between 5.8 and 6 meters).

Carbon-Steel Poles   These poles probably have the lowest first cost and the highest maintenance cost of all metal types.   They require

Figure 14-42 Aluminum poles have demonstrated an ability to withstand weathering over a number of years. This pole at the Venetian Causeway in Miami, Florida, has been in use for more than 20 years. [The American City & County; *Pfaff & Kendall photo*]

Figure 14-43 The utilitarian wood pole retains its popularity in many areas. [The American City & County]

regular painting or galvanizing to protect them from corrosion. They are generally used in locations requiring poles of moderate height.

Low-Alloy–Steel Poles   These poles make use of a relatively new product developed by the steel industry, distinctive for its unusual color and for its ability to resist weathering and corrosion. It contains copper, nickel, and chromium and weathers to a brown color after 2 or 3 years of exposure. The producers market it under the trade names CorTen (United States Steel), Yoloy (Youngstown Sheet and Tube), and Republic 50 (Republic Steel Co.). During the weathering process, one side develops color faster than the other because of prevailing sun and wind. The poles can be painted if desired.

Wood Poles   Wood poles have supported power and communication lines longer than any other type has. They also support street lights in areas where their plain, utilitarian appearance is not a handicap. When chemically treated, wood poles should last for as much as 40 years. In a limited number of areas, the large pileated woodpecker can quickly carve a hole that can weaken this type of pole dangerously.

Wood poles need not be strictly utilitarian. Manufacturers are able to fabricate them into pleasing shapes, frequently protected with a glass-fiber coating. They also will embed a plastic conduit in a slot in the pole to supply power to the light fixture when the power is transmitted in underground cables.

Cast-Iron Poles   This type of pole is still used in areas that want to retain the nostalgic atmosphere of the past. Cast-iron poles can be provided with intricate and flowery designs and with fluted shafts.

Chapter Fifteen

Labor Negotiations with Municipal Unions

WILLIAM S. FOSTER

No city or county government of any size can afford to ignore the growing militancy among its employees. This militancy has become as much a part of the mangement of urban services as have the operation and maintenance of equipment, the provision and inventorying of materials and supplies, the scheduling of work details, and the design of maintenance and repair facilities.

Although the large-scale effect of the unionization of municipal employees is relatively new, strikes of city employees have occurred sporadically for many years. With the present strong trend and the apparently permanent place that the union movement has earned for itself in city and county governments, negotiating patterns should be identified.

In view of the vital importance of urban services to the economic and social health of the community, negotiations are aimed at preventing a strike if at all possible. Frequently prevention is not possible, and a strike must be endured.

We as a people discover new chemical elements, develop new alloys, split the atom, and harness its power. We produce such spectacular television documentaries as *Men on the Moon* and, more recently, *Rock Hunting on Mars.* But we seem unable to develop bargaining procedures between management and labor that do not involve the ancient and crippling effect of a strike, either in the public or in the private sector.

Labor negotiations in the public sector have emerged from outright illegality during the Roosevelt years to respectability or at least acceptance today. The International City Management Association (ICMA), the organization representing professional city and county adminis-trators, has expressed the policy that public employees have the right to choose whether or not they will organize and seek to bargain collec-tively. ICMA holds that this right must be regulated by democratic principles, and this is an important consideration.[1]

Prevention of strikes is the immediate goal, so that the people in the community will not be denied the services necessary to ensure that the community is economically and socially viable. However, the long-range goal is to establish a harmonious and constructive relationship between the urban government and its employees for the good of all.

Ineffectiveness of Strike Bans

Efforts to block the organization of municipal employees into unions and especially to outlaw strikes in the public sector have been almost uniformly unsuccessful, as similar efforts have been in the private sector. A study by the Public Service Research Council[2] shows convincingly that efforts to outlaw strikes of municipal and county employees by requiring compulsory bargaining have had the effect of increasing strike activity. The most dramatic example quoted in the report is that of Pennsylvania. In the 12 years prior to passage of the state's compulsory-bargaining act, its urban governments experienced 72 strikes, or 6 per year. These involved 43,086 workers and caused the loss of 97,017 person-days. In the 4 years after the act was passed, the same governmental units ex-perienced 282 strikes, or 73 per year. These involved 117,718 workers and caused the loss of 1,500,000 person-days.

Mayor Kevin White of Boston has warned that binding arbitration imposed by state legislation means that someone other than the elected city council or county commissioners will set the local tax rate. Massa-chusetts, incidentally, is one of the states with laws that require binding arbitration.

NEGOTIATIONS

Negotiations with union bargaining representatives in the public sector differ from those in most private-sector bargaining. One important point is economic. A strike in most industries can produce a great financial hardship on the industry involved. In the local-government sector, in contrast, a strike simply means that the municipality stops pay-ing the employees' wages. As far as the governmental unit is concerned,

[1] *Draft Statement on Management/Labor Relations,* International City Management Associa-tion, October 1976.

[2] *Public Sector Bargaining and Strikes,* Public Service Research Council, 8320 Old Court-house Road, Vienna, Va. 22180, 1976.

a strike becomes something of an economic advantage. However, depending on the inconvenience that the strike produces, it can be an economic and social hardship for the public. Moreover, the economic advantage soon becomes a luxury that is difficult for a community to afford. Many will attest that in a strike no one really wins.

Negotiations in the public sector also tend to be more open and probably will become completely open as so-called sunshine laws become more widespread. These laws require all meetings of local government officials to be open to the public, and labor negotiations fall into this category. The public has a direct stake in the outcome of the negotiations and properly should be completely informed of their progress. In the private sector, in contrast, union and management conduct negotiations behind closed doors. Management also is reluctant to disclose complete financial and managerial details of its operations.

Many will argue that the increased use of "sunshine" for labor relations in the public sector presents problems. Management's main concern is to see that prenegotiation instructions to and from city officials are not subject to sunshine exposure.

Advantages of Labor Negotiations

Certain spinoff advantages accrue to urban governments that have been lax in operational policies when they negotiate a labor contract with the unions. To do so successfully, urban managements must be well informed about their own operation, and many managements are not.

They must know their operating costs and how they have changed; and they must know their wage costs and how they have varied and also how they compare with those in neighboring governmental jurisdictions. They must know the costs of fringe benefits provided to the employees and how these compare with those provided elsewhere. They must document such items as group insurance and its cost to the municipality.

As a group, urban governments do not document and disclose their financial situation as well as they should to be prepared for meaningful negotiations. A study by Coopers and Lybrand, a nationally known accounting firm, has shown that 76 percent of the cities whose records the firm examined do not disclose the actuarially computed value of vested benefits over the total pension fund or the net balance-sheet accruals. Since pensions are important in the negotiations and since many pension funds in the public sector appear to be headed for financial trouble, this is a significant weakness in these financial reports.[3]

If labor negotiations stimulate municipalities and counties to put their financial houses in order, the overall benefits will be substantial, and

[3] *Financial Disclosure Practices of the American Cities,* Coopers and Lybrand and the University of Michigan, 1976.

the ability of governmental units to negotiate from a sound base will be enhanced. Nevertheless, urban management must remember that unions traditionally doubt the limitations of municipal budgets and disregard pleas of financial distress.

Urban-Management Rights

Management in the public sector has certain rights and obligations in the labor-negotiating field, actually more rights than do those in the private sector. The labor lawyer James Baird strongly urges that a well-prepared municipality or county learn about them and use them.[4]

First, if the city's work force is presently nonunion, the city has a right and a duty to create working conditions that will convince employees that they do not need to unionize. This would require setting wage scales and fringe benefits that compare favorably with those offered both in the private sector and in neighboring governmental units. It also means establishing a grievance procedure that the employees will consider fair, effective, and impartial, possibly one involving a respected third person outside the governmental unit. Supervisors should be identified and provided with authority that will make them feel that they are actually a part of management.

Baird warns that management does not, legally or morally, have the right to dismiss or discipline employees for advocating a union. Management's right is to ensure that its own employment policies will make unions less attractive.

Secret Ballot for Union Recognition

Management has the right to refuse a union demand for recognition and bargaining power when that demand is not supported by an election using a secret ballot. Unions often offer petitions and signed authorization cards supporting their demands for recognition. The signers undoubtedly have faced pressure from those advocating the union, and this pressure could not be present with a secret ballot.

In the private sector, unions win a little more than half of all secret-ballot elections, and if management contests the elections, they win much less. Among white-collar workers, when management makes no effort to get in touch with its employees, unions have won the elections by a ratio of more than 5:1. When management has been in touch with its

---

[4] James Baird, "A 'Bill of Rights' for Municipal Management," *The American City*, July 1973, pp. 47–49. James Baird is an associate with the firm of Pope, Ballard, Shepard, & Fowle of Chicago. He served as legal assistant–attorney adviser to Sam Zagoria and to Frank W. McCulloch, chairman of the National Labor Relations Service of the National League of Cities, United States Conference of Mayors, and National Association of Counties.

employees, either individually or in group meetings, unions have won about half of the elections. When management has reached its employees both personally and by written messages, unions have lost substantially, with management winning by more than 2:1. In this period, however, public-employee unions win more elections than they lose.

Disadvantages of Forming a Union

Management has the right and the obligation to point out the disadvantages of establishing a union. At least five issues can be presented to stress management's arguments: (1) as union members, employees are obligated to pay agency-shop dues; (2) union members are subject to the possibility of fines and assessments; (3) employees may find that the international union may take over the local group through trustee arrangements; (4) employees as union members will discover that they are subject to stringent rules in union constitutions; and (5) employees should be constantly reminded by management that union membership is no guarantee of raises, shorter hours, or increased job security.

Management, says Baird, has a right and an obligation to transmit these messages through letters, posters, supervisory discussions, and speeches. It can and should use them in newspaper stories, advertisements, radio and television presentations, and any other legitimate medium available.

Negotiation Procedure

Because of the growth of unions in the municipal employment area, many unions have gained recognition as bargaining agents for city and county employees. Consequently urban-government management must conclude wage agreements with them. Mayor Ronald R. James of San Jose, California, faced this situation, and he had the advantage of experience in the field. He had studied labor negotiations at Stanford University, and later had conducted bargaining negotiations with the Teamsters' Union in behalf of the trucking and warehousing industry, which was his business. So when he met the union representatives, he conducted his negotiations from the strength of his experience.[5]

James recommends that urban-management negotiators bargain hard. He believes that union members lose respect for negotiators who supinely accept every demand. Moreover, the members will be more likely to support the administration at election time if they know that the administration is a hard bargainer but that it will bargain.

Mayor James advises paying for negotiating experience and backing

[5] "When You Negotiate with Municipal Labor Unions," *The American City*, June 1971, p. 140.

the negotiators solidly. The union may be expected to try to separate urban officials from their negotiating team. Charges of bad faith, unwillingness to meet, and other accusations should be accepted. Nor should one be surprised by aggravating techniques such as slowdowns, mass coffee breaks, synthetic sickness, and slow response to telephones. All this is simply the union's method of applying pressure.

Communications between the city council and the team of negotiators should be kept open. All press conferences should be taped. Some newspaper reporter, no matter how careful, is liable to misquote a management statement and create serious complications. In any case, management should avoid any action that appears to be an attempt to negotiate through the press.

In bargaining, the first meeting should be devoted to agreement on working rules for behavior at subsequent meetings and on the time and place of subsequent bargaining sessions. At the second meeting, the management team should receive written proposals from the union negotiators, thus giving management time to study the proposals and to determine the cost of each of them and its effect on management's ability to administer municipal services effectively. The management team should identify the proposals that it can accept, those that it feels it must reject, and those that appear to be subject to resolution by compromise.

Then, and only then, should the management team offer to the union negotiators, item by item, its counterproposals. Management should submit its proposals line by line, sentence by sentence, and paragraph by paragraph, as in any important contract. The management team should avoid negotiating away such administrative responsibilities as work-crew sizes, work time, scheduling, and similar details.

Defense of Civil Service and the Merit System

Union negotiators can be expected to attack civil-service benefits and the merit system. Jerry Wurf, president of the American Federation of State, County and Municipal Employees, once said: "Civil Service is a useful mechanism, but we have to remember that the civil service system is the managerial system of the boss—he owns it. Our experience with the civil service commissions has been that, with a couple of notable exceptions, they are nothing but the flunkies of the boss."[6]

This suggests that union negotiators are afraid of the merit system and civil service. Skilled workers can challenge union organizers by asking why they should pay initiation fees, assessments, and dues to a union when they get similar advantages through civil service and the merit system.

---

[6] A. L. Leggat, "Don't Slough Off Merit Systems at the Bargaining Table," *The American City & County*, October 1975, p. 112.

Negotiating Rights

Management has the right, Baird advises, to demand a concession from union negotiators for every concession that its negotiating team makes. For example, a concession on wages can be accompanied by a guarantee of additional employee productivity, more realistic work crews, and adherence to lunch periods and established reporting and quitting times.[7] Baird also advises that during the negotiations rights that cannot be bought back at a reasonable price may be taken unilaterally after an impasse has been reached. He warns that this procedure entails risks, but he asserts that no doubt exists that management has the right to take this action.

The management negotiating team should attempt to anticipate union demands. It should consider the demands seriously and prepare serious counterproposals. As a negotiating measure, management should prepare a list of contract violations that have occurred during the last contract period.

In the past, union negotiators in the municipal field have been unimpressed by the argument that the local government cannot afford the demands for wages and fringe benefits presented in the negotiations. Jerry Wurf once told city managers, meeting in New York, that city councils always can raise the money. Subsequent evidence rather clearly shows that in an increasing number of cases he is wrong.

Compulsory Arbitration

Compulsory arbitration is a judicial type of hearing that receives testimony, hears witnesses and cross-examines them, and is conducted by an arbitrator who should be satisfactory to both sides. In selecting an arbitrator, local governments should attempt to get one who is sympathetic to and knowledgeable about the problems of municipalities. Some arbitrators are not.

Once the arbitrator has been selected, the administrator's representatives should treat him or her with respect. They should be on time at all meetings, avoid making arbitrary objections to the evidence presented, and let the opposition speak without interruptions. When they present evidence, it should be clear and easily understood. The presentation of management's case should also be clear.[8]

The management team must be prepared with good, clear, and convincing exhibits and a well-documented presentation. If money is being discussed, the budget director should be called. If a point of law is being negotiated, the city attorney should testify. If the issue under negotia-

[7] Baird, op. cit.

[8] "How to Alienate Arbitrators and Lose Cases," *International City Management Association Newsletter*, Supplement No. 1, *Labor Relations*, October 1976.

tion borders on management rights and the retention of management policies, the personnel director and the chief of civil service should be on hand.

STRIKE PREPARATIONS

If negotiations do not result in a contract, the local government must be prepared to take a strike. If the negotiations have been sufficiently open so that the public is well informed and if the added financial burden that would be required by the union demands has been pointed out in terms of increased taxes, the public probably will be ready to support the opposition to the strike by its local government.

A strike of municipal employees is a relatively new experience in most cities. The one "advantage" is that it makes the public aware of public services and of the staff of workers who provide them and help the city to function. Unfortunately too large a segment of the public takes these services and the workers for granted.

Need for Public Support

Management must be prepared to show the public that the wage scales and fringe benefits paid the workers are equal to those in comparable cities. It must show that the wage and benefit demands made by the striking employees will produce measurable financial hardships that the public should not have to assume and that the demands intrude on the ability of the local government to manage its affairs effectively.

Preparation of a Plan

If the local government is faced with a strike, it should make some type of plan that will do what it can toward maintaining service or providing alternative service to reduce public inconvenience. A first step in the plan, apparently minor but actually important, is to obtain keys to the shops, maintenance yards, buildings, and gas pumps. This is an elementary step that is often overlooked. Locks should be changed if required.

Management must concentrate some part of the strike plan on subjects such as (1) treatment of nonunion employees, (2) security of the physical plant, (3) payroll arrangements for those qualified, (4) a policy for rehiring strikers, and (5) generally strong, visible security for municipal services. Under the strike plan, management must make sure that its administrative policies will not induce immediate supervisors to be attracted to the union along with rank-and-file employees.

Park Strike Plan

The East Bay Regional Park District of Oakland, California, faced a strike of its 250 employees, who demanded a 68 percent wage increase, restrictions on management, control of hiring policies, and seventy other points.[9]   The strike plan developed by Christian Nelson, chief of parks, enabled the district to survive the 60-day ordeal and still maintain the park system.

His first step was to work out a management compensation plan and put it in writing.   Management personnel would have to carry the bulk of the operating load and should not be taken for granted.   Next, he polled his work force to see how many would remain on the job.   His poll showed that 18 would try to do the work previously performed by 250 employees.

He refused to be friendly with the strikers, and at the same time he did not overreact to tire slashing, death threats, and other intimations of violence.   He provided pay for extra security to protect those who stayed on the job.

Nelson believes that one should act decisively.   One should be ready with court restraining orders when they are needed.   The door should be opened for those who want to work, and these workers should be treated loyally.

Nelson concentrated on key parks where the public was frequently in attendance.   He organized his crews so that those who remained were visible.   He reorganized the work into zones so that the available work force could handle it, and he placed faith in the people who continued working.   Sanitary facilities in the park system were kept in good order to avoid trouble with the board of health.   Nelson appealed to the public for help, issued bags, and encouraged people who used the parks to keep certain areas clean.   He made it a point to be helpful to returning employees.

Strike Lessons

Nelson reported that no one really won.   The employees settled for a 15 percent raise instead of a 68 percent increase, and thirty-eight employees, primarily in the supervisory class, withdrew from the union. The one important lesson for park management, as well as for all other municipal managers, is that anyone in responsible charge of urban parks must possess knowledge and skills beyond those of a turf specialist. This lesson can be applied to all aspects of municipal services.

Under present conditions, all candidates for responsible posts as supervisors or administrators must be able to deal effectively with unions.   Candidates may be skilled and knowledgeable technicians, but if they have no concept of human relations, they will be ineffective.

Refuse-Collection Strike Plan

A workable plan for maintaining the service of solid-waste collection and disposal can be extremely difficult in large metropolitan areas.   The

[9] Gary M. Chamberlain, "Do's and Don'ts of Preparing for and Surviving a Strike," *The American City & County,* December 1975, p. 10.

service is labor-intensive, and in large metropolitan areas disposal points are often at remote locations. Nevertheless, a strike plan might entail points such as these:

1. Try to provide sites for householders and businesses so that they can dispose of the solid wastes themselves.

2. Investigate the possibility of placing large portable containers at strategic locations so that residents and businesses can put the wastes in them.

3. Explore the question of whether businesses and industry can make use of private haulers to care for their solid-waste collection and disposal needs.

4. Remind the union negotiators that private firms are available and anxious to collect and dispose of the refuse under contract and that the entire refuse-collection force therefore might be abolished.

5. If a management-rights article containing a no-strike clause and a right to subcontract has been inserted in the contract, much of the strike-plan action will have its needed effectiveness.

Public Support

The experience in Berkeley, California, illustrates how public support aids the municipal management team. In Berkeley the fire fighters went on strike, although all other segments of the municipal work force accepted the city's wage proposals. The strike continued for 22 days. During that period, local citizens assisted the supervisory firemen who operated the trucks and other fire-fighting equipment and extinguished the fires. Fortunately most of the fires were confined to garages, brush, and empty warehouses.[10]

Undependability of State Support

Reliance on assistance from the respective state government in helping to maintain needed urban services during a strike crisis is speculative at best. Attitudes of the various state governments toward the trend to municipal unions and toward the affected cities themselves are sufficiently unclear to make support undependable. By classic definition, the city is a creature of the state. But the state government is sensitive to political pressures and undoubtedly would look with reluctance on becoming embroiled in a labor dispute, especially in states with strong labor movements. As a notable example, Mayor John Lindsay of New York fared badly a few years ago when he asked for help from Gov. Nelson A. Rockefeller in attempting to settle a dispute with refuse-collection workers.

[10] Al Leggat, "Mixing Management and Meditation," *The American City & County*, December 1975, p. 68.

Union Loss of Political Influence

Following guidelines such as those outlined above does not automatically mean success in negotiations with municipal labor unions. Management often complains that it did everything that responsible people recommended and still lost. However, the guidelines will assure union negotiators that they will not automatically receive whatever they ask for simply by breaking out picket signs.

In the past, the movement toward unionization of municipal employees has been strong and has been received sympathetically by the general public. But 1976 may have represented a temporary turning point in the public's attitude toward these unions. Labor expert Al Leggat advises that public-employee unions have less voting influence than they have had in years. Union members today, he says, have better education than the rank-and-file union members of the past. They understand issues more clearly and have less enthusiasm for the recommendations of the international unions. Union endorsement of a slate of candidates generally follows a study of whether the slate will win in any case and is primarily a matter of climbing onto the election bandwagon.[11]

Union Setbacks

The San Francisco experience reinforces Leggat's opinion. San Francisco's former mayor, Joseph Alioto, found himself confronted with a series of strikes of municipal workers. The strikes were considered illegal under California law. Nevertheless, Mayor Alioto concluded an agreement with the striking workers on terms that the public considered capitulation.

In a ground swell of protest, San Franciscans changed the city charter to make striking by a city employee result in automatic dismissal. The charter change removed the mayor's power to declare an emergency, and it denied the mayor the authority to settle wage disputes unilaterally. It further placed the salaries of city employees under a strict formula based on wage rates in other large California cities.

In the same year, San Diego voters approved a change in their city charter stating that striking city employees are to be fired and will not be reinstated. If the employees wish to return to work, they can be rehired only at entry level.

Also, Mayors Wes Uhlman of Seattle and Peter Flaherty of Pittsburgh were successful in facing down strike-prone city workers and won strong

[11] Al Leggat, "Unions Losing Clout at the Polls," *The American City & County,* October 1976, p. 40. Leggat at one time was associated with the political action program of the United Auto Workers. Later he became labor-relations director of the city of Detroit, and he is now labor consultant to the state of Florida and labor adviser to St. Petersburg, Florida.

public support for their efforts. Public employees in Seattle lost badly in an effort to have Uhlman recalled.[12]

If the city administration enjoys public support, its ability to oppose what it considers to be excessive demands of striking employees always has been successful. Shortly after World War II DeLesseps Morrison, newly elected mayor of New Orleans, found himself faced with a strike of refuse collectors. He appealed for support to the students of Tulane University, who responded by performing the collection and disposal service during this emergency. Many of those students are now executives in the New Orleans business world and occasionally recall how housewives would bring coffee and doughnuts to them when they made the collections. The strike ended fairly quickly.

At one time, employees of the Seattle water and electric services threatened to go on strike. Seattle is a strong labor town, and one of the members of the city council was also an official in the Seattle Building Trades Council. When faced with the strike threat, the city council announced that it was prepared to shut down both the water and the electric utilities, to lock all doors, and to walk away. The union made the gesture of an offer, stating that it would provide enough water and electricity to operate schools and hospitals as well as similar critical services. The city council, however, was fully aware that this would require energizing the entire electric system and providing water for the entire distribution system; so the council members were unimpressed by the offer. Before the strike deadline, the union retreated and concluded an agreement. This was rather brutal bargaining, but it proved successful.

On two occasions, New York suffered cruel strikes, first by the Transport Workers' Union and second by the sanitation workers. Both caused virtual breakdowns in the city's services and great damage to its reputation. New Yorkers, however, remained apathetic about both events.

Importance of Remaining Calm

Finally, many have urged municipal management not to become emotionally involved with the strike operation. Those who go on strike or are threatening to do so are the same workers who have performed for the good of the community in times past and have served loyally and often heroically when disaster has struck. They have wives, families, hopes, and aspirations. Moreover, when the strike is in progress, their pay stops, and they would not be on strike unless they felt that they have grievances that the city management has not corrected.

And as Al Leggat instructs in every public-employee supervisory class

---

[12] "Public Employee Strikes," *The Christian Science Monitor*, Oct. 12, 1976, p. 13.

he teaches, do not overlook the power of the wives of the employees. Keep them informed of their husbands' welfare in public employment. Communicate with employees' homes in peaceful times and in strike situations.   Wives of municipal employees walking in a picket line are powerful.   They and their baby carriages with youngsters holding sharply worded signs are a television reporter's delight.

One must be flexible, advises Mayor James of San Jose, and keep a sense of humor.

Chapter Sixteen

Municipal-Service Performance Goals

WILLIAM S. FOSTER

Performance standards, in the last analysis, must take into account the wishes of the people being served. If the public wants a certain standard of service, even though an available alternative would be less costly and more effective, and has expressed a willingness to pay the extra cost, it has a right to this less efficient service.

Of course, this principle must be followed with caution. Prof. John F. Collins, former mayor of Boston, has said that every public official, whether elected or appointed, if he or she is to serve the best interests of his or her city, must be ready to make decisions that entail the risk of defeat at the next election or of dismissal from an appointive office.[1] One of the statements frequently attributed to the late Al Smith, former governor of New York, was "Not what the public wants, but what the public ought to have." Nevertheless, the wishes of the public will predominate.

Standards vary among communities. Some communities demand a neat, attractive appearance, with roadways carefully maintained. Others, even those whose people are prosperous and well educated, appear less concerned with appearance and accept a somewhat-littered environment. Some want well-lighted streets, and others actually prefer darkened ones.

Standards also can vary in a single community as time passes. As an example, a community that has been satisfied to have snow removed only in the business districts and on key arterial streets may now de-

---

[1] Private communication between John F. Collins, professor of urban affairs, Massachusetts Institute of Technology, and the author.

mand that the service be enlarged to clear all streets after every snow-storm.   Continued rising expectations and desires are understandable human characteristics.

Quality of Life

One frequently hears the term "quality of life" applied to an urban environment.   Political scientists and others who have made the most serious attempts to measure this elusive quality appear to pay only casual attention to the services that an urban government provides for its residents.   Yet if one examines these services closely, it is apparent that they have a direct effect on the parameters that the investigators choose.

The political scientist, the behavioralist, the sociologist, and others conducting studies of the quality of life tend to make broad groupings within their parameters.   The traffic parameter will embrace the condition of the roadway surface, identified by the urban administrator as road and street maintenance.   Similarly, the community-health parameter will include water supply and distribution, the reliability of the waste-water system, and the thoroughness of the collection of solid wastes, as well as the effectiveness of the park system.   Public safety will include the adequacy of street lighting and the reliability of the water supply for fire protection.   Without the effective performance of the services discussed in the chapters on these services, the quality of life in an urban environment would be dismal.[2]

Moreover, when people start disliking their local government, according to Brett Hawkins, they begin complaining about the condition of the streets, the adequacy of sewerage, street lighting, traffic congestion, and water supply.   The standard of these services is one of the fundamentals that the public uses to determine whether the quality of life in a community is good.[3]

Identification of Goals

In a lighthearted manner, Federal District Judge Frank J. McGarr once enunciated what he called McGarr's first law: "Whatever government does, it does more or less badly."[4]   Those who provide public services have heard this criticism frequently and with some annoyance.   Government does not always perform "more or less badly," any more than the

[2] For representative studies of the quality of life in an urban environment, see Martin V. Jones and Michael J. Flex, *The Quality of Life in Metropolitan Washington, D.C.,* Urban Institute, Washington, 1970; *Measuring Potential for the Quality of Life,* research directed by George A. Wing, Indiana University, Division of Business and Economics, South Bend, Ind., 1971; *The Quality of Life in the United States,* Midwest Research Institute, directed by Ben-Chieh Liu, Kansas City, Mo., 1973.

[3] Brett Hawkins, *Nashville Metro,* Vanderbilt University Press, Nashville, Tenn., 1966.

[4] Richard E. Friedman, "Coping with the Bureaucracy," *Chicago Bar Record,* January–February 1977, p. 212.

private sector always performs with excellence. Frequent call-backs of automobiles, appliances, and, in one instance, pretzels are indicative of poor work in nongovernmental services.

Jerry Wurf, long-time president of the American Federation of State, County and Municipal Employees, once told city managers meeting in New York that they had no reason to apologize for the management that they provide and that labor unions have had ample opportunity to appraise management in both the public and the private sector.[5]

In a more serious vein, Judge McGarr went on to say that the objective of government is to act with "clarity of purpose, brisk efficiency, dedicated personnel, and a notable record of success." His first objective, clarity of purpose, can be represented by the goals that every local government should set for itself and that each municipal service should establish for its operations.

To set these goals and to enlist public support for them, the community can employ two techniques:

1. A survey of opinions of what citizens expect from their municipal services

2. A detailed and formalized response to citizens' complaints

Citizen Survey   Gallup and Roper, the national polling organizations, have been able to predict with great precision the outcome of national elections by careful interviews with only 1600 selected people.

Macon, Missouri, a small city near the Ozark hills, pinpointed its civic goals with a citizen survey and followed the survey with community action that attained at least some of the goals. This action revitalized the people and won an All-America Cities award for the community. Port Arthur, Texas, a city of moderate size, did the same and won the same award. Tulsa, Oklahoma, a large city, followed the same path and won similar recognition.[6]

St. Petersburg, Florida, a city that also has won All-America Cities recognition, makes use of a citizen survey on an annual basis. Its surveyors interview 625 households out of a population of 125,000. The households are selected professionally to help ensure their representative character; the questionnaire is eight pages long.

The St. Petersburg questionnaire does not examine as many municipal services as some communities would like to survey, and it may be more detailed than many communities feel would be necessary. Nevertheless, it can be adapted to each community's needs without particular difficulty. St. Petersburg spends between $6000 and $9000 on each survey, using interviewers who call on the households personally or

[5] Floor comments at the annual meeting of the International City Management Association held in New York in 1969.

[6] William S. Foster, "All-America Cities: Democracy at Work," *National Civic Review*, April 1974, p. 178.

ST. PETERSBURG CITIZEN SURVEY   City 12-76

Hello, my name is _____. I work for Suncoast Opinion Surveys and I would like to speak
to the youngest male (oldest female) 18 years of age or over who happens to be at home. (TO QUALIFIED
RESPONDENT): The City of St. Petersburg has asked us to conduct an independent survey of Citizens to
help the City improve its services. (SHOW I.D. AND LETTERS ONLY WHEN NECESSARY.) Here's the first
question I'd like to ask: (TIME INTERVIEW BEGAN: _____)

1. How long have you lived in   6-1( )Less than 3 months   (TERMINATE)
    St. Petersburg?   2( )3 to 11 months
                                           3( )1 to 5 years
                                           4( )More than 5 years
                                           5( )Don't know

1a. Would you consider yourself a permanent   7-1( )Permanent
    resident or a seasonal resident of   2( )Seasonal
    St. Petersburg?

2. Would you rate the following services performed or provided by the City of St. Petersburg as
    Excellent, Good, Fair or Poor?

	Excellent	Good	Fair	Poor	Don't Know
2a. Police services	8-1( )	2( )	3( )	4( )	5( )
2b. Fire services	9-1( )	2( )	3( )	4( )	5( )
2c. Plays, musical performances, exhibits, and other activities	10-1( )	2( )	3( )	4( )	5( )
2d. Cleanliness of city streets	11-1( )	2( )	3( )	4( )	5( )
2e. Park maintenance	12-1( )	2( )	3( )	4( )	5( )
2f. Noise pollution control	13-1( )	2( )	3( )	4( )	5( )
2g. Condition of city streets	14-1( )	2( )	3( )	4( )	5( )
2h. Library services	15-1( )	2( )	3( )	4( )	5( )
2i. Water service	16-1( )	2( )	3( )	4( )	5( )
2j. Sewer service	17-1( )	2( )	3( )	4( )	5( )
2k. Senior adult services	18-1( )	2( )	3( )	4( )	5( )
2l. Garbage collection	19-1( )	2( )	3( )	4( )	5( )
2m. Bus service	20-1( )	2( )	3( )	4( )	5( )

3. About how often have you ridden on   21-1( )Almost daily
    St. Petersburg City buses in the   2( )At least once a week
    past 12 months? Would you say   3( )At least once a month   (Go to #5)
    (READ RESPONSES 1-5):   4( )Less than once a month
                                               5( )Not at all
                                               6( )Don't know   (Ask #4a-j)

(ASK ONLY OF NON-RIDERS)
4. Please tell me which, if any, of the following are reasons you do NOT ride city buses more often?

	Yes, reason	No, Not reason	Don't Know
4a. Service not frequent enough	22-1( )	2( )	3( )
4b. Bus stop not close enough to home	23-1( )	2( )	3( )
4c. Takes too long to go by bus	24-1( )	2( )	3( )
4d. Too many transfers required	25-1( )	2( )	3( )
4e. Buses don't run on schedule	26-1( )	2( )	3( )
4f. Fares are too high	27-1( )	2( )	3( )
4g. Poor waiting conditions at bus stops (no shelters or benches; muddy or dusty)	28-1( )	2( )	3( )
4h. Danger of crime at bus stop	29-1( )	2( )	3( )
4i. I don't know when and where buses run	30-1( )	2( )	3( )
4j. Prefer to go by automobile (or bike)	31-1( )	2( )	3( )

5. Do you know the location of the public   32-1( )Yes   (Ask #5a)
    bus stop CLOSEST to your home?   2( )No
                                                 3( )Not certain

    (IF "YES", ASK:)
5a. Is this location convenient for you   33-1( )Yes, convenient
    and other members of this household?   2( )No, not convenient
                                                 3( )Don't ride bus; doesn't matter
                                                 4( )Don't know

6. The City of St. Petersburg recently established an office of Crime Prevention to provide citizens
    information and instructions on crime prevention measures citizens can take to protect themselves,
    their homes and businesses.

6a. Have you personally seen or heard anything   34-1( )Yes, have
    about the Office of Crime Prevention or any   2( )No, have not
    of its programs such as Operation Identifica-
    tion, Vacation Alert, Neighborhood Alert?

6b. If "YES", how did you learn about the service? 35-1( )Neighborhood presentation or speech
                                                       2( )Public display
                                                       3( )Business or home security inspection
                                                       4( )School alert program
                                                       5( )TV, radio, newspapers, or billboards
                                                       6( )Other: (specify)_____

6c. Have you taken any measures to improve the   38-1( )Yes
    physical security of your home or business   2( )No
    as a result of seeing or hearing about any
    of these Office of Crime Prevention programs?

Figure 16-1 The St. Petersburg, Florida, citizen survey makes a detailed investigation of
public opinion on governmental services.

7. Have you driven an automobile in
    St. Petersburg in the last 12 months?

    39-1( )Yes, have driven (Ask #7a-c)
    2( )No, don't drive   (Skip to #8)
    3( )Don't know

7a. Would you say finding a satisfactory
    parking space in DOWNTOWN St. Petersburg
    is HARDLY EVER a problem, SOMETIMES a
    problem, USUALLY a problem, or don't
    you ever try to park downtown?

    40-1( )Hardly ever a problem
    2( )Sometimes a problem
    3( )Usually a problem
    4( )Don't park downtown
    5( )Don't know or don't remember

7b. Did you receive a traffic ticket for an
    ACCIDENT or MOVING VIOLATION (i.e.
    speeding, reckless driving, etc.) in
    St. Petersburg during the past 12 months?
    (IF "YES", ASK:) How many tickets did
    you receive this past year?

    41-1( )No, no tickets
    2( )Yes, one ticket
    3( )Yes, two tickets
    4( )Yes, three tickets
    5( )Yes, four or more tickets
    6( )Not a driver
    7( )Don't know

7c. Referring to traffic signals; that is,
    red lights, flashing lights, etc., do you
    feel St. Petersburg has generally too many
    signals, too few or the right number of signals?

    42-1( )Too many
    2( )Too few
    3( )Right number
    4( )Don't know

8. Would you say the enforcement of traffic
    laws against MOVING VIOLATIONS in St.Peters-
    burg is generally too strict, generally not
    strict enough, or about what it should be?

    43-1( )Generally too strict
    2( )Generally not strict enough
    3( )About right
    4( )Don't know

9. Are you ever bothered by traffic noises
    in this neighborhood? (IF "YES", ASK:)
    Are you bothered by traffic noise Almost
    Daily, At Least Once a Week, or Less
    Than Once a Week?

    44-1( )No, never bothered
    2( )Yes, almost daily
    3( )Yes, at least once a week
    4( )Yes, less than once a week
    5( )Don't know

10. Are you ever bothered by polluted air
    in this neighborhood? (IF "YES", ASK:)
    Are you bothered by polluted air
    Almost Daily, At Least Once a Week, or
    Less Than Once a Week?

    45-1( )No, never bothered
    2( )Yes, almost daily
    3( )Yes, at least once a week
    4( )Yes, less than once a week
    5( )Don't know

11. Would you say the amount of street lighting
    at night in this neighborhood is about right,
    too low (need more lighting), or too bright
    (more lighting than necessary)?

    46-1( )About right
    2( )Too low
    3( )Too bright
    4( )Don't know

(If home has NO SIDEWALK across front of property;
Ask #12 and 12a)
12. Would you like or not like to have
    sidewalks constructed on this block?

    47-1( )Yes, would like   (Ask #12a)
    2( )No, would NOT like (Go to #13)
    3( )Don't know

12a. IF new sidewalks were constructed on this block,
    would you be willing to pay the cost for the
    sidewalk IN FRONT OF YOUR HOME? (IF "NO", ASK:)
    Would you be willing to share the cost with the
    City?

    48-1( )Yes, would PAY cost
    2( )Yes, would SHARE cost
    3( )No, would not pay

(If home has SIDEWALK; ASK #12b)
12b. Are the sidewalks in this neighborhood
    in good condition?

    49-1( )Yes
    2( )No
    3( )No sidewalks in this neighborhood
    4( )Don't know

13. Would you say the streets in your
    neighborhood do NOT need ANY repair,
    need SOME MINOR repair or need
    MAJOR REPAIR?

    50-1( )Need no repair
    2( )Need some minor repair
    3( )Need major repair
    4( )Don't know

    INTERVIEWER -- RECORD TYPE OF STREET

    51-1( )Black top/asphalt
    2( )Brick
    3( )Concrete
    4( )Shell
    5( )Unpaved
    6( )Other:_____

14. Do you or any other member of this
    household have a library card for the
    St. Petersburg Public Library System?

    52-1( )Yes, have card
    2( )No, don't
    3( )Don't know

15. About how often during the past 12 months
    have you or members of your household (in-
    cluding children) used the St. Petersburg
    Public Library including the Main Library
    its branches, mobile vans or telephone
    reference service? Would you say.......
    (READ RESPONSES 1-4)?

    53-1( )At least once a week
    2( )At least once a month
    3( )Fewer than 4 times in last 12 months
    4( )Not at all
    5( )Don't know; don't remember

16. Turning now to neighborhood cleanliness, would you say your neighborhood is usually Very Clean, Fairly Clean, Fairly Dirty or Very Dirty?

54-1( )Very clean
2( )Fairly clean
3( )Fairly dirty
4( )Very dirty
5( )Don't know

---

17. In the past 12 months, did the collectors ever miss picking up your trash and garbage on the scheduled pick-up days? (IF "YES", ASK:) How many times would you say this occurred?

55-1( )No, never missed
2( )Yes, 1 or 2 times
3( )Yes, 3 or 4 times
4( )Yes, 5 or 6 times
5( )Yes, _____ times
6( )Don't know; don't remember

---

18. In the past 12 months, did the collectors ever spill or scatter trash or garbage you set out? (IF "YES", ASK:) How many times would you say this occurred?

56-1( )No, never spilled
2( )Yes, 1 or 2 times
3( )Yes, 3 or 4 times
4( )Yes, 5 or 6 times
5( )Yes, _____ times
6( )Don't know; don't remember

---

19. Have you or any member of your household used one of the six brush collection points located throughout the city during the past 12 months?

57-1( )Yes
2( )No
3( )Don't know

---

20. During the past 12 months, did you or members of your household see any rats on your block? (IF "YES", ASK:) About how many times were rats seen?

58-1( )No, never
2( )Yes, 1 or 2 times
3( )Yes, 3 or 4 times
4( )Yes, 5 or 6 times
5( )Yes, _____ times
6( )Don't know; don't remember

---

21. Have you or any member of your household used any of St. Petersburg's Municipal POOLS in the past 12 months? Have you used any of its PARKS? RECREATIONAL CENTERS? BEACHES? PLAYGROUNDS?

21a. (IF "YES", ASK:) Generally speaking, would you rate St. Petersburg Municipal (type of facility) as Excellent, Good, Fair or Poor?

21b. (IF "NO, NOT USED", ASK:) What is the MAIN reason you have not used any of St. Petersburg's (type of facility) ?

	Pools	Parks	Recreational Centers	Beaches	Playgrounds
Yes, USED (1)	59-1( )	60-1( )	61-1( )	62-1( )	63-1( )
No, did NOT USE (2)	2( )	2( )	2( )	2( )	2( )
Can't remember (3)	3( )	3( )	3( )	3( )	3( )
IF "YES":					
Excellent (1)	64-1( )	65-1( )	66-1( )	67-1( )	68-1( )
Good (2)	2( )	2( )	2( )	2( )	2( )
Fair (3)	3( )	3( )	3( )	3( )	3( )
Poor (4)	4( )	4( )	4( )	4( )	4( )
Don't know (5)	5( )	5( )	5( )	5( )	5( )
IF "NO":					
Don't know about them (1)	69-1( )	70-1( )	71-1( )	72-1( )	73-1( )
Too crowded (2)	2( )	2( )	2( )	2( )	2( )
Too hard to get to (3)	3( )	3( )	3( )	3( )	3( )
Busy with other activities (4)	4( )	4( )	4( )	4( )	4( )
Use private facilities (5)	5( )	5( )	5( )	5( )	5( )
Age/health problems (6)	6( )	6( )	6( )	6( )	6( )
I don't enjoy (7)	7( )	7( )	7( )	7( )	7( )
Other (8)	8( )	8( )	8( )	8( )	8( )
Don't know (9)	9( )	9( )	9( )	9( )	9( )

---

22. During the past 12 months have you or any member of your household attended any performance, sports event, show, exhibition, rock shows or other presentation or meeting at St.Petersburg's Bayfront Center? (IF "YES", ASK:) Approximately how many times did you or they attend?

74-1( )No, have not attended
2( )Yes, once or twice
3( )Yes, three or four times
4( )Yes, five or six times
5( )Yes, seven or more times
6( )Can't remember

---

23. What would you say are the MAIN reasons you and members of this household have NOT ATTENDED Bayfront Center activities and performances more often? (DO NOT READ ANSWERS, BUT MARK ONE WHICH COMES CLOSEST TO REASON GIVEN BY RESPONDENT.)

75-1( )Too busy; not enough time to go
2( )Too expensive; don't have money
3( )Too old; poor health
4( )Only go to performances I like
5( )Just not interested
6( )No transportation; no bus after show
7( )Afraid to go out at night
8( )Don't go out; prefer to stay at home
9( )Prefer other activities
10( )Other: (specify)_____

24. Do you feel the parking facilities at Bayfront Center are adequate or not adequate? How about
    City bus service to and from the Bayfront Center?

	Adequate	Inadequate	Don't Know
Parking facilities...................78-1( )		2( )	3( )
Bus transportation..................79-1( )		2( )	3( )

25. Which of these activities and uses would
    you like to see MORE OF at the Bayfront
    Center?
    (SHOW CARD "B")

6-1( ) Serious Music/Dance Performances
2( ) Lectures/Art Shows
3( ) Sports Events
4( ) Popular Music
5( ) Religious Gatherings
6( ) Musicals/Dramas
7( ) Rock Shows
8( ) Films
9( ) Other: (specify)_____

26. I am going to read a list of activities and I would like for you to tell me if you are VERY
    INTERESTED, FAIRLY INTERESTED or NOT REALLY INTERESTED in the activity. Let's start with
    classical symphony concerts. Would you say you are VERY INTERESTED, FAIRLY INTERESTED or
    NOT REALLY INTERESTED in classical symphony concerts? How about ......?

    (INTERVIEWER: Whenever a respondent indicates he/she is either "Very or Fairly Interested" in
    an activity, ask the following question and record reply in the space indicated below:)

    In St. Petersburg do you feel you have sufficient or insufficient opportunity to experience
    __(name of activity)__ ?

	INTEREST LEVEL				OPPORTUNITY		
	Very Int.	Fairly Int.	Not Int.	Don't Know	Suff.	Insuff.	Don't Know
Classical symphony concerts.........15-1( )	2( )	3( )	4( )	30-1( )	2( )	3( )
Contemporary music concerts.........16-1( )	2( )	3( )	4( )	31-1( )	2( )	3( )
Choir/chorus concerts...............17-1( )	2( )	3( )	4( )	32-1( )	2( )	3( )
Opera...............................18-1( )	2( )	3( )	4( )	33-1( )	2( )	3( )
Traditional theatre performances....19-1( )	2( )	3( )	4( )	34-1( )	2( )	3( )
Experimental/contemporary						
theatre performances..............20-1( )	2( )	3( )	4( )	35-1( )	2( )	3( )
Classical ballet performances.......21-1( )	2( )	3( )	4( )	36-1( )	2( )	3( )
Modern dance performances...........22-1( )	2( )	3( )	4( )	37-1( )	2( )	3( )
Exhibits of art of the past.........23-1( )	2( )	3( )	4( )	38-1( )	2( )	3( )
Exhibits of contemporary art........24-1( )	2( )	3( )	4( )	39-1( )	2( )	3( )
Important living artists............25-1( )	2( )	3( )	4( )	40-1( )	2( )	3( )
Art and craft classes...............26-1( )	2( )	3( )	4( )	41-1( )	2( )	3( )
Fine films..........................27-1( )	2( )	3( )	4( )	42-1( )	2( )	3( )
Historic architecture tours.........28-1( )	2( )	3( )	4( )	43-1( )	2( )	3( )
Fine literature.....................29-1( )	2( )	3( )	4( )	44-1( )	2( )	3( )

27. Overall, would you rate arts and cultural
    opportunities in St. Petersburg; that is,
    fine art, music, theatre, etc., as
    Excellent, Good, Fair or Poor?

45-1( ) Excellent
2( ) Good
3( ) Fair
4( ) Poor
5( ) Don't know

28. The City of St. Petersburg, in conjunction with the Junior League of St. Petersburg, recently
    initiated a program called "Project Concern". This program attempts both a long-term and short-
    term approach to crime prevention by providing citizens in two high-crime target areas in the
    downtown and southside areas of the city more ready access to available governmental services,
    assistance to youth in terms of job placement assistance and related activities and a concen-
    trated program of citizen education and information on crime prevention measures.

28a. Have you seen or heard anything about "Project
     Concern", its two centers or any of its programs
     such as job fairs, crime prevention presentations,
     assistance to crime victims, etc.?

46-1( ) Yes
2( ) No
3( ) Don't remember

28b. The program presently focuses its services
     on assistance to victims and special services
     for those who have committed crimes or might
     be more likely to commit crime. Do you feel
     the program should concentrate on.....? (Read
     response 1 and 2)

47-1( ) Assistance to victims or potential
         victims or
2( ) Assistance to offenders or potential
     offenders
3( ) Don't know

28c. The program is concentrated in two geographic
     areas of the city. Do you feel the type of
     services provided by Project Concern should or
     should not be offered on a city-wide basis?

48-1( ) Yes, city-wide
2( ) No, NOT city-wide
3( ) Don't know

29. Turning now to police protection and
    public safety, how safe would you feel
    walking alone in this neighborhood at
    NIGHT, Very safe, Reasonably Safe or
    Not Safe at All? (Repeat for "DAY")

NIGHT	DAY
49-1( ) Very safe	50-1( ) Very safe
2( ) Reasonably safe	2( ) Reasonably safe
3( ) Not safe	3( ) Not safe
4( ) Don't know	4( ) Don't know

30. Are there some parts of St. Petersburg where you would LIKE TO GO OR USED TO GO AT NIGHT but do NOT because you would NOT feel safe?

51-1( )Yes, some parts (Ask #30a)
   2( )No   (Skip to #31)
   3( )Don't know

(IF "YES", ASK:)
30a. Which parts of St. Petersburg are these? (DO NOT READ ANSWERS, BUT MARK ONE WHICH COMES CLOSEST TO REASON GIVEN BY RESPONDENT.)

52-1( )Downtown St. Petersburg
   2( )Southside St. Petersburg
   3( )Central Plaza
   4( )Webb's City
   5( )Bayfront Center
   6( )The Pier
   7( )Williams Park
   8( )All Areas of City
   9( )"This" or "My" Neighborhood
  10( )Other: (specify)_____

---

31. In the past 12 months, did anyone break in or was there strong evidence someone tried to break into your home?

55-1( )Yes, broke in
   2( )Yes, tried to break in   (Ask #31a-c)
   3( )Yes, both
   4( )No, neither   (Go to #32)
   5( )Don't know

(IF "YES", ASK:)
31a. How many times did this occur? (Break-ins or attempted break-ins)

56-1( )One
   2( )Two
   3( )Three
   4( )Four or more
   5( )Don't know

31b. Were all incidents reported to St. Petersburg Police? (IF "NO", ASK:) How many were not reported?

57-1( )Yes, all reported (Go to #32)
   2( )No, one not reported
   3( )No, two not reported
   4( )No, three not reported
   5( )No, four or more not reported
   6( )Don't know

(IF ANY NOT REPORTED, ASK:)
31c. What was the main reason for NOT notifying the police? (DO NOT READ ANSWERS, BUT MARK ONE WHICH COMES CLOSEST TO REASON GIVEN BY RESPONDENT.)

58-1( )Didn't want to go to court
   2( )Didn't think it was important enough
   3( )Didn't think it would do any good
   4( )Didn't want to get involved
   5( )Didn't want to get anybody in trouble
   6( )Afraid my insurance would go up
   7( )Other:(specify)_____
   8( )Don't know; don't remember

---

32. How many motor vehicles do you and members of your household own?

59-1( )One
   2( )Two
   3( )Three or more   (Ask #32a-d)
   4( )None (Go to #33)
   5( )Don't know

(IF OWN VEHICLE(S), ASK:)
32a. During the past 12 months, and in St.Petersburg, did anyone steal or use any vehicles belonging to members of this household without permission?

60-1( )Yes, did steal or use
   2( )No   (Go to #33)
   3( )Don't know

32b. How many times did this occur?

61-1( )One
   2( )Two
   3( )Three
   4( )Four or more
   5( )Don't know

32c. Were all incidents reported to the St. Petersburg Police? (IF "NO", ASK:) How many were NOT reported?

62-1( )Yes   (Go to #33)
   2( )No, one not reported
   3( )No, two not reported
   4( )No, three not reported
   5( )No, four or more not reported
   6( )Don't know

(IF ANY NOT REPORTED, ASK:)
32d. What was the MAIN REASON for NOT notifying the police? (DO NOT READ ANSWERS, BUT MARK ONE WHICH COMES CLOSEST TO REASON GIVEN BY RESPONDENT.)

63-1( )Didn't want to go to court
   2( )Didn't think it was important enough
   3( )Didn't think it would do any good
   4( )Didn't want to get involved
   5( )Didn't want to get anybody in trouble
   6( )Afraid my insurance would go up
   7( )Other: (specify)_____
   8( )Don't know; don't remember

---

33. To rob means to take something from a person by force, fear or by the threat of force. Did anyone rob or try to rob you or a member of your household in the past 12 months in St. Petersburg?

64-1( )Yes   (Ask #33a-c)
   2( )No   (Go to #34)
   3( )Don't know

(IF "YES", ASK:)
33a. How many times did this occur?

65-1( )One
   2( )Two
   3( )Three
   4( )Four or more
   5( )Don't know

33b. Were all incidents reported to the St. Petersburg Police? (IF "NO", ASK:) How many were NOT reported?

66-1( )Yes   (Go to #34)
   2( )No, one not reported
   3( )No, two not reported
   4( )No, three not reported
   5( )No, four or more not reported
   6( )Don't know

(IF ANY NOT REPORTED, ASK:)
33c. What was the MAIN REASON for NOT notifying the police? (DO NOT READ ANSWERS, BUT MARK ONE WHICH COMES CLOSEST TO REASON GIVEN BY RESPONDENT.)

67-1( )Didn't want to go to court
   2( )Didn't think it was important enough
   3( )Didn't think it would do any good
   4( )Didn't want to get involved
   5( )Didn't want to get anybody in trouble
   6( )Afraid my insurance would go up
   7( )Other: (specify)_____
   8( )Don't know; don't remember

34. Considering serious physical attacks to in-
     clude such things as beatings, knifings,
     shootings and so forth, in the last 12 months,
     were you or any member of your household
     seriously physically attacked in St.Petersburg?
     (By someone who was NOT a member of your family
     or household?)

     68-1( )Yes   (Ask #34a-c)
        2( )No   (Go to #35)
        3( )Don't know

     (IF "YES", ASK:)
34a. How many times did this occur?

     69-1( )One
        2( )Two
        3( )Three
        4( )Four or more
        5( )Don't know

34b. Were all incidents reported to the
     St. Petersburg Police? (IF "NO", ASK:)
     How many were NOT reported?

     70-1( )Yes   (Go to #35)
        2( )No, one not reported
        3( )No, two not reported
        4( )No, three not reported
        5( )No, four or more not reported
        6( )Don't know

     (IF ANY NOT REPORTED, ASK:)
34c. What was the MAIN REASON for NOT
     notifying the police? (DO NOT READ
     ANSWERS, BUT MARK ONE WHICH COMES
     CLOSEST TO REASON GIVEN BY RESPONDENT.)

     71-1( )Didn't want to go to court
        2( )Didn't think it was important enough
        3( )Didn't think it would do any good
        4( )Didn't want to get involved
        5( )Didn't want to get anybody in trouble
        6( )Afraid my insurance would go up
        7( )Other: (specify)_____
        8( )Don't know; don't remember

35. In the last 12 months, has anyone vandalized;
     that is, intentionally damaged your home, car
     or other property or that of members of your
     household in St. Petersburg?

     72-1( )Yes   (Ask #35a-c)
        2( )No   (Go to #36)
        3( )Don't know

     (IF "YES", ASK:)
35a. How many times did this occur?

     73-1( )One
        2( )Two
        3( )Three
        4( )Four or more
        5( )Don't know

35b. Were all incidents reported to the
     St. Petersburg Police? (IF "NO", ASK:)
     How many were NOT reported?

     74-1( )Yes   (Go to #36)
        2( )No, one not reported
        3( )No, two not reported
        4( )No, three not reported
        5( )No, four or more not reported
        6( )Don't know

     (IF ANY NOT REPORTED, ASK:)
35c. What was the MAIN REASON for NOT
     notifying the police? (DO NOT READ
     ANSWERS, BUT MARK ONE WHICH COMES
     CLOSEST TO REASON GIVEN BY RESPONDENT.)

     75-1( )Didn't want to go to court
        2( )Didn't think it was important enough
        3( )Didn't think it would do any good
        4( )Didn't want to get involved
        5( )Didn't want to get anybody in trouble
        6( )Afraid my insurance would go up
        7( )Other: (specify)_____
        8( )Don't know; don't remember

36. In the last 12 months, has anyone committed any
     other crimes against you or any member of your
     household in St. Petersburg, such as "Peeping
     Toms", bicycle theft, bad checks, stolen hubcaps,
     and so forth?

     76-1( )Yes   (Ask #36a-d)
        2( )No   (Go to #37)
        3( )Don't know

     (IF "YES", ASK:)
36a. What were these crimes?

     77-

36b. How many times did this occur?

     78-1( )One
        2( )Two
        3( )Three
        4( )Four or more
        5( )Don't know

36c. Were all incidents reported to the
     St. Petersburg Police? (IF "NO", ASK:)
     How many were NOT reported?

     79-1( )Yes   (Go to #37)
        2( )No, one not reported
        3( )No, two not reported
        4( )No, three not reported
        5( )No, four or more not reported
        6( )Don't know

     (IF ANY NOT REPORTED, ASK:)
36d. What was the MAIN REASON for NOT
     notifying the police? (DO NOT READ
     ANSWERS, BUT MARK ONE WHICH COMES
     CLOSEST TO REASON GIVEN BY RESPONDENT.)

     80-1( )Didn't want to go to court
        2( )Didn't think it was important enough
        3( )Didn't think it would do any good
        4( )Didn't want to get involved
        5( )Didn't want to get anybody in trouble
        6( )Afraid my insurance would go up
        7( )Other: (specify)_____
        8( )Don't know; don't remember

37. In the past 12 months have you had any direct
     contact with a St. Petersburg Police Officer
     for any reason such as calling for assistance,
     reporting a crime, or being stopped by the
     Police? (IF "YES", ASK:) What type of
     contact did you have?

     6-1( )No, no contacts
        2( )Yes, response to call for assistance
        3( )Yes, I was stopped by the police
        4( )Yes, at a crime prevention meeting
        5( )Yes, contacted by an officer in an
             investigation
        6( )Yes, other: (specify)_____
        7( )Don't know; don't remember

38. Would you rate the speed in responding to calls of the St. Petersburg Police as Excellent, Good, Fair or Poor? How about the courtesy of St. Petersburg Police? Professionalism?

	Excellent	Good	Fair	Poor	Don't Know
a. Speed in responding to calls......................8-1( )		2( )	3( )	4( )	5( )
b. Courtesy...9-1( )		2( )	3( )	4( )	5( )
c. Professionalism.................................10-1( )		2( )	3( )	4( )	5( )

39. Do you think the police in St. Petersburg are generally fair in their handling of people?
- 11-1( )Yes
- 2( )No
- 3( )Sometimes Yes/Sometimes No
- 4( )Don't know

40. Do you think the amount of police patrolling in your neighborhood is too much and could be reduced, is about right now or is not enough and should be increased.
- 12-1( )Too much
- 2( )About right
- 3( )Not enough
- 4( )Don't know

41. Do you have any complaints with the TASTE, ODOR, APPEARANCE OR PRESSURE of your drinking water? (IF "YES", ASK:) Which -- Taste? Odor? Appearance? or Pressure?
- 13-1( )Yes, taste
- 2( )Yes, odor
- 3( )Yes, appearance
- 4( )Yes, pressure
- 5( )No, no complaints
- 6( )Don't know

42. Do you happen to have a fire extinguisher in your home? (IF "YES", ASK:) How many do you have?
- 17-1( )One
- 2( )Two   (Ask #42a & b)
- 3( )Three or more
- 4( )No, have none   (Go to #43)

42a. Where is/are your fire extinguisher(s) kept in your home?
- 18-1( )Kitchen
- 2( )Garage/carport
- 3( )Other: (specify)_____

42b. Do you happen to know what type of fire extinguisher(s) you have?
- 20-1( )Soda ash
- 2( )Carbon dioxide (CO_2)
- 3( )Other: (specify)_____

43. Do you have a heat or smoke detector system in your home? (IF "YES", ASK:) Which -- heat, smoke or both?
- 22-1( )No, do not have
- 2( )Yes, heat
- 3( )Yes, smoke
- 4( )Yes, heat & smoke

44. Were you aware the St. Petersburg Fire Dept. provides free home fire inspections on request? (IF AWARE OF PROGRAM, ASK:)
- 23-1( )Yes, aware   (Ask #44a)
- 2( )No, not aware   (Go to #45)

44a. Have you used this fire inspection service in the last 12 months?
- 24-1( )Yes, have   (Go to #45)
- 2( )No, have not   (Ask #44b)

(IF AWARE BUT HAVEN'T USED, ASK:)
44b. Why have you not used this service?
- 25-_____
  _____

45. If a fire broke out in your home, how would you most likely report the fire?
- 27-1( )Own phone
- 2( )Neighbor's phone
- 3( )Fire call box
- 4( )Other: (specify)_____

46. During the past 12 months did you ever get in touch with the City of St. Petersburg to complain about something like poor city services or a rude city employee or for ANY reason?
- 28-1( )Yes   (Ask #46a-c)
- 2( )No   (Go to #47)
- 3( )Don't know
- Voluntary Comments:

46a. How many different problems or situations did you complain or contact the City about?
- 29-1( )One
- 2( )Two
- 3( )Three
- 4( )Four or more
- 5( )Don't know

46b. Which department or official did you contact INITIALLY?
- 30-1( )St.Pete Serv.& Info.Center/City Hall or MSB
- 2( )Mayor or Councilman
- 3( )City Manager's office
- 4( )Police
- 5( )Other: (specify)_____
- 6( )Don't remember

46c. Were you generally satisfied with the City's responses? (IF "NO", ASK:) What was the MAIN thing you were dissatisfied with? (INTERVIEWER: MARK REASON CLOSEST TO THAT GIVEN BY RESPONDENT.)
- 31-1( )Response not yet completed
- 2( )Yes, satisfied
- 3( )No, never responded to my request
- 4( )No, never corrected problem
- 5( )No, too much "runaround", "red tape"
- 6( )No, had to keep pressuring them for results
- 7( )No, personnel were discourteous
- 8( )No, other: (specify)_____
- 9( )Don't know

47. During the past 12 months, did you contact
anyone with the City of St. Petersburg to
seek information or service such as having
your water turned on, obtaining a building
permit and so forth?

32-1( )Yes   (Ask #47a-c)
2( )No   (Go to #48)
3( )Don't know
Voluntary Comments:

47a. How many different problems or situations
did you complain or contact the City about?

33-1( )One
2( )Two
3( )Three
4( )Four or more
5( )Don't know

47b. Which department or official did you
contact INITIALLY?

34-1( )St.Pete Serv.& Info.Center/City Hall or MSB
2( )Mayor or Councilman
3( )City Manager's office
4( )Police
5( )Water Dept.
6( )Sewer Dept.
7( )Other: (specify)_____
8( )Don't remember

47c. Were you generally satisfied with the
City's response to your inquiries?
(IF "NO", ASK:)
What was the MAIN reason you were
dissatisfied?
(INTERVIEWER: MARK THE REASON
CLOSEST TO THE LISTED REASONS.)

35-1( )Response not yet completed
2( )Yes, satisfied
3( )No, City DID NOT provide requested service
4( )No, City COULD NOT provide requested serv.
5( )No, took too long to satisfy request
6( )No, too much "runaround", "red tape"
7( )No, personnel were discourteous
8( )Other: (specify)_____
9( )Don't know

48. Thinking back over the past year, were there
any complaints which you would have liked to
make to City officials but DIDN'T?
(IF "YES", ASK:)
What was the MAIN reason you did NOT make
the complaints?
(INTERVIEWER: MARK REASON CLOSEST TO
REASON GIVEN BY RESPONDENT.)

Voluntary Comments:

36-1( )No
2( )Yes, didn't think it would do any good
3( )Yes, problem not worth time or effort
to complain about
4( )Yes, thought official already knew
about problem
5( )Yes, thought someone else had or would
report problem
6( )Yes, didn't know where or how to complain
7( )Yes, reported it to other people
8( )Yes, other: (specify)_____
9( )Don't know

49. Which of the following do you consider to
be your BEST source of information about
services and activities of the City of
St. Petersburg? (READ RESPONSES 1 - 6)

37-1( )Newspaper
2( )Television
3( )Radio
4( )Utility bill inserts
5( )Friends or neighbors
6( )Governmental mail-outs
7( )Other: (specify)_____
8( )Don't know

50. During the past year, have you or any members
of your household attended any meeting or hearing of city council or other city government
groups?
(IF "YES", ASK:)
50a. Do you feel your attendance at these meetings
or hearings was time well-spent?

39-1( )Yes   (Ask #50a)
2( )No
3( )Don't know

40-1( )Yes
2( )No
3( )Don't know

51. Do you feel you could have a say about the
way the City Government is running things
if you wanted to?

41-1( )Yes
2( )No
3( )Don't know

Finally, a few questions about you and your family.

52. What are the ages of all other members of
this household? (IF NECESSARY, ASK
RESPONDENT'S AGE)

42-Respondent's age:_____
43-Others' ages:_____
44-_____

(HAND CARD "A")
53. Please give me the LETTER on this card
which comes closest to your TOTAL household income before taxes last year?

45-1( )A-Under $5,000
2( )B-$5,000 to $9,999
3( )C-$10,000 to $14,999
4( )D-$15,000 to $19,999
5( )E-$20,000 and over
( )Interviewer Estimate

54. Are you renting or do you own your
residence?

46-1( )Rent
2( )Own

Check whether interviewed:

47-1( )Male   48-1( )White
2( )Female   2( )Non-white:_____

Housing type: 49-1( )Single family
2( )Duplex
3( )Multi-family, less than 10 units
4( )Multi-family, 10 or more units

5( )Residential hotel, rooming
or boarding house
6( )Mobile home
7( )Other: (specify)_____

So that my office may call you to check my work if it wants to, may I have your name and telephone
number:

Name: _____   Address: _____

58-1( )Number:_____
2( )Refused
3( )No phone

I hereby attest that this is a true and honest interview:

INTERVIEWER: _____   Date: _____   Time interview ended: _____

reach them by telephone.   Then analysts study the responses on the basis of demographic, social, and economic groupings.   The surveyors confine the interviews to a maximum of 30 minutes, and no household has ever refused to be interviewed.

These surveys identify goals that may have been overlooked, give information on progress toward goals that already have been identified, and provide persons who sometimes are called the "silent majority" with the opportunity to express themselves on the quality of the governmental services they receive.   Frequently a survey represents the first time that these citizens have been consulted about the operation of their city.

Response to Citizen Complaints   The second goal-identifying technique, the prompt processing of citizen requests, complaints, and comments, is also an effective means of measuring the thoroughness of municipal-service performance.   Most people dislike making complaints and will do so only when they consider that a condition has become intolerable. Consequently when they make a call to what they believe is the proper city office, they do so with a great sense of irritation and with doubts, often expressed forcibly, that the municipal forces actually will take corrective action or that the city employee responding to the call really cares about the inquiry.

A procedure developed by James W. Morgan when he was commissioner of public works in Birmingham, Alabama, proved able to turn the liability of an angry citizen into the asset of a civic supporter.   It was so successful that ultimately the people of Birmingham elected him mayor.

Under the Morgan plan, the city employee receiving the complaint thanks the citizen submitting it and assures him or her that the problem will be investigated promptly and that he or she will be informed of the action taken.   Then a form letter signed by the commissioner goes to the complainant, again thanking him or her for concern for the welfare of Birmingham and advising that action is being taken.

A memorandum then goes to the appropriate department head, who is instructed that the matter be investigated and corrective measures undertaken and that a report be delivered to the commissioner's office stating what has been done to respond to the complaint.   The commissioner sends a final letter to the complainant stating what has been done and asking whether conditions now are satisfactory.   Mayor Morgan displayed with satisfaction communications from those who had been indignant with the city government and later became its staunch supporters.

Not only does this method enable the city to document complaints and corrective action.   It also identifies persons who make frivolous and numerous complaints that do not justify corrective action. In addition, the method brings to light issues of a more serious nature: a bridge that should be replaced, roadways that should be widened, parks that should be created. Since these are capital-construction items, they provide the city with an opportunity to explain their status to the complainants and to outline what is needed to put such improvements in the capital budget. Finally and perhaps most important, the method provides evidence to show how well municipal services are performing.

In responding to complaints or requests for information one study[7] emphasizes that the citizen must be assured that (1) he or she has access to his or her local government, (2) he or she has confidence that the disposition of the complaint will be satisfactory, and (3) the personnel of the local government will treat him or her with courtesy.

Photographic Evaluation

The goal most obvious to the public is a good appearance, and a photograph is convincing evidence to the public in demonstrating how well a neighborhood is attaining an attractive, litter-free appearance. Moreover, photographs can disclose the standard of service provided by other maintenance activities. They show whether the street is in good repair, whether street cleaning has been thorough, whether refuse collection has been careless and sloppy, and whether snow removal has been effective. They show whether traffic lanes are well marked and they can be used to illustrate maintenance in park systems.

Four photographic evaluation techniques exist; all have been designed primarily to measure the amount of street litter. The systems currently available are as follows:

1. Urban Institute method of evaluating street areas
2. Project Scoreboard, Fund for the City of New York, used to evaluate street areas
3. Gilson "litter count," designed to document all objects with a minimum size equal to that of a cigarette package, used to evaluate commercial areas
4. Photometric index, developed by the American Public Works Association, for use on streets, parking areas, and certain private property[8]

The first two systems can survey an entire block but depend on the opinion of those making the survey to determine the litter-free rating. Thus they contain a subjective element that may raise doubts in the

[7] *Measuring the Effectiveness of Basic Municipal Services,* Urban Institute and International City Management Association, Washington, February 1974.
[8] Richard H. Sullivan and Tim Kipp, *Photometric Index Study,* for Keep America Beautiful, Inc., American Public Works Association, Chicago, November 1975.

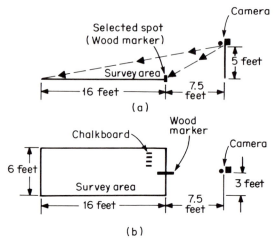

Figure 16-2 All photographs for the photometric index are taken with the camera located in this manner: (*a*) profile; (*b*) plan. [*American Public Works Association*]

minds of the public.   Both make four classifications of litter conditions. The first divides them into increments of 1.   The second uses increments of 0.25.

The third system apparently was designed to appraise the condition of sites of commercial activity and employs no standard size.   It also de-

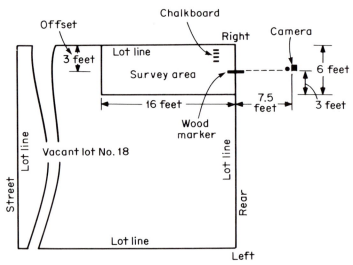

Figure 16-3 If the photograph is to record the litter index of a vacant lot, the camera will be located as shown. [*American Public Works Association*]

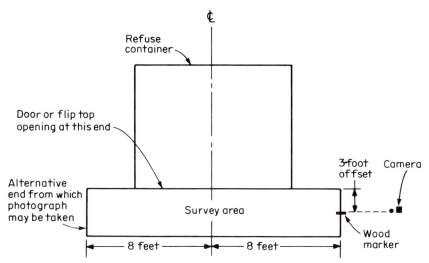

Figure 16-4 If the photograph is to record the index of littering around a bulk-refuse container, the camera can be placed as shown. [*American Public Works Association*]

pends on the judgment of the surveyor, who must count the litter in a "representative" area and then extend this figure to the number of square feet in the entire area being surveyed.

The fourth system, which seems the easiest to use and the least liable to error, samples a site extending 16 feet (4.9 meters) along a block face and 6 feet (1.8 meters) wide. Sites are drawn on a random basis within the area being surveyed.

To make the photometric study, the surveyor places a camera 7½ feet (2.3 meters) from one end of the selected site and 3 feet (0.9 meter) from one side. The camera is placed 5 feet (1.5 meters) above the ground. A wood marker is placed in the center of the end nearest the camera,

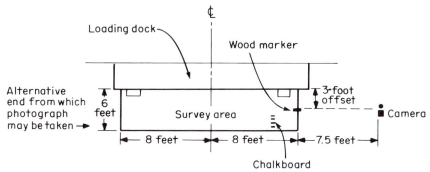

Figure 16-5 If the photograph is to be used to survey litter at a location such as a loading dock, the camera can be located according to this diagram. [*American Public Works Association*]

and an identifying chalkboard is placed on the survey area to identify the site. Prior to taking photographs, the surveyor lays out a standard area 16 feet long and 6 feet wide with white markers, dividing it into ninety-six squares each 1 foot (0.3 meter) on a side. The surveyor then takes a photograph of the site, with the camera placed as described, and makes the exposure into a transparency that can be placed over photographs of litter scenes requiring evaluation. The number of squares containing discernible litter is the index for that specific area.

Surveyors can adopt the same general system to estimate the littered condition of vacant lots, loading ramps, areas adjacent to large refuse containers, and similar locations.

Street-Maintenance Goals

The goal of road and street maintenance is simple. The roadway surface should provide a smooth, comfortable ride. It should drain well, and shrubbery should not obscure vision at intersections and in other areas.

Responsible supervisors should drive over all the streets in the community at least once and preferably twice a year to look for flaws or incipient flaws. They should be equipped with tape recorders so that they can identify areas needing attention. On high-traffic arteries, a "bumpometer" will locate irregularities that are not visible by more casual inspection.

If a bumpometer is available and supervisors choose to use it to evaluate the entire street system, the results will enable them to document priorities for future street work on an impartial basis. The public is inclined to accept a chart from a meter in preference to the subjective opinion of a supervisor.

Street-cleaning Goals

To the public and to most local governments, the primary goal of an effective street-sanitation program is basically cosmetic. Consequently the most convincing evaluation of street cleaning appears to be accomplished by the photometric method.

This may change if those charged with the prevention of water pollution gain sufficient authority. As discussed in Chapter 6, fine material on the street surface, not immediately visible, contains sufficient oxygen-demanding pollutants to pose a pollution problem after every rain. However, this type of pollution is difficult to measure and agencies for water-pollution control do not seem anxious to control it.

To make the sweeper operation more visible, especially in residential areas, and to assist the public in recognizing that street-cleaning work is in progress, those in charge should arrange to have sweepers painted an eye-catching color, probably yellow because this is the color noticed most quickly. If attention is drawn to the sweeper in this manner, people will see it when it travels through residential areas and recognize that it is performing its cleanup work.

Supervisors also must provide the sweepers with operators who adjust their brooms correctly and are meticulous in their sweeping operations so that the sweepers pick up all the debris and do not leave trails of uncollected dirt. When measuring productivity, supervisors should encourage thoroughness of work rather than an increased number of curb miles traversed. It obviously is counterproductive to call attention to a service such as this and then to perform it badly.

Waste-Water Collection and Storm-Water Drainage Goals

The basic goal of waste-water collection and storm-water drainage is reliability. If failures occur in either one, the public generally is affected immediately and often is greatly inconvenienced.

Clogged sewers and sewer breaks cause waste-water backups, flooding basements and family rooms and generating odors as well as depositing waste-water solids in the areas. The public does not want these mishaps to occur at all. When they do occur, the goal of the sewer-maintenance crew is to correct them immediately, treating them as a type of emergency. A review of complaints will permit a municipality to determine how well this service is progressing toward its goal of no breaks or clogged sewers at all.

The goal of storm-water–drainage maintenance depends to some extent on where the problems arise. In some areas such as south Florida and parts of Texas with excessively flat topography and with few houses equipped with basements, flooded streets can occur frequently because of the difficulty of providing drainage. Nevertheless, the public dislikes flooding.

If a street subject to flooding serves a residential, business, or commercial district in an area that is drained more easily, the frequency of flooded conditions becomes a matter of public concern. Records should show a continual decrease of such conditions, with the ultimate goal of eliminating them completely.

Package Sewage-Treatment Plants

The operating goals of small waste-water treatment plants are an effluent that meets sanitation requirements and an operation that does not create nuisance odors. The problem with such small privately owned plants is that the owners frequently do not give them the attention that they require, and consequently the local government must exercise some control over them for the protection of the community.

While detailed technical instructions should be followed for plants of this nature, there are some general policies which should correct most problems in plants that appear to be in trouble. The plants function under aerobic conditions when they are performing as the designers anticipated. This means that the pollution-destroying bacteria thrive in the presence of air.

If the plants generate disagreeable odors, this means that anaerobic bacteria have been allowed to develop, and these multiply in the absence of air. To prevent these odor nuisances from developing, the operators therefore should increase the volume of air in the treatment process. One set of guidelines that has proved successful in ensuring good performance is as follows:

1. Provide enough air to maintain at least 0.4 milligram per liter of dissolved oxygen in the effluent.

2. Operate the plant blowers 24 hours per day.

3. Operate the plant with sludge-return lines at maximum flow.

4. Keep air diffusers unplugged for the entire length of the aeration tank.

5. Scrape the sides and bottom of the hopper-bottomed clarifiers at least twice a week.

6. Be sure that the skimmers are functioning properly at all times. Grease and other skimmings should be buried.

7. The sludge should be wasted to the holding tank when the 30-minute sludge-settling test rises to the vicinity of 80 or when the sludge blanket threatens to overflow the weirs.

The guideline instructions emphasize that the sludge test and the dissolved-oxygen test are the most important control features.[9]

Goals for Snow and Ice Control

To the public, the goal of snow and ice control should be to maintain the streets free from snow and skidproof regardless of the weather. To some persons, it also means that this should be accomplished without the use of salt.

To those entrusted with the work, the goal means that the local government should have available sufficient operators and equipment to meet all but a "disaster" storm, possibly one expected every 100 years, and to gear the program to the use of salt but on a sparing basis.

Most persons engaged in this work welcome legislation that prohibits all but the most essential traffic during heavy storms. People do go out, regardless of weather; they abandon their cars when the drifts immobilize them; and at times they suffer badly because they refuse to wear clothes suitable for the weather. Some die because of exposure.

[9] F. Richard Kapp, "Assistance Given for Obtaining Optimum Results by Small Sewage Plant Operators," *The Overflow,* January–February 1977, p. 4, P. O. Box 1030, Kissimmee, Florida 32741.

Generally, the public in snow-belt areas will accept snow and ice with a certain amount of stoicism. People farther south, in contrast, have reacted fearfully to snows that northerners would consider mild. Nevertheless, all people become uneasy with the appearance of snow and ice, knowing that they will be accompanied by accidents, injuries, and deaths. Consequently some administrators send plows and spreaders to distribute salt and abrasives out earlier than is absolutely necessary to assure the public that corrective measures are being taken.

Records that help document the effectiveness of snow and ice work would include items such as the following:

1. Number and intensity of storms
2. Snowfall at each storm and total snowfall for the year
3. Number and intensity of ice situations
4. Number of vehicles marooned by snow
5. Accidents, injuries, and deaths attributed to snow and ice storms
6. Vehicles for snow and ice control utilized in each storm
7. Emergency measures required

Solid-Waste Collection Goals

From the public's standpoint, the goals of solid-waste collection are reliability, promptness, neatness in performance, and quietness in the collection work. From the standpoint of those performing the work, efficiency of operation rates high. The service makes intensive use of labor, and a conscientious administrator strives to use the labor effectively.

The photometric evaluation of street conditions discussed above can be used to document the appearance of streets and to disclose such unaesthetic conditions as waste spillage from trucks. Other factors or parameters that can be recorded on a regular basis and summarized annually to illustrate progress toward collection goals are the following:

1. Missed collections, indicated from complaint inquiries
2. Spillage during collections, indicated from complaints and from other sources
2. Property damage attributed to collection crews
4. Injuries to solid-waste collection crews
5. Objectionable noise, indicated from complaints

Traffic-Control Goals

The goal that the public sets for its traffic-control engineers is simple. Traffic must move smoothly and safely and at reasonable speeds, and a driver must be able to find a convenient parking stall at his or her destination. The public can be impatient with traffic conditions and unreasonably demanding in traffic control. A participant at one public meeting said: "I want to be able to drive into town whenever I feel that I should.   I do not want to be hampered by traffic congestion.   I want to park within a block of where I want to go.   And I do not want to pay."

The attainment of such a goal is obviously difficult, if not impossible, because the traffic engineer has no way of governing the volume of vehicles that enter the traffic network at any given time.   Nevertheless, the goal of making it possible for traffic to move smoothly and safely at reasonable speeds and to ensure parking space at the end of the journey is worthwhile even though elusive.

To measure progress toward such a goal would require documenting traffic conditions as thoroughly as possible and to note changes from year to year.   These are some of the parameters worth recording:

1.   Peak and off-peak travel times between strategic points in the traffic network

2.   Duration of peak traffic congestion and its comparison with off-peak periods

3.   Number of accidents and their severity, that is, property damage, injuries, and deaths translated into vehicle-miles traveled

4.   Availability of both off-street and on-street parking

5.   Frequency with which traffic lanes are blocked by construction and maintenance work

6.   Air-pollution problems arising from vehicular exhaust

7.   Noise generated by traffic

8.   Adequacy of pedestrian trafficways

Water-Distribution Goals

For the public, the goals of water supply and distribution are simple. The supply should be ample and dependable.   The water should be tasteless and odorless, without ingredients that are harmful to health.   It should be reasonably soft and cool.   Its cost should not be excessive.

For the local government, the goals are more detailed.   The volume of water must be sufficient not only to satisfy domestic, commercial, and industrial requirements but also for fire protection.   The pressure should be maintained at not less than 30 to 40 pounds per square inch (107 to 276 kilopascals) throughout the system.   Fire hydrants must be reliable, as must be the valves in the system.   Water mains must be free from leaks so that as much as is practicable of the water that has been purified and pumped at rather substantial cost actually will be used by the customers.   Water rates must be adequate to make the system economically viable.   Most water administrators strongly want all services to be metered.

Park-Maintenance Goals

The primary goal of park systems is to encourage constructive use. Harold M. Olmsted, a descendant of the greatest park planner of the

United States, Frederick Law Olmsted, whose most highly acclaimed work was Central Park in New York, has often repeated his ancestor's advice: parks must be used and not merely looked at.   The park-utilization coefficients and other factors discussed in Chapter 12 can document the extent of the use and indicate the need for future facilities as well as their types.

Summary

With goals such as these and with adaptations of them for specific conditions in various local areas, the maintenance services provided by local governments should be able to play a strong role in supporting a community's efforts to improve the quality of life for its people.

An anecdote attributed to the Chinese philosopher Confucius illustrates the value of good, responsive government.   According to the story, the philosopher met a woman weeping by the side of a road. When he inquired about her trouble, the woman said that a man-eating tiger had slain her husband and four sons.   When Confucius asked her why she did not move from the village, she responded that she would not because the government there was good.   This prompted Confucius to state that bad government is more to be feared than a man-eating tiger.

Appendix

To determine the velocity and volume of flow by a graphic solution to the Manning formula discussed in Chapter 9, "Sewer Maintenance," use Figure A-1 to make the calculation when the pipe is flowing full. Then use Figure A-2 to determine the solution for partially full conditions.

As an example, let us assume a 24-inch sewer placed at a slope of 0.1 percent, or 0.0010 foot per foot of trench. Assume a constant Manning n of .013 and a flow depth of 6 inches.

From Figure A-1, move upward along the .0010 ordinate until it intersects the 24-inch line. By interpolation between the two velocity diagonals, the velocity is 2.4 feet per second. Moving along the abscissa at this point discloses a discharge volume of 7.0 cubic feet per second.

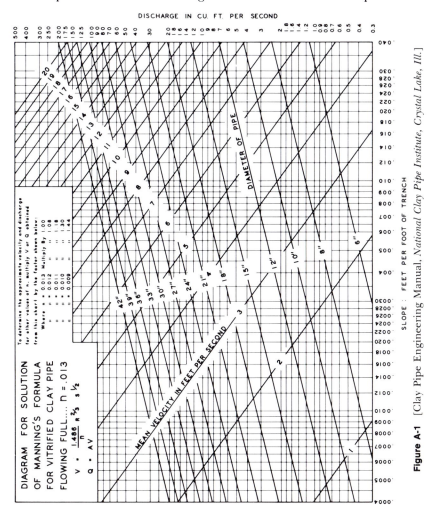

Figure A-1 [Clay Pipe Engineering Manual, *National Clay Pipe Institute, Crystal Lake, Ill.*]

From Figure A-2, the ratio of the 6-inch depth of flow to the pipe diameter (*d*/*D*) is .25. Since the dotted curves apply, .25 intersects the discharge curve at .125, and the velocity curve at .64.

Applying these factors to the results when the pipe is full produces a discharge of 0.875 cubic foot per second and a velocity of 1.54 feet per second.

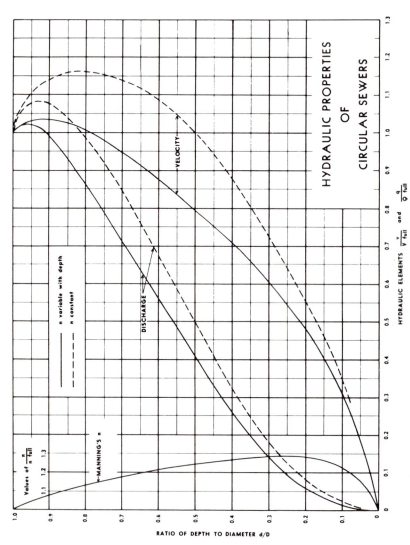

Figure A-2 [Clay Pipe Engineering Manual, *National Clay Pipe Institute, Crystal Lake, Ill.*]

Index